Trudeau

Trudeau

THE EDUCATION OF A PRIME MINISTER

JOHN IVISON

SIGNAL

McCLELLAND
& STEWART

Library and Archives Canada Cataloguing in Publication data
is available upon request.

ISBN: 978-0-7710-4895-1
ebook ISBN: 978-0-7710-4897-5

Jacket design by David A. Gee
Jacket photo © 2018 Bloomberg Finance LP/Getty Images

Text design by Leah Springate

Typeset in Bembo Book by M&S, Toronto
Printed and bound in Canada

Published by Signal, an imprint of McClelland & Stewart,
a division of Penguin Random House Canada Limited,
a Penguin Random House Company
www.penguinrandomhouse.ca

1 2 3 4 5   23 22 21 20 19

Penguin
Random House
Canada

For Dana

CONTENTS

THE VISION OF THE ANOINTED

JUSTIN TRUDEAU'S TWITTER BIO used to read: "Changing the world, a little bit every day." His government has tried to live up to that ambitious agenda since being elected with 184 of the 338 seats in the House of Commons in the election of October 2015—with decidedly mixed results.

Canadians are generally in favour of making poverty history. But they are modest people, not accustomed to their leaders having such lofty aspirations. In the past they have voted for prime ministers like Jean Chrétien, who were more interested in staying in power—leaders who believed that good government is boring government. In the country's largest province, Ontario, Bill Davis won four elections in a row, following his own advice: "Bland works." As former prime minister Kim Campbell said when assessing Davis's record, "He did nothing in particular."[1] That is the antithesis of Trudeau's approach to government. His first mandate was characterized by sweeping schemes and massive government spending to reconstruct a new Canada in the image of his own progressive leanings.

Justin Trudeau, the eldest son of former prime minister Pierre, was elected on a promise to transform a country that was designed to withstand change. When he emerged from Rideau Hall as Canada's twenty-third prime minister on an unseasonably warm day in November 2015, the atmosphere was providential and full of possibility. As Trudeau walked around greeting well-wishers and posing for selfies, it overwhelmed the senses—like the moment Dorothy entered Technicolor in *The Wizard of Oz*. The sun burned the trees as this most telegenic of prime ministers unveiled a cabinet composed for the first time ever of an equal number of men and women, not to mention a cohort of turban-wearing Sikhs, a former Afghan refugee, and an Indigenous justice minister. It was as if Ottawa's clean-cut leading man—dubbed by the British tabloids as the "sexiest politician in the world"[2]—had cast his cabinet with a view to the movie version that might follow.

The bright and cheery symbolism resonated after the severe, austere Harper years. The country was gripped in a euphoric pandemic of optimism—a belief that politics could make a positive difference. But as he unveiled the priorities for his government—"real action" on climate change; a "renewed nation-to-nation relationship with Indigenous people"; a pledge to make the 2015 election the last held under the first-past-the-post system—there was a sense that Trudeau was setting goals that were too ambitious, too impractical, and often beyond his ability to deliver. Too late—expectations had shot to infinity and beyond.

In the years after his historic victory, an accumulation of missteps and controversies has sparked accusations that he presides over a government that values style over substance and talk over action—that he is prime minister of a "government of glossy, toothy, touchy-feely phonies."[3] Canadians are divided by their chameleon prime minister. Polls suggest that since the 2015 election, the number of people who disapprove of him has at times constituted a majority, up from less than one third when he was first elected.[4] Trudeau promised to be a transformative leader, but his critics contend that he just plays one on television. They argue that he is more likely to be a transitional prime minister than one who will leave an indelible mark on Canada.

As a rebuttal, Liberals point to innovations like a gender-balanced cabinet and an "inclusive growth" strategy to suggest they will be as impactful over time as his father's introduction of bilingualism and multiculturalism. "On the cabinet, we recognized and articulated a consensus that was already happening but nobody had articulated. I really believe that is what political leadership is," said Gerald Butts, Trudeau's former principal secretary and best friend. "Notwithstanding all the stuff written about it since, Germany, France, and Spain have all done the same thing we did."[5]

When he entered politics, Trudeau came across as a frivolous person with no fixed principles and a party trick that involved throwing himself down a flight of stairs. As a backbench opposition member, he was considered a parliamentary lightweight. But as his political ambitions ripened, so did he. The former drama teacher with the d'Artagnan moustache put away the melodrama, the jeans, and the skateboard that used to accompany him into the House of Commons and took his place alongside more established political heavyweights as leader of the Liberal Party. He showed he could lead a team of able people, many more able than himself.

He has spent his life in the limelight since the visiting American president Richard Nixon raised a toast "to the future prime minister of Canada—to Justin Trudeau" at a gala at the National Arts Centre in Ottawa when he was less than four months old.[6] Canadians feel that they know him. But his public persona as the first prime minister of the Instagram age is a one-dimensional, condensed version of the real man. The exhausting torrent of images showcasing him as a dynamic and outgoing leader fail to capture his complexity, far less offer a guide to his performance.

In the peerless first volume of his biography of the prime minister's father, Pierre Elliott Trudeau, John English said the seeming contradictions in the life of the elder Trudeau were more often consistencies.[7] The son shares many of the apparently paradoxical gifts passed on by his father—intelligence (contrary to the assertions of his critics, who have mistaken naiveté for stupidity) and discipline, but also spontaneity and risk-taking. One apparent inconsistency is that he has what friends say is a "rhino hide," perhaps the legacy of growing up as Pierre Trudeau's son, and therefore either hated or fawned over. "He immediately discounts those people [his critics]. I've never seen a politician with a backbone and a rhino skin like this one," said an Ottawa veteran who has worked for five Liberal leaders.[8]

Yet there is an almost adolescent need to be adored. In this way, he differs from his father. While Pierre was, in the words of Marc Lalonde, his closest adviser in the 1970s, "like an oyster that opened with great difficulty,"[9] the son has perfected the art of grip-and-grin retail politics. Watching him sprinkle his stardust around a room is an enlightening experience—smiling eyes are locked, there is a hand on the arm or a double-hand clasp for the women, a firm grip on the shoulder for men. "He move[s] through the crowd like someone doing an easy crawl through lake water," said writer Ian Brown.[10] As one close adviser told Brown, his life in the public eye led the younger Trudeau to conclude that he wasn't going to have a variety of personalities, dictated by different circumstances: "He doesn't have this onstage light that he flicks. Because he lives his whole life onstage."[11]

This book was not conceived as a definitive biography of Trudeau or his time in office. There is simply not enough supporting documentation to make conclusive judgments. But it is meant to offer glimpses behind the curtain and insights into a ministry that promised to offer open government and soon discovered it could either be open or it could govern. We are left to rely on anecdotal accounts from the people around the prime minister—and on the author's own observations, as someone who has chronicled his political progress for a decade or more, including a number of one-on-one interviews down the years.

Dozens of Trudeau's friends and political colleagues were interviewed for this book. Many were still working in government or had commercial sensitivities and so preferred to talk on a non-attributable background basis. Those interviews suggest a leader who is good at understanding the feelings of others and playing on them. He tends to be impulsive, overemotional, and at times sanctimonious. But, as part of his political metamorphosis, he has added conviction and discipline to his ability to know what to say, how to say it, and to whom, for maximum effect. On a good day, he is a formidable politician.

One of the central contentions of this book is already apparent: that Trudeau's greatest strengths are also his greatest weakness; that the famous name, lifetime of privilege, and impulsiveness are as liable to hurl him from office as they were to get him there in the first place. He has proven to be a polarizing figure—in broad terms popular with women and young voters, but disliked in a visceral way by men, particularly older men, who dismiss him as a fop and a phony—someone who got to be where he is because of his name and not his achievements.

Even some of his own caucus and staff admit they were late converts —casualties of the "I-knew-his-father" syndrome. "I'm fifty-four years old and I remember when Justin Trudeau was born," said Ben Chin, former chief of staff to finance minister Bill Morneau and a founding member of Team Trudeau. "It makes me predisposed to saying, 'I'm not impressed by you. I knew your father. You're not going to fool me into thinking you're your father.' I wanted to be skeptical of him. It took me several years of getting to know him and hearing his views and arguing stuff back and forth to come to realize that was my problem. He wasn't saying to me, 'Like me because I'm my father's son.' He was saying, 'These are things I believe in.' It was my problem not his."[12]

But many men, and perhaps a growing number of women, have not undergone that conversion. The traits that carried him to power have, at times, threatened to undo him. He may have been more prescient than he knew when he read a First Nations prayer at his brother Michel's memorial that contained the line "I seek strength, not to be greater than my brothers, but to fight my greatest enemy, myself."[13]

Another hypothesis of this book is not even particularly controversial: that the Trudeau government has not been very effective at implementing policies, often because it is too focused on communications and not enough on making things happen after they've been announced. People who have watched the prime minister at close quarters say the capriciousness in his personality means the initial idea is more interesting than following up on the implementation. "He's much more about 'What's new?'" said one senior Liberal staff member. "He's good at getting people super-excited, setting bold visions. But it creates real challenges in execution."[14] Trudeau clearly revels in the liturgical aspects of being prime minister but is less enthralled about the actual exercise of government. Yet, while he is a man of good intentions, he will be judged on results. And those results have been disappointing for many —a triumph of symbolism over action.

For a majority government, the Liberals have made disappointing progress with their parliamentary agenda—excluding appropriation bills (which always pass), just 39 per cent of their legislation had received Royal Assent by the end of June 2018—far fewer than the average of 60 per cent for majority governments in previous parliaments over the past two decades.[15] One Liberal MP explained that the new government exhibited naiveté by allowing the opposition parties to impose the parliamentary agenda—unlike the iron fist that controlled procedure in the Harper years. "Once we'd got elected, people thought it would be just like the village council—everybody would get together and make Canada a better country. It was all peace, love, unicorns, and rainbows. Harper ran it like Robert Mugabe, but we went to the other side. The first piece of business we undertook at the human resources committee was a study by Niki Ashton of the NDP to review Employment Insurance. So we're out of power for ten years and the first thing we see is a motion by the third party," he said.[16]

Yielding power on the committees and turning loose the Senate as a partisan chamber did not make for the effective use of power. Nor did having the time and energies of so many key people in this most centralized of governments focus almost exclusively on the Canada–U.S. relationship for the better part of two years—an unavoidable consequence of the election of Donald Trump.

Then there have been the broken promises. The Liberals ran on a platform that promised "modest" deficits of around $20 billion over four years, with a "credible plan" to balance the budget in 2019. Instead, runaway spending has seen deficits amount to $80 billion in that time period, with no plan for the budget to return to balance. The reason? "They like spending. They just like it," said one senior Liberal staff member, unhappy with, and noticeably distancing himself from, the profligacy of his own government. "The economy was so good in 2017, we could have balanced within three years if we had shown a bit of discipline—and still have done meaningful stuff. But a different choice was made."[17] Namely, to spend the $6 billion windfall of unexpected tax revenues on pre-electoral goodies.

One MP said successful Liberal governments have often exhibited creative tension between the prime minister and his finance minister—think Chrétien and Paul Martin or Pierre Trudeau and John Turner —with both pulling at the blanket from different ends. But a number of Liberal moderates lament that lack of challenge function provided to a free-spending prime minister by his finance minister, Bill Morneau. "Finance has become a vassal state," said the MP.[18]

The Harper Conservatives considered one of their greatest successes to be their reduction of Ottawa's capacity to launch national social programs by cutting the goods and services tax by two points. The goal was, in the words of Republican tax reform advocate Grover Norquist, to shrink government until it was "small enough to drown in a bathtub."[19] But that logic works only if the government of the day cares about living within its means. This government boasts proudly of its record on lifting children out of poverty, thanks to its massive increase in the child benefit. But the surge in social spending will be paid for by future generations.

This is not a ministry that has faced adversity—whether fiscal, economic, or over national unity—on the same scale as many of its predecessors. Growth was robust in 2017, at 3 per cent, and was respectable in 2018, at 2 per cent. Unemployment has been bumping against record lows, below 6 per cent for much of the Liberals' time in office. This is more likely the result of a buoyant U.S. economy than Canadian government policy. But what is not reflected in those numbers is what tax expert Jack Mintz called the "slow bleeding of Canada"[20]—the impact on the country's competitiveness of Liberal fiscal and environmental policies. Jobs, capital, and head office functions have not gushed south of the border, but a gradual seep is evident as companies seek to move profits and people to the U.S., where corporate and personal tax rates are lower, and where resource projects in particular are more likely to get swift approval. Foreign direct investment in Canada has slowed in recent years—even before Trump's tax cuts took effect. The worry for many investors, and voters, is that Trudeau is a prime minister more interested in taxing than generating wealth; that he believes the private sector is a golden goose that can't be killed.

A third assertion of this book remains unproven: that the Liberal government has made a fundamental miscalculation by thinking Canada is a more "progressive" country than is the reality—and that it can govern in perpetuity as long as it dominates the left-of-centre vote. There is an absolute conviction that Canadians share Trudeau's devotion, bordering on dogmatism, for an activist agenda to transform Canada into a more egalitarian society by government fiat. Trudeau is not the first politician to think voters mirror his or her beliefs, but he and his closest advisers are guilty of what American conservative thinker Thomas Sowell called "The Vision of the Anointed" in his 1995 book of the same name. Sowell talked about the "special state of grace" for those "Teflon prophets"—the "Anointed"—who predict future social, economic, or environmental problems unless there is government intervention. "Those who accept this vision are deemed to be not merely factually correct but morally on a higher plane. Put differently, those who disagree with the prevailing vision are seen as being not merely in error, but in sin," he said.[21] The "Benighted," who don't buy into the vision, are dismissed as uninformed, irresponsible, or motivated by unworthy purposes. It's a description written twenty years before the advent of the Trudeau Liberals that perfectly captures the way they see themselves and their opponents.

William A. Macdonald, a sage corporate lawyer who has watched Canadian politicians come and go for more than half a century, advises that "nothing is ever only one thing—no one thing is ever everything."[22] And Trudeau himself says his father taught him that the world is too complicated to be explained by one overarching ideology. But Macdonald is not alone in thinking that Trudeau has got the nature of Canadian politics wrong—that it is more centrist than progressive left; that the vast majority of Canadians would be more comfortable with a governing party that merely promoted Canada as the best place in the world to live, to earn an income, and to build wealth and businesses. "Post-war Canada is the product of progressive Conservatives and conservative Liberals," Macdonald notes, "both of whom believed that economic advances and social advances went hand-in-hand. I don't think the Trudeau people get that."[23]

The philosophical underpinning of the Trudeau government's approach is John Stuart Mill's *On Liberty*, which predicted that great things could be achieved "if the superior spirits would but join with each other" for social betterment. In this perspective, grand visions to reconstruct society are possible and what Sowell called an "omni-competence" on the part of government is assumed. "Intractable problems with painful trade-offs are simply not part of the vision of the Anointed," Sowell observes. "Problems exist only because other people are not as wise or as caring, or not as imaginative or bold as the Anointed."[24]

Trudeau's narrow ideological world view operates like an old-fashioned mechanical calculator, spitting out basic solutions to complex problems. The answers are rarely questioned and expensive policies are often enacted with the standard explanation of politicians giddy at the prospect of spending other people's money: "We can't afford not to."

But there are many, many Canadians who are far more comfortable (whether they know it or not) with the philosophical leanings of writers like Adam Smith, the Scottish economist. He took issue with the "man of system . . . so enamoured with the supposed beauty of his own ideal plan of government that he cannot suffer the smallest deviation from any part of it. . . . He seems to imagine that he can arrange the different members of a great society with as much ease as the hand arranges the different pieces upon a chess board." But as Smith pointed out more than 250 years ago, in the great chess board of human society, "every single piece has a principle of motion of its own, altogether different from that which the legislature might choose to impress upon it."[25]

After three years in power, Trudeau was discovering that the game of human society does not always go harmoniously. "I think the problem is they have shifted from the aspirational left to the identity left," said pollster David Coletto of Abacus Data.[26] His research suggests that since the election of 2015, Liberal support has remained steady among those who self-identify as left or centre-left, but that it has leaked from people in the middle who are more concerned about the cost of living, lack of accessibility to housing, and rising interest rates than setting the world to rights.[27] "Instead of dealing with that issue, the prime minister is travelling around the world, trying to be a beacon of hope and optimism for everyone in the era of Donald Trump, when those people in the middle would just like him to come home and do something about their rising anxiety around the cost of living," said Coletto.[28]

One measure of the government's priorities was its decision to merge cabinet committees that mull ideas and legislation before they're set before full cabinet. In summer 2018, the lead economic committee—on growing the middle class—was incorporated into another committee on diversity and inclusion. While there are committees on reconciliation with Indigenous Canadians and on the environment, there are now none exclusively focused on driving economic growth. Gerald Butts denies that the priorities of the Trudeau government have shifted. But a number of Liberal MPs interviewed for this book perceive a drift leftward—and it has made them nervous. "There has been a relentless attempt to woo left-of-centre voters. I think, in retrospect, the centre-right voter has not been catered to, or has been ignored. But we're the party of the middle. Our brand has to be in the centre," said one senior caucus member.[29]

Trudeau was elected promising to be the great unifier, the leader who would forge consensus and bridge partisan divides after the partisan Harper years. Conservatives are not your enemies, he told Liberals, they are your neighbours. But years of playing identity politics, with its baked-in hostility toward anyone deemed "privileged," has cleaved fresh breaches, disharmony, and estrangement. Stephen Harper did a lot of things that made his opponents resentful. But, despite riding to power on a wave of good intentions, the Liberals—through their attempts to control Parliament, their lack of transparency, abuse of process, torqueing of public policy, and programs for partisan advantage—have been no better than the Conservatives. "Of course they don't see it that way," wrote journalist Andrew Potter. "No one ever does, because people tend to interpret their own behaviour in light of what they see as their true motives. And because they see their motives as fundamentally good, the Liberals give themselves a pass for engaging in the behaviours for which they (and the press gallery) crucified Harper."[30]

The SNC-Lavalin scandal in early 2019 was a perfect example. Trudeau was accused of obstructing justice for pressuring his then-attorney general, Jody Wilson-Raybould, to strike a special plea bargain with the Montreal engineering company accused of bribery and corruption overseas. Many Canadians viewed the story as blatant abuse of the rule of law and the prosecutorial independence of the attorney general's office. Partisan Liberals looked the other way, viewing any transgression as a necessary evil to secure votes in Quebec, win the election, and enact more of their enlightened policies.

But even for some Liberals, the focus has shifted over time. They were elected on a "fairness" agenda, which in 2015 meant making taxes more "fair" for the middle class—people with aspirations who want to make their own way in life and keep more of their income. The definition of "fairness" is now more likely to appeal to people engaged in the culture wars over inclusiveness, Indigenous issues, and climate change. Among the believers in the identity agenda, there is a sense of certainty about everything that many of us would like to feel about anything.

This thin-skinned sectarianism has manifested itself most visibly on social media. Butts maintains that Twitter, in particular, is a game. "I hold out the possibility that I could be wrong about anything at any given time. That's not the person I play on Twitter," he said.[31] But there is little evidence that Trudeau's righteousness is synthetic. The conclusion drawn from talking to many centrist Liberals is that the crusade for reconciliation and equality has not healed divisions but created new ruptures; that the pendulum has swung too far, too fast. The Liberal Party should be in clover—Canada has enjoyed a period of decent economic growth, historically low unemployment, a New Democratic Party that is on the ropes, and an untested, unknown Conservative leader. Yet confidence is in short supply.

Former prime minister Stephen Harper, in his 2018 book *Right Here, Right Now*, contends that we are living in an age of disruption that will morph into the kind of populism seen in the United States and the United Kingdom if traditional political approaches, both conservative and liberal, are continued. In his view, a world of rapid and unpredictable change means that "ordinary" people are not interested in parties that offer market-oriented, socially progressive solutions—rather they tend toward the economically interventionist, socially conservative policies that leave them less vulnerable. "That is what opened the door to the populists of the right. They have appealed to such voters by emphasizing their conservative social values, while being less committed to market economics," he wrote.[32]

Whether his prediction applies to Canada remains debatable. But what is clear is that voters across the country are dissatisfied and ungratified by their options. If Harper's logic holds, the electorate will hardly have become more enamoured by Trudeau's tendency to apologize to what he considers marginalized groups for historical slights done to them. The former prime minister contends that the underlying presumption that blames Western society for all ills makes left-liberalism vulnerable because it is "way off-side" with the majority of working people. In part, Trump's election was a reaction to the perceived "apologetic tenor" of the Obama years. The unwritten assumption is that a similar phenomenon may yet occur in Canada. Decent people everywhere endorse apologies for wrongdoing but can see through the virtue signalling evident in overapologizing.

It will have been noted in the Prime Minister's Office that, while 29 million Canadians were governed by provincial Liberal governments when Trudeau came to office, that number has dwindled to just 1.6 million after right-leaning governments were elected in Ontario and Quebec and British Columbians voted for an NDP government. Obviously, the circumstances in each case were specific, but fatigue with the Liberal Party was evident in each, especially in Ontario. None of this precludes future electoral success, especially if voters consider the alternatives uninspiring. The prime minister is constantly reminded he is not running against perfection but against a number of flawed opposition leaders. Yet it is a fair criticism of this most quixotic of prime ministers that he spends too much time tilting at windmills in order to undo perceived injustices; that in his efforts to spark socio-economic inclusive growth, he is more focused on the social than on the economic. It is clear that for many people who voted for the Liberals with enthusiasm in 2015, the thrill has gone.

This book will explore the extent to which Trudeau's ambition to change the world a little bit at a time has been realized. The conclusion is hard to escape that he entered politics as a man of promise but has emerged as a man of promises that have failed to materialize.

ONE

PASSION OVER REASON

JUSTIN PIERRE JAMES TRUDEAU was born on Christmas Day, 1971, at Ottawa Civic Hospital, the first son of the sitting prime minister, Pierre Elliott Trudeau, and his wife, the former Margaret Joan Sinclair. The two had married the previous March. Margaret was twenty-nine years younger than her husband and was striving to make the adjustment to the structured life of a prime ministerial spouse. But she was a vivacious presence in official Ottawa and won many over with her beauty and kindness.

Sharon Sholzberg-Gray, whose late husband, Herb, was in Trudeau's cabinet, said that the prime minister was touched when he saw her with her newborn son in October 1971, just two months before his own child was expected. He must have relayed the news to Margaret because the next day, Sholzberg-Gray received a hand-knit baby outfit and a hand-written note, saying that it was made in preparation for her own child but she wanted to pass it on as gift.

Justin's grasp of politics is likely innate—inherited not only from his father but also from his maternal grandfather, James "Jimmy" Sinclair, the Scots-born former fisheries minister in the government of Liberal Louis St. Laurent in the 1950s. In fact, Justin said he later followed the outgoing campaign style of Sinclair rather than that of his father, "because it suited my personality."[1]

The family lived at 24 Sussex Drive, the prime minister's official residence, until they were forced to move to Stornoway, the residence of the Official Opposition leader in 1979, after Trudeau senior lost to Joe Clark's Conservatives. Justin was enrolled at nearby Rockcliffe Park Public, the school his mother had attended when Jimmy Sinclair moved his family to Ottawa while he was in cabinet. Life in the tight-knit Rockcliffe community seems to have been fun for Justin and his younger brothers, Alexandre, known to everyone as Sacha, who was also born on Christmas Day, in 1973, and Michel, born on October 2, 1975. Justin —or RCMP code name Maple 3—enjoyed a privileged but relatively normal early childhood, taking the bus for the short trip to school every day, even if it was followed by an RCMP cruiser.

He sometimes bristled at the living conditions—on one occasion, the twelve-year-old gave his RCMP minders the slip and took off on his bike through the Rockeries, near Rockcliffe Park. His father was furious. "Dad said: 'Look, these guys have a job to do and you just made it a lot more difficult.' I never did that again," Justin recounted.[2] But there was some freedom to be a normal boy. A photograph from the front page of the local *New Edinburgh News* in 1981 shows the three brothers and four young friends on their bicycles, playing in the lanes of the affluent, old neighbourhood in early spring. "The lane is our favourite place," it quoted Justin as saying, in what must have been one of his earliest press interviews.[3]

One former schoolmate at Rockcliffe Park remembers "a nice kid —a little precious and theatrical for sure—but a good athlete and a good guy." The friend recalled attending St. Brigid's Roman Catholic church in Ottawa's Lowertown. The three Trudeau boys would show up each Sunday in a stretch limousine and would often drive their friends home afterward. "He wasn't arrogant. I don't remember him ever playing the Daddy trump card. But he didn't have to—he drove around in a limo."

The friend said one incident in particular sticks in his memory from a time when they were seven or eight. A group of boys, including future

Friends star Matthew Perry, would play sports after school in the Rockcliffe Park gym. "I don't know why I did it to this day, but I told Justin it was cancelled. He got on the school bus and went home and about twenty minutes later the RCMP detail wandered into the gym and asked where he was. When they couldn't find him—panic. The whole school was on lockdown. Cops everywhere. If there'd been helicopters, they'd have been out there too. When they found out he was safe, they asked why he'd gone home. 'Because my friend told me it was cancelled.' Boy, I took a lot of shit for that."[4]

Life changed for all three of the boys in May 1977, when Pierre and Margaret separated. Justin was just five years old. Trudeau dwells on the split at some length in his memoir, *Common Ground*, saying that while both parents exerted wonderful influences on him, "like every child of divorced parents," he was shaped by their breakup.[5]

Despite becoming an icon of social liberalism for heralding his "just society," Pierre could not escape the traditionalist mindset drummed into him as a child. The difficulties of co-parenting with someone so much older were apparent in Margaret's complaint that, post-split, when she was living a short walk from 24 Sussex in New Edinburgh, she had to intervene to set up a television in the prime minister's residence so the boys could watch Saturday morning cartoons. "Pierre is a very old-fashioned father. . . . He tried to give me the argument that the brain can actually be damaged by the waves," she told the *Ottawa Citizen*.[6]

Pierre's only account of the breakup in his memoirs is typically understated. "I was a neophyte at both politics and family life at the same time. I married late in life, our three boys—Justin, Sacha and Michel—arrived fairly quickly, and I was learning about marriage and parenthood at the same time as I was learning about the workings of politics. So perhaps it was a little too much for me, and, regrettably, I didn't succeed that well."[7] In her 2010 book about her battles with mental illness, *Changing My Mind*, Margaret said Pierre was widely seen as a man who did pirouettes, but what he really did, hour after hour, was work. "Unless it was an official occasion, we never went to the ballet or the theatre. For him, his life was perfect. . . . For me, it wasn't enough. I wanted and needed to play."[8]

And she did. After helping Pierre campaign during the 1974 general election, she recounted how she succumbed to "severe emotional stress" that prompted increasingly erratic behaviour—including a trip to New York, where, as Pierre's biographer John English said diplomatically, she "came under the spell of Senator Edward Kennedy, who enthralled her completely."[9] Her depression lapsed in 1975, when she became pregnant with Michel, but problems recurred in the summer of 1976, as Margaret defiantly smoked marijuana in front of the RCMP detail and, in one fight with her husband, ripped the letters off a treasured quilt emblazoned with Pierre's personal motto: "Reason over Passion."

Justin said living life in the public eye played a part in the failure of the marriage. "Its effect is neither insurmountable nor necessarily traumatic, but it demands that you maintain a state of mind that enables you to handle steady pressure and periodic hassles," he said in *Common Ground*. While his father "revelled" in the hardships, taking them as a personal challenge, for his mother, the experience was quite different, made intolerable by a mental health condition that Margaret later revealed was diagnosed as bipolar disorder.[10]

Pierre's "monastic perfectionism" at home suited him but drove his wife out of 24 Sussex, which she referred to as "the crown jewel of the federal penitentiary system."[11] On March 4, 1977, their sixth wedding anniversary, she decided to leave Pierre for a ninety-day trial separation and headed to Toronto to attend a concert by the Rolling Stones. As she recounted in her memoir, *Beyond Reason*, she invited the Stones to party in her hotel room after the show, where they drank, played dice, and smoked hashish. The story made headlines around the world, with London's *Daily Mail* blaring: "Canada's First Lady Shocks the World and Trudeau Orders His Wife: Come Back Now."[12]

It's clear from his memoir that his mother's jet-set period in the 1970s left a lasting mark on her eldest son, who said he will never be able to fix the things that went wrong with his childhood.[13] He recalled that when he heard his parents arguing, he would "escape" by reading an Archie comic and dream of growing up in the mythical neighbourhood of Riverdale, where no one got divorced. He said he learned the "futility of trying to please everyone around you," and noted, "I sort of locked into the idea that if I could be the perfect son to both of my parents, well maybe that would be enough to keep them together. And ultimately, obviously, it wasn't. . . . That was a lesson about limitations." [14]

But he suggested that, while he was angry during his youth that he could never do enough to keep his mother near him, he has since come to terms with the past. "[We] shared a close mother–child bond and I appreciated that she treated me in a special way—not because I was the first born, but because she sensed that I had inherited much of her personality, including her zest for adventure, her joy of spontaneity and her need to connect emotionally with people around her." [15] He also addressed head-on the cruel refrain from critics that he has his mother's brains. "I know what my political opponents are trying to do when they say I am my 'mother's son,' more than my father's. They are appealing to those old misunderstandings and prejudices about mental illness. Like everyone, I take after my parents in different ways and I am immensely proud of both of them." [16]

Seamus O'Regan, a friend since the early 2000s, attributes Trudeau's early experience with mental illness for his compassion with people who are suffering. O'Regan was drinking too much and fighting depression, particularly after he left his job on CTV's morning show, *Canada AM*. He was elected as an MP in his native Newfoundland in 2015 but was juggling the job and his illness until he got a note in the House of Commons from Trudeau, asking him to come to the PM's office. "Ultimately, he was crucial to putting me on the straight and narrow . . . God love him," notes O'Regan. "He said, 'We fought too hard to be here, you fought too hard to be here, go and get well and you'll be fine.'" Of Trudeau, O'Regan says, "It takes a lot to confront a good friend, even when it's plainly obvious it needs to happen. . . . Tons of credit to Margaret Trudeau for being as open as she was in the eighties and nineties, when it was not cool to talk about depression and bipolar. But [Justin] as a kid had to deal with this, very early, very early. It opened my eyes to a part of him that is intensely private but, when he hauls it out, there's an enormous amount of empathy there."[17] Trudeau's intervention proved pivotal. O'Regan went into rehab and has been sober ever since. He was promoted into the cabinet in a 2017 shuffle.

Justin Trudeau's upbringing may have been unconventional, but nothing about the Trudeau story is conventional, which is what makes it compelling. He may have called his autobiography *Common Ground*, but he remains a most un-common man. How many people could say they walked onto a stage at a Liberal convention as their father was serenaded toward retirement by Paul Anka singing "His Way"? The answer is three. As the crowd cheered, and many cried, Justin, Sacha, and Michel emerged with "Trudeau" inscribed on their caps. "I want my kids to see that the line of business their dad was in had some importance in the country," said Pierre, in his address.[18]

Trudeau says he experienced childhood in Ottawa but grew up in Montreal, where Pierre and the boys moved after his retirement from politics in 1984. The family moved into an art deco home on avenue des Pins that Pierre had bought in 1979 for $230,000, and Justin was enrolled at his father's alma mater, Collège Jean-de-Brébeuf, a Jesuit school in Pierre's time but non-denominational by the time his son arrived. The school provided Trudeau with an early grounding in life and politics. "I learned at Brébeuf not to give people the emotional response they are looking for when they attack me personally. Needless to say, that skill has served me well over the years," he said.[19]

The teenage years are fraught for most kids, and Trudeau seems to have been no exception. "As a teenager, I was too skinny, had terrible skin and big glasses and a nose that didn't fit my face," he told *Chatelaine*'s #TheManSurvey project, noting further that he went through puberty at an all-boys school and when girls arrived he had no ability to engage with them: "I had no game. I was hyper self-conscious and deeply insecure."[20] He built up a core group of friends, including Marc Miller, who later became a Liberal MP in Montreal, and took refuge in "nerdy showmanship"—juggling balls or riding a unicycle.[21] Miller agrees that Trudeau wasn't cool back in the early 1980s, but notes "no one is cool at that age." He remembers there being an immense power shift in grade eleven, when girls arrived at Brébeuf, from the thinkers to the better-looking guys. "None of us was in either group," he said.

Trudeau's nerd claims may not resonate with the "selfie-king" image he has projected in recent years. But Miller said that the theatrical escapades with the unicycle or juggling were more the exception than the norm. "People have trouble understanding that he is fundamentally a very introverted person, a private person, because they see someone who is very capable of very high-quality speaking and obviously someone who is comfortable in crowds. But he's probably most comfortable reading a book on his own, as opposed to going out drinking with the boys," he said.[22]

It was at Brébeuf that Trudeau's formative views on Quebec sovereignty and language took shape—heavily influenced by those of his father. He recounted how, in class debates, the sovereignty side argued that independence was necessary for Quebec to reach its full potential. Trudeau argued that, as the son of a Québécois francophone who had served as prime minister for more than fifteen years, he failed to see how the province was being disadvantaged. "The compelling economic arguments against breaking up Canada at a time when the world was moving towards freer trade and more open borders clinched the deal for me. Where were the benefits? What would be the rewards? Seeing none, the whole sovereignty argument seemed extremely weak to me," he said in *Common Ground*. A report from CBC's *The National* from 1990 featured a confident Justin gearing up for a college referendum at Brébeuf, very much in the minority in his defence of federalism. Interviewed by CBC's Neil Macdonald after the vote, a fresh-faced, gum-chewing eighteen-year-old Justin gave the trademark Trudeau-family shrug and dismissed the caustic response to his arguments. "I've never been affected by peer pressure. Never," he said.[23]

While not intimidated by his contemporaries, Trudeau was decidedly discouraged by the presence of his father, which stalked the hallways of Brébeuf like Banquo's ghost. Once, when trying to be helpful, Pierre showed his son his report cards from the school, dating back to the 1930s—a line of straight As. The realization that the son was not like the father sparked a teenage rebellion that manifested itself in a form of "subconscious defence mechanism." He detailed some of this in *Common Ground*: "It worked like this: 'If I choose not to give a project all of my effort, I cannot be judged negatively based on the result.' My father strove for, and succeeded in reaching, tremendous heights of achievement. I chose not to try nearly as hard, so why should anyone be surprised when my marks failed to match his?"[24] Miller said his friend is a smart person who is consistently underestimated. "But his ability to apply himself was never there. He did just enough to get by, to get his dad off his back and to pursue his own passion. But he was never a guy you were going to see sitting in a library doing a Ph.D. for five years," he recalled.[25]

While we all mature from the teenage versions of ourselves, it is clear his father was the yardstick against which Trudeau judged himself—then and, most likely, now. The deduction that can be made is that his "just getting by" way of doing things was a reaction to, and rebellion against, his father. It doesn't take a team of Viennese psychologists to arrive at the conclusion that Trudeau's childhood experiences left him craving parental affection and approval—feelings for which politics can act as a placebo (until suddenly it doesn't). Little seems to have given him more pleasure than being told by his mother, Margaret, that, upon returning from a rafting trip with his son in 1992, Pierre said, "You know, I never realized it but Justin is really very good with people."[26] The younger Trudeau's inclusion of the anecdote in his memoir suggests that laurels were hard won in the Trudeau household.

In the decade between his CBC appearance at Brébeuf and his emergence into the national consciousness at his father's funeral, Trudeau attempted to lay down his own path. He did so under the media radar and we are reliant on his own account for much of the detail of these formative years.

His erratic grades extinguished hopes of going to McGill Law, but he scored well enough to gain entry to arts at McGill, to study literature. It was there that he was introduced to Gerald Butts, the razor-sharp son of a Cape Breton coal miner who served as vice-president of the McGill Debating Union and who would go on to do his master's thesis on James Joyce's *Ulysses*. The two met on the steps of what is now the William Shatner University Centre, after being introduced by a mutual friend named Jonathan Ablett, whose father had worked in the Privy Council Office under Trudeau's father. "The thing that struck me about Justin the first time I met him was how normal he was," said Butts. "People ask me, 'What's his greatest achievement?' I say that he has grown up in the most abnormal circumstances imaginable, maybe the most unusual of anyone in the country, and he's a normal dude."[27]

Butts convinced Trudeau to join the debating society, and they bonded on the return trip from a competition against a Princeton University team that included future U.S. presidential candidate Ted Cruz.[28] "Conspiracy theorists see a plan [to run the country] from the beginning, but we mostly hung out, drank beer, and shot pool," remembered Butts.[29] Neither young man was particularly political. "My first exposure to politics was when I went to his dad's Charlottetown Accord speech in October 1992. If you find the *Montreal Gazette* from that day, Justin and I were his dad's security detail—really long-haired versions of both of us pushing reporters away."

Butts would go on to become principal secretary for Ontario premier Dalton McGuinty and, later still, would serve in the same role in Trudeau's Liberal government. He had been planning to study for a Ph.D. on the philosopher Hegel but became involved in politics working on papers for then Liberal senator Allan MacEachen (Pierre Trudeau's former finance minister). In 2000, Butts was subsidizing his doctoral studies by running focus groups for the Liberal-associated polling firm Pollara when he became so infuriated with the Ontario government of Mike Harris that he contacted McGuinty's office. He rose to become director of policy and, as reporters in the cozy press gallery at Queen's Park could attest, was an architect of the platform and the sweeping victory in the 2003 provincial election. Butts recalls Trudeau visiting him during his time at Queen's Park and was showing him around the premier's office when they bumped into a young intern. "He introduced himself to Justin and said he'd just become a Canadian citizen that day." The intern was Ahmed Hussen, a former Somali refugee whom Trudeau appointed as his immigration minister in 2017.

Trudeau and Butts remained as tight as two coats of paint since those early days, serving in each other's wedding parties and constantly consulting and advising one another. "Gerald is not just a best friend, he is my closest advisor as leader of the Liberal Party of Canada," Trudeau said in *Common Ground*, which was published before the 2015 election.[30]

His English literature degree at McGill exposed Trudeau to a range of writers—he cited William Blake, Aldous Huxley, and Wallace Stevens in his memoir. He credits his wide-ranging reading habits for helping to preserve his political personality as an "open-minded centrist," just as many of his contemporaries pledged themselves to the *Communist Manifesto* or *Atlas Shrugged*. He quotes one of his father's favourite sayings—Thomas Aquinas's admonition, "I fear the man of a single book" —for persuading him that life is too complicated to be explained by an overarching ideology,[31] even if his critics contend he is less open-minded and centrist than he might profess.

Trudeau's enthusiasm for Canadian politics was stoked during his second year at McGill during the referendum campaign surrounding the Charlottetown Accord that sought to bring Quebec into the Canadian Constitution as a "distinct society." Trudeau, like his father, emerged as one of the few Quebec federalists who opposed the accord, siding with the Péquistes. Trudeau said he took to wearing a T-shirt that read: "My No is a federalist No."[32]

Three years later, Quebec was again plunged into constitutional crisis, this time over the province's second referendum. This was another pivotal event in the life of the impressionable young man. The No side won by just 54,288 votes, ensuring that Quebec stayed in Canada. If half of those voters, plus one, had cast their lot with the separatists, Canada would have broken up. "And what message would we have offered the world?" asked Trudeau. "If even a country as respectful of its diversities as ours had failed to reconcile its differences, what hope would the rest of the world have of getting along? To this day, that question is one that drives me."[33]

It is reasonable to suggest that the younger Trudeau, like his father, became a passionate advocate of greater protection for individual rights as a reaction against what he saw as an outdated ethnic nationalism. After leaving McGill with a B.A. in English literature, Trudeau headed east and . . . kept going. Like most bumptious young men, he wanted to travel to let the world see him. He had travelled with his father as a child and recalled meeting British prime minister Margaret Thatcher, German chancellor Helmut Schmidt, and Swedish prime minister Olof Palme, who gave him a reindeer-hunting knife. The first dead body he saw was Russian leader Leonid Brezhnev, in 1982.

But this was an altogether less exalted trip. In September 1994, he met with old Brébeuf friends Marc Miller, Mathieu Walker, and Allen Steverman (the latter two both now Montreal doctors) in London and set off for Africa on an overland expedition. In a beaten-up old truck, they drove through Morocco, Mauritania, Mali, Burkina Faso, Ivory Coast, Ghana, Togo, and Benin over the course of two and a half months. Miller said Trudeau relished the relative anonymity, noting, "He's a guy who, whether he likes it or not, was born with a camera in his face—he's someone of note in Canada. But we went through Africa and no one knew who he was. I think that was extremely liberating for him."[34]

There were adventures along the way—different members of the group were robbed, they were tear-gassed at a soccer stadium in Ivory Coast, Miller beat the village strongman in an arm wrestle in Mali, and they had their last case of bad Moroccan beer confiscated at a border post in Mauritania, only to pass through customs and be given the opportunity to buy it back (which they did). The trek ended in Benin and the group flew to Finland, where they spent Christmas in Helsinki. Miller returned to Montreal to start his law studies, but Trudeau headed to Russia, where he crossed the steppes on the Trans-Siberian Express. He then spent some months touring Asia before heading home to Canada. By the end of his year-long sojourn, he was in a position to concur with Mark Twain's famous observation that travel is fatal to prejudice, bigotry, and narrow-mindedness.[35]

But it also brought home to him something he claims to have taken for granted in Canada: that, wherever he went, there was a clear majority and minorities who were always "others"—exceptions to the national identity. In Mauritania, for example, they had only abolished slavery thirteen years prior to Trudeau's trip there. "In contrast, our modern Canadian identity is no longer based on ethnic, religious, historical or geographic grounds. Canadians are of every possible colour, culture and creed, and continue to celebrate and revel in our diversity," he said in *Common Ground*.[36]

It should be borne in mind that Trudeau's memoir was written with one eye on the pending 2015 election, during which the refrain "Canada is strong not in spite of our differences but because of them" was heard nightly in campaign venues across the country. But it seems plausible that this was not merely pre-election pandering, and that the twenty-three-year-old did experience some kind of epiphany—that justice, equality, and tolerance were not as revered in the places he visited as they were at home.

The year of travelling also seems to have instilled in Trudeau a wanderlust, and within months of returning to his father's home on avenue des Pins in Montreal, he felt the urge to travel again, heading west this time. Finding work as a snowboarding instructor and part-time doorman at Whistler's Rogue Wolf nightclub, he said he realized he had a talent for engaging kids. This led to his enrolling at the University of British Columbia's Faculty of Education and completing a twelve-month education program, before accepting a job at West Point Grey Academy, a private co-ed school in Vancouver, where he taught French, drama, and math. Trudeau spent two and a half years at the academy, indulging his own predilection for brain-teasers and math puzzles. He said his "unorthodox approach" made him popular with the students but less so with the conservative school administrators. After a disagreement over an article written by a student in the in-house newspaper for which Trudeau was responsible, and the subsequent closure of the newspaper, he decided to leave West Point Grey and move to the Vancouver public system at Sir Winston Churchill Secondary School.

But for Trudeau, life on the left coast was drawing to a close, the consequence of two devastating personal tragedies—the loss in November 1998 of his twenty-three-year-old younger brother, Michel, in an avalanche while backcountry skiing in British Columbia's Kokanee Glacier Provincial Park, and two years later the death of his "invincible" father.

Trudeau said he spoke to Michel a week before his death. To ask his brother not to go out in the backcountry would have been to deny the life Michel had chosen to lead, he said. Kokanee Lake was at the bottom of the mountains, and an early-season avalanche knocked Michel into the depths of the lake, where he drowned. His body has never been recovered. In his memoir, Trudeau recalled how Michel had rebelled against his father's influence, called himself "Mike," and gone to Dalhousie in Halifax to study, before heading west. He said the two brothers had been close as kids but had drifted apart as adults, as Michel had set out to forge an identity distinct from the rest of the Trudeau family. Justin wrote about how he still misses a brother who was able to find a "calm zone, a private place" that eludes many people—including, his words suggested, himself.[37]

By Christmas of that year, Pierre Trudeau was hospitalized with a case of pneumonia. His eldest son's opinion was that his father was never the same man after Michel's death. His mother also suffered debilitating grief at losing her youngest son. "Michel's death and its impact on my parents affected me deeply," Justin wrote. "I spent long days in contemplation and long nights dealing with the loss of Michel, my mother's struggles and the reality of my heretofore invincible father's deterioration."[38] Justin's memoir makes clear how profoundly the devout Pierre was affected by the death of his son: "One day," he recalled, "my father suggested to my mother: 'If there is no afterlife, then nothing I have done in my life matters at all.' It may have been the most profoundly sad thing my father ever said."[39]

But while Michel's death weakened his father's faith, Justin said it had the opposite effect on him. He attended an Alpha course, an evangelistic program that seeks to explore the basics of Christian faith through discussion. "I was suspicious that the course would consist of proselytizing for one sect or another," he wrote. "But I discovered this wasn't the case at all. Instead it was about developing the humility necessary to admit that we cannot get through life's most difficult challenges on our own. Sometimes we need God's help."[40]

By the spring of 2000, Pierre Elliott Trudeau was dying—he had been diagnosed with prostate cancer and had decided not to pursue treatment. Justin spent the summer with him in Montreal, reading him Shakespeare. He died in late September. And it was Shakespeare whom Trudeau said he had on his mind as he was getting ready to head to Notre-Dame Basilica to give the eulogy that marked his re-emergence into the Canadian consciousness. The fresh-faced twenty-eight-year-old opened with a line from the Bard's *Julius Caesar*: "Friends, Romans, countrymen . . . ," inspired by his intention to praise, not bury, his father.

The eulogy was an audacious performance—overwrought, to be sure, but replete with the three-legged stool of Aristotelian rhetoric: ethos, pathos, and logos. He captured his audience and made them laugh and cry. He spoke clearly in English and French and reinforced the life lessons instilled by his father—"genuine and deep respect for every human being, notwithstanding their thoughts, their values, their beliefs and their origins." He concluded by adapting a Robert Frost poem: "The woods are lovely, dark and deep. He has kept his promise and earned his sleep. *Je t'aime, papa*"—before laying his head against the coffin, as he choked back tears.[41, 42] It was another torrid way-post for a young man not yet thirty, who had seen his parents divorce and who had buried his brother and then his father. But it undoubtedly shaped his temperament and resolve. What else could life pitch that was more difficult?

The bulk of the coverage the next day was laudatory, with the *Globe and Mail* claiming Trudeau had captured the hearts of the country. (The *National Post* was typically contrarian, with Peter Scowen deeming the eulogy a "treacly, over-acted" embarrassment and scoffing, "He squinted his eyes for emphasis, he raised and lowered his voice for dramatic effect, he gesticulated like a third-rate modern dancer. It felt not so much like being in the presence of a new generation of Trudeau greatness, as like being on *Romper Room*, listening to a story about a magic bean."[43])

The prospect of a career in politics had been raised with Trudeau before the funeral—and he had said it did not interest him. "I'm passionate about politics because I'm passionate about life. But this is not my direction. I don't read the newspapers. I don't watch the news. . . . So much of politics is posturing and playing for the crowd, playing for the cameras. It's not something I feel any interest in," he wrote in an opinion article—undermining the case that he didn't much care for the media.[44] It is more than a little comical that such a disclaimer should come from someone who has proven so proficient at posturing and playing for the crowd.

Despite Trudeau's apparent reluctance, some fine judges of political horse flesh had already spotted his potential. Tom Axworthy, who had been Pierre Trudeau's chief of staff and had known Justin from birth, said he saw echoes of the father in the son, noting, "He has a tremendous communications ability in both languages, a natural eloquence and flair that his dad certainly had. Those genes were passed on."[45] After the funeral, Trudeau said he was approached to run for the Liberals but that he was determined to stay away from the traditional political world, avoiding all Liberal events.

Yet he said his new-found public image encouraged him to push causes he believed in, such as avalanche safety and, increasingly, issues affecting young people. His father's old friend Jacques Hébert had launched Katimavik in the 1970s as the country's pre-eminent youth services program. The idea of joining this organization and promoting volunteerism in both official languages appealed to Trudeau's emerging sense of civic engagement. Within a couple of years, he was chairing Katimavik's board and had persuaded Jean Chrétien's Liberal government to increase its funding to $20 million a year. Elizabeth Gray-Smith, the daughter of Pierre's cabinet colleague Herb Gray, worked as Justin's press aide one day while he was promoting Katimavik in Ottawa and remembered, "The day culminated with a big speech at the auditorium at Lisgar High School. He got up on stage and you could hear a pin drop. That takes skill, that takes charisma. I was blown away—I went home and told my dad, 'This guy's going to be prime minister.'"[46]

Seamus O'Regan was introduced to Trudeau by his CTV colleague Ben Mulroney, son of another former prime minister in 2001. "We just hit it off," said O'Regan. "He was naturally curious, had a great sense of humour, and connected the dots on a bunch of different stuff. He was a great conversationalist, almost a Newfoundlander, which is the highest praise I can give. Believe it or not, there was a refreshing lack of ego. The guy's not lacking for confidence, but he's not over-confident. I would never accuse him of being cocky."[47] O'Regan invited Trudeau to the 2002 Juno music awards, which were being held in St. John's, Newfoundland and Labrador, and it became clear that the eulogy for his father had transformed him into a celebrity. "Rock stars wanted to be with him—he was completely flattered by it all," said O'Regan. "People could almost feel he was going to do something. . . . I hate the notion of it—I don't like the sense of inevitability or fate. But there was a whiff of it. Undeniably, there was a whiff of it."[48]

The desire to be closer to his grieving mother and a vague feeling that it was time to settle down persuaded Trudeau to move back to Montreal, where a teaching job proved hard to find with his B.C. credentials. In another instance of the kind of career non sequitur that had marked his progress through life up to that point, he decided to park his teaching ambitions and study engineering. He presented it as a new intellectual challenge and something entirely unexpected, "at least for those who didn't know me well."[49] In the fall of 2002, he enrolled at the Université de Montréal's École Polytechnique to study engineering.

It was during this time that he met Sophie Grégoire, when they co-hosted a children's foundation gala. A former classmate of Trudeau's younger brother Michel, Grégoire was a well-known Quebec TV and radio host and Holt Renfrew personal shopper when they met. A stylish brunette, she described herself as "passionate, spontaneous, extroverted" and a "bonne vivante" in a 2001 interview with Quebec showbiz magazine *7 Jours*. The interview revealed that her parents had nicknamed her "The Tornado" and that she had tried her hand at deep-sea diving, tennis, ballet, jazz, pottery, and the flute. On men, she had "no tolerance for cowardice" and didn't like "wet noodles."[50]

The couple met again for dinner at Montreal's Khyber Pass Afghan restaurant, and as the date drew to a close, Trudeau said he felt a "giddy sense that Sophie would be the last woman I ever dated, a feeling so strong, I actually said: 'I'm 31-years-old. Can we just skip the boyfriend/ girlfriend part and go straight to engaged, since we're going to spend the rest of our lives together?'"[51] It was a stark contrast to the indecision that hobbled his professional life. Trudeau is frank about the "joy for spontaneity" he shares with his mother. An informal proposal on a first date suggests the impetuosity of a poet. But his instinct appears to have been unerring on this occasion.

They were married on May 28, 2005, in Montreal. "A Hollywood wedding this was not," wrote gossip columnist Shinan Govani, who frowned over Trudeau's "unorthodox beige tuxedo" and gushed about Sophie's deeply décolleté gown "that matched the colour of the Veuve Clicquot that was being generously passed around." He went on to declare, "These nuptials were notable for their non-over-the-top-ness and the guest list not made up overwhelmingly of back-scratching political hacks or two-bit celebrities spread out like cream cheese on the couple's big day cracker. These were, more or less, the couple's close friends and family." Govani noted presciently that at one point Trudeau was seen talking to his friend Seamus O'Regan, about whom there were rumours of political aspirations. "A preview of a Cabinet meeting from 2015?" he mused.[52] (He was out by a couple of years—Trudeau appointed the MP for St. John's South–Mount Pearl as veterans affairs minister in August 2017.)

The couple departed for their honeymoon in Mauritius in Pierre's 1960s Mercedes-Benz convertible, with a single red rose on the back of the car. Trudeau was frank in his own memoir that the fairy-tale romance has had its rocky patches. "Our marriage isn't perfect and we have had difficult ups and downs, yet Sophie remains my best friend, my partner, my love. We are honest with each other, even when it hurts," he said.[53] Both Trudeau and his wife have been asked about rumours of extramarital affairs since their wedding. Trudeau dismissed the speculation, as any good politician would. But in an interview with the *Globe and Mail*, Grégoire Trudeau admitted they had been to marriage counselling, though she wouldn't elaborate on why.[54] When she spoke to *Global News*, she was even more candid. "I can tell you right away that no marriage is easy," she said. "I'm almost kind of proud of the fact that we've had hardship, yes, because we want authenticity. We want truth. We want to grow closer as individuals through our lifetime and we're both dreamers and we want to be together for as long as we can. I'm happy that we had to go through that."[55]

O'Regan said the relationship between Justin and Sophie was "passionate and intimate" from day one. "They both knew very early on this was going to happen. I'd never seen him like that. It was evident she was special. . . . She was very comfortable with him and the whole scene. I don't think politics was necessarily something that was natural to her, but the wackiness that was ever-present in his life was something she could adjust to. She could occupy that world with him, which is not easy to find," he observed. "When the two of them are together, and they're both energetic about something, there's almost a hurricane of energy. She brings that out in him." O'Regan said Grégoire Trudeau has struck a fine balance by enjoying the public persona but not becoming enthralled by it. But he acknowledged that the pressures on the marriage are intense. "It's as you'd expect if you're the prime minister and you marry an extremely intelligent, wilful, creative person who wants to make her own mark on the world," he said.[56]

Trudeau acknowledged the difficult life of the political wife, remarking, "Whether it's Michelle Obama or Melania Trump or Hillary Clinton, there's a whole cottage industry of people willing to criticize the choices that a spouse makes. . . . Sophie does an extraordinary job being an amazing mom for the times I'm not as present as I'd like to be, a great partner and manages to bring forward her voice on important issues that matter to her. But it's never easy."[57] Like any couple, they argue on some things and search for compromise on others. "We even make sure we get little date nights now and then. We get a quiet corner of the restaurant and Canadians are lovely in not bothering us more than they have to," he said.[58] O'Regan said he thinks their relationship is strong enough to weather inevitable storms, noting, "I think what they have underneath all of that is just too strong. I really do. I think the love is quite real."[59] Another close friend agreed that the couple's relationship is solid: "Staying married is a choice we make every day. I have nothing but respect for the way they have managed their unique circumstance. As for the rest, it is nobody's business."[60]

As the courtship blossomed, Trudeau was still floundering in his professional life. He concluded that his engineering studies were "an intellectual indulgence" and left the program. Meanwhile, he was dabbling with the volunteer sector (as chair of Katimavik and a board member of the Canadian Avalanche Foundation); the media (in a weekly segment on French radio in Montreal); and public speaking on youth and the environment. He signed up with the Speaker's Spotlight bureau and quickly found he was in demand—earning $290,000 in 2006 and an eye-watering $462,000 in 2007, according to the *Ottawa Citizen*.[61] To bolster his speaking career, Trudeau realized he needed a deeper understanding on environmental issues, so in the fall of 2005 he decided to continue his education by pursuing a graduate degree in environmental geography at McGill. (This was another degree he didn't finish, abandoning it to focus on politics.)

He also dabbled in acting, appearing as World War One hero Talbot Papineau in a CBC Television drama production. The producers were looking for a dashing Quebecer to play the bilingual, bicultural Rhodes scholar who died in the battle of Passchendaele, aged thirty-four—and Trudeau's name came up. "I'm excited about it. This is something completely new for me—and, geez, I hope I don't suck," he said.[62] He needn't have worried—he gave what was widely regarded as a creditable performance, aided by his affinity with the character. "I would be incapable of playing a role that wasn't very much me, and that was why I was sort of safe with this," he commented.[63] His biggest challenge as an actor was to tone down his natural exuberance. "What I tend to do is overdramatize a bit, but that was quickly nipped in the bud. In some of the voiceover work we did, Brian [McKenna, the director] was like 'Justin, don't slip into melodrama, keep it straight, keep it real.'"[64] It would not be the last time Trudeau was criticized for being too theatrical.

While his dance card was full, and money was not an issue—during the Liberal leadership race in 2013, Trudeau conceded that he'd "won the lottery" by being born into a wealthy family and revealed that his inheritance was worth $1.2 million—his pursuits were aimless. Perhaps unconsciously, Trudeau was again following in the footsteps of his father. Stephen Clarkson and Christina McCall, in their biography *Trudeau and Our Times*, concluded that Pierre was a mythological "eternal boy" who attempted to delay adulthood and prolong adolescence. Once he'd completed his schooling, he spent a decade and a half writing articles, driving fast cars, travelling the globe, and escorting beautiful women. Former classmates envied him: "Most of us married fairly early and started to raise a family and you had to earn money for that. As a rich bachelor, Pierre was able to spend years 'finding himself,'" said one.[65]

Justin's oscillation between coasts and careers was less glittering—he seems to have tried to resist the tractor beam of Liberal politics by exploring all the alternatives. But by the time of Paul Martin's election loss to Stephen Harper's Conservatives in January 2006, his involvement with youth and environmental advocacy had pulled him into the orbit of electoral politics. "The more I spoke with young people all over the country, the more I began to gravitate toward a life of advocacy," he remembered. "It was becoming increasingly clear to me that the issues youth cared about—education, the environment, their generation's economic prospects—needed a stronger voice in the public sphere. I also began to feel that a generational change was approaching, one that might open up new possibilities."[66]

He contacted Tom Axworthy, who was heading up the Liberal Party's Renewal Commission after Martin stepped down as leader. The offer to help was accepted and he was named as the head of the party's youth task force on renewal. He later recalled that he had taken out a party membership but that a career in politics remained a "far-off possibility," despite the hopes of those Liberals holding out for a saviour who could capture the *Zeitgeist* in the way his father did in 1968. From the outset, he wanted to be recognized as someone who had developed his own expertise, rather than as someone trading on his father's reputation. "This isn't me choosing to leverage anything out of this. This is really me saying: 'How can I help?' I'm saddled with a name that has positive connotations for some people and hugely negative connotations for other people. All I'm saying is, I've been an activist for quite a while around youth issues and if I can weigh in on this, I really should."[67]

Axworthy described Trudeau's involvement as a step toward the Liberal Party. "He will be in the company of some very seasoned political folk and some world-class thinkers. We'll see how he does but I'm pretty confident about it."[68] His confidence was well placed. Engagement in the renewal process proved to be catnip for the Liberal Party's newest member. He was clearly thinking seriously about the personal metamorphosis required by politics, even before the leadership convention in December. The *Globe*'s Roy MacGregor reported him saying, in November, "I've got to quit using 'I' so much. I've got to quit using 'I' so much."[69]

Trudeau's initial finding as head of the youth task force was that the most pressing challenge was to get young people to vote at all. While there were many passionate young activists, they tended not to involve themselves in elections. Overcoming the cynicism about politics was to become a dominant theme in the 2015 election campaign, but it was to have less impact in 2006.

Trudeau initially said he didn't intend to endorse a leadership candidate, but he ended up backing Ontario provincial cabinet minister Gerard Kennedy, in part because of his public service record outside politics as head of Toronto's Daily Bread Food Bank. Trudeau said he felt the Liberal Party was in a deeper hole than many realized and that it needed a leader from a new generation, someone from outside the federal party, to reinvigorate it.[70]

It was as part of Kennedy's team that he came into contact with Katie Telford, who worked as Kennedy's chief of staff at Queen's Park and was national campaign director for the leadership bid. Trudeau had asked to meet with Telford for dinner before the convention, and they engaged in heated debate about the issue of recognizing Quebec as a nation. Telford hadn't known what to expect from the man with the famous name, and she apparently registered surprise at his knowledge and passion. As he left the restaurant, he offered an aside: "I'm not quite what you thought I was, am I?"[71]

At a dramatic delegated leadership convention in Montreal in December 2006, Kennedy lost out to eventual victor Stéphane Dion as the standard-bearer of those who did not want Bob Rae or Michael Ignatieff to win. The sense that a Rae or Ignatieff victory would split the party allowed Dion to come up the middle and triumph. For Trudeau, the weekend in Montreal was pivotal to his decision to launch his own political career. He said he loved the ideas, values, and policy-making involved, but recalled his mother's words of caution that a politician's life comes with incredible personal cost.

And then there was Pierre. "The association with my father was never a reason for me to get into politics," Trudeau revealed. "It was, rather, a reason for me to avoid entering the political arena."[72] As Butts told the *Globe*, "That polarity is what he must deal with every time he opens his mouth. He's not dealing with his father's looming figure but a ghost."[73] The thought of being measured according to his father's achievements was a burden Trudeau struggled with, even in adulthood. Roy MacGregor summed up the contrasting personalities: "The father was sewn up so tightly, nothing ever got out he did not wish to be seen, the Jesuit Spartan micro-managing his own emotions. The son sometimes bursts through the stitches, the inside exposed for anyone within hearing distance."[74]

The younger Trudeau also expressed exasperation at the impression among many Canadians that he was vacuous. "What am I supposed to do?" he asked. "Recite pi to the 10th decimal? Ask them to throw me a line of poetry and have me finish the poem?"[75] But he said his time mixing with Liberals at the Palais des congrès in Montreal persuaded him that when it came to campaigning, he was Jimmy Sinclair's grandson—"the ultimate retail politician." He recalled, "The experience of the convention had taught me something: I had political skills independent of my last name. I'll not pretend the name didn't make a difference but it wasn't all I had. Not by a long shot."[76]

At the age of thirty-five, it was time to embrace adulthood—and, perhaps, destiny.

TWO

TESTING THE WATER WITH BOTH FEET

AT VARIOUS POINTS DURING his decade or more in politics, Trudeau has implied that his critics are guilty of cynicism, when in fact they are more often culpable of nothing worse than realism. This tendency toward self-righteousness, even when he's wrong, was evident early on in his political career, when he chided the media for suggesting that he coveted the Liberal nomination in the Montreal riding of Outremont —even though his own memoir later made clear that he had actively sought the relatively safe seat. In February 2007, Trudeau confirmed that he would seek the nomination in the much tougher riding of Papineau, a seat that had been Liberal but which at that time was held by respected Bloc Québécois MP Vivian Barbot. "There is no question that I wanted to do this," he admitted, "that I wanted to fight for it. I'm not the kind of person who enjoys getting handed things, despite what the newspapers like to say."[1]

Yet, as he revealed in his memoir, before he announced he would run in Papineau, he had wanted the nomination for the nearby Outremont riding. It had been vacated by the late Jean Lapierre, Paul Martin's Quebec lieutenant, and Trudeau had even made representations about the vacancy. "I called Stéphane [Dion] again and told him I was interested in running for him, and that I thought Outremont would be a good fit," Trudeau said.[2] It seems the newspapers got it just about right.

Outremont was the riding where he lived with his wife, Sophie, in their new $1.2 million home; it was where his baby son, Xavier, would live after his birth on October 18, 2007. The problem was that neither the local riding association nor the leader's office wanted him to run there. Trudeau described the atmosphere as "outright toxic."

In the end, he was forced to look elsewhere—a decision that may have been consequential, given that the NDP candidate in the Outremont by-election was well-known former provincial Liberal cabinet minister Tom Mulcair, who proceeded to steam-roll all opposition and take the seat. It is one of those quirks of providence that Mulcair did not get the chance to smother Trudeau's political career before it was able to oxidize and, ultimately, engulf his own. But in blocking Trudeau's candidacy in Outremont, Dion inadvertently set in train events that would culminate in the "Orange Wave" of successful NDP candidates throughout Quebec in 2011.

Trudeau ended up seeking the nomination in Papineau, a diverse north-end riding where the immigrant population is around 40 per cent and which, according to the 2016 census, has the second-lowest median family income of any riding in Canada. Jean Lapierre, who left politics to become a commentator, said Trudeau had to prove to Quebecers that he had "something in his belly." To do so, he would have to overturn the impression that he had "never done anything with his two hands."[3] But Trudeau was up for the challenge of wrestling back a seat that had been Liberal from 1953 until Barbot won it for the Bloc in the 2006 election. "What better way to prove my worth?" he asked.[4]

Dion's team was determined to do Trudeau no favours, and he was forced to fight a tough, contested nomination race against a popular local city councillor, Mary Deros, and an Italian-language newspaper publisher, Basilio Giordano. There was trepidation in the Liberal establishment in Quebec that Trudeau might hurt the party's efforts in the province at a time when the Conservatives and even the NDP were showing signs of life. The Liberals had been buffeted by the sponsorship scandal, the illicit and even illegal use of public funds intended for federal government advertising in Quebec. The feeling was that the province had to be wooed, not subjected to the kind of tough love synonymous with the Trudeau name. Justin had made known his opposition to the Conservative motion in the House of Commons in 2006 that recognized the Québécois as a nation within Canada, calling it "an old idea from the 19th century . . . based on smallness of thought."[5]

But Trudeau was more focused on local issues than grander constitutional questions—and quickly found that he had a natural affinity for retail politics. "After experiencing the drama and manoeuvring of the 2006 Liberal leadership convention, this brand of up-close-and-personal politicking quickened my pulse. I'm a social being by nature. I'm also someone who enjoys physical activity, which campaigning in Papineau required in large degree," he said.[6] A standard observation by the political veterans interviewed in the course of the research for this book is how natural Trudeau is with people, despite describing himself as an introvert who learned how to be gregarious. "I've never seen anything like it," said one person who has worked on many campaigns over the past twenty years. "He's holding hands with this little old lady for forty-five seconds and she's beaming and saying, 'I met you when you were four'—the type of stuff that makes most politicians think, 'Shoot me now.' But he's loving it. I can't think of another word for it than 'gifted.' I was constantly floored by how good he was."[7]

Trudeau recognized that politics is a tactile business and that he needed to spend his days knocking on doors and walking around the neighbourhoods of Papineau if he was going to triumph. But while he might have been born into politics, Trudeau was never taught its arts. His opponents were using their supporters to tap into local community groups, and the electoral math was pointing toward a humiliation. Fortunately for Trudeau, help arrived in mid-March, when veteran political organizers Reine Hébert and Franco Iacono joined the campaign team. Hébert brought in Louis-Alexandre Lanthier, a Montreal native who had worked on Parliament Hill for, among others, Ken Dryden. The new team not only increased membership sales but schooled the would-be candidate in the rudiments of campaigning. Instead of striding through the riding in his sunglasses, he was trained to walk more slowly behind a campaign team member, who would offer an initial greeting to people that allowed Trudeau to follow up once the startled residents had lifted their heads. And instead of offering a quick "hello" or "pleased to meet you," Lanthier urged him to introduce himself by name, or risk being regarded as "some friendly oddball who randomly shook their hand."[8]

On one occasion, Trudeau was given the kind of briefing book common on Parliament Hill—the type his father would have brought home by the box-load while he was prime minister. "Imagine this is the first time I've seen one of these. What would you like me to do with it?" he asked his advisers. It was a light-bulb moment for the political veterans, who realized the elder Trudeau had not mixed political and family time. "We really were starting from scratch," said Lanthier.[9] Yet, while the stagecraft required honing, the natural showmanship was already in evidence. Those closest to him say Trudeau feeds off the energy of crowds in a way that less instinctive politicians are unable to do. Lanthier recalled the 2011 campaign, when Trudeau did an event with then leader Michael Ignatieff: "When Michael came into the room, people were running up to him and hugging him. By the time he got to the green room, he was exhausted. It drained every bit of energy from him. Justin said, 'Michael, you have to learn how to let the crowd invigorate you. If they drain you, you're not going to last.' Justin had figured that out for himself."[10]

The focus on a street-level campaign paid off. Supported by his wife, Sophie, his brother, Sacha, and his mother, Margaret, he won the nomination on the first ballot—precluding the prospect of his two local rivals combining forces to defeat him on the second ballot. It's impossible to know how many in the packed Montreal college gym backed him because of his family name. But he leaned heavily on his father in his speech, noting that the Park Extension neighbourhood that was part of the Papineau constituency had been in Pierre's Mount Royal riding when he was sent to Ottawa for the first time in 1965. "We are all children of the Charter, and of that we are immensely proud. So you can understand how proud I am to be able to say that your prime minister was also my dad."[11]

The response to his speech on the night put the new candidate on notice about what to expect from a media unimpressed by his pedigree. In the *Montreal Gazette*, veteran columnist Don Macpherson compared Trudeau to a sixties tribute band, noting, "Although he sometimes complains about the burden of expectations he inherited along with his father's name and fortune, his seven-minute speech before the vote was about his father and his Charter of Rights. It was not about his own program or record of accomplishment, leaving one to conclude that he has neither to offer."[12]

The nomination victory immediately placed an additional burden on Trudeau—party discipline. Accustomed to speaking his mind, he made a speech to teachers in New Brunswick during the week of his victory that questioned the existing system of English and French school boards, suggesting that it would be more cost-effective and better for students if they merged. He also compared sovereigntists to children who whine and complain to get more attention. The comments were raised with Dion in Ottawa, where the Liberal leader said his new candidate's words didn't reflect the party's official position and that he personally would not have talked about his political opponents in such a disrespectful fashion. "He is new. He will no doubt have to make his thoughts more precise," said the leader, in a smack-down that must have stung the self-regard of the political neophyte.[13] Trudeau apologized, but not before Bloc Québécois leader Gilles Duceppe pounced on the comments, suggesting they showed a lack of knowledge about jurisdictions —education being a provincial responsibility—and an "arrogant attitude" toward French Canadians. Despite being a politician who has become synonymous with digital media savvy, it would not be the last time Trudeau was caught saying something in one part of the country that spread quickly via the Internet and tripped him up in another.

The nomination team broke up after Trudeau's victory, but he persuaded Lanthier to come back as full-time campaign manager. In those pre–fixed-election-date, minority-government days, an election could break out at any moment and it was anticipated that Stephen Harper might call one in the fall of 2007. In the event, it didn't come until the following year, but Trudeau and Lanthier made good use of the intervening period. The strategy was to have Trudeau act as if he was already the member of Parliament for Papineau, attending every church bazaar, bingo hall, and community event he could. The riding was divided into three parts—strong Bloc Québécois francophone territory in Villeray, Liberal-friendly Park Extension, and the swing area of Saint-Michel, with its large Italian and Haitian populations.

The luxury of time, combined with his strength with people, meant that Trudeau was able to swim against a tide that swept away Dion's leadership and his ill-fated Green Shift, the ecological fiscal reform that he pioneered. The Liberal Party's pollster Michael Marzolini tried to persuade Dion that the focus groups appraising the plan that would lower income taxes and raise levies on greenhouse gases were not convinced. "The focus groups were bad. Marzolini told the leader's office, 'Don't do this, don't do this, don't do this.' But Dion insisted and they did it anyway," said one person who was party to the discussions.[14]

Yet in Papineau, Trudeau was defying the receding Liberal tide. He had started door-knocking in the neighbourhoods in Villeray and Saint-Michel that had been lost by less than 10 per cent in 2006. The response was predictable—that Satan would be seen skating to work before the son of Pierre Trudeau was winning their vote. But Trudeau was a disarming presence on the doorstep, according to those who watched his campaign up close. He would say to supporters of separation that, while they would always differ on the issue of Quebec, they might agree on the environment or health care—and that they were almost certainly united in opposition to the Harper Conservatives. In the eighteen months between winning the nomination and the election, he was able to hit those polls twice, and the second time around, the response was less hostile. "My thought was 'That person is not going to vote for us but I'm not sure that person is going to vote at all now,'" recalled Lanthier.[15]

Shopping for votes in multicultural Papineau, at a time when the "reasonable accommodation" debate in Quebec was at its height, forced the novice candidate to scrutinize his own belief system. Should he, for example, turn down the volume on his advocacy of certain aspects of the Charter of Rights when talking to socially conservative new Canadians? One reason for his success, and for his occasional failures, is that he has never been good at dissembling. So, instead, he addressed the issue head on—against the advice of his more seasoned advisers.

He talked about gay marriage in a speech at a Pakistani-Canadian mosque, where support for the Charter was high, given that it entrenched the freedom to practise religion. "But guess what? Those rights that protect you also give gays the right to marry and give your daughter the right to marry a non-Muslim. The Charter of Rights protects freedoms for everyone. You can't pick and choose the rights you want to keep and leave behind the ones you don't like."[16] The idea that multiculturalism is a social contract that sees newcomers buy into Canadian values in return for respecting aspects of their culture has been as constant as the north star in Trudeau's firmament of beliefs—hardly surprising, given his lineage.

Another recurrence has been his ability to test the depth of the water with both feet. As he admits, this happens most often when he tries to be witty or clever. Disregarding the golden rule, adopted by politicians at all times in all places, not to answer hypothetical questions, Trudeau replied at length to a query on his website asking if an extraterrestrial would be protected by the Charter. The rookie politician thought it would underline his commitment to diversity to say yes—prompting a La Presse cartoon that featured Trudeau telling E.T. that he had Charter rights, while E.T., looking suspiciously like Stéphane Dion, gave him the finger.

On September 7, 2008, Stephen Harper visited the governor general's official residence and asked Michaëlle Jean to call a general election.

The official campaign launch, in late September, contained both the sub-lime and the ridiculous sides of the Trudeau candidacy—the confluence of those who saw him as the second coming and those who "dismissed him as a charlatan who invokes his family name to trade up."[17] He greeted the crowd of three hundred attendees in ten languages; knocked the Conservatives for cutting support grants for artists (a disastrous pol-icy by Harper that played well for the opposition parties in Quebec and arguably denied the Conservative leader his majority); and summarized the Liberal Green Shift—"It's simple: pollute and get penalized."

Supporters inside the storefront committee room on Saint Denis Street talked about witnessing a future prime minister. But outside, a group of fifty "street sovereigntists" objected to his opposition to the idea that the Québécois constituted a nation. Secretly, though, the pro-testers said they were rooting for Trudeau. "We like him because he makes funny and awkward statements," said François Gendron, spokes-person for les Jeunes Patriotes du Québec. His election "could even help our cause."[18]

The hard work was paying off for Trudeau, to the extent that he felt comfortable enough to take some time off from the ground game in Papineau to help the ailing Dion campaign, which was tanking badly. Trudeau looked like he'd leapt from the pages of *People* magazine as he warmed up a campaign rally in North Bay. "Here's the man who in seven days will be the next prime minister of Canada . . . Stéphane Dion!" And Dion looked as if he'd just stepped from the pages of *Current Sociology* as he gave the crowd his trademark goofy grin and a wave that raised the arm of his suit up to his elbow.[19]

The dismal nature of the campaign was captured by the sight of a Liberal supporter at a rally carrying one thunderstick. The meltdown in financial markets meant that the election had become about the econ-omy and leadership—neither of which were Dion's strengths. The day before he was introduced by Trudeau, Dion had to be asked three times in a cTv Halifax interview what he would do about the looming eco-nomic crisis. The Liberal line was that Dion had had trouble hearing the question; cynical journalists suggested it was only the hard questions that he had trouble hearing. The Green Shift policy was a disastrous strategic mistake—too complicated and punitive for Canadian voters in 2008. But voters don't vote for or against policy platforms. They vote for leaders they can trust—whom they feel comfortable supporting. Dion was not that leader and the Liberals went down to defeat, losing eighteen seats.

Papineau was one of the few bright spots, with Trudeau winning his seat by 1,200 votes to become one of only two new Liberals heading to Ottawa. It was an impressive performance—an outsider in every way in one of the poorest ridings in Canada, he won because he proved, in Jean Lapierre's words, that he had "something in his belly" and that he was prepared to get his hands dirty—literally, in the case of the annual spring clean-up at Parc Jarry in the riding.

In his memoir, Trudeau made clear how important his election was to diffuse the dilettante narrative and finally grant him legitimacy. "I had earned the right to sit in the House and no one could ever take that away from me," he declared.[20] He may have displayed the "overwrought elocution of a poor thespian"[21] and championed the Charter rights of extraterrestrials, but he added glamour and excitement to an otherwise dull race. Elderly matriarchs dashed off to install their teeth when he turned up on their doorsteps unannounced. If he was eccentric, he had at least persuaded the voters of Papineau that he was their eccentric.

Between his election in 2008 and his re-election in 2011, Trudeau was surprisingly low-key. The focus was on issues important to the residents of Papineau—immigration and visa requests, Employment Insurance problems, and so on, according to Lanthier, who as executive assistant and close adviser was like a shadow to the young MP for nearly seven years. Trudeau used the time as a backbench opposition MP to learn the issues and skills that were to prove crucial when he became leader. One MP colleague said Trudeau did not make his mark as a backbencher. "He didn't distinguish himself in Question Period or in caucus interventions. You didn't get the sense this guy was on the make. He was unfailingly polite and decent. But had he not had the last name he has, you wouldn't have thought about him one way or the other," he said. "In retrospect, I wonder if he was just keeping his powder dry."[22]

Another colleague from those days agrees that Trudeau didn't make much of an impression. He didn't engage on the bigger issues of the day. "What I found interesting about Justin was that, while Pierre Elliott Trudeau hated constituency work, his son loved that personal contact and solving immigration or pension problems. He really worked on the constituency issues, and you'd see him with a big green folder in the House, signing cards," he said.[23] Rodger Cuzner, the veteran MP from Cape Breton, Nova Scotia, was party whip at the time. "I found out early, he showed up, worked hard, knew his files and always wanted to prove he was capable. He had to do a little bit more than anyone else and he always did a little more than anyone else," he said.[24]

The two files on which the rookie MP was most active were youth programs and immigration. One of his first actions in Parliament was to introduce a motion to create a national policy for youth volunteer service. He quickly discovered that support for ideas is based not on their merits but rather on which party came up with them. In his first major speech in Parliament, Trudeau called for more financial support and programs to encourage young people to get involved in their communities. "Young people get a bad rap, often, for being apathetic, disconnected, cynical about the world," he said after introducing his motion calling for the creation of a national youth service policy. Before he had even heard the details, Bloc youth critic Nicolas Dufour described the proposal as one worthy of Trudeau's father because it infringed on Quebec's jurisdiction.[25] The motion was crushed by the Conservatives and the Bloc.

He also learned the art of not walking over his own message in media scrums. Trudeau had a tendency to engage in long, rambling interviews that would often veer off into areas where the party leadership would prefer him not to go. While he lamented the halcyon days of his father's era, when politicians and reporters engaged in free-form debates, he quickly fell into line with the demand for message discipline and recited talking points. Despite his mostly low-key approach on Parliament Hill, he was open with reporters about his ambition to one day become prime minister. "Do I hope my path takes me in that direction? Absolutely," he said.[26] But he did not actively pursue that ambition in his first term as an MP, and he was a bit-part player in the drama that saw a coalition of Liberals and New Democrats, supported by the Bloc Québécois, attempt to usurp Stephen Harper as prime minister in late 2008.

Harper sniffed the danger and avoided a vote of non-confidence by asking the governor general to prorogue the House of Commons and end the parliamentary session. The legitimacy of a government formed from parties that had just lost a general election, and which would be propped up by a party that wanted to break up the country, was always dubious. The prorogation acted like a time-out and stalled any momentum the coalition force had built up. Their cause wasn't helped by an amateurish television address by Stéphane Dion, who was still Liberal leader, delivered to television networks an hour after their deadline and of substandard, cellphone-like quality. Jean Lapierre said the video looked like it had been made by a high school kid,[27] and it undermined the credibility of a coalition that had been built with the intention of saving the country from the "incompetence" of the Harper government.

After the failure of the coalition to oust Harper, Dion resigned. A new leadership convention was scheduled for May 2009. Michael Ignatieff, Bob Rae, and New Brunswick MP Dominic LeBlanc emerged as interested parties. There were whispers that Trudeau might stand. He even topped one poll of potential replacements for Dion. But he later said he had never had any intention of running and that he was so "uninterested in leadership squabbles," he took a neutral role.[28] Aside from political considerations, Trudeau had more pressing domestic issues on his mind. On February 5, Sophie gave birth to Ella-Grace Margaret Trudeau, a sister for fifteen-month-old Xavier.

Trudeau continued to keep his head down in the run-up to the 2011 election. The only time he caused a stir outside his riding was when he fell foul of the People for Ethical Treatment of Animals (PETA), which complained about a Christmas card that showed the Trudeau family wearing jackets with thick fur trim, with the kids nestled under a fur blanket. It would not be the last time Canada's most photogenic political family would be criticized for their choice of apparel.

Back in Ottawa, a deal saw Ignatieff, the Canadian-born academic and author who had spent most of the previous thirty years outside the country, emerge as leader. The ensuing disaster for the Liberal Party is dealt with in a page and a half of Trudeau's memoir, which is a good indication of how close to the action he was. "Michael's lack of intuitive feel for Canadian politics—perhaps a product of his many years living outside the country—left him vulnerable," Trudeau wrote.[29] Both he and Ignatieff himself blamed the Harper Conservatives for denying the Liberal leader "standing," or a fair hearing, by unleashing ads that suggested he was "just visiting" and was only in it for himself. But the ads worked because they accurately reflected the mood of Canadian voters.

In his part-memoir, part-exorcism, *Fire and Ashes*, Ignatieff admitted that he didn't really know much about politics when he was nominated to run in Etobicoke, Ontario. He claimed that his experience as leader educated him, but most observers of his time in the position would likely agree that politics wasn't really his thing. "Great politicians make contrivance look uncontrived—all the human skills in politics involve artifice but the artifice must be concealed with ease and grace," he said.[30] Ignatieff never mastered that art, but he might have been thinking about Trudeau when he wrote this advice (although it is indicative of their relationship that the younger Trudeau is not once mentioned in the book).

A particularly revealing passage gives vivid description to this inner incongruence Ignatieff suffered. "I have never been so well dressed in my life and never felt so hollow," he wrote. "I would say that some sense of hollowness, some sense of a divide between the face that you present to the world and the face that you reserve for the mirror, is a sign of sound mental health. It's when you no longer notice that the public self has taken over that trouble starts . . . you'll soon surrender your whole life to politics. You become your smile; the fixed rictus of geniality that politics demands of you. When that happens, you've lost yourself."[31] It is interesting that, in his own memoir, Trudeau expressed no such doubts. On the contrary, he said he found his calling in "public service through politics."[32]

During the 2011 election campaign, the Liberals drew big, enthusiastic crowds and Ignatieff was in his element as a performer and orator. He relished the opportunity to take his message to Canadians, but the tour stuck to big cities where the Liberals knew they could draw a crowd. He ended up preaching to the converted. "Our party became an echo chamber," he remarked. "All we were hearing was the sound of our own voices."[33] The result was the worst defeat in the party's history. Harper finally gained his majority, the NDP became the Official Opposition, and the Liberals were reduced to 34 seats. A decade earlier, the party had enjoyed a comfortable majority of 172 seats and then proceeded to lose support gradually in four subsequent elections. Trudeau was re-elected in Papineau, but there was little to celebrate. "In a sense I wasn't really all that surprised," he recalled. "I had felt in my bones that the party's connection to the country had grown perilously weak, and that this was the inevitable conclusion of a long period of disconnection and decline."[34]

Immediately after the election, Trudeau called his old friend, Gerald Butts, and said he was thinking of quitting. Butts advised him to give it some time and see whether his mind was changed after watching the Conservatives run a majority government. Ignatieff stepped down the morning after the crushing defeat, and this time Trudeau did not shut down talk of his interest in running for the Liberal leadership. He said the party had four or five years to rebuild and reconnect with voters and remarked that he would have to weigh up whether he could balance his personal and political duties. But he cautioned against the party pinning all its hopes on a leader deemed to have "star power."[35]

He headed off to Tofino on Vancouver Island, on vacation with his family, to think about his future. His inclination was to leave politics.

He told Butts that he didn't want to spend the next ten years doing something that might not amount to anything. He said he'd tried his best, but the party wasn't listening about the need for root and branch reform, and he didn't want to become a footnote in history. By October 2011, Trudeau was telling reporters that he would not run for the leadership because he barely saw his young family as it was.

But many Liberals did not take the statement as conclusive proof that he was out, noting that there were plenty of signs that he remained engaged. For example, in the same month he admitted, "The intellectual challenge of rebuilding the party from scratch is actually something I quite relish."[36] But if there were large numbers of Liberals urging him to run, support within the party was far from universal. Bob Rae, who emerged as interim leader, cautioned him that leader of the Liberal Party was not an entry-level position.[37]

Further doubts were raised by Trudeau's performance in the final Question Period of 2011 in the House of Commons. At one point, Peter Kent, the Conservative environment minister, belittled his NDP critic, Megan Leslie, for not attending the recent conference on climate change in Durban, South Africa. This inflamed the opposition parties, since the government had decided not to accredit any of their members, making it hard for them to attend. Trudeau couldn't contain himself. He leapt to his feet and shouted, "You piece of shit!" at Kent. According to Lanthier, it was a calculated move—as are many of Trudeau's seemingly impromptu schemes. "He didn't come into the House knowing this was going to happen, but he wanted to call that minister on it. He'd had enough, he got mad, he waited until everyone stopped clapping so that it was the perfect moment to blurt it out," he said.[38]

When tempers had subsided, Trudeau apologized for his use of language that was "decidedly unparliamentary." Kent, somewhat ungraciously, called for a more abject apology. When foreign minister John Baird, a noted parliamentary pugilist, rose to speak, it seemed weeping gelignite was about to be added to an already blazing conflagration. But his point of order ended up defusing the incident. "I'd just like to wish everyone a Merry Christmas and peace on earth," he said.[39] It was a fitting end to a tumultuous parliamentary calendar and a lesson for Trudeau that outrageous behaviour is more likely to attract attention and ridicule than political disciples. The "piece of shit" incident did little to detract from the impression of many Canadians heading into 2012 that Trudeau was a frivolous political lightweight.

The man himself was all but convinced his political race was run.

THREE

LIVING IN THE LIMELIGHT

"I'm amazed by how many people go into politics because they want to be loved. I do think there are people who go into politics because they like the cameras and the microphones but they can't sing or dance."

STEPHEN HARPER, address to the Stanford
Graduate School of Business, February 2018.[1]

THE FORMER PRIME MINISTER didn't mention Justin Trudeau by name in this address, but you didn't have to be Hercule Poirot to pick up on the clues. Trudeau had ruled himself out of the race to succeed Michael Ignatieff, but the Liberal policy convention in Ottawa in January 2012 was pivotal in making him reconsider. It is tempting to believe that the adoration that greeted him there was irresistible to someone so drawn to the cameras and microphones.

Gerald Butts refutes the idea that Trudeau is addicted to the limelight. "Nobody believes this, but Justin is a really shy guy and a learned extrovert," he said. "There's a big difference between being self-aware and self-absorbed. Justin Trudeau is the most self-aware person I've ever met in my life. From a very young age, he's been accustomed to seeing himself as other people see him."[2] But, by his own admission, Trudeau enjoyed the attention at the Liberal convention. The highlight for at least one delegate was shaving off Trudeau's d'Artagnan moustache, after winning the privilege in a charity raffle. "Holy shit, I'm shaking," she said, fortunately after she had put down the razor.[3]

Trudeau said he was impressed and invigorated by the enthusiasm on display. The convention elected a dynamic forty-two-year-old president, Mike Crawley, who beat former deputy prime minister Sheila Copps in a close vote that signalled the Liberals were ready for generational change. Crawley endorsed ambitious plans to professionalize fundraising; supported a resolution to legalize marijuana, proposed by the party's noisy and numerous youth wing; and backed a new, no-fee class of "supporters" who would be given a voice in choosing the new leader. The latter innovation would turn out to be Trudeau's ticket to power, scaring off other potential candidates and swamping those who did run through effective use of social media.

Websites such as Canada Loves Justin Trudeau had already emerged, and there was increasing pressure on him to reconsider running. Liberals were, in the words of one delegate, looking for a new, younger person to lead the party, not "some old re-tread."[4] Trudeau dismissed speculation he might run as a media concoction, telling former Michael Ignatieff speechwriter and Liberal blogger Adam Goldenberg, "There is no talk of leadership. . . . You've got to get the media to actually do their homework and write actual stories and actually talk about something other than who gets to be head of that, or who gets to run this." But in reality, he later recalled that as he sat in the convention centre, he was starting to "seriously entertain the thought that I could lead them."[5]

Trudeau may have started to believe that he might be ready to lead. But there were absolutely no signs that the country, beyond a small group of his closest friends, was ready to be led by him. Tom Pitfield, the son of Michael Pitfield, who was clerk of the Privy Council for two stints during Pierre Trudeau's time in power, has known Justin his whole life, as the Trudeaus and Pitfields were family friends. Tom went to Rockcliffe Park Public School in Ottawa, where he was close with

Michel, and after the youngest Trudeau passed away, Tom became more friendly with his older brother.

Pitfield had worked in the Senate before moving into the information technology business at IBM. But he retained his love of politics and policy, which in 2006 led to him co-founding Canada 2020, a progressive think-tank based on the Centre for American Progress in the United States, with fellow Liberals Tim Barber, Eugene Lang, and Susan Smith. He had become friendly with Gerald Butts, and they decided to gauge what interest there might be in a Trudeau leadership bid. Butts had been focusing on his roles as Premier Dalton McGuinty's principal secretary in the Ontario government and, from 2008, as the chief executive of World Wildlife Fund Canada. But he had always been an unofficial sounding board for Trudeau.

Pitfield and Butts went to see Pierre Trudeau's former principal secretary, Jim Coutts, in Toronto, to convince him to pay for a poll for the prospective candidate to see if there was any interest in him. "The anecdotal evidence was that there wasn't—people who didn't know him perceived him as his father's son," said Pitfield. "We tried to counter this in leadership by focusing on Justin's strengths—avoiding his last name entirely—even using a lower-case 'j' in the graphical treatment of his logo to make him feel more personable. His website was justin.ca because that's what people called him—still do." On the way home from Toronto, Pitfield ran into Trudeau in the airport. "I sat down beside him and he asked, 'What are you doing here?' I answered, 'Funny you should ask, I was just seeing Coutts.' 'Oh, what were you seeing Coutts about?' he asked. I said: 'You.'"[6]

But the early signals were not auspicious. In his short parliamentary career, Trudeau had said little of substance on the great issues of the day. Nobody knew his views on Canada's relationship with the U.S., his thoughts on international trade, how he might reshape the federation, or his proposals for helping Canada compete on the global stage. Further, Trudeau's performance did not win him the respect of his parliamentary colleagues. Criticism across the aisle should always be taken with a pinch of salt, but the comments of former immigration minister Jason Kenney were withering and apparently heartfelt. "If I were a Liberal, as I used to be, I wouldn't be inclined to vote for a guy who has zero executive experience, zero governing experience and zero record of putting forward substantive ideas to address the tough issues of the day," he said. "In the several years I have been in Parliament with Justin Trudeau, I don't remember him saying a single thing about growth and job creation."[7] Kenney's opinion actually turned even more sour after he left Ottawa in a bid to become leader of Alberta's official opposition in 2016. "The guy was my critic in opposition for three years," he said in 2018. "I don't think he has the foggiest idea what's going on. This guy is an empty trust-fund millionaire who has the political depth of a finger-bowl."[8]

Commentators pointed out that if he did have leadership ambitions, it was time to ditch the jeans, the skateboard, and the unparliamentary language, along with the funny little moustache. But instead of proving to his doubters that he had the gravitas to govern, he challenged a Canadian senator to a boxing match on live television.

In the weeks before he turned forty on December 25, 2011, he had adorned himself with a Haida-image tattoo on his shoulder and decided he wanted to take part in a real live boxing match. Trudeau had trained as an amateur boxer since his early twenties, but he'd never fought formally. As he approached forty, he told friends that one of his bucket-list ambitions was to take to the ring just once. He signed on for the Ottawa-based white-collar cancer charity event Fight for the Cure in October 2011 and set out to find a Conservative to be his opponent. He approached Conservative MPs Rob Anders and Peter MacKay, but neither was tempted. As he joked to Liberal MP Dominic LeBlanc, "Who knew I'd have such a hard time finding a Conservative who wants to punch me in the face?"[9]

Eventually, he came across Patrick Brazeau, a Conservative senator from an Algonquin community who boasted of a black belt in karate and a background in the Canadian Forces. It may have seemed like reckless conceit on the part of Trudeau, but what his father's principal secretary, Jim Coutts, said of Pierre often applies to his son too: "Trudeau did and said little publicly that was not carefully rehearsed in advance."[10] If Pierre's presence and charisma were carefully constructed, so too were those of his son, who saw the fight as a building block for his ambitions. "I wanted someone who would be a good foil, and we stumbled upon the scrappy tough-guy senator from an indigenous community," he told *Rolling Stone* magazine in 2017. "He fit the bill, and it was a very nice counterpoint. I saw it as the right kind of narrative, the right story to tell."[11] Brazeau said he took the words as a compliment, but they landed Trudeau in hot water with Indigenous activists, who called them "super-arrogant, super-racist" and "really disgusting."[12]

Everyone who knew and cared for Trudeau advised him against the match-up. The campaign team was resigned to him appearing on posters with a broken nose—and that was if he were still sufficiently compos mentis after the fight to debate politics. Sophie Trudeau was terrified, her husband said, but he reassured her he was confident it was going to go well. "I had a level of confidence in myself and an understanding of my own abilities, so that I was able to reassure Sophie. But she was still nervous—it's never fun to see someone you love getting punched in the face," he said.[13]

Trudeau shared his confidence with some of his colleagues. Rodger Cuzner, the MP from Cape Breton, was sitting in front of him in the House of Commons two days before the fight and recalled their conversation: "I said, 'Are you all set to go?' He said, 'I'm going to win.' I thought to myself, 'You're getting your lights knocked out.' Brazeau was a tough guy, he was brought up in a community where they didn't fight after school, they fought during school. But Justin said, 'No, listen. I've trained hard, I've got a great coach, we've talked about the game plan and we'll stick to it. I'm going to beat him.'"[14] Still, as heavyweight boxer "Iron Mike" Tyson once observed, "Everyone has a plan until they get punched in the face."

The fight took place in Ottawa on March 31, 2012, and the prevailing wisdom among people who knew nothing about boxing was that the burly senator would make mincemeat of his slighter opponent. The Brazeau camp, including representatives of the Sun News Network, who turned up with their cameras to witness the massacre, had not talked to Trudeau about the rigorous training regime he'd signed up for in a Montreal gym. Nor did the boosters of "Brass Knuckles" Brazeau have an accurate read on his fitness level. The late Doug Finley, Brazeau's senatorial colleague, said he feared the worst for his fellow Conservative when they shared a smoke outside the venue just prior to the fight.

The first round went according to plan—at least the plan of right-wing polemicist Ezra Levant, who was commenting on the bout for Sun News. The "Shiny Pony," Levant's nickname for Trudeau, took some heavy shots and in the post-bout interview admitted to "seeing stars." Brazeau said he approached the tilt as more of a street fight than a boxing match. "I hit him with a right and I saw his eyes roll back," he said.[15]

"He hit me harder than I'd ever been hit before," Trudeau said.[16]

"This is a one-round fight," opined Levant. "Brazeau's seen more fights in a month than Trudeau has in his life."[17]

But in the second round, Trudeau's three-inch height advantage and superior conditioning paid off—Brazeau was punched out. "The Shiny Pony is a stallion. All that ballet training has paid off," shouted Levant.

"Just when I was beginning to wonder how much more I could take, he stopped landing those big punches," Trudeau recalled. "I could hear him huffing and puffing and suddenly, I was connecting my punches and swatting away his."[18]

"I had nothing left in the tank," said Brazeau. "He was obviously a lot better trained than I was. I underestimated him and didn't give him enough credit prior to the fight."[19]

In the third round, after a third standing eight count, the referee called the fight. In his post-bout interview with Levant, Trudeau had the last laugh. "This must really be eating you up inside, Ezra," he chuckled.[20]

Days later, in the foyer of the House of Commons, the loser was forced to undergo the humiliation of having his hair cut off by the winner.

Brazeau said he called Trudeau the day after the fight to congratulate him and the Liberal MP had said he would only cut off an inch, in recognition of how symbolic long hair is to Indigenous people. But Brazeau said he was happy to lose his flowing locks and donate the hair to be used in wigs for cancer patients, in honour of his mother, who had died of cancer.

It was ridiculous, puerile even—two overgrown schoolboys in shiny shorts battering each other until they bled. But the display of true grit transformed Trudeau in the public eye—he became his father's son, having been disparagingly dismissed as his mother's boy prior to that. Ironically, the self-styled twenty-first-century feminist had proven his worth in the most primitively masculine way possible. There was no question he had shown physical bravery, mental strength, and grace under extreme pressure. He had demonstrated he was prepared to learn from others who were better qualified—in this case his coach, Ali Nestor Charles—to reach his goal. He'd arrived better prepared than his opponent and had executed on his strategy. "It said to me that he takes calculated risks—not foolhardy risks," remarked one member of the tight-knit Liberal team. "It said he knows what he knows and he knows what he doesn't know. And it said he has incredible discipline—that if he had to train two hours a day, he would train two hours a day."[21]

Most importantly for the Liberals, it gave them a victory over the Conservatives—the first in a very long time. "It provided a base of confidence for himself and for others—it showed people he could take hits and could focus on one issue, at a time when people were saying he was not really focused," said one of his closest aides. "We had people like Mauril Bélanger (the late Ottawa-Vanier MP) who came to say, 'If he goes for the leadership, I'm there.' For some reason, it reached people."[22] It had been a long time since the compact band of Liberal MPs had had much to laugh about in the House, but Trudeau's victory gave birth to one of Rodger Cuzner's periodic bursts of poetic fantasy during members' statements in the House—"The Thrilla on the Hilla":

The blows came from everywhere, pummelled and pounded
It looked like the senator thought he was surrounded
He was dazed and confused, the ref twice stopped the fight
He got hit with so many lefts, he was begging for a right
In less than six minutes, it was all over and done
A TKO victory, the good guys had won.[23]

The aftermath was less heart-warming for Brazeau, who spiralled badly downward after his defeat—a string of scandals and lows followed, including being suspended from the Senate in the expenses scandal and an abortive suicide attempt. However, after breach of trust charges were dropped, he returned to the Senate, where he continues to sit as an independent. He said his defeat had very little to do with what happened subsequently in his personal and professional life, although it upset Conservative colleagues who lost money on the fight. "After the fight, I was alone and defeated and the same thing happened in my life," Brazeau revealed. "But it taught me to be patient, and not underestimate people. Six years later, I'm still waiting for a thank-you from the Liberal Party. I truly believe that if I'd won, Justin Trudeau would not be prime minister."[24]

By the summer, Trudeau was telling people he would run for the leadership "if I have to," even as he talked to Butts about how a leadership bid might look. An informal network of supporters was already growing, as Trudeau's office kept a cluster of interested people up to date on his movements. "I told him, 'I'm going to keep feeding this group of people," said one aide. 'Whenever you decide what you want to do, you have a base to start from.'"[25]

Despite the enthusiasm for Trudeau to run, anyone watching his performance in the first half of 2012 would have been well aware that he was, at best, a work in progress as leadership material. In February, he was on the receiving end of criticism after suggesting that Quebec separatism could be acceptable given the divisive politics of Stephen Harper. He emerged from Question Period to clarify the comments and gave one of the more bizarre media scrums in recent Hill history. With dramatic flourish, he repeatedly referred to himself in the third person and generally sounded as if he were less interested in other people than he was in himself. "Does Justin Trudeau want Canada to separate? Of course not. Will Justin Trudeau fight with his very last breath to ensure this Canada stays the Canada we know it can be? Of course," he said, in a display of thespianism that would have had his former director Brian McKenna reminding him to "keep it real."[26]

At a charity rugby match on Parliament Hill in June, while other MPs, reporters, and Canadian international rugby players huddled at half-time, Trudeau was giving television interviews at centre field. It raised questions about his leadership credentials. Could he play in a team, much less lead one? Could he share the credit, form friendships with former opponents, and keep a coalition of jousting Liberals intact? The answers to those questions were not readily apparent in the summer of 2012.

In the shadows, Butts had left his position as Canadian president of the World Wildlife Fund. "My plan was not to leave WWF, but I was frankly surprised and overwhelmed by how saturated the coverage was and how insatiable the appetite was for everything associated with it," he said. "It became super-clear to me that I couldn't run a national charity and chair this campaign. The board was getting nervous, the government was putting on pressure, and I said, 'I don't want this thing to become politicized.'"[27]

He had quietly pulled together a small team to map out a leadership bid, should Trudeau decide to take the plunge. It included Katie Telford, Daniel Gagnier, a former chief of staff to premiers of Quebec and Ontario, and Tom Pitfield. Butts was looking for a new political challenge after helping on McGuinty's re-election in 2011, and he had flirted with Mark Carney when the governor of the Bank of Canada was contemplating a leap into politics. But if Trudeau was in, he told the *Globe*'s Ian Brown, he had always liked his chances. "Because he has the nation's ear and they're interested in what he has to say—and they'll give him a fair hearing."[28]

One person involved in the early discussions said Trudeau's indecision was prompted by Sophie, but his memoir makes clear that his own painful personal experience as the scion of a political family also weighed heavily. He recalled that his father had once told him he should never feel compelled to run for office. "Our family has done enough," he said.[29]

But pressure was growing. The NDP had lost its talismanic leader, Jack Layton, to cancer the previous summer. Layton had led the party to its best election result in its history in 2011 and would have proven a tricky opponent for any Liberal leader in 2015. "Had Jack Layton lived, it might have been a different world," said one senior Liberal staff member, who was present as the third-place Liberals discussed the prospect of a merger with the NDP.[30] The New Democrats elected Tom Mulcair as their leader at a convention in March 2012. But the idea of electoral cooperation between the two parties was floated by leadership contender Nathan Cullen, and there was support in both parties, including from Jean Chrétien and former NDP leader Ed Broadbent, for some kind of deal. The idea was debated at a three-day retreat organized by Butts, Pitfield, and Telford in July 2012 at Mont Tremblant, Quebec, which brought together potential supporters of a Trudeau leadership bid.

One person who attended the founding meeting of Team Trudeau said that between twenty-five and thirty people were there, split into two very distinct groups—on one hand, friends and family of Justin; on the other, political professionals who would form the core of the leadership campaign. On the friends and family side were Sophie, Butts, Telford, Sacha Trudeau, Marc Miller, and Tom Pitfield (who had brought up brisket and smoked meat from Montreal) and his wife, Anna Gainey, who would later become Liberal Party president.

On the other side were a sprinkling of former MPs, including Omar Alghabra and Navdeep Bains, in a group that was very Ontario-centric. But there was a noticeable dearth of Westerners, with only three attendees coming from west of the Ontario–Manitoba border: Ben Chin, Bruce Young (a lobbyist at Earnscliffe Strategy Group in Vancouver), and Richard Maksymetz (an experienced political organizer who was the B.C. finance minister's chief of staff). This group called attention to the animus that still existed in the West toward the Liberal Party, thirty years after Pierre Trudeau's National Energy Program, which was aimed at lowering energy costs in eastern Canada at Alberta's expense.

Very few of those who attended the meeting straddled the two groups, and the integration was not smooth. There was friction between Justin's brother, Sacha, and a number of the political operatives. "He struck me as a really bright guy who didn't know what he was talking about when it came to the nuts and bolts of politics," said one person at the table. "He was trying to forcibly insert himself, and at the start he was made the Quebec organizer to placate him. But he was a disaster and had to be replaced."[31] Sacha Trudeau declined to be interviewed for this book, but one person there said he was not replaced; rather, he left on his own terms. "What Sacha realized was that he didn't really want to do it and I don't blame him," the source said. "He'd lived the first half of his life in his father's shadow and didn't want to live the second half in his brother's shadow. He could have been Bobby Kennedy if he'd wanted to. But he didn't want to."[32]

Justin confirmed later that his brother didn't have a formal role in the campaign, "other than being my brother and someone I love and trust." When asked to describe how he and Sacha were different, Trudeau replied, "I'm very good at trusting people. He's very good at mistrusting people. And we form a good balance that way."[33] Trudeau's closest Quebec adviser post-Tremblant was Robert Asselin, who had worked for Stéphane Dion, Pierre Pettigrew, and Paul Martin when the Liberals were in power and for Michael Ignatieff while the party was in opposition. He would later work for Bill Morneau in Trudeau's government.

The subject of merging with the NDP was raised at a campfire discussion, and some sympathy toward the idea was expressed by those whose priority was to get rid of Stephen Harper. But that provoked an impassioned response from those present who were not prepared to see the death of the Liberal Party, with its 150 years of history, on their watch. Butts and Telford pointed out that a merger would not auto- matically see the new party accumulate support from people who had previously voted NDP or Liberal. As they noted, in the 2011 federal elec- tion, many Liberals in the Greater Toronto Area voted Conservative to prevent the NDP "Orange Wave" from sweeping through the country's largest city.

Trudeau's view centred on his belief that the party couldn't allow the desire for power to trump policy and principle. He said he couldn't support the NDP policy calling for the repeal of the Clarity Act, which would make it easier to break up the country. And there were areas of economic policy disagreement on trade, foreign investment, and resource development that were too wide to broach. "We definitively put to rest the idea of a merger," he later recalled.[34]

The rest of the discussion centred on what kind of leadership cam- paign Trudeau would run, if he committed to entering the race. "It's not like there was a platform being formed, but I had the sense that Gerry [Butts] had the narrative that would end up becoming 'the mid- dle class, and those working hard to join it,'" said one person who was there.[35] Butts said that theme was related strongly to the diagnosis of what was wrong with the Liberal Party—that it had lost touch with regular people and was not connecting with people like his and Telford's middle-class parents. "We felt that was connected to a stagnation in the economic prospects of the average family," he noted. When it was pointed out that median incomes were actually rising at the time, he dismissed the statistics as being skewed by the resources boom in the first decade of the century, commenting, "The stats look better than they really are because of commodity prices." He later observed, "We were articulating an as yet unarticulated consensus which, again, is what political leadership looks like."[36]

Butts had emerged as a controversial figure for those who detest Trudeau and all his works—a Cyrano de Bergerac type of figure who wrote all the prime minister's best lines and pulled the strings from behind the scenes. In fact, the relationship was much more symbiotic than that. Butts had a deeper policy background than Trudeau, dating back to his time with Dalton McGuinty's Ontario government, but close observers of the relationship say Trudeau had his own convictions on the Charter, Quebec, the environment, gender, and the role of the federal government. The principal differentiation is that he was the front man. As Trudeau told the *Globe and Mail* in a lengthy pre-election profile, "I set the frame. . . . And I'll figure out how to get it across to people."[37]

The third member of the triumvirate that would go on to run the country is Katie Telford, the petite, data-driven political operative Trudeau had first met as part of Gerard Kennedy's leadership bid. Trudeau once said that he and Butts need a boss and that this is Telford's role: "Katie is the grown-up around me and Gerry. She's the one who is exceedingly well-organized and she thinks things through in a far-seeing and broad way. She thinks about the deeper consequences when Gerry and I are trying to outsmart each other."[38]

Butts said Telford was the obvious choice to bring in to lead Team Trudeau when he started recruiting. "We both walked away from politics with the same lesson [Butts from McGuinty's office; Telford from Stéphane Dion's]. We didn't think you had to be bad people, that the shark tank that the Liberal Party of Canada had become, with a bunch of self-interested people who wanted to kill each other for marginal advantage, that it didn't have to be like that. What we both admired about Justin was that he wanted to win with integrity, or lose. It's what we still believe."[39]

The tightness of the relationship between the three would provide stability in the transition from opposition to government. "Why do the three of us work? Honestly, because we really, deeply trust each other," said Butts. "Every time Katie Telford or Justin Trudeau opens their mouth to disagree with something I am saying, I immediately think there is as good a chance as not that they are right and I am wrong."[40] Butts' resignation over the SNC affair created serious disequilibrium at the apex of government. Trudeau is said to have tried to fill Butts' role—to unspectacular effect. But the concentration of decision-making would provoke considerable resentment among those who would grow to believe that power was overcentralized in the hands of Telford and Butts.

Back in Tremblant, the decision was taken to build on Liberal credibility on the economy, which had been hard-won in the 1990s but frittered away in more recent campaigns. A Trudeau-led party would be pro-growth and would support free trade, fiscal discipline, and foreign direct investment. Most importantly, Trudeau said that a party under his leadership would speak to the anxiety felt by the middle class, which he claimed was seeing its debts growing as incomes stagnated.[41]

Finally, Trudeau asked the delegates to the Mont Tremblant congress if they were prepared to sign up for a campaign that ditched the party's internecine rivalries—and many of the characters associated with the Chrétien–Martin civil war—to build a political movement around new Liberal supporters who might not have joined a traditional party. "I looked around the room and asked everyone another simple question: 'Are you up for that?' One by one, the group said yes. They were in and they were in for the right reasons. I would make it official a couple of months later but Sophie and I decided then and there that we were in too," Trudeau recalled.[42] As Sophie later told journalist Susan Delacourt, "I think it was at that moment, when people were just simply being themselves and we were all looking at each other and chatting about life and about politics and about everything around the fire outside. And it was just like, 'yep, this is going to work.'"[43]

Pitfield said the energy was tangible. "That moment of realization that this was actually going to happen . . . everybody was very excited about it. It was like going into battle," he said.[44] The people who knew Trudeau best realized the significance of his decision. "He's a determined person—he decides something and goes after it, as was evident with the boxing thing. There are not a lot of people out there who decide they are going to become prime minister," said Pitfield.[45] It seems the floundering and indecision that characterized his life before politics were firmly in the past. One caucus colleague said he believes what changed Trudeau's mind was the direction in which Stephen Harper was taking the country, noting, "I really think that Justin made the decision to run for his kids, in terms of the country he wanted them to grow up in. I don't think he had the desire to run—he'd seen it up close and personal. But I think some of the things Harper did made him change his mind."[46]

With that critical decision made, the group got to work, preparing not only for a leadership race but also for a general election. "We knew that, barring a Biblical cataclysm, he would win the race. We had polls showing name recognition at 80 to 85 per cent—a tremendous advantage right there," said one person involved in the leadership effort. "It was the easiest internal contest any of us had ever been involved in. Seven out of ten people I talked to were on board in the first two minutes of any conversation."[47]

As word leaked out, the field of serious candidates melted away. Bob Rae, the party's interim leader, had been considering a run but demurred. There were rumours around other heavyweights like Ontario premier Dalton McGuinty, Bank of Canada governor Mark Carney, former deputy prime minister John Manley, and ex–New Brunswick premier Frank McKenna. But once Trudeau committed, it was clear that he would swamp the field with his ability to tap into his tens of thousands of followers on social media. If they could be encouraged to sign up as no-fee Liberal supporters, they would be able to vote him in. Trudeau acknowledged this himself when he said the leadership was "just a step along the way."[48]

In the event, there were other contenders. Marc Garneau, the Montreal MP and former astronaut, was the most serious candidate in a field that included a mix of existing, former, and aspiring MPs—Joyce Murray, Martin Cauchon, Martha Hall Findlay, Deborah Coyne, Karen McCrimmon, George Takach, and David Bertschi. Standing in the way of the Trudeau juggernaut proved to be a career-limiting option for most of the candidates. Only Garneau, Murray, and McCrimmon eventually made it into the Liberal caucus, and only Garneau and Murray ended up in cabinet. Unlike Abraham Lincoln, Trudeau did not buy into the concept of a team of rivals. Garneau knew his only chance was to take on Trudeau in a one-on-one debate and hope that his opponent was as unprepared as his critics said he was. Like any good front-runner, Trudeau denied him that opportunity.

The campaign launched officially on October 2, 2012, in Papineau. The message was a woolly mix of "hope and hard work"—an ill-defined plan for growth that would work for the middle class. But it contained the vaulting ambition that Canadians have come to know and love (or loathe), with its reference to German writer Johann Wolfgang von Goethe: "Make no small dreams, they have not the power to move the soul."[49] The launch was short on specifics, but the main themes of the 2015 election campaign were already present: it was time to write a new chapter in the Liberal Party's history, turfing a government that had lost touch with fairness and diversity in favour of nasty divisiveness. Trudeau's speech included the idea that Canada could not choose between a strong economy and a healthy environment—the premise that formed the basis for the "grand bargain" on a pipeline and a carbon tax that came later. The theme of a thriving middle class was also marbled throughout the speech. "It provides realistic hope and a ladder of opportunity for the less fortunate. A robust market for our businesses. And a sense of common interest for all," Trudeau said.[50] This is the sense of common ground that critics, some of whom are Liberal Party MPs, argue has been lost in the years since.

At the behest of the Westerners in his team, he made his first stop in Calgary to "confront the ghosts closely associated with my father"— namely the National Energy Program introduced by Pierre Trudeau that had created such divisions between Alberta and Central Canada. He told a skeptical crowd that resource development was one of the handful of issues that defined Canada's success as a country. The following month, he would articulate that policy even more clearly in an op-ed, published in Postmedia's papers, that supported the acquisition of Calgary-based oil company Nexen by Chinese state-owned enterprise CNOOC on the grounds it would create middle-class jobs. The stance was at odds with the prevailing public opinion, even among Conservatives, but was consistent with the belief Trudeau expressed during his visit to

Calgary that "there's not a country in the world that would find 170 billion barrels of oil in the ground and leave them there."[51]

After Calgary, Trudeau's team devised a tour that would see him hit parts of rural Canada that he would not be able to visit during a general election campaign. He passed much of the winter of 2012–13 in a van in small towns in Quebec, Saskatchewan, and New Brunswick. "He spent a lot of time in rural Canada, knowing full well he'd never go back when things mattered more," said one campaign staff member.[52] In the interior of British Columbia, the name Trudeau evoked memories of the "Salmon Arm salute," the one-finger greeting Pierre Trudeau directed at demonstrators pelting his railway car with tomatoes in 1981. During a boisterous stop in Kelowna, the younger Trudeau was asked what he had learned from his father. "When in the B.C. interior, wave with your whole hand," he replied.[53] He was greeted by large, curious crowds and the affection was later reciprocated. In 2015, former fighter pilot Stephen Fuhr became the first Liberal elected in a Kelowna riding in forty-three years.

By the time it was all over, Trudeau had visited 154 different ridings. During this rigorous tour, Trudeau revealed himself to be a disciplined campaigner with an iron constitution—it was clear already that the fit forty-year-old would campaign longer and harder than his two more mature rivals in the 2015 election. "He is without exception the hardest-working colleague I have in that caucus," said Dominic LeBlanc, who accompanied him on much of the New Brunswick tour—a province the Liberals swept in 2015. "He never complains about a day of six or seven events. And he has no vanity about hard work."[54] As one weary political aide remarked, "There's a reason we're all worn out."[55]

But the main takeaway from the tour was that Trudeau knew instinctively that political campaigns are exercises in emotion rather than reason —something that his father, with his "Reason over Passion" motto, preferred to ignore. In Rothesay, New Brunswick, there was polite enthusiasm for a rather uninspiring stump speech. But the real magic happened when Trudeau worked the room, with his trademark double-hand clasp for women and a firm grip on the shoulder for men. His eyes were constantly fixed on the voter, as if he had a lifelong fascination with the subject under discussion.

Pat Darrah, a seventy-seven-year-old veteran Liberal who once organized for Trudeau's father and sported an original pin from the 1968 election campaign, commented that, in his experience, politics turned in cycles, noting, "I think it's time for a new cycle. The youth of the country want to see a more human side to government." The agent of that change, in his opinion, was Trudeau. "There's a great warmth to him," he said.[56]

The rock star analogy was taken literally on some occasions. One campaign aide recalled being approached at an event by two young women who asked if he knew which hotel Trudeau was staying in: "I said, 'Yes.' One said, 'Do you think he'd want to have a threesome with us afterwards? Can you ask him?' I said, 'No, I'm not going to ask him that.'"[57]

The candidate held four events that day in New Brunswick—a chilly Tuesday in February—and drew one thousand people, testimony to crowd-pulling power possessed by few others in Canadian politics. At the time, this was news to Hill reporters, long underwhelmed by Trudeau's presence in Parliament. But it was no surprise to the Liberal MPs who flocked to support his campaign. "They would bring him out to a spaghetti dinner and the room would be packed. I think because they knew him, they knew if you scratched the surface, the intelligence was there," said one member of the Liberal team.[58]

It wasn't glamorous. But during an interview in the dingy bowels of the Capital Exhibition Centre in Fredericton, Trudeau spoke with conviction about his belief that Canada needed political leadership that built on a broad sense of common purpose, rather than one that emphasized the things that divided people. He was confident in the belief that he had what it took to provide that leadership. "If I didn't believe I did, I wouldn't be spending five days a week away from my young family; I wouldn't be criss-crossing the country and sitting in back rooms like this," he said.[59]

He even tried to play down the image of the wealthy trust-fund kid by addressing "misconceptions" about the size of the estate left by his father. Documents showed that his inheritance was worth about $1.2 million in 2011, according to the *Ottawa Citizen*, and he had earned more than $450,000 for public speaking that year. He agreed he had "won the lottery" by having a wealthy family, but that dividends from the family holding company, which topped out at around $20,000 one year, were not enough to live off.[60] The documents did suggest that Trudeau was not immune from the financial pressures buffeting other Canadians after the great recession. In the years since becoming an MP, his speaking income had tailed off (though it was still a healthy $72,000 in 2012). With Sophie staying home with their growing family, the Trudeaus had decided to downsize by selling the house in Outremont for $1.6 million in order to buy a smaller home for $777,000 (with a $622,000 mortgage) in nearby Mont Royal.[61] But even as he sought to defuse the impression he was affluent, he acknowledged that he could not personally identify with the middle class he was championing. "I'm not middle class. I don't pretend I am," he said.[62]

By mid-March, Marc Garneau had withdrawn from the race. He had reached the conclusion he could not win, after his own polling showed 72 per cent support for Trudeau.[63] The Liberal Party said it had nearly three hundred thousand members and supporters signed up— with the Trudeau camp claiming it had the backing of more than half of them. (The party had entered the campaign with just thirty thousand members.)

Butts and Telford had run a campaign that lifted many of its lessons from philosophical fellow-travellers Barack Obama, with his "citizen engagement," and Tony Blair, with his "third way." The guiding principle was that to effect change, leaders needed to tap into a nationwide, grassroots volunteer movement. But engaging such a broad-based group of supporters was likely to create its own difficulties, as Trudeau acknowledged. "Obama's big mistake, or the big challenge he faced following the 2008 election was . . . keeping mobilized these millions of people who came out to vote for him in the first place," he said.[64] The Liberals have since faced their own struggles in this regard. Governing a country as complicated as Canada has taken its toll on the enthusiasm of existing supporters, evident in the faltering number of donors in the first quarter of 2018.

But in the spring of 2013, the Trudeau campaign was able to dismiss such concerns. With a small army of twelve thousand volunteers, and access to the data of the thousands who signed up as supporters, the Trudeau campaign was able to engage in a conversation with voters using social media. The thousands of email addresses, names, and birthdates amassed during the campaign gave Trudeau "the bare bones of a rebuilding effort," he said.[65] In his launch speech, Trudeau had argued that a simple leadership change could not solve all the Liberal Party's problems. It all smacked a bit of Monty Python's *The Life of Brian*. The more Trudeau proclaimed he was not the Messiah, the more Liberal members became convinced he was—and, having previously followed a few, they were in a good position to know.

The surprising thing was that they were right. Trudeau immediately solved all the problems that had taken the Liberal Party to the brink of extinction: he projected a sense of the country that reconnected the party in Quebec; that reached beyond the downtown cores of Canada's major cities; that closed the funding gap with the Conservatives; that streamlined a clumsy party structure without provoking civil war; and, most importantly, that persuaded Canadians in all walks of life that government could be part of the solution. Even before he was confirmed as leader, the Liberals were ahead in the polls. Gerald Butts described the articles of faith that fed this wellspring of hope. "Justin and I are both very traditional philosophical liberals, in that the individual is paramount and government ought to be in the business of expanding opportunities for individuals," he said.[66]

On April 14, 2013, Trudeau was confirmed as party leader, winning the support of 80 per cent of the 104,552 votes cast. The campaign marked a coming of age for Trudeau. In his launch speech, he said it was time for his generation of Canadians to put away childish things and get down to the serious, "very adult" business of building a better country.[67] And in his victory speech, he made clear that the in-fighting between so-called Chrétien and Martin Liberals was over. "The era of hyphenated Liberals ends right now,"[68] he said.

Over, too, were Trudeau's salad days, when he was "green in judgment, cold in blood."[69] Just as his father had gone to Ottawa in 1965 with a reputation as a charming but unreliable dilettante, only to impress with his work ethic and encyclopedic knowledge of his files,[70] so now his son had to prove his doubters wrong.

FOUR

NO SMALL DREAMS

IN POLITICS, SOME DAYS you are the dog, and some days you are the tree.

In his first few months as Liberal leader, Trudeau found himself on the receiving end of a deluge of derision from his more experienced political opponents after making a number of unforced rookie errors. The Harper Conservatives had made a tradition of getting their retaliation in first with new Liberal leaders, and Trudeau was no exception. No sooner had he been crowned than the Conservatives launched a TV attack ad featuring slow-motion images of the new leader performing a mock striptease at a 2011 event for the Canadian Liver Foundation. But it backfired spectacularly when broad-based support emerged for the idea of an aspiring political leader taking off his shirt for charity.

Though the ad failed to leave a mark, Trudeau wasted little time in bruising his own reputation. In the wake of the horrific Boston Marathon bombing, he responded by saying it was essential to look at the motivating factors behind the attack. The new Liberal leader's use of the phrase "root causes" was leapt upon by Stephen Harper, who ridiculed him for what the prime minister said was a weak response to terrorism.[1] The Tories set out to capitalize on the gaffe by launching a debate on terrorism in the House of Commons. "This is not a time to commit sociology," said Harper.[2]

As tensions rose between the parties after the arrest of two Canadians accused of trying to derail a VIA train, the Conservatives blanketed ridings with flyers portraying Trudeau as an inexperienced lightweight.[3] The attack ad, which suggested Trudeau was "in over his head," failed to resonate with people in isolation, but the leader's comments soon injected new life into the claim. Trudeau's parliamentary tenure had begun innocuously enough when he made his first appearance as leader in Question Period. He gave notice about the Liberals' fixation on the pocketbook issues facing the middle class when he asked about tariff increases on Chinese products in the recent budget that would raise the cost of tricycles, "little red wagons," educational materials, and clothing for young children. It was a low-key but effective debut that was aimed at the suburbs Trudeau needed to win over. He had played down the melodrama and managed to mix it up with the more established heavyweights, Harper and Tom Mulcair, without looking out of place.

Yet there were already concerns that he was going to have to make major changes to the way he spoke in front of the cameras if he was going to avoid being eviscerated. Trudeau had promised to do politics differently, but he soon found that the emotional vocabulary open to politicians is limited for a reason. As playwright John MacLachlan Gray noted, when normal people enter politics, they transform themselves into cartoons because they are no longer permitted to express embarrassment, angst, mortification, anger, surprise, wonder, or doubt.[4]

Spin doctors in the Trudeau camp were already concerned that he could sometimes "say the right things, the wrong way." Yet even they were hard pressed to explain away his next blooper. In an interview with *La Presse*, he said he favoured keeping the existing representation in the Senate because it favoured Quebec. "We have 24 senators from Quebec and there are just six from Alberta and six from British Columbia. That's to our advantage," he said—comments that may have gone down well in his own riding but that, not surprisingly, upset people in the West, making it all the harder for the new leader to build a truly national party.[5]

The comments also obscured an early and important policy position —that a Liberal government would try to improve the Senate rather than abolish it, as the NDP proposed, or create a rival to the House of Commons by electing its members, as the Conservatives were proposing in a reference to the Supreme Court. Trudeau's idea was to improve the appointments process so that the Red Chamber was filled with non-partisans rather than the bagmen and hacks who had clogged its benches over the years. But the point was lost amid the howls of outrage from Western premiers. "I think if you want to be a national leader, you have to act like a national leader and, if you don't, it means you don't understand what it means to be one," said Alison Redford, the then Alberta premier.[6]

Trudeau started to look like a cork dancing in a torrent he couldn't control when news broke about his lucrative speaking career in mid-June. Trudeau's carefully cultivated image of sunny benevolence exploded amid revelations that he was in a dispute with a charitable foundation in New Brunswick. The Grace Foundation had paid Speakers' Spotlight, the agency representing Trudeau, $20,000 for him to appear in June 2012. They had hoped for a sellout crowd to raise funds to buy furniture for a home for the elderly in Saint John, but sold only 120 tickets, worth a total of $6,000, which barely covered the venue rental and advertising costs. The charity incurred a $21,000 loss, which was clearly their problem—Trudeau declined to refund the foundation on the basis that all contractual obligations had been fulfilled. But it did not reflect well on the new Liberal leader, who was made to appear as generous as a pawnbroker for refusing to bend on repayment—at least initially (after the story broke, Trudeau said he would either reimburse or "work with" organizations he spoke to as an MP).

A trickle of other stories about his speaking engagements emerged, including one where he spoke at an Ontario Public Service Employees Union event as "Justin Trudeau MP" alongside Conservative Gary Goodyear and New Democrat Peggy Nash. But while his parliamentary colleagues were not paid, Trudeau received $20,000. Charlie Angus, the prickly NDP MP from Northern Ontario, summed up the broader public mood when he remarked that he'd just given a speech and received a baseball cap and a coffee mug. "This is not a side business. It's what I'm expected to do," he said.[7] At the time, Liberal insiders were talking about the Justin Trudeau project as being a long-term, two-elections endeavour. The sense was that the party may not be best served by winning power before their man was ready—and he was showing few signs of that.

Another mini-storm was brewing with the retirement announcement of Bob Rae, the former NDP Ontario premier who had steadied the Liberal ship as interim leader after the 2011 election loss. It was widely assumed in Liberal circles that George Smitherman, a former provincial minister who had represented the same Toronto Centre riding provincially, was a shoo-in for the nomination for Rae's seat. The Liberal leader had promised open nominations in every riding, and Smitherman was well-placed to mobilize support. He had some baggage from his time as Ontario's health minister, but he was popular in the riding and tight with the people around Trudeau (he had given Butts his first job in politics).

But the Trudeau team was intoxicated by a book called *Plutocrats: The Rise of the New Global Super-Rich and the Fall of Everyone Else*, by Canadian journalist Chrystia Freeland. Its themes of income inequality and the hollowing out of the middle class played right into the redistributive "fairness" narrative being pulled together by Butts. Trudeau had, in speeches and in op-eds, been fleshing out the idea that the Liberal Party, which in his words, used to be the party of upward mobility and equal opportunity, needed to be that party again. Trudeau had met Freeland at a Toronto signing for *Plutocrats* eight months earlier, when he'd been a mere leadership hopeful. When Rae announced his retirement, Butts approached her about running, but she turned him down. She was married with three kids and was working in Manhattan for Thomson Reuters. But Trudeau was not to be dissuaded and called her himself. She admitted that her reply that time was a "soft no."[8] After talking it over with her family, she decided to accept.

Trudeau had told her "there were no guarantees" and it would be a "contested nomination" but that there was no way he was letting her lose the chance to run. The leader's office shipped in a huge team of experienced organizers, including some from the Ontario premier's team, to smooth her passage. To ensure that Freeland's candidacy was not swamped by Smitherman's local machine, the former deputy premier of Ontario was quietly persuaded to look elsewhere. Equivocation on the open nomination promise was a warning sign that other democratic reform pledges—electoral reform, loosening the grip of the Prime Minister's Office, and so on—might also end up being sacrificed at the altar of political expediency. It would not be the last time that the reality failed to live up to the rapturous campaign oratory. Trudeau may not have fulfilled his agent-of-change rhetoric in this instance, but he did secure a crucial member of his team and a future foreign affairs minister. Freeland duly won the nomination and the Toronto Centre by-election later that fall. She subsequently moved to the next-door riding of University-Rosedale for the 2015 election, vacating her seat for another big Trudeau "get"—future finance minister Bill Morneau.

Morneau was a well-known businessman—executive chair of Canada's biggest human resources firm, Morneau Shepell, and was chair of the C.D. Howe Institute when Butts met him through the Young Presidents' Organization. "He decided he wanted to run and we needed a Bay Street type," said Butts,[9] who denied that Morneau came on board with the understanding that he would be finance minister if the Liberals formed a government. "We were really disciplined in not offering anything to anybody—not even once, not even to Chrystia, was anybody offered a cabinet post. In the first go-round, some people probably thought they were up for one, like Bill Blair for instance. But we were religious about not offering those things," he noted.[10]

Trudeau's powers of persuasion when it came to the recruitment of high-profile candidates proved to be impressive. Adam Vaughan, a former journalist turned Toronto city councillor, took just two days to dump his secure job to run for the third party, on the promise he could help create federal housing policy.

THE NEW LEADER CONTINUED to be criticized by the Conservatives for being a blank canvas, without policies or principles, but a plan was quietly taking shape, though one not ultimately without its setbacks.

For example, Trudeau had been hesitant about legalizing pot when the Liberal youth wing had proposed it at the 2012 convention, expressing doubts about even decriminalization. "It's not your mother's pot," he said, in reference to the impact on brain cells of today's cannabis—a turn of phrase that might have mystified those with more traditional matriarchs. But by the summer of 2013, he said his opinion had evolved to the point where he advocated the regulation, legalization, and taxation of pot. With the NDP in favour of decriminalization, it was a significant shift to capture the votes of progressive Canadians. Trudeau insisted he was not advocating the use of pot—a point he undermined somewhat when he admitted he'd smoked marijuana after being elected as an MP. "We had good friends over for a dinner party, our kids were at their grandmother's for the night and one of our friends lit a joint and passed it around. I had a puff," he said. He was unrepentant when he was asked about it later. "I am not a consumer of marijuana but, yes, I've already tried it." [11]

That was a gift for the Conservatives—after all, it was illegal and hypocritical (Trudeau had actually voted in favour of tougher marijuana possession laws). But for a generation who were used to being told by their politicians that they'd smoked pot but "didn't inhale," it was a refreshing admission. On this occasion at least, the precarious level of frankness was calculated. While Trudeau's team recognized that they needed to add message discipline to his quiver, they also wanted to make his transparency a trademark.

It was an astute call. The Liberals had already identified issues that might resonate with Millennials who had not bothered to vote in previous elections, such as electoral reform (during the leadership debates, Trudeau had advocated the preferential ballot system, where voters rank the candidates instead of choosing one).[12] Trudeau maintained that Millennial voters were not disengaged but were simply waiting for the right leader. The research suggested that he was on to something. Young people rejected authority and felt no duty to vote. They were less willing to defer to institutions or parties (only one in four eighteen- to twenty-nine-year-olds identified with a party, compared to four in ten of over-sixties). But they could be attracted by a leader who displayed openness, introspection, and empathy, suggested Michael Adams, president of Environics, at which point their attachment could be intense, if prone to change.[13]

The gamble on the pot admission paid off—as had Trudeau's boxing challenge to Patrick Brazeau and countless other lesser wagers. But as canny *Toronto Star* columnist Tim Harper noted, he was "flying awfully close to the flame."[14] Harper was not alone in thinking that Trudeau's apparent determination to fill dead air was an Icarus-like accident waiting to happen. But the Liberal calculation was that boredom, as much as cynicism over scandals like the one unfolding over Senate expenses, explained the modern disillusionment with politics.

It was perhaps fortunate for Trudeau that, just as he was settling into his new role, the Harper Conservatives were distracted by the biggest public embarrassment that had ever befallen them. It emerged that the Senate's lax expenses regime had been stretched to the breaking point by some senators. The travel and living expenses of four in particular —Conservatives Mike Duffy, Pamela Wallin, and Patrick Brazeau, and Liberal Mac Harb—led to the first three being suspended from the Upper House and to Harb retiring. But it was the revelation that Duffy had repaid erroneously claimed housing expenses of $90,000, with a cheque written by Stephen Harper's chief of staff, Nigel Wright, that lit the blue touch-paper.

The independently wealthy Wright admitted giving Duffy the money but said he did so in the interests of the taxpayer. Harper denied any knowledge of the affair and Wright was forced to resign. The saga grievously wounded Harper's reputation for probity, as the accusation he levelled at Paul Martin during the sponsorship scandal—if he knew, he was corrupt; if he didn't, he was incompetent—came back to haunt him. The affair rumbled on right through the 2015 election, contributing to the sense that it was time for change.

If voters were growing cynical about the Harper Conservatives, Trudeau set out to ensure that they were never bored with him and his party. In late August, he succeeded in knocking the Senate saga off the front pages, at least temporarily, by announcing via Twitter that Sophie was once again pregnant and that the family would need another seat in their canoe. Hadrien was born on February 28, 2014, and has proceeded to enliven Trudeau-family photo opportunities everywhere, from the caucus room to the White House to a dull signing ceremony in India where he performed an exasperated face-plant.

As the Senate expenses scandal reclaimed the headlines, Trudeau attempted to lay the building blocks for the narrative that would form the main thrust of his election campaign two years later—a middle class beleaguered by a sense of rising income inequality, wage stagnation, increasing costs, and unsustainable personal debt. This was home ice for Harper—he had recently boasted to the British Parliament that the average middle-class family was paying $3,300 less in federal taxes since the Conservatives were elected, thanks to income tax cuts, a lower GST, and a suite of boutique tax credits. This was the prime minister who had provided unflappable, unemotional leadership during the near cataclysm of the Great Recession.

A study of the Harper years by former Bank of Canada governor David Dodge and economist Richard Dion suggested that Canada's economic performance was driven mainly by global developments that affected exports in particular. But real GDP growth between 2006 and 2015 was higher than in the United States or across the rest of the G7. The unemployment rate, at 7.1 per cent over that same period, was marginally higher than that south of the border. But real disposable income per capita increased at double the rate in the U.S.[15] After the scare of the U.S. sub-prime mortgage collapse, the Canadian economy recovered and, if growth was sluggish, voters could remind themselves that they'd flirted with disaster and eating dog food.

This was the economic battlefield on which Trudeau chose to fight. It struck many as being akin to the Charge of the Light Brigade—a Nanos Research poll suggested that Harper outpolled Trudeau two to one on the question of "competence" (even while the Liberal leader had the advantage on "trust").[16] It was assumed that Trudeau would have to match Harper on deficits and try to remain revenue neutral on taxes. But the Liberals had a tactical manoeuvre up their sleeves that liberated them from Harper's orthodoxy.

As Dodge and Dion pointed out in their study, after the recession Harper sacrificed economic growth, in particular public investment, in order to improve a debt position that was already solid.[17] After recording deficits that topped out at $55.6 billion in 2009–10, the Harper government pledged to get the budget back into the black before the election and even introduced balanced-budget legislation to enshrine the idea in law. While at the September 2013 G20 meeting in St. Petersburg, Russia, he committed Canada to a debt-to-GDP ratio of 25 per cent by 2021, down from 34 per cent at the time.[18]

In sharp contrast, the idea of deliberately taking the country back into deficit to spur growth was taking shape in Liberal minds. "On economic policy, we were influenced a lot by circumstances to be honest —long years of low growth after the recession of '08," said Robert Asselin, the veteran political adviser who was involved in drawing up the economic plan. "We needed to help and came to the conclusion that it should come from two things—infrastructure spending and consumer spending, through the child benefit. It was largely successful when you look at the evidence."[19]

Another theme that was to become central to the Liberal plot line was also hinted at when Trudeau spoke at the Calgary Petroleum Club that fall. His speech expressly supported the Keystone XL pipeline from

Alberta to refineries in Texas and Illinois, which was being blocked by the Obama administration—an endorsement that was greeted with nods of approval from the who's who of Calgary's business elite.

But there was considerably less enthusiasm for his next proposal— "a national approach to pipelines and development, within an overall framework that includes a policy that puts a price on carbon pollution." He did not flesh out the "national energy strategy," with its implication of a carbon tax, which sounded a bit too much like the hated National Energy Program imposed on Alberta by his father—a fact that he acknowledged. "The irony of this is not lost on me," he told the Petroleum Club. "I really wish it didn't have to fall on some guy called Trudeau to propose a national anything."[20]

There was no detail on pricing carbon and, given the fate that had befallen his predecessor, Stéphane Dion, and his ill-fated Green Shift, it was a precarious decision to drop the prospect into the debate. But the mention of carbon pricing was not a trifle—the decision to run on the grand bargain of "a clean environment and a strong economy" had already been taken.

The combination of increased interest in the Liberal Party under its new leader and the constant drip of unsavoury revelations related to the Senate expenses issue pushed the Grits into the lead in most opinion polls in the fall of 2013. The feeling of darkness at noon among Conservatives, who felt they had a good story to tell on the economy that was being eclipsed by the Senate scandal, was epitomised by a sour little speech given by Harper at the party's policy convention in Calgary in early November. He took aim at his perceived enemies— "elites," "ivory tower theorists," bureaucrats, and the media. "Our opponents accuse us of being unfair, nasty and ruthless. . . . Friends, in terms of our opponents, I couldn't care less what they say." It was with particular relish that he singled out Trudeau. "Could Justin Trudeau run the economy? In 2015, we're not choosing the winner of *Canadian Idol*. The only trade Justin Trudeau has been working on is the marijuana trade," he said.[21] These barbs would have been less likely to become embedded if Trudeau hadn't validated them by saying something inane.

The forum was bad enough—a "ladies night fundraiser" in Toronto, where well-to-do women were urged to pay $250 a head to "really get to know the future prime minister" over cocktails. The Warholian invitation portrayed the Liberal leader as a teen heart-throb—and, by implication, the female audience as giddy fan-girls. The response was caustic. "This isn't just demeaning. It's stupid. Stupid, stupid, stupid. All issues are women's issues," said NDP MP Megan Leslie on her Facebook page.

But what was said was even more dumb. The informality of the event went to Trudeau's head and he apparently forgot there were television cameras in the room that would relay his ruminations to an audience less enamoured with him than the $250-a-head adulators. When he was asked what other country he admired, he mused aloud about the virtues of communist China. "There's a level of admiration I actually have for China because their basic dictatorship is allowing them to actually turn their economy around on a dime and say 'we need to go green.'"

Who knows where the comment emerged from, but Trudeau, like his father, seems to be intrigued by dictatorships. Pierre Trudeau took his sons to visit China in 1990, just after the Tiananmen Square massacre and, according to Justin's brother Sacha, Pierre referred "very delicately" to the "sad difficulties" China had recently faced. "China," he told his sons, "is an ancient land, with its own internal imperatives . . . outsiders simply cannot know what is best for China, or how it needs to travel down its chosen path."[22]

Once free of the embraces of the uptown girls, Trudeau realized he'd gaffed and issued a rather lame tweet that said Canada is the best country in the world. "I will never trade our freedoms," he said. But the sand had already been thrown in the gears. Expressing admiration for China's dictatorship and lack of democracy could not be presented as calculated frankness—rather, it was a textbook example of Trudeau's greatest strength being his greatest weakness. His tendency toward transparency encouraged people to trust him—a wonderful commodity for politicians. As Republican strategist Frank Luntz told a gathering of influential Conservatives in 2006, his research suggested that people would rather vote for someone they trust than someone who agrees with them on the ten issues they care about most.[23] But Trudeau's tendency to babble like an accident victim in shock undermined his efforts to portray himself as a plausible alternative to Harper. The China comments were symptoms of "a cluttered and undisciplined mind," said columnist Andrew Coyne.[24]

None of this, however, was disastrous for the Trudeau brand. He was still in the honeymoon phase as leader, and he was making friends as he travelled around the country holding large rallies attended by lapsed Liberals, such as the one thousand supporters who turned up to the Victoria Conference Centre on a Tuesday night in mid-January. Trudeau was unapologetic when it emerged he had missed two out of every three Question Periods that fall because he was on the road, leaving the forensic grilling of Harper over the Senate scandal to able interrogator Tom Mulcair.[25] Few could have argued seriously that the new leader's time was better spent in Parliament rather than bonding with Canadians outside the Ottawa bubble in the months after his victory.

But 2014 was shaping up to be a different story. The pressure was building on Trudeau to be visible in the House and to offer some substance around the vague ideas he had floated on pot and carbon, to explain how he intended to build a stronger economy, and to comfort an anxious middle class. The new year was going to require some tough decisions from the rookie leader—a sense of purpose and a resoluteness that had been conspicuous by their absence up to that point.

Nobody—least of all the senators who sat in the Liberal caucus—expected the hammer that came down in late January.

FIVE

JUST NOT READY

THE SENATE EXPENSES IMBROGLIO proved to be a very Canadian scandal—there was no sex and no one was found guilty of doing anything wrong. Duffy, Brazeau, and Harb were subsequently charged with criminal offences (Wallin was never charged), but after a high-profile trial, Duffy was exonerated and the charges against the other two were dropped. While there were some questionable expense claims, the milquetoast Canadian version couldn't compare to the 2009 U.K. parliamentary expenses scandal for sheer hoggishness. The British iteration resulted in six ministerial resignations over false accounting charges, a Conservative MP who claimed taxpayers' money to clean the moat of his country estate, and a Labour MP who went to jail for claiming housing expenses on a mortgage that had already been repaid.[1] As *The Daily Mash* satirical website suggested, the MP in question, Elliot Morley, had become the first person in the history of the world to forget he'd paid off his mortgage and should perhaps have eaten more oily fish.[2]

While the Canadian version was a limited and modest affair, it did discredit all the denizens of the Red Chamber, already in disrepute with the public on account of being unelected, underworked, and untouchable until age seventy-five. A looming investigation into the broader expenses claims of senators by Auditor-General the late Michael Ferguson persuaded Trudeau to take a very agricultural approach, along the lines suggested to the author by a farmer from Steinbach, Manitoba: "If there's moisture in the grain, you have to throw out the whole load— the whole batch is tainted."[3] Trudeau decided he couldn't take the risk that some Liberal senators might have caught something nasty that could be passed on to the rest of the party.

Without warning, on the morning of Wednesday, January 29, he gathered his Liberal senators and announced that he was expelling all thirty-two of them from the caucus. At the same time, he said that as prime minister he would inaugurate a non-partisan appointment process— taking the prerogative of Senate appointments away from the head of government for the first time since Confederation. He then departed abruptly to hold a press conference, leaving his mortified chief of staff, Cyrus Reporter, to explain the decision to people with whom he'd worked closely for two decades. "It was all kinds of awkward," said one person familiar with the meeting.[4]

It was also a bold surgical solution to the problem that was the Senate —one that did not require provincial consent, which was unlikely to be forthcoming in any case. Some senators tried to put a brave face on the news. The Liberal leader in the Senate, James Cowan, admitted he had not been consulted but said that Trudeau had "set us free." Others were less stoical. "I'm still a Liberal. I've always been a Liberal. I've been a Liberal for 38 years," said Senator Mobina Jaffer.[5] A number of those affected carry grudges to this day and can be relied upon by opponents to help delay or question the wisdom of government legislation in the Upper House.

It was, according to people close to Trudeau, an extremely tough decision. "He had to go and tell a bunch of people who had worked with his dad, 'Sorry guys, you're out.' He came back upstairs to the leader's office after that and he felt the weight of doing it. He didn't do it lightly," said Alex Lanthier, one of his closest aides.[6] Trudeau had long been criticized for being too cautious on the Senate, by arguing that he wanted to improve it rather than get rid of it or make it a rival to the House of Commons by electing senators. That led to charges that he championed the status quo. No one could say that any longer, after his difficult conversation with a roomful of lifelong Grits like David Smith, Dennis Dawson, Grant Mitchell, and Terry Mercer. Trudeau admitted he had personal relationships, even friendships, with most of the Senate caucus. "But I didn't get into politics to do the easy thing," he said.

Though it may have been a tough call for Trudeau, the shift in process changed the face of the Senate for the better. There was a prospect that the policy changes might yield ruinous, unintended consequences for the Senate—along the lines of Prohibition or the introduction of the cane toad in Australia. But while Liberals sometimes grumble about their agenda being delayed in the Red Chamber, the changes have been largely beneficial for Canadian democracy.

Within two years of being appointed, the Independent senators group was the largest in the Upper House. As the appointments process unfolded, there were criticisms that many new senators were Liberal in all but name, given the preponderance of social workers, women's issues experts, and human rights activists. The Conservatives complained that, under Trudeau's regime, not only would senators be unelected, but those who appointed senators would be unelected. But the Independents have proven themselves true to their name on a number of high-profile occasions, such as when they sent the physician-assisted dying bill back to the House with amendments in June 2016, and the occasion when they forced a major climb-down by the Liberal government on a budget implementation bill that same year.

Most notably, there was the time in the summer of 2017 when a heated stand-off took place between the House and the Senate, after the Red Chamber refused to pass the government's budget as written. Some senators were unhappy that the Liberals had stuffed the plans for their new Infrastructure Bank into the budget and had included an escalator tax on beer that would see prices rise in perpetuity, without the requirement for another vote. The Senate sought to amend the budget and the House refused to accept the amendments. On that occasion, the Senate acquiesced, but not before confirming "its privileges, immunities and powers as provided under the Constitution to amend legislation, whatever its nature or source."[7] Trudeau was put on notice that he had created a Frankenstein's monster that might one day seek revenge on its creator.

As the party approached its biennial policy convention in Montreal in February 2014, Trudeau and his advisers were in a buoyant mood. They had assumed they would have to spend a year fighting with Mulcair and the NDP for the right to be considered the default alternative to Stephen Harper. But they were well ahead of schedule.[8] The party released a seven-minute video in early February that offered the broadest hints yet about how they intended to beat Stephen Harper on the economy. It was not for those with a sugar intolerance, given that it featured a syrupy animation of an old Wilfrid Laurier tale of the wind and the sun, in which each entity tried to get a traveller's coat off. The beating sun eventually triumphed, proving that "persuasion is superior to force" and "kindness trumps aggression."[9]

"It's time to revisit sunny ways," intoned the Liberal leader, giving birth to a cliché that would be banned from any future political drinking bingo game due to overuse. But it was useful in suggesting that Trudeau didn't intend to campaign solely on the merits of his haircut. While the middle class was tapped out, the federal government had room to invest, Trudeau said in the video. The suggestion was that Ottawa had a role to play by investing in growth, rather than consumption, particularly through use of strategic investment in infrastructure. Skeptics pointed out that many of the new Liberal team had come of age at Queen's Park, where Dalton McGuinty's government was similarly well-intentioned with its green energy experiment that, because of the whopping subsidies provided to wind and solar producers, sent hydro bills soaring. But the video did suggest a Trudeau Liberal Party that was not just about a debonair leader afloat on a sea of platitudes.

The three thousand or so delegates at the party convention in the Montreal Palais des congrès—the site of the leadership convention in 2006—were giddy at the prospect of a return to government. The polls had them in first place, and the leader's speech conveyed the feeling that there had never been a more exciting time in Canadian politics. Trudeau's plan was to appeal to centre-right voters on the economy, while pushing progressive issues like the legalization of pot and the decriminalization of physician-assisted death, which the party endorsed enthusiastically. The clearest appeal made in his keynote speech was aimed at former Conservative voters. "Canadians who voted Conservative aren't your enemies, they're your neighbours," he said.[10] But the more the leader dropped hints about how he might govern, the louder came the calls to define those policies—and put a price on them.

The Liberal faithful had been warned that *debt* is a dirty word since the former finance minister Paul Martin was known as "the deficit slayer." Yet they appeared ready to follow their new leader's belief that debt may not be so bad after all, as long as it was used to stimulate growth. The intellectual backstop to this idea was Larry Summers, the former U.S. treasury secretary, who spoke at the convention in Montreal. His idea of "secular stagnation"—the idea that Japanese-style economic torpor is the new normal in North America—was to have a profound impact on the Canadian political landscape. In Summers's opinion, market mechanisms to ensure full employment and strong growth had failed, and so governments were obliged to juice demand with "productive investment."

But if Liberal delegates drunk, figuratively and literally, on the prospect of a return to power were easy to persuade, it was much less clear that Trudeau would be able to convince voters to shift from their zero-tolerance attitude toward deficits. Jim Carr, a future cabinet minister but then a Liberal candidate in Winnipeg, acknowledged that convincing voters to plunge deeper into debt would be a tough sell. "Winnipeg built city parks 100 years ago that are now regarded as the jewel of its green space. But all those city councillors lost their seats. You have to be brave to advocate positions that don't have immediate payback," he said.[11]

The political risks were to manifest themselves in Conservative attacks focused on comments Trudeau gave to CPAC's Peter Van Dusen in a post-budget interview, when he said that in a growing economy "the budget would balance itself."[12] In typically cunning fashion, the Conservatives clipped the Liberal leader out of context, omitting the qualifier about the importance of a growing economy, and attempted to portray Trudeau as the Forrest Gump of fiscal planning for claiming that budgets balance themselves.

But worries over rationalizing deficits were concerns for the future, as the Liberals enjoyed their first feel-good moment in close to a decade. Trudeau, looking more Moores menswear than Billabong, sought to reassure his party that he was not in over his head. He was still ranked unfavourably by voters when compared to Harper on economic management. But as Jennifer O'Malley Dillon, Barack Obama's former deputy campaign manager, told the convention, Obama had faced a similar problem in 2012—and triumphed. On that occasion, Obama was up against Mitt Romney, a successful business leader who voters felt had a stronger economic sense. Yet, according to O'Malley Dillon, Obama had convinced voters he was on their side and would create a better future. While Romney talked about economic woes, Obama had a positive message about fairness and opportunity.[13] It was a lesson Trudeau took to heart—that empathy mattered more than technical competence.

The new leader was still on a steep learning curve. For example, he couldn't resist the temptation of appearing on *Tout le monde en parle*, the popular Quebec talk show that has proven the graveyard of politicians much more circumspect than Justin Trudeau 1.0. He was asked whether Canada should do more in Ukraine, where the Russian military had made several incursions after the annexation of Crimea. He answered that the situation was very worrying, "especially because Russia lost in hockey and they'll be in a bad mood." Trudeau realized immediately he'd stepped in it and attempted to rationalize making fun of a volatile situation where eighty people had died already. "That's trying to bring a light view to the situation that's extremely serious," he said with a sheepish grin that made him look like a little boy caught cutting the cheese.[14]

The gaffe was pounced on by the Conservatives, another sign that Harper had already identified Trudeau, rather than Mulcair, as his greatest threat. "There is a pattern here of supporting communist dictatorships," said Chris Alexander, the citizenship and immigration minister, casting back to Trudeau's admiring comments about China.[15] The Liberal leader emerged to apologize after he returned to Ottawa and said he had visited the Ukrainian embassy to express his regret to the ambassador in person. "Canadians are open to having people who aren't tightly scripted, who are willing to talk like people talk, and from time to time take risks and from time to time apologize or withdraw their comments," he declared.[16]

NDP MPs grumbled in private about encountering a sense of destiny on the doorsteps—voters said they liked the NDP but felt Trudeau was fated to be prime minister. No matter how many times Mulcair targeted Trudeau as a serial flip-flopper who showed poor judgment, voters seemed prepared to extend him the benefit of the doubt. Perhaps it was his age and relative experience; perhaps it was his last name. Either way, what Trudeau had is an indispensable commodity for any politician.

But the *Tout le monde* interview and its aftermath was a sobering episode for the young leader. He emerged from it bloody, if not bowed. It was another formative experience—he'd already decided to be less available. Now he would be less open and he would stick to the script. One Liberal candidate in a by-election that summer noticed a rigour and discipline that was previously lacking. "He was very regimented, no bullshit small talk, all business. When we hopped on a plane, he was on his iPad reading briefing notes. Every time we were going to meet with the media, he'd do his twenty-minute thing in a holding room asking what angles he was likely to be asked about. It was a very rigid regime. It struck me as kind of like the perception of his dad—a Jesuit-style regimen," he said. That restraint extended to his personal time. As the leader of the third party, he did not travel with a large entourage —usually just his former executive assistant, Tommy Desfossés, and photographer Adam Scotti. But at the end of the day, when the others went for a drink, Trudeau would head off to bed. "Then he'd be up at 6 a.m. in the gym at the hotel," said the Liberal candidate.[17]

Up to that point, the main thrust of the Liberal message had been economic, but in early May, Trudeau issued a statement that made clear he intended to be equally active on social issues like abortion. The day before the massive March for Life anti-abortion rally on Parliament Hill, Trudeau announced that new Liberal MPs would be expected to vote against any new restrictions on abortion access. It was a warning shot, fired over the heads of candidates with "pro-life" views who were considering a run for the party. The party had always had a cadre of MPs and members who were anti-abortion, but the leader was adamant in his pro-choice opinions and said that, despite his pledge about open nomination races, anti-abortion candidates would no longer be welcome to run. Liberal insiders pointed out that the move was forced upon the leader by the emergence of thirty-five to forty candidates with "pro-life" views, mostly in Western and rural ridings. "It was all cost and no benefit. We didn't want to have to deal with this in the middle of a campaign," said one senior Liberal.[18]

The policy had an impromptu air about it, as if it were made up on the spot during his scrum in the foyer of the House. It later emerged that Trudeau was debating with himself whether to reveal a policy that had only just been decided upon. When asked if future abortion votes would be whipped or free, as they had been in the past as issues of conscience, he responded, "That is an issue that [long pause and gaze into the distance] . . . I've committed . . . well it's a tough one. . . ." He proceeded to say that all future MPs would have to vote pro-choice, but existing MPs would be grandfathered "to a certain extent."[19]

The reaction was visceral. The Catholic Church accused Trudeau of "trying to patrol the conscience of the people."[20] *Calgary Herald* columnist Naomi Lakritz summed up the negative coverage that followed: "He doesn't seem to have any fine mesh in his brain through which his thoughts pass."[21] Lakritz wasn't alone in her opinion. John McKay, the veteran Toronto-area Liberal MP who favoured restrictions on abortion but had already been nominated, was caught on tape calling Trudeau's decision a "bozo eruption."[22] NDP leader Tom Mulcair, whose caucus was even more flatly opposed to reopening the abortion debate than the Liberals, pointed out the difficulties of having a "two-tiered system" in caucus.[23]

Trudeau spent the next month trying to contain the damage caused by his announcement. In a letter to party supporters, he acknowledged that the policy may have come "as a surprise," but he said it was intended to ensure that Liberals "vote as one" in the House of Commons. He insisted that the party remained open to Canadians with opposing views and that he understood that some people had trouble with the decision. "I empathize and I care deeply that you are working hard to reconcile your beliefs with this party policy," he said. "Canadians of all views are welcome within the Liberal Party of Canada."[24]

Yet, over time, any sense of equivocation, far less accommodation, disappeared. And the Liberal reputation as a big tent party departed with it. While Trudeau campaigned on the principles of equality and diversity of belief, it became increasingly clear that some beliefs were more equal than others. It was a classic example of the special role Trudeau saw for himself and the rest of the Anointed—of rescuing the Benighted from their own opinions.

The summer of 2014 was a moment of respite for all the political parties, as they gathered their strength for the thirteen-month sprint to the electoral finishing line. The only time Trudeau made the headlines was when an intruder broke into his Ottawa home in late August, while his family slept. But this was less a national security incident than the case of what police called a "very intoxicated nineteen-year-old" blundering into the wrong house.[25]

As the leaves started to turn red in the early fall of 2014, it was a time of contemplation for everyone. Most polls suggested that the Liberals were in majority government territory. The Conservative claim that Trudeau was incapable of leading a G7 nation through uncertain times was not resonating with voters, who felt that the Liberal leader might be able to learn on the job. The deluge of Conservative attacks should have reduced Trudeau to the status of a children's entertainer in the public eye, yet the damage was limited. Bruce Anderson and David Coletto at Abacus Data issued a report that suggested Conservative attempts to make Trudeau's competence the ballot question were not working and were likely to become less effective as the economy improved and the risk factor in contemplating change was reduced.[26]

But the real problem for the Conservatives was not their line of attack on their chief rival—it was the slipping popularity of their leader. In his memoir, *Fire and Ashes*, Michael Ignatieff had lamented that Canadians appeared to have an inordinate amount of patience with Stephen Harper's excesses. "You would have thought contempt of Parliament and contempt for democracy would be issues that would arouse the patriotic ire of citizens beyond the precincts of the chamber. You would be wrong," he said.[27] Yet by late summer 2014, the polls suggested that Canadians had tired of Harper's idiosyncrasies. Fewer than one in five Canadians in the Abacus poll said that the Conservatives deserved to be re-elected, something Anderson called an "enthusiasm shortage," noting further, "Harper's biggest problem is not the economy or policy mix but the sense that he is closed-minded to other opinions, is not a compromiser and is hyper-partisan."[28] Harper's colourless message had been heard so often over the previous decade that it became like living next to the highway for many Canadians. Compared to Trudeau's "sunny ways," it began to look very monochromatic indeed.

Yet just when it seemed that the Liberals had secured the position as the most plausible alternative to the Conservatives, they reminded Canadians why they'd been sent into exile in the first place. As Brad Lavigne, Jack Layton's former adviser, noted in his book *Building the Orange Wave*, the Liberal Party of old was a brokerage party that stood for nothing, except staying in power. "They can be in favour of free trade one day and against it the next. Every core principle is on the table. What you stand for today is what your pollster told you yesterday."[29] This sense that Trudeau and his party were on all sides of every issue damaged the Liberals in the polls—ten months after polls showed them with a clear lead, most public surveys had them back in third place, ten points off their year-highs.

The culprits were head-scratching policy positions on two issues— opposition to the deployment of fighter jets to fight the Islamic State of Iraq and Levant (ISIL) terror organization, and support (with certain reservations) for the Conservatives' new anti-terror legislation, Bill C-51.

The first misstep was Trudeau's refusal to support a government motion to join the U.S.-led airstrikes against ISIL because, he said, past interventions in the region had failed. Alarmed by the territorial gains made by ISIL in Iraq, U.S. Secretary of State John Kerry secured the support of nine countries at the NATO summit meeting in Wales in early September to launch a coordinated response. Harper agreed to commit six CF-18 fighter jets, an air-to-air refuelling tanker, two surveillance aircraft, and seven hundred Canadian Forces personnel, including special forces to help enable airstrikes. But, with one eye on the election and the potential unpopularity of the intervention in Quebec, the Liberals said they would not support the six-month mission.

Predictably, the NDP said it would oppose sending troops overseas, on the questionable basis that the fight against ISIL was the continuation of failed U.S. policy in the region going back to the 2003 invasion under President George W. Bush. "All the horrors unfolding before our eyes are as a result of that failed mission," said leader Tom Mulcair.[30]

The Liberal position was more curious—essentially that ISIL should be stopped, just not by Canadians. Trudeau spoke about "a military role of a non-combat nature"—that is, the Liberal Party would not support the combat mission but would support the troops when they arrived in the combat zone. He dismissed the impact of "a few aging warplanes" and then spectacularly flubbed the biggest issue to confront him since becoming leader.[31] In a question-and-answer session at the Liberal-friendly Canada 2020 conference in Ottawa, run by founding Team Trudeau member Tom Pitfield, the Liberal leader said Canada should concentrate on providing humanitarian aid, "rather than whipping out our CF-18s to show them how big they are"—an off-colour bit of improvisation that added to the impression he was not serious enough to be a prime minister at war.[32]

The Liberals had traditionally supported Canadian military interventions while in opposition. The mission against ISIL was supported by many Liberal grandees like Bob Rae, Irwin Cotler, and former foreign affairs minister Lloyd Axworthy, under the "responsibility to protect" doctrine. The decision not to do so on this occasion was decried as a transparent attempt to appeal to progressive voters in Quebec, where the NDP held fifty-five of seventy-five seats—criticism that appeared to be borne out a year later when, once safely ensconced in government, Trudeau withdrew the fighter jets but kept the other aircraft in theatre and tripled the number of troops on the ground.

The decision to oppose the mission was taken in anticipation that airstrikes wouldn't resolve the situation and that ground troops would be required. In fact, the depraved human rights abuses committed by ISIL, and the success of the bombing mission by the coalition—the U.S., Saudi Arabia, France, U.K., Germany, Bahrain, the United Arab Emirates, Australia, and the Netherlands—meant that the intervention remained popular and it was the parties that opposed it that looked incoherent. One poll suggested that two thirds of Liberal voters supported the mission.

Up to that point, nothing much had stuck to Trudeau, but the decision to back away from confronting an enemy as odious as ISIL found him offside with the prevailing mood in the country and caused the momentum to shift. The unscripted penis joke clearly didn't help. There are few more important decisions for a politician than sending a nation's armed forces to war. But protecting civilians from terrorist attacks is right up there—and again Trudeau got it wrong.

The morning of Wednesday, October 22, began like any other pleasant fall day in the Canadian capital—typically safe and tranquil. I was just about to deliver a speech five minutes from Parliament Hill when a friend, whose office overlooked Elgin Street, emailed to say there had been a shooting at the War Memorial, just below his window. CTV journalist Evan Solomon and I sprinted along Sparks Street to be greeted by chaos at the Cenotaph, instead of the usual tourists milling around the guard ceremony.

A police officer was shouting into his radio: "DND member down!" Four people were pumping the chest of a fallen figure in a kilt—Corporal Nathan Cirillo, a reservist from Hamilton, who was one of two ceremonial guards. The friend emailed me again, saying he was in a state of shock, having seen a gunman pump three shots, two at close range, into the back of Cirillo. "He had a black and white Palestinian type head scarf over his face that he pulled down after the shooting, then he held up the gun and shouted something I didn't hear," he said.[33]

What he shouted was "*Allahu akbar.*" The gunman was Michael Zehaf-Bibeau, a thirty-two-year-old drug addict of Libyan descent from Montreal. After leaving Cirillo to bleed to death, he raced back to his car, U-turned up Wellington Street, abandoned the car, and ran onto Parliament Hill. There, he commandeered the ministerial car of Conservative MP Michelle Rempel, which was idling in front of the East Block building, and drove to Centre Block, before bursting into the building, where he wrestled with House of Commons security officer Constable Samearn Son. After a scuffle in which Son was shot in the leg, Zehaf-Bibeau ran toward the Library of Parliament at the north end of the building.

If he had turned left into the Reading Room, halfway down the Hall of Honour, he would have interrupted the weekly Conservative caucus meeting and would have been able to pick off the prime minister and the entire cabinet; if he'd turned right into the Railway Room, he could have slaughtered the NDP Official Opposition. As it was, the intrepid parliamentary sergeant-at-arms, Kevin Vickers, and four brave RCMP officers, Curtis Barrett, Richard Rozon, Martin Fraser, and Dany Daigle, combined to overpower and kill Zehaf-Bibeau before he could do any more harm.

The four RCMP officers formed an Immediate Action Rapid Deployment—a diamond formation used in life-threatening situations where waiting for backup might result in more deaths. With Barrett at the apex, the four officers walked toward the north end of the hall with weapons drawn. After seeing movement at the Library of Parliament door, they heard a gunshot and Barrett said he felt the percussion and shockwave of a bullet going past him.[34] Vickers was taking cover against a wall and the distraction of the RCMP officers allowed the sergeant-at-arms to break cover and fall to the ground while firing. At the same time, Barrett was firing as he walked toward the gunman. The combination of a team of brave Canadians prepared to put their lives in the line of fire ended the threat, with thirty-one shots hitting Zehaf-Bibeau.

But Canada was in shock. The shooting on Parliament Hill came just two days after Warrant Officer Patrice Vincent had been run over and killed by Martin Couture-Rouleau, a twenty-five-year-old Muslim convert in Saint-Jean-sur-Richelieu, Quebec. A country that had almost felt itself immune from the outrages being perpetrated around the world was suddenly dragged out of its cozy complacency.

A visibly shaken Stephen Harper, who had been spirited by staff members into a small electrical utility closet in the Reading Room during the shooting, said in a nationally televised address that his government would take "all necessary steps" to keep Canadians safe. As life returned to a degree of normalcy, Harper told the House of Commons that the law and policing powers needed to be strengthened. The legislative manifestation of that pledge emerged in early February 2015—the anti-terror bill, C-51. Harper launched the bill at a campaign-style event where he attacked the opposition parties for their perceived lack of resolve. "Every time we talk about security, they suggest that somehow our freedoms are threatened," he said. "[But] violent jihadism is not a human right, it's an act of war."[35]

With the Parliament Hill shootings still fresh in the nation's memory, the Liberals decided to signal their consent before even seeing the draft legislation, albeit with the reservation that they might amend the law if they won government. But again, Trudeau called it wrong. The Liberals were the party of the Charter, but they were prepared to vote for C-51, which was widely criticized as an infringement on individual liberties and Charter rights. On close inspection, it looked to many people as if Harper had overreached and was politicizing the security of Canadians. Groups like the B.C. Civil Liberties Association pointed out, regarding preventative detention, that individuals could be held on suspicion that they "may" carry out a terror attack, lowering the evidentiary threshold from "will." There were concerns about the expansion of powers for CSIS, the federal spy agency, giving it the ability to intervene to reduce threats. The bill also criminalized statements that "knowingly advocate or promote the commission of terrorist offences." At the same time, one glaring omission in the bill was the lack of parliamentary oversight for the expanded security apparatus. A number of provisions in the bill were clearly open to Charter rights challenges, which made it all the more curious that a Liberal leader with the name Trudeau was ready to vote in support of the legislation.

Having studied the bill, Mulcair took the principled position that he could not support it. The NDP lived up to former prime minister John Diefenbaker's definition of the role of the Opposition—"It must be vigilant against oppression and unjust invasions by the Cabinet of the rights of people. It finds fault, it suggests amendments, it asks questions and elicits information; it arouses, educates and moulds public opinion by voice and vote."[36] Mulcair called the bill "sweeping, dangerous, vague and ineffective." The wording was sufficiently obtuse, he argued, that it could permit CSIS to investigate anyone who challenged the government's social, economic, or environmental policies.[37] The suggestion was dismissed as a typical NDP conspiracy theory by Harper. But, having given the Conservatives a free pass, presumably on the grounds that he believed the legislation would be popular with Canadians, Trudeau was reduced to attacking the NDP for opposing the bill. "The NDP has not once in its history supported anti-terror measures," he said.[38]

He did identify the issue of parliamentary oversight as a core weakness of the bill—as academics Kent Roach and Craig Forcese pointed out, the maxim in the security sector when dealing with powerful covert state agencies is "Trust but verify." Yet, by siding with the Conservatives, Trudeau had undermined the opposition's role of preventing the shortcuts through democratic procedure that governments try to take. The upshot was that the polls kept ticking downward, as Canadians tried to figure out what a Trudeau government would mean for the country in the wake of disjointed, jumbled policies on defence and terrorism.

The big policy miscalculations were compounded by some caucus management issues that might have been ignored had the polling numbers been more healthy. But for the Liberals in the fall and winter of 2014–15, every error was magnified.

In October, Trudeau was approached by a female NDP MP who relayed an accusation of harassment against Liberal MPs Scott Andrews and Massimo Pacetti on behalf of herself and another NDP MP. With little in the way of internal investigation, Trudeau suspended the two Liberals and blocked their candidacy in the next election. The case came on the heels of the dismissal of Jian Ghomeshi as a CBC Radio host after allegations of sexual abuse and the emergence of a broader national discussion on the subject of sexual harassment. But while Ghomeshi's case went to trial, where he was acquitted of five charges (the sixth was withdrawn after he signed a peace bond and apologized to his accuser), the two Liberals were initially afforded little due process. Both MPs denied the allegations, but their careers were effectively over, even before Toronto lawyer Cynthia Peterson had been appointed to conduct an independent investigation. After Peterson reported, Trudeau said the actions were serious enough to expel them permanently, but the finding was a formality.

The summary nature of Trudeau's decision left some Liberals muttering about it being a Queen of Hearts–like trial—sentence first, verdict afterward. The absence of due process suggested confirmation bias on Trudeau's part when faced with emotionally charged gender issues. It also hinted at the same ruthlessness he had shown in jettisoning the Liberal senators.

An even more bizarre decision in February 2015 appeared to vindicate the Conservative charge that Trudeau lacked the judgment to run the country. For reasons best known to himself, Trudeau put his own credibility on the line by appearing at a press conference with former Conservative MP Eve Adams, who had decided to cross the floor and join the Liberals. It was hardly a coup on a par with the 2005 defection of Belinda Stronach, who saved Paul Martin's Liberals from a spring election they didn't want by tipping the numbers in a non-confidence vote.

Adams, by contrast, had been a lightning rod for controversy during her time as a Conservative MP. Her then boyfriend, Dimitri Soudas, had been forced out as executive director of the Conservative Party after being accused of meddling in a nomination race in a safer seat where Adams wanted to run (her existing seat of Mississauga Brampton South was seen as increasingly unwinnable). She proceeded to upset colleagues in neighbouring ridings, as she held photo opportunities in schools and hospitals in the constituency where she wanted to run. "It's the opposite of teamwork," remarked one MP.[39]

She then used glowing endorsements from six cabinet ministers in the nomination race in the new, safer Oakville riding, even though they were intended for use in Mississauga. Three of the ministers refused to back up their endorsements when contacted by media. In a messy nomination contest with a local chiropractor, allegations of ineligible members and bullying behaviour flew back and forth until, eventually, the national candidate selection committee disqualified both hopefuls from running.

In short, the Conservatives were happy to be rid of Adams and it was a mystery why Trudeau embraced her so enthusiastically. There was speculation that the real prize was Soudas, who knew where the bodies were buried in the Conservative Party because, as Harper's communications director and Quebec fixer, he'd buried many of them. The Liberals sent a senior staff member to help Soudas root through his basement in search of useful information, but with little success, according to one person familiar with the expedition.[40] But for the prospect of unquantifiable partisan gain, Trudeau took a very public reputational hit that made him look like just another cynical political hack. He was forced to endure the humiliation of sitting straight-faced as Adams rhapsodized about how the Liberals were the only team she'd ever wanted to play for. She complained about how she could no longer support "mean-spirited leadership that divides people" and how she was committed to working with "someone who inspires, not with fear-mongers and bullies."[41]

The growing sense of unrest among some Liberals crystallized around the decision to embrace Adams as part of the Liberal caucus. "Justin talks about 'doing politics differently,' but what we have is the same old hypocrisy," said one MP. "Every nomination is being managed and it's brewing negativity. The Eve and Dimitri thing reinforced a lot of grumbling on the ground."[42] Mike Colle, the provincial Liberal member for Eglinton-Lawrence, where Adams decided to run, said the move was an "affront" to all Liberals.[43] Perhaps fortunately for Trudeau, Adams proceeded to lose the Liberal nomination for the riding to a smart young federal prosecutor, Marco Mendicino, who went on to beat Conservative finance minister Joe Oliver. Notably, it was the first time Trudeau and the team around him did not get their own way. Worse, the opportunistic flirtation with Adams did little to reverse the sense that the Liberals under Trudeau had blown it.

Part of the problem was that Trudeau was keeping his powder dry for the election—which meant that he talked about concepts rather than specifics. In February, he hinted at broad-based tax relief when he said he would cancel the Harper government's $2 billion proposal to allow couples to income split for tax purposes. Trudeau pointed out that the plan would help better-off Canadians, while he intended to "invest in the middle class, and those working hard to join it." But you would have had to have been a code-whisperer to discern that he intended to use the money for a middle class tax cut and for an enhanced child benefit.

Another consequence of the dip in the polls was that it slowed down a candidate recruitment campaign that had been proceeding smoothly until the shooting on Parliament Hill. "If you can sum up nominations in one sentence, it is 95 per cent dependent on where the public polling is," said one senior campaign insider. The team identified bright young candidates from various political and ethnic backgrounds. Maryam Monsef was a twenty-nine-year-old Afghan migrant who had nearly knocked off the mayor of Peterborough, Ontario, in a mayoral race when she was approached to run for the Liberals. Initially, she said she had no interest in running, but she was exactly the kind of fresh face the party was seeking. She was persuaded and ended up winning a tight nomination race, taking the seat in Peterborough from the Conservatives and then later being appointed as Trudeau's first minister of democratic reform.

Amarjeet Sohi was a popular Indian-Canadian city councillor in Edmonton, who had once been imprisoned and tortured for advocating land reform in the Indian state of Bihar.[44] He was at first reluctant to enter the race. Yet he too was talked around and won the nomination for Edmonton Mill Woods, took the seat from the Conservative incumbent, and was then appointed to cabinet as the first minister for infrastructure and communities. But in the months before the election, the conveyor belt of talent seized up. "In 2014, people were coming out of the woodwork. But the last three months, trying to round up the last thirty to forty candidates was really difficult," said the campaign insider.[45]

Liberal prospects were not improved by the "Orange Chinook" that swept through Alberta in early May. The NDP in that province had been like the fossil fish that everyone had thought was extinct until it was recalled to life by a province-wide repudiation of the Progressive Conservatives, who had been in power since 1971. Rachel Notley became the province's first NDP premier, and the victory led to an upswing in fortunes for the federal party, as the prospect of Mulcair repeating the feat became a real possibility. At the turn of the year, the NDP had been demoralized by defections, retirements, and an inability to move the dial of public opinion. But a relaunch of Mulcair, highlighting his middle-class background and his thirty-five years of public policy experience reintroduced him to voters who were beginning to struggle with

Trudeau's decisions. "We put doubt in the minds of the jury," said one senior New Democrat—doubt that was fomented by Trudeau himself.[46]

The Conservatives were seasoned practitioners at kicking their opponents in the guts and, as the Liberal poll numbers tumbled, they attempted what they hoped was the coup de grâce. Ignoring the NDP, who were starting to edge ahead in the polls, the Tories released an attack ad that urged viewers to agree with the conclusion "Justin Trudeau—just not ready." The ad featured a workplace setting with a group of people— an older white man, a middle-aged Asian man and white woman, and a younger white woman—looking through a pile of resumés. The younger woman said Trudeau's application included his photo but that his experience included nothing about balancing a budget or making a payroll. "But didn't he say budgets balance themselves?" the older woman interjected. She later suggested that being prime minister is "not an entry-level job." But there was also a surprising aside from the younger woman, who said, "I'm not saying 'no' forever, but not now." The Asian man's comment was the most damning of all, with its implication that the Liberal leader was just a good-looking dimwit: "Nice hair, though."

Kory Teneycke, the Conservative Party spin doctor, indicated the media spend on the ad would be significant. "This is how Justin Trudeau is viewed by the public," he said. "He's viewed as a likeable guy but not a very serious guy. . . . He's the type of person who loves the celebrity side of the job—taking selfies at funerals, bouncing babies on his hand and doing political rallies."[47]

In the wake of the devastation wrought on the careers of Stéphane Dion ("He's not a leader") and Michael Ignatieff ("Just visiting"), Trudeau could have been excused if he stopped buying green bananas for the office fruit bowl. Perhaps the only silver lining for the Liberals was that Trudeau had talked his way into the punchlines of a thousand pundits —as a leader so dense, light bent around him. The only way was up.

SIX

THE ROAD TO RIDEAU HALL

THE FIGHT BACK BEGAN in the unlikely setting of Dinty Moore's diner in Aylmer, Quebec, in the first week of May 2015. Trudeau invited the media to join him in the short journey across the Ottawa River from Parliament Hill, and it wasn't to partake in the excellent Gateau Au Chocolat "La Bombe."

Instead, he unveiled a package of income tax cuts and child benefit payments that would be paid for—or not, as it turned out—by a $3 billion tax hike on the wealthiest Canadians. The "Fairness for the Middle Class" package would prove to be the central plank in the Liberal election platform, with its pledge to create a new tax bracket of 33 per cent for Canadians earning more than $200,000 a year, up from 29 per cent. More revenue would be saved by cancelling Conservative fiscal measures, including scrapping the planned income-splitting tax credit and the doubling of the tax-free savings account limit. Instead, the Liberals said they would lower the amount of income tax paid by those in the $44,700–$89,400 bracket—a move Trudeau said would benefit every taxpayer by $670 per year.

The tax hike for the wealthiest Canadians was intended to pay for the middle-bracket cut—that chimera of finance ministers everywhere, the "revenue-neutral" tax cut. The increase raised the combined federal–provincial tax take in six provinces, including Ontario and Quebec, to over 50 per cent—the psychological barrier which, if broken, tends to yield diminishing returns, as high earners seek to avoid handing over more than half of each additional dollar earned. Fairness was, it seemed, an elastic concept. (In the event, the first promise broken by the Liberals in office was this one—tax avoidance measures by those earning more than $200,000 meant that there was a net cost of $1.2 billion to the treasury for the middle-bracket cut.)

But the real meat in the "fairness" tax sandwich served up at Dinty Moore's was the new income-tested Canada Child Benefit (CCB), an incredibly generous measure that earmarked an extra $4 billion on top of the $18 billion the Conservatives were already spending on child care. It would prove a very attractive offering, outbidding the Harper Conservatives on tax breaks and allowing the Liberals to claim that 90 per cent of households would be better off. By the Liberals' reckoning, a family with an income of $45,000 and two kids would be $4,000 better off each year than under Harper's plan.[1]

The CCB was positioned as the opening salvo in a bidding war for the affections of voters. But it was part of a coherent package aimed at targeting resources at low-, modest-, and middle-income families, and it reflected the feeling that economic growth was leaving people behind in precarious employment and without adequate pension coverage. Combining the CCB with an expansion of the Canada Pension Plan, an enriched Working Income Tax Benefit, and a retooled Canada Student Grant targeted at lower-income families, the Liberals attempted to create what in effect was a guaranteed annual income for different groups like seniors and parents with kids. "I don't think people understand how transformative it is in terms of the amount of cash going to low-income families, how it changes the quality of life in a significant way for people making $40,000 a year to have an extra $700 a month. That's real money," said one person involved in designing the new package of measures. "All together we created a package that isn't as generous as Denmark, but it's different from the U.S. It was a very attractive and coherent package and even three years later, the Liberals haven't gotten credit for it."[2]

There was an unsavoury tinge of class envy to the launch of the Fairness package—with disparaging references to "the wealthy" and a zest to address income inequality by making high earners poorer. "The Canadian dream has been taken from too many, for the benefit of too few, for too long,"[3] Trudeau said at the launch, positioning himself as a latter-day Robin Hood. The messaging became smoother when the election campaign began in earnest, with Trudeau reverting to the lines he'd used in a recent speech on liberty, where he had said the job of a leader is to bring people together. "You do not divide them against one another," he said.[4] The experience in the U.K. and elsewhere was that voters realized that well-heeled taxpayers helped to pay for the welfare system and did not appreciate income disparities being turned into a class war. The message for much of the election campaign was softened to ask the wealthy to "pay a little more" to help those with less. The softer tone resonated and delivered some of the highest-income ridings in Canada into the red column. But that sense of resentment against success has resurfaced from time to time in the Trudeau government, notably in the proposal to target the wealthy in small business tax reforms in 2017—"them and us" rhetoric that demonized the wealthy.

Yet on the sunny May day in Aylmer, there was a sense that Trudeau was back in the game, even if it would take some months before that became apparent in the polls. He spoke in specifics rather than in platitudinous fables about "sunny ways"; he looked relaxed, spoke without notes, and was in command of his brief. Trudeau had been spending five or six hours a week in debate preparation, and the training was clearly paying off. Most importantly, he had established the narrative that Canada had become less fair under Harper, that the middle class was struggling, and that the economy was not growing. The data didn't back up this contention—economists pointed out the idea that middle-class dreams had turned sour under Harper didn't fit the facts. Median after-tax income had reached record highs in the years prior to 2015, in part because the share of government transfers going to the middle-income quintile had risen substantially.[5]

But the country was heading through the looking glass into an election campaign—a world of cabbages and kings where nothing is what it seems to be because everything is what it isn't. The Conservatives were already claiming that the Liberal plan would raise taxes for two million families—which would have been some feat, if true, given the massive amounts of money Trudeau was pledging to spend on child benefits. The launch of the Fairness package brought to mind an old episode of the British sitcom *Yes Minister*, where the hapless minister is told the difference between a "brave" decision and a "courageous" one: the former could lose the government of the day votes; the latter could lose the election. Trudeau had just made an extremely courageous decision.

There were vigorous internal debates about the thrust of the Liberal campaign. Behind the scenes, there was speculation that Trudeau might replace Gerald Butts with David Herle, who had run Paul Martin's campaigns federally and Kathleen Wynne's provincially in Ontario.

Elsewhere, there were concerns about the dangers of pushing marginal tax rates over 50 per cent when the prevailing argument was meant to be about "fairness." But there was agreement that the Liberals should attack the Conservatives where they lived, on the home turf of tax cuts and child care, taking care to outbid the Tories for the voters' affections, and that required revenue. The plan was adjusted according to the economic circumstances of the day. Those circumstances in early summer 2015 included a fifty-dollar-a-barrel oil price; the first quarter of negative growth since 2011[6]; an unemployment rate that had risen to 6.8 per cent; and seven consecutive months of declining exports. Much of the commentary that greeted the tax package was positive—it was simple, didn't require lengthy negotiations with the provinces, and could prove stimulative for the economy. The knock on it was that it was hugely expensive and would leave few dollars available for infrastructure, fighting climate change, and other worthy causes, if the Liberals stuck to the pledge to also balance the budget. That would prove to be a big "if."

The Fairness event was the unofficial launch of the battle for hearts and votes. Within days, all three major parties were running television commercials—the Liberals and Conservatives selling tax breaks and child benefits, the NDP flogging its national daycare plan. The Liberals had ceded daycare to the NDP as an expensive proposition they couldn't afford to fund. As the summer wore on, they found themselves increasingly vulnerable to NDP leader Tom Mulcair on Bill C-51, the anti-terror legislation the Liberals had chosen to support and change, if elected. The issue had not faded away and was becoming a point of differentiation between the two parties in the big cities, where they were most often in direct conflict.

One nominated Liberal candidate in Nova Scotia, former Canadian Forces veteran David MacLeod, resigned in protest of the party's decision to back the legislation. In a letter to Trudeau, he gave his reasons. "Having opposed oppressive political systems in the name of Canadian democracy, I refuse to support any entity complicit in the creation of a repressive act which assaults Canadian liberty," he said.[7] In Perth, Ontario, lifelong Liberal mayor John Fenik sought the NDP nomination, after concluding that Mulcair represented a more potent progressive threat to Harper than Trudeau (he eventually lost to Conservative Scott Reid).

Invigorated by Rachel Notley's victory in Alberta, the NDP increasingly believed it was the little party that could. And sure enough, support was surging—by early June, ten successive opinion polls had the party in first place. This reversal of fortune started to produce bizarre outcomes. The Truth and Reconciliation Commission into Canada's relations with its First Nations released its list of ninety-four recommendations in early June. While Mulcair was circumspect, presumably with one eye on having to enact the recommendations as prime minister, Trudeau promised to implement them all. If he had managed to read them, he certainly hadn't costed them.

But Trudeau and his team realized they couldn't let the NDP momentum go unchallenged and had to pivot their campaign to take on Mulcair. Attack dogs like Toronto MP Adam Vaughan were dispatched to NDP events to point out that the New Democrats wanted to reopen the

Constitution in order to abolish the Senate, and to make it easier for Quebec to separate by repudiating the Clarity Act to set the threshold for independence at 50 per cent plus one.

In a further response to the NDP threat, Trudeau released a package of thirty-two democratic and government reforms ahead of schedule in mid-June—measures the Liberals claimed would "restore democracy in Canada." Central to the plan was introducing a new way to elect future governments. "We are committed to ensuring that the 2015 election will be the last federal election using the first-past-the-post system," he said at a press conference in Ottawa's historic Château Laurier hotel, flanked by more than 150 of his candidates. If asked, most voters would have said the problem was the politicians, not the voting system, but electoral reform had its enthusiastic advocates, particularly among Millennials. Trudeau had supported the preferential ballot system during the Liberal leadership race, but said that, if elected, he would launch a "national engagement process" that would look at all the alternatives to the status quo, including proportional representation, after which his government would legislate.

The other measures—ranging from giving backbench MPs more power to balancing the cabinet with an equal number of men and women—were designed to provide contrast with a Conservative government that Trudeau portrayed as authoritarian, secretive, and disrespectful toward taxpayers. There were promises to save home mail delivery, open up public access to government documents, and close loopholes in political financing. A good number of these ideas proved either impractical or unpalatable once the Liberals were in government. But as someone involved in attempting to implement the agenda after the election noted, "These were third-place promises. This sprawling platform was created by a third-place party that had been out of power for a decade and was throwing stuff at the wall. When someone asked, 'How are we going to do all this stuff?' the response was 'We'll only have to if we get elected.'"[8]

Canadians were not standing around their barbecues debating the merits of mixed-member voting over ranked ballots. But they wanted something different, and this was something. Three out of four voters said they felt it was time for change, and the only consolation for the Conservatives was that the NDP was siphoning votes from the Liberals.

On the day of the "open and fair elections" launch, Trudeau was in a prickly mood, bristling at the suggestion he could not realistically connect with middle-class voters whose cause he championed because he had never lived their experience first hand. "I was a high school teacher. I am a strong advocate for women's rights and I'm not a woman. That's an argument I summarily reject, particularly since I've spent the last three years building a political party, almost rebooting it from scratch," he responded.[9] Despite his protestations, there was an obvious disconnect between the wealthy trust-fund kid and his reverence for the middle class, a cohort to which he clearly did not belong.

This overcompensation was apparent in his relentless pursuit of income redistribution. In the House of Commons, Stephen Harper claimed that Conservative tax reductions had helped every family in the country. Trudeau responded that helping every family was not fair. "What is fair is helping those who need it most. A $2 billion tax break that favours the wealthiest families . . . that is the prime minister's plan," he said.[10] The rhetoric verged on an open declaration of class war. The motivation may be a matter of debate, but there can be no doubt that Justin Trudeau is an intensely ideological person who holds the sincere belief that the common people of Canada, if not the world, need his help.

The Liberals were still falling in the polls, as the Conservative carpet-bombing took its toll. But Trudeau's irritation with the way things had been going seemed tempered by the announcements that put him back in the mix. He'd added some policy beef to his undoubted political talents and let slip enough detail to suggest that the forthcoming tele-vised leaders' debates would not prove the Waterloo his opponents were anticipating.

The official starting gun for the forty-second general election campaign was fired by Stephen Harper on Sunday, August 2. With the election date set for October 19, it promised to be a marathon seventy-eight-day slog—the longest since 1872. All three major parties had a shot at victory—the first Nanos Research poll of the campaign had the Conservatives at 31 per cent support, the NDP at 30, and the Liberals at 29. But those numbers disguised undercurrents that were already moving voter sentiment. As Mulcair noted, the country was flirting with recession and there was a sense on the doorsteps that Harper had outstayed his welcome. The PM's portrayal of Stéphane Dion and Michael Ignatieff as risky gambles had paid off, but in 2015 he was facing two leaders who were more popular than he was. And as Harper's former campaign manager, Tom Flanagan, has written, political attacks are far less effective when the target is more esteemed than the source of the attack, which was certainly the case in the 2015 election campaign.[11] In particular, it became increasingly hard to portray Mulcair as a "socialist and protectionist" when he was proclaiming his devotion to balanced budgets.

But if the tide was turning against the government, one time-honoured Conservative tactic was working—the evisceration of a Liberal leader, thanks to an advertising blitz with the "Justin Trudeau—just not ready" spot. Gerald Butts, Trudeau's key adviser, recalled the impact with a shudder. "I sat through those focus groups at Bay and Bloor in Toronto, with a mix of 416 and 905 [downtown and suburban GTA] voters, who should have been core target Liberal voters. They were asked, 'What do think of Justin Trudeau?' 'Well, you know, he's just not ready,' they said, parroting the Tory line. But people want Justin to do well. He's the only candidate in the history of the country who could have survived what the Tories did to him," he said.[12]

Twin counterpunches got the Liberals back in the game. The first was the release of a television commercial that disregarded the orthodoxy that politicians should never repeat their opponents' attacks. The spot directly addressed the Conservative contention that Trudeau was "not ready" by featuring the Liberal leader walking against a backdrop of Parliament Hill, saying he was "not ready to watch hard-working

Canadians lose jobs and fall further behind." The spot was filmed at Major's Hill Park on one of the hottest days of the year, with Trudeau in a white shirt, sleeves rolled up, speaking directly to camera. "It was a thousand degrees that day and we spent the whole day shooting. Justin had three white shirts that got soaked after five minutes—there was a rotation of them hanging in the trees to dry," said Butts.[13] He called the "ready" ad the "most effective in Canadian political history"—but then, he wrote it. What is undeniable is that it blunted the Conservative attacks by dealing with them head-on. "When we showed that ad, it was like someone threw on a light switch," noted Butts.[14]

The second counterpunch was the leaders' debate. Kory Teneycke, Harper's spokesperson, coined one of the most memorable lines of the campaign when he said that Trudeau would probably exceed expectations if he came on stage with his pants on. Teneycke is one of Canada's smartest political strategists, having worked as communications director for the Harper government and as an election adviser to current Ontario premier Doug Ford. But the intended zinger made Trudeau's task easier—it was round one against Brazeau all over again. All he had to do was avoid being knocked out and he would be in good shape to come off the ropes later in the fight. On debate night, he did that and more—appearing energized and on top of his subject matter, forcing Harper onto the back foot on the economy ("The contraction is almost exclusively in the energy sector," the prime minister said, conceding that there was a contraction[15]).

Butts said he'd never been as nervous as on the day of the debate. "[Trudeau's] last few debate preps were brutal," he said. Former Ontario finance minister Dwight Duncan was playing Mulcair in the debate prep, Liberal MP David McGuinty was playing the role of Harper, and former deputy prime minister Sheila Copps acted as Elizabeth May. On the day before, in a full dress rehearsal at a studio on York Mills Road, Duncan said Trudeau was on top of his files, looked confident, and presented well.[16] But the next day, at a last-minute run-through, Butts said the Liberal leader was just "dialling it in." Duncan said that, to him,

Trudeau looked like a man who was already ready to get into the ring for the prize fight—that he'd prepared sufficiently and was confident of victory. But the lacklustre performance created a chill among Trudeau's advisers. "We cancelled the last debate and he and I went for a walk in Trinity Bellwoods Park," said Butts. "A bunch of people recognized him and came over to say, 'We're pulling for you, we're counting on you.' I don't know where he found it from, but on the night he was awesome."[17]

During the debate, Trudeau drew blood in his tussle with a tentative Mulcair, who appeared to have abandoned his prosecutorial style, honed in Question Period interrogations of Harper, in favour of making the case for the defence. In particular, the Liberal leader attacked Mulcair's admission that he'd recognize a referendum result in Quebec where 50 per cent plus one of the population voted to separate. In one segment, Mulcair asked Trudeau ten times, "What's your number?," referring to the percentage of the vote in a referendum that could facilitate Quebec's separation from Canada. Finally, Trudeau hit back: "I'll give you a number. Nine. My number is nine. Nine Supreme Court justices said one vote is not enough to break up this country."

It landed like an upper cut to the NDP leader's jawline. Tom Pitfield recalled that in the Liberal war room, Trudeau's sixty staff leapt into action. "As soon as Justin said, 'My number is nine,' we were out buying into YouTube and every media channel on the planet. After the *Maclean's* debate, we were the second largest broadcaster in Canada—we knew that people were going to form their impressions of Justin immediately after and we wanted to make sure the impressions they had were of a guy who was serious. We were buying cheap and we were buying lots," he said. "We spent more than four times as much as Stephen Harper's Conservatives did on online voter contact and digital advertising."[18] For Trudeau, the strategy of going after his two more experienced rivals paid off. The photo op the next day, of Trudeau sparring at a Toronto boxing gym, was symbolic, suggesting he was still standing after the first round and had plenty of energy left.

For the Conservatives, things were going less well. The inscrutable workings of providence resulted in the first weeks of the campaign coinciding with witness testimony at the trial of Senator Mike Duffy. Nigel Wright, Harper's former chief of staff, was on the stand for six days. While Wright corroborated the prime minister's version of events—that Harper was unaware Wright was inking a personal cheque for $90,000 to Duffy—questions about ethics dogged the Conservative leader on the campaign trail. It was a reminder to voters about the more pernicious side of Harper's brand of executive democracy.

Part of the reason the Liberals were able to rescue themselves after falling into third place in 2015, in a way they were unable to in 2011, was that they had a much clearer view of their audience. In 2011, they had paid nearly $1 million to polling company Pollara for four hundred live calls a night. In 2015, they brought their polling in-house, hired Pollara analyst Dan Arnold, and used the savings to conduct four times as many live calls. "That gave us credible numbers in the regions," said one person involved in the campaign. "We could detect what was happening in Peel region or in Laval, or detect differences in the north and south side of Calgary. We had a $5 million budget for the ground game and we did four or five times more polling for cheaper. It made a 100 per cent difference when it came to making our decisions on where to send Trudeau and deploy our resources." [19]

The other innovation was the adoption of cutting-edge voter information technology. Katie Telford, who co-chaired the national campaign, and Tom Pitfield had orchestrated the modernization of the party's database, online canvassing, and fundraising. Pitfield had spent time with the Obama campaign and brought home the lesson that making a digital campaign work required the creation of a digital culture. "The party had Liberalist [a voter identification database] through both failed campaigns—Ignatieff and Dion. The reason it failed is that they had no culture, they just had a platform. I have Photoshop on my laptop, but I couldn't make a garage sale sign. They didn't buy into it, they didn't use it, nobody took it, owned it, and made sure all the pieces worked. You need to get the whole organization working around it because it's holistic or it's nothing," he said.[20]

After the dry run of the leadership campaign, the Liberals had their digital tools ready in 2015. Pitfield preached the message that people could not be persuaded to vote Liberal on digital media if they were hostile, but Trudeau's authenticity online could win people's attention and spark a relationship with people who could see themselves voting for him. And if they became motivated, digital made it easier to communicate with other people. "The more you're engaged, the harder it is for parties to convince you that their version of reality is a better version," he said. "You need to be campaigning two years out—and that's what Trump has figured out too. It makes you harder to dislodge. There's a community of like-minded people out there that you're trying to get into the party and one of the things digital does really well is help you find them. Once you've introduced yourself and built a relationship built on trust, you can start engaging them around common values and get them out to vote."[21]

Pitfield said that Trudeau became the digital tool's greatest advocate and its toughest critic. "He understood the importance of getting stake-holders in the party to embrace digital tools, but he was also adamant they were no substitute for engaging people face-to-face at the door," he explained.[22] On the ground, Richard Maksymetz was in charge of campaign mobilization and political operations. The Liberals reconfig-ured Barack Obama's platform and flew his former field director to Ottawa once every six weeks to ensure it was operating smoothly. The technology updated the existing, but flawed, Liberalist voter identifica-tion and relationship management system, by layering on information gained on the doorsteps, now input by cellphone, about how likely people were to vote and who they might vote for. Voter identification had been the secret sauce for the Conservatives for over a decade and helped to explain their superior fundraising capability. But in 2015, the Liberals were at least competitive.

In the fog of electoral war, it wasn't at all clear at the time, but the turning point in the campaign came at the end of August, when Mulcair promised that the first ever NDP budget would be balanced. The New Democrats had established a discernible, though clearly not insurmountable, lead in the polls, and Mulcair wanted to blunt Harper's attacks about reckless spending with the image of a moderate, competent public administrator. But the decision was to prove fateful for the NDP leader, who inadvertently handed the agent-of-change baton to Trudeau and allowed him to make more ambitious promises. No sooner had Mulcair taken the pledge than a Nanos poll emerged showing that Canadians believed the country was already in recession, with a majority supporting the idea that the federal government should run a deficit to stimulate growth.[23] "Mulcair made a huge mistake," said Robert Asselin, who helped draft the Liberal platform and later worked as a senior adviser to Bill Morneau. "If he'd said he was going to put more into the economy, people would have seen the contrast with Harper. The fact that he wanted to help people but spend no money made no sense."[24]

Trudeau took full advantage, telling an audience in Belleville, Ontario, that the Liberals would not make balancing the budget their top priority. "We will balance the budget, but how long that takes will depend on the mess that Stephen Harper has left behind. This country needs a plan for growth," he said.[25] The Liberal leader was suddenly on the same page as public opinion. "I don't recall any platform-specific stuff moving the needle," said one campaign insider, "aside from that deficit pledge, which had been worked out in the spring, on the assumption that on September 1, second-quarter results would come out and we would be in a technical recession. We had planned on running a deficit if we were in a recession. I think we won because people thought we were in recession."[26, 27] The upshot was that, while Mulcair was constrained within the Conservatives' fiscal framework, Trudeau had billions and billions of shiny, new dollars to spend.

The next day, he made clear what he intended to spend his newfound, borrowed wealth on—a doubling of the infrastructure budget to $125 billion over ten years to stimulate demand in the economy. That was more than five times the amount Mulcair had promised on infrastructure. The increase would mean deficits of less than $10 billion in each of the following two fiscal years, with the budget returning to balance by 2019, he said—a commitment that proved to be the second promise broken by the new government. But the voters weren't in on the joke that these were "third-place promises." "The growth will eliminate Harper's deficit and we will balance the budget in 2019," said Trudeau, with the confidence of every spendthrift politician down the ages.[28]

There was no great outcry from economists, a number of whom had been co-opted by the Liberals to explain that a $2 trillion economy like Canada's could weather small deficits, particularly if they were used for "productive investment" like infrastructure. What they did not explain was that there was every prospect the Liberals had gotten their sums wrong, given that the platform was drawn up without all the sophisticated modelling available to the Department of Finance. As the transition team discovered when they came to power, the books were $12 billion worse than had been anticipated in the spring budget, so none of the parties would have managed to balance the books in 2015–16 without cutting costs to the bone.

As one insider said, "My distinct recollection when Finance officials briefed the transition team was we weren't even close. We would tease [platform architect Mike] McNair and say, 'Your costings were shit.' But growth was not what was projected in the Conservatives' spring budget, and oil was down. It would have been difficult for them to stay in surplus."[29] Harper must have known this as the campaign wound its way into its second month, even as he told voters there was "little to zero risk" of deficit in the 2015–16 fiscal year. But he didn't let that deter him from attacking his younger rival for "having no idea what he's talking about" when it came to deficits. The fact that he himself had used stimulus spending to counter recession, running up a $56 billion deficit in 2009, was disregarded as he blasted Trudeau and his plan to "spend more on everything."

But Harper's keen political antennae were clearly tuned to the rising fortunes of the Liberals, particularly in Ontario, at the expense of the

NDP. A Léger poll in early September showed the NDP still leading in public support, but the party's high numbers in Quebec masked slippage elsewhere. The New Democrats had reached the same conclusion and were resorting to increasingly desperate attacks on the Liberals, such as the press release suggesting that Justin Trudeau didn't care about battered women and would oppose their plan to combat violence against women. The Liberals hit back by wondering who Mulcair admired more: "Karl Marx or Margaret Thatcher?"—an odd question raised by the NDP leader's "praising" of Thatcher's economic policies and then "boasting" about the NDP being a member of the Socialist International.[30] The reason for the hostilities was simple—less than a third of voters had decided who to vote for, giving the two opposition parties the prospect of doubling their support if they could pummel the reputation of the other into the dirt.

To take the pulse of voters, I travelled coast to coast visiting twenty-two ridings in seven provinces between Halifax and Vancouver in the last month of the campaign. It became clear that even in traditionally deep-blue ridings like South Shore–St. Margaret's, stretching south from Halifax along Nova Scotia's rocky coast, there was a sense that it was all over for Harper. Melvin, a Boutiliers Point senior, was repairing his lawn mower in his yard when NDP candidate Alex Godbold showed up and asked if he was thinking of voting for the New Democrats. "Oh probably. I've been listening to some of this stuff. But Harper there— he's got to go," he said.[31] Not all the good people of Boutiliers Point were New Democrats—the seat was eventually won by Liberal MP Bernadette Jordan. But, importantly in a riding that had been Tory for all but four of the previous fifty years, none were Conservatives.

In Montreal in late September, there was a sense that people were waiting to see which party was more likely to unseat Harper before deciding how to cast their vote. Liberal insiders say they were convinced by early September that they were going to win the election, but that confidence had not percolated down to street level, where two out of three said they had not yet decided whether to vote Liberal or New

Democrat. In polls, the NDP maintained their lead over the Liberals, but the cracks were showing. "The winnability factor is the key in Quebec," said pollster Jean-Marc Léger, and it was becoming clear that much of the rest of the country was backing red.[32]

Trudeau's presence in Montreal announcing that a Liberal government would boost the budget for CBC/Radio-Canada by $150 million a year, double the annual budget of the Canada Council for the Arts, and increase funding for Telefilm Canada and the National Film Board undoubtedly helped. Elections everywhere, but particularly in Quebec, resemble auctions, and the Liberal Party has long been adept at bidding for votes.

But the key event in Quebec was the backlash against a Federal Court decision to recognize the right of Muslim women to take the oath of citizenship in a niqab, which bolstered the Conservatives and Bloc Québécois in their attempt to exploit discomfort in the province about religious accommodation. Harper said he would appeal the ruling and later announced a "barbaric cultural practices" hotline, a cynical and inflammatory attempt to gain advantage in the emerging contest of identity politics. Mulcair and Trudeau came out in support of the court's decision—but the NDP leader had more to lose. In the French-language debate, Bloc leader Gilles Duceppe said he could hardly be accused of dividing Quebecers on the issue of the niqab, since 80 per cent agreed with him. It was the final nail in the NDP campaign—the party that had won fifty-eight of seventy-five seats in the province in 2011 was now aligned with a policy that was highly unpopular. Support melted away—down to 34 per cent in Quebec from around 50 per cent earlier in the month. It was a principled finale to a campaign that had, up to that point, been mildewed by caution and pragmatism in an attempt to protect a lead that evaporated anyway.

Quebec jumped for the Liberals, in large measure because it was clear that they were winning in seat-rich Ontario. In Waterloo, Ontario —the bellwether of Canadian federal politics, given its record of voting on the side of the winner in nine of the previous eleven elections—the untested thirty-four-year-old Bardish Chagger was running against seven-year veteran Conservative Peter Braid and city-councillor-turned-NDP-candidate Diane Freeman. While canvassing in a new subdivision, Chagger encountered a man named Mikey on his doorstep. He told her he was not interested in talking. "I hate how government takes money out of my pocket—it drives me bananas," he said, as he made to close the door on her. Undeterred, she stuck her foot in the door and launched into her sales pitch about how the Trudeau Liberals were intent on doing politics differently, emphasizing how she would represent her constituents, not just repeat her leader's message. Mikey would later send out a Tweet: "Bardish passed the front door test—hard work pays off. You have my vote."

Canvassing with candidates is never a scientific way for a journalist to gauge voter intent. Mikey could well have been a Liberal volunteer, although it didn't seem likely given the vehemence with which he cursed politicians. But what was clear in every region of the country was that people had decided they'd had enough of the Conservatives and that the anti-Harper vote was coalescing around the Liberals (Chagger won by more than ten thousand votes in Waterloo and was later appointed government House leader).

The platform was broad enough to allow candidates to pick and choose the parts that played well in their riding. In Mississauga-Malton, for example, Navdeep Bains talked less about the carbon pricing that might increase gas prices, and more about investments in public transit and family reunification for immigrants. He spent most mornings hanging out at the local GO train station, handing out "Tired of your long commute?" flyers. The Liberals ended up sweeping the commuter suburbs around Toronto.

The irony of an election that was meant to be about slow growth in the economy was that many of the problems voters wanted government to address were related to growth that was out of control—gridlock and soaring house prices. Voters might have worried about recession, but after-tax incomes were hitting all-time highs, as cities like Vancouver,

Winnipeg, and Toronto prospered. The election really came down to the way Canadians wanted to be governed and what kind of country they wanted it to become. Overwhelmingly they wanted optimism and change, and Justin Trudeau presented himself as the best vehicle for that.

The Liberals ran a Teflon campaign that was barely rocked in the final days when co-chair Daniel Gagnier was forced to resign for advising TransCanada Corp. on how to lobby the new government on the subject of pipelines. Concerns about how the Liberals could possibly fulfil all their promises were brushed aside—candidates were rarely asked about such inconvenient details amid the truthy "hope and change" sales pitch. As exasperated NDP candidate Peggy Nash said about her party's message, "Somehow, it's not punching through."[33]

The Liberals outflanked the NDP on social policy and outbid the Conservatives on taxes. The platform proved a compelling package for voters and energized a large volunteer army at the door. The leader performed better than expected in debates and on the hustings—not only did he remember to put his pants on, he was in command of his briefs. The team he assembled was impressive and diverse—people who had done something with their lives, like former Toronto police chief Bill Blair, high-flying Bay Street executive Bill Morneau, and decorated military veteran Harjit Sajjan.

The NDP, meanwhile, snatched defeat from the jaws of victory. Megan Leslie, the animated MP for Halifax, inadvertently summed up all that was wrong with the campaign when she responded to a question at an all-candidates debate: "It may not be sexy but it's good governance."[34] Canadians, it turned out, were in the mood for something a bit more seductive than good governance. Many voters remained dubious about Trudeau's credentials, but they opted for what they saw as the least bad option—inadvertently confirming the quip made by the Liberal leader's father that "there are no spectacular choices in a country like Canada."[35] The outcome was a resounding rejection of Stephen Harper and his command-and-control style—and an affirmation of Trudeau's contention that it was time for change.

In the dying days of the campaign, Harper, the law-and-order prime minister, was grubbing for votes with Rob Ford, the mayor of Toronto. It was an undignified end to ten years in power that had, at its best, provided steady, common-sense administration at a time of global economic dislocation. The mood was encapsulated by normally polite Canadians going out of their way to be rude to Conservative candidates in shopping malls. "I couldn't care less what you say and I hope you don't make it," said one man in a North Vancouver mall to Conservative MP Andrew Saxton. "Andrew should own this riding, but there is a 'Harper effect,'" whispered one of his team.[36] The collapse of the NDP vote had not helped Harper's cause. But as one resigned Conservative put it, "This is what happens when you're mean to so many people for so long."[37]

The Liberals' own polling had suggested a week before the election that a majority was in the bag. On the day, Dan Arnold, the party's polling guru, was predicting 177 seats, including every riding in Atlantic Canada except the one held by the NDP stalwart Jack Harris in St. John's, Newfoundland and Labrador. In the event, they won that too, en route to taking 184 seats, with 39.5 per cent of the vote, compared to 99 seats for the Conservatives (31.9 per cent of the vote), 44 seats for the NDP (with 19.7 per cent), 10 seats for the Bloc (with 4.7 per cent), and 1 seat for the Greens (3.5 per cent). At one point, the ticker on one TV channel was showing the Liberals winning 33 seats out of 32 in Atlantic Canada, as the results came in for the Quebec riding of Gaspésie–Îles-de-le-Madeleine, which is in the Atlantic time zone.

It was a stunning vindication of sticking with a strategy that had at times seemed destined to make Trudeau a historical footnote. In the end, he won a majority of seats in Quebec; took back the Greater Toronto Area; and won seats in Winnipeg, Calgary, Edmonton, and Vancouver. It was the ideal platform from which to heal all the wounds and divisions accumulated over the Harper years. "I will be the prime minister of all Canadians," Trudeau pledged in his victory speech.

There were few signs of buyers' remorse in the days that followed the election. Many Conservatives acknowledged that they had run out of steam. It seemed the country had what it wanted most, which was a change in tone. For a brief moment in time, Canada was at peace with itself. Writing about Pierre Trudeau, the journalist Richard Gwyn might just as easily have been describing Justin when he observed, "He not only mirrored the prevailing liberalism of Canadians, he personified it and magnified it."[38]

SEVEN

BECAUSE IT'S 2015

WINSTON CHURCHILL IS SAID to have spent the "best years of his life composing his impromptu speeches."[1] The best lines always appear effortless but are in fact the product of much thought and discussion. So it was with Trudeau's shrug and casual response to a question about why he had insisted on putting an equal number of men and women in his first cabinet. "Because it's 2015," he said smugly, standing against the backdrop of his new team in front of Rideau Hall, after their swearing-in. The crowd roared its approval in the background. The response appeared improvised but was far from it. "Like most things that have happened in the last five years, we made it up on the spot and we've been talking about it for years," said Gerald Butts.[2] As political scientist Alex Marland noted in his book *Brand Command*, the Liberal brain trust was obsessed with promoting an image of political leadership that was the antithesis of the command-and-control style of the Conservatives. But that did not mean they had forsaken a Harper-era mainstay—distorting the truth by using spin.[3]

A CBC behind-the-scenes news report from the day of the swearing-in ceremony showed Liberal PMO staff discussing how the cabinet would walk up the driveway of Rideau Hall to meet the governor general in front of cheering crowds the Liberals had called on to attend. There was a carnival mood, as Trudeau and his newly sworn-in cabinet took part in Canada's blessing—the peaceful transfer of power. The sun was blazing with unseasonal warmth on the early November morning. Hadrien Trudeau ran into his father's arms, as if on official photographer Adam Scotti's cue. That had also been planned—Trudeau had asked that his children wait by the fountain in front of Rideau Hall and he would greet them with outstretched arms. The sight of Trudeau taking selfies, hugging ministers, kissing his wife, and cuddling his kids was digital media gold—"calculated facets of the Trudeau brand intended to feed the notion of a kinder, sunnier government."[4]

The thirty-member "cabinet that looks like Canada," in Trudeau's words, was packed with people with fascinating back-stories. Kent Hehr, elected in Calgary, had struggled to get his life back on track after being paralyzed in a drive-by shooting; Harjit Sajjan was elected in British Columbia after he helped reduce the influence of the Taliban in Afghanistan using techniques learned fighting gang violence as a member of the Vancouver Police Department; Carla Qualtrough, the visually impaired human rights lawyer was a three-time Paralympic Games medalist in swimming before getting elected in Delta, B.C.; Maryam Monsef, an Afghan immigrant, had narrowly lost in her first foray into politics when she ran for mayor in Peterborough as a twenty-nine-year-old.

It was a cosmopolitan band of people from a variety of backgrounds with one thing in common—the vast majority had never sat in the House of Commons before being sworn in. The desire for gender, geographic, and ethnic balance meant that a number of seasoned MPs and new recruits were not invited to sit around the table—former solicitor general Wayne Easter, retired lieutenant general Andrew Leslie, former Indian affairs minister Bob Nault, and ex-immigration minister Judy Sgro were among those overlooked.

Trudeau's task in choosing ministers was also helped by the fact that the caucus was stuffed with mediocrities who thought they were Socrates. The slow-down in candidate recruitment—the consequence of the Liberals dipping in the polls in early 2015—had, in the estimation of one insider, lowered the quality: "Some people who got in were borderline idiots."[5] One veteran of the parliamentary precinct noted the new government's fascination with fresh faces. "There's a bias in this government against anyone older than forty. The problem with that is that you're always discovering age-old problems for the first time," he said.[6]

There were some old hands, too—Ralph Goodale at Public Safety, Marc Garneau at Transport, Scott Brison at Treasury Board, Stéphane Dion at the renamed Global Affairs, Lawrence MacAulay at Agriculture, John McCallum at Immigration, Judy Foote at Public Services, Navdeep Bains at Economic Development, Dominic LeBlanc as Government House Leader, and Carolyn Bennett at Indigenous and Northern Affairs.

The new chief of staff, Katie Telford, and principal secretary, Gerald Butts, had government experience at Queen's Park. Both had been part of a transition team that nearly started life in government on the back foot, after proposed co-chair Daniel Gagnier's forced resignation. Butts made a last-minute call to Marc-André Blanchard, then chief executive of law firm McCarthy Tétrault, and asked him to step in as francophone co-chair, alongside former senior bureaucrat Peter Harder.[7] Some of the rookies, like Jim Carr at Natural Resources, Jane Philpott at Health, Jean-Yves Duclos at Social Development, Chrystia Freeland at Trade, and Bill Morneau at Finance, had distinguished careers that had exposed them to politics.

There were question marks over the new prime minister himself, who had never managed anything bigger than the Katimavik youth charity. Yet Seamus O'Regan, who was appointed to cabinet in 2017 but who had served on the Katimavik board with Trudeau, said there were never any doubts about who was in charge. "He's authoritative, he's forceful, and he attracted people who knew they would be listened to," he said. "He listens genuinely. But they are tightly managed. He watches the clock. He doesn't allow himself to ramble on and he doesn't like people who speak just for the sake of speaking. He's ruthlessly disciplined on time. I love that and totally respect that, after ten years at CTV, where if Christ himself came back, he'd get three and a half minutes on *Canada AM.*"[8]

The new government was going to need discipline and brevity. If it was going to be transformative, not just transactional, it would also need all of Trudeau's rookies to perform spectacularly. Unfortunately, the new prime minister's rhetoric would outpace the abilities of a number of his new cabinet members. MaryAnn Mihychuk, the only female Liberal elected between the Ontario and B.C. borders, was a former cabinet minister in Gary Doer's NDP government in Manitoba. She found herself in the federal cabinet as employment minister, but a number of MPs said she had problems getting the job done. First, she lost responsibility for the employment insurance file, and then, after approving a $1.1 million upgrade to her office, she was demoted from the ministry in the shuffle of January 2017.

Mihychuk wasn't the only one in over her head. Derek Burney, Canada's former ambassador in Washington, had also acted as Brian Mulroney's chief of staff in a previous life. He said Trudeau's decision made life hard for a government coming out of the gate. "Gender equity in cabinet put more of a constraint on them, in terms of their ability to manoeuvre, than acted as an asset. If your caucus is three-to-one male and you make females as 50 per cent of your cabinet, you're already putting yourself behind the eight ball," he said.[9]

But those travails were in the future. On the day of the swearing-in ceremony, Trudeau and his cabinet were energized by the powerful symbolism—which was just as well. To borrow from the fictional spin doctor Malcolm Tucker in the television series *The Thick of It*, they had a to-do list longer than a Leonard Cohen song.

Over the course of the first month, Trudeau had to put in place his plan to withdraw Canada's fighter jets from Iraq, figure out how to make good on his campaign commitment to accept twenty-five thousand Syrian refugees by the turn of the year, attend the G20 summit in Turkey in mid-November, then head immediately to the Philippines for the Asia-Pacific Economic Cooperation meeting, where the massive Trans-Pacific Partnership trade agreement was high on the agenda. Trudeau had barely enough time to head home for a change of underwear before he was obliged to head to London to meet the Queen, then head to the Commonwealth leaders' summit in Malta and the climate change conference in Paris. In the space of one week, his plane spent thirty-six hours in the air, flying 33,231 kilometres to Turkey and the Philippines.[10]

The message the new prime minister would spread at all these summits was that those who had worried that Canada had lost its compassionate and constructive voice during the Harper years should worry no more: "On behalf of 35 million Canadians, we're back."[11] It was an early example of the self-congratulatory tone that has helped to alienate many of those thirty-five million Canadians. The sense that Canada had been away was presumptuous—between 2001 and 2014, the armed forces suffered 158 fatalities in Afghanistan, one of the highest casualty rates per capita among the coalition members. But the Liberals' pledge to "restore Canada's leadership" in multilateral organizations like the United Nations, through a commitment to international peace-keeping operations, was a departure from Stephen Harper's grudging sense of obligation to the UN, where Canada would not "go along to get along" and would only "go along" if the direction was in keeping with the government's interpretation of freedom, democracy, and rule of law.[12]

The self-proclaimed "new era in Canadian international engagement" was welcomed in Canada's foreign missions and by foreign service officers in Canada. When Trudeau visited the Lester B. Pearson building on Sussex Drive in Ottawa, the headquarters of the foreign affairs department, he was greeted by an outbreak of euphoria, as the supposedly neutral public servants cheered him and his new foreign minister, Stéphane Dion. When he said he was touched by their enthusiasm, the crowd applauded.[13]

In the early going, Trudeau's Rotary Club optimism about Canada's leadership capabilities was not matched by action. But the rhetoric was received particularly well in the White House, where President Barack Obama was winding down his second term. Relations between the two leaders, personally and on policy, were warm from day one, despite the irritants of the Keystone XL pipeline, which Obama announced he would not approve, and Canada's withdrawal of its fighter jets from the air campaign against the Islamic State in Iran. According to Roland Paris, Trudeau's foreign policy adviser, Obama did not seem perturbed about the withdrawal when the two men met for the first time in Manila. "The fact that Trudeau simultaneously recommitted Canada to the anti-ISIL coalition and pledged to boost Canada's training role likely helped to defuse any concerns," he said.[14]

The new PM's hectic schedule turned out to be a blessing—allowing him to meet and begin to form personal relationships with the leaders of most of the world's major powers, including the U.K., France, Germany, Italy, Japan, and China. He also met Vladimir Putin of Russia on the margins of the G20 in Turkey. The Liberal plan was to normalize diplomatic relations with Russia that had been restricted under Stephen Harper—but only after Canada's opposition to Putin's adventures in Crimea and Ukraine had been conveyed. There was no formal meeting scheduled, but Trudeau approached Putin in a meeting room at the end of the summit and delivered the message that Canada would continue to oppose Russia's interference in Ukraine and that it expected Putin to fully implement the Minsk peace accords.[15]

In Paris, Trudeau engendered much goodwill thanks to his vow to fight climate change at home and overseas and the commitment to earmark $2.65 billion to help developing countries in their own transition to a low carbon economy. "Canada is back, my good friends," he said in his address, touching his heart with his hand. "We're here to help."[16] Columnist Andrew Coyne scoffed, "For fans of self-serving humbug, Trudeau's speech was the trifecta: the glib sloganeering, the false humility and the gaudy theatricality"—but all from a country that produced just 1.6 per cent of the world's emissions of greenhouse gases. "In substantive terms," noted Coyne, "it matters not a whit that 'Canada is back.'"[17]

Trudeau said that the new NDP government in Alberta was putting in place a carbon pricing regime that would limit the development of the oil sands and would provide the platform for a national climate change plan. The new government used the opportunity of the Paris conference to signal its virtue to the world, with Trudeau at the head of a three-hundred-person delegation of politicians and bureaucrats—double the size of the U.S. contingent. The travel, hotel, and per diem costs for 155 of those delegates was nearly $1 million—with three mid-level bureaucrats racking up $12,000 over two weeks on meal claims alone.[18] Catherine McKenna, the environment minister, billed $6,600 for a French freelance photographer to take pictures of her at the conference. The government had been in office for less than a month, but it had started as it meant to go on, with the spending taps turned to "gush." And for all the hoopla, the emissions target set by the Harper government—a 30 per cent cut from 2005 levels by 2030—remained the same.

Saskatchewan premier Brad Wall, who was in Paris with the Canadian delegation, foreshadowed the dispute that would crystallize later in the mandate by sounding a more cautious note than many of his fellow politicians in Paris. He said that Western Canada's energy sector had already shed jobs and he was keen to ensure that new climate policies caused "no net new harm."[19] The Trudeau government would make much of its reconciliation of the environment and the economy, but the truth was that they were never in harmony.

At home, the nation expected the Liberals to deliver on their extensive laundry list of promises—some of which were in their power to enact, like the Canada Child Benefit, while many others, such as the infrastructure spending, required careful negotiation with premiers and mayors. This might have been a good time for the new prime minister to manage expectations and remind people that politics in Canada is the art of the possible—and that not much is possible. Instead, within a week of the cabinet being installed, ministers were issued mandate letters with commitments they were obliged to meet that outnumbered the hundreds already in the platform. "If you accept the election platform was written by and for a party that was in third, and whose goal was to become second, you can promise hundreds of different things —it's not a governing document," said one Liberal who has worked for three different ministers in five portfolios. "But then they caught the bus and I thought 'Okay, the first thing they'll do in transition is crank expectations down.' But no, they made the election platform promises into mandate letter commitments and published them. So rather than bring expectations down, they cranked them even higher. Trudeau had so much capital in the bank, that's the time he could have brought expectations back into line with reality and not have paid a heavy price."[20]

The most glaring misalignment between good intentions and realistic deliverables was on the promise to build a "renewed nation-to-nation relationship" with Indigenous people. In one particular moment of irrational exuberance in an interview with APTN, the Indigenous television network, Trudeau said he would give First Nations a veto over development on their territory—going much further than the right to be consulted demanded by the courts.[21] Trudeau had already promised he would implement all ninety-four recommendations of the Truth and Reconciliation Commission, including the one that required the Pope to apologize for Canada's residential school system. Many others were similarly beyond Trudeau's ability to deliver.

Yet at the Assembly of First Nations chiefs meeting in early December, he received a number of standing ovations for his promise to be a "partner" to Indigenous Canadians. He announced an inquiry into murdered and missing Indigenous women—which subsequently proved to be a tortuous and unsatisfactory experience for all concerned, including the families of the victims—and pledged to end the 2 per cent cap on increases in Indigenous education funding.

But he also said that his government would never "impose a solution from the top down," meaning that structural reforms were unlikely to accompany the planned no-strings-attached cash injection. That commitment drew particular praise from the chiefs, resistant to the idea that they might lose power and funding. The new prime minister further endeared himself by suspending a Harper-era financial transparency obligation that allowed the federal government to withhold money from First Nations that failed to disclose audited financial statements, including how much the chief and band councillors were paid. Most bands had abided by the law to disclose their finances, but a few scattered First Nations did not, presumably because the chiefs were paying themselves fat salaries. One case exposed because of the act was that of Chief Ron Giesbrecht of the eighty-member Kwikwetlem First Nation, who pocketed $914,000 in salary—the equivalent of $1.6 million for someone who pays tax on income. One band councillor said that if it hadn't been for the transparency act, they never would have known the extent of Giesbrecht's remuneration package.[22] Taxpayers and band members had a right to that information, but in order to buy the quiescence of the chiefs, the Trudeau government overturned the legislation.

Trudeau maintained that no relationship was more important to him than the one with Indigenous peoples, just as previous Liberal governments had raised false hopes by saying they would introduce major reforms to land claims policy, Indigenous justice, and education. The promises in the 1983 Liberal Red Book were broken by Jean Chrétien once in power, and the fiscal pressures already apparent in late 2015 meant that Trudeau's commitment to enact all ninety-four recommendations of the Truth and Reconciliation Commission was already in jeopardy. As the late Michael Ferguson, the auditor general, said in his spring 2018 report, "incomprehensible failures" explain why the federal government can't create better conditions for its Indigenous people. In short, the bureaucracy is "broken" and doesn't do a very good job of delivering services to its citizens.[23]

Trudeau was animated by the Indigenous file, despite it becoming increasingly obvious it was not a winner for the government in any way. The attempts to improve the relationship between the government of Canada and its Indigenous population were sincere, and there were some signs things were on a better path. But in many ways, the son repeated the mistakes of the father. Pierre Trudeau wanted to shatter the old political systems and dreamed of a new "participatory" politics. But as his principal secretary Jim Coutts noted, citizens expected Trudeau to lead, not debate. In its first years, Pierre Trudeau's government brought forward twelve priorities for study—far too many for even a new majority government—when Coutts said it would have been wiser to concentrate on four or five very specific ideas.[24] The elder Trudeau might have won John Lennon's approval as "beautiful" and a man who could bring peace to the world during the former Beatle's visit to Ottawa in December 1969,[25] but three years later he lost his majority and nearly lost power, clinging on to a plurality by two seats over Robert Stanfield's Progressive Conservatives. As his biographer John English put it, "The effervescence of Trudeaumania cloaked a flat economy."[26]

As he entered office, the younger Trudeau faced a similarly becalmed economy, the result of low commodity prices and stagnant growth globally. Just two weeks after the sunny day at Rideau Hall, Bill Morneau, the new finance minister, was obliged to rain all over the new Liberal government's parade. His fiscal update dampened some of the post-election euphoria with a bucket of cold reality that illustrated how badly the economy had deteriorated since the 2015 budget. As we have seen, the transition team was told in the wake of the election triumph that the books were $12 billion worse than anyone outside the finance department had assumed. It was abundantly clear that the promise of "modest" $25 billion cumulative deficits over the three subsequent fiscal years, before the budget was returned to balance, was in grave peril. Morneau said it was too soon to say what the government might do, but he reiterated a commitment to implementing the promises in the platform and said merely that he aspired to budgetary balance in 2019.

The first blatant broken promise was the disintegration of the platform prediction that the plan to raise taxes on the top earners would pay for the $3.4 billion cut for the middle class—a failure that had been predicted by just about every expert who had looked at the behaviour of taxpayers when the marginal rate rises to over 50 per cent. Morneau was forced to concede in early December that reducing the middle bracket for nine million Canadians would not be revenue neutral, as the platform had claimed, and would in fact cost $1.2 billion a year, as high earners decided to earn less or make more efforts to avoid payment. But in the warm glow of the Liberal honeymoon, such picayune issues were ignored.

In contrast, Trudeau's presence at the temporary processing centre at Toronto's Pearson Airport for the arrival of the first government-organized plane-load of Syrian refugees from Beirut received sweeping coverage. A Canadian Forces plane, loaded with 163 refugees, landed at Pearson in the wee hours of December 11. Trudeau and Ontario premier Kathleen Wynne were there to hand out winter coats, gloves, and hats to refugees like sixteen-month old Madeleine Jamkossian and her family. "You are home," said Trudeau. "Welcome home." Earlier, he had told airport workers that "tonight matters, not just for Canada, but for the world."[27] But it also mattered for the government's credibility.

The Liberals had promised to bring in twenty-five thousand refugees by the end of the 2015 calendar year, but the logistical challenges meant that only six thousand or so arrived by New Year's Eve. John McCallum, the immigration minister, argued that the exact timing was less important than the ultimate result, and by early 2018, fifty-two thousand Syrians had arrived in Canada, with one couple even naming their newborn son Justin.[28]

Their failure to hit ambitious targets was frustrating the new prime minister and his closest advisers. The Conservatives had organized their own foreign trips and managed relations with the provinces. So when Trudeau went overseas for four international summits, then sought to convene a first ministers' meeting, the public service struggled to respond, according to one senior official in the Prime Minister's Office. Neither did the bureaucracy know how to prepare briefing books for Question Period, another function that political issues management staff in the PMO undertook under Harper. "A lot of muscles have atrophied. We're pulling political levers and finding out the levers are not attached to anything," said one person in the Prime Minister's Office.[29] The upper echelons of the bureaucracy took umbrage at this criticism. "We pulled off four summits in three weeks—there was impeccable support from the Department of Global Affairs and the embassies, which responded heroically," said one deputy minister.[30]

But the Liberals were clearly aware that they were vulnerable to the criticism of promising more than they could ever deliver. To try to combat the perception, the PMO adopted the system of running government called "deliverology," pioneered by British bureaucrat Sir Michael Barber during Tony Blair's Labour government. Barber was invited to a cabinet retreat in January 2016, and the role he had played in Britain was assigned in Canada to Matthew Mendelsohn, a former deputy minister in the Ontario government, as the head of the "results and delivery unit" in the Privy Council Office. Butts and Telford had adopted the approach at Queen's Park with Dalton McGuinty's Ontario Liberal government. The concept attempted to ensure that election promises were kept by requiring cabinet ministers to check in regularly with the prime minister and with public servants to see where they were in delivering any given promise. In essence, it was adopted to allow the centre to keep an eye on far-flung ministries. In Barber's world, bureaucrats needed to ask what their program was trying to achieve, how they planned to achieve the goals, how they would know if they went off track, and how would they adjust things if they did go off track.[31]

Mendelsohn's role was to collect data from departments and ministers, as part of a continuous assessment, and to report on progress to the prime minister. The hope was that the extra discipline would encourage the public service to be more focused on outcomes than on process or rules. "Part of it was the culture of Ottawa, which isn't very well connected to the rest of the country. It's a company town and the ADMs [assistant deputy ministers] are married to other ADMs. They don't know what's happening at the United Way in Vancouver. Results and delivery has been helpful in making people think carefully about the delivery chain and understanding it from tip to tail," said one person involved in the system's design.[32]

That enthusiasm was not uniform across government. The public service may have favoured the new ministry over its predecessor, but its real preference was for what *Yes Minister*'s Sir Humphrey called "respon-sible"—that is, bureaucratic—government. "There was a lot of eye rolling and resistance," said one senior political staffer. "It's dissipated somewhat but has not become an overwhelming part of our corpo-rate culture. It's a bit like gender-based budgeting. In some respects it's a political play—and it requires bureaucrats to do work they don't want to do."[33]

As part of deliverology, the government made public its "mandate letter tracker," which looked at the 364 commitments the prime minis-ter had made in his missives to ministers,[34] and assessed whether they had been completed, were underway, or were not being pursued. The only problem was that the website offered a much rosier performance picture than the independent website Trudeau Meter, which tracked election campaign promises. For example, in late 2017, the govern-ment's tracker judged the commitment to balance the budget in 2019–20 to be "underway, with challenges," even though it was clear as early as December 2015 that the pledge had been abandoned. The exercise revealed the flaws in self-appraisal—any analysis compiled by bureau-crats, almost genetically programmed to pursue a quiet life, meant that the best gloss was put on things. But what the status report did reveal was that running a federation like Canada was hard work and no amount of sunny ways and Aesop's fables made it less so.

The file that would make this more apparent than any other was the quest to build pipelines to ship Canada's oil bounty from its source in Alberta to foreign markets. The issue had been a burr under the saddle of the Harper government, which had made very little progress in get-ting a pipeline to saltwater built, despite having given the official green light to Enbridge's Northern Gateway project, which proposed to build a 1,177-kilometre pipeline from Bruderheim, Alberta, to the coast at Kitimat, British Columbia. The hostility from First Nations, environ-mentalists, and many municipalities remained entrenched, and Trudeau had made known his opposition to a pipeline that traversed the Great Bear rain forest, the remote expanse of central and northern B.C. that environmental non-government organizations renamed to galvanize international support for its protection (without consulting local residents). But he had also long supported the Keystone XL pipeline, which was planned to run from Alberta to refineries in Illinois and Texas, and which had become a potent symbol for environmentalists battling fossil fuel extraction. Jim Carr, the new natural resources minister, was given the job of selling the grand bargain of "a clean environment and a strong economy"—the dual policy of a national carbon pricing regime and building a pipeline to the coast.

In late January 2016, news broke that the government would require a new assessment process for pipelines that would include a separate climate test to determine their impact on greenhouse gas emissions. The new test clearly had the potential to delay multi-billion-dollar projects already before the regulator, the National Energy Board, such as Kinder Morgan's plans to more than double the capacity of its existing Trans Mountain pipeline to Burnaby, B.C., and TransCanada Corp's ambitious Energy East project to ship crude from Alberta to Saint John, New Brunswick, from where it could be sold to Asia. Trudeau told the House of Commons that the existing regime wasn't getting the job done, and pipelines would not be built without community acceptance, especially from Indigenous people, who were winning case after case in court on the basis of their right to free, prior, and informed consent. But there were worrying portents for those Canadians concerned about the country's competitive position and its failure to extract a world price for its oil—a discount caused by transportation bottlenecks that economists at Scotiabank estimated would cost the oil sector $15.6 billion in revenue in 2018.[35]

The transitional rules introduced by the Liberals that would be in place until they could introduce more comprehensive legislation required that the "upstream" greenhouse gases from the mining of the bitumen be taken into consideration, not just the emissions produced by the pipeline itself. This was not the approach Trudeau took when he came out in support of Keystone XL. The U.S. State Department had concluded that the oil sands would be developed, regardless of whether Keystone was built, so attributing greenhouse gases from extraction did not make sense—reasoning Trudeau accepted when he said the pipeline was in the national interest. "It is in keeping with what I believe is a fundamental role of the government of Canada: to open up markets abroad for Canadian resources and to help create responsible and sustainable ways to get those resources to markets," he told the Petroleum Club in Calgary. But that logic did not apply to Energy East, with predictable consequences. The pipeline was much further behind in the regulatory process than Kinder Morgan's project (the National Energy Board had completed its hearings into Trans Mountain and its decision was pending, while hearings into Energy East hadn't even started).

Concern about the transitional rules saw an interesting exchange in the House of Commons, bearing in mind subsequent events. The then Conservative House leader, Andrew Scheer, accused Trudeau of bringing in his own NEP, the "no-energy program." The new prime minister responded that he intended to pursue a non-aligned status and be a "responsible referee," not a cheerleader for any project in the pursuit of "social licence." Yet as events unfolded, he would in due course become not just the cheerleader for, but the owner of, a pipeline.

If a camel is a horse designed by committee, as comedian Allan Sherman once put in, then Canada is a country fashioned and frustrated by its geography. No one would deliberately set out to build a country where the national interest is so often subverted to the local. Federalism is the greatest inhibitor of federal power, and the trick, as former federal NDP leadership candidate Brian Topp once said, is "finding the thread that unites the pearls."[36] Trudeau quickly discovered that the thread was fraying, as the Alberta government and industry claimed pipelines were crucial to their future, while Quebec and B.C. were staunch in their opposition.

In Quebec, the provincial Liberal government introduced an injunction to ensure that the project met provincial environmental regulations, adding another layer of red tape. Despite the fact that Energy East was popular in Atlantic Canada, where the Liberals had picked up thirty-two out of thirty-two seats; despite it taking oil off the rails, preferable after the Lac-Mégantic rail disaster that killed forty-seven people when a train carrying crude derailed and exploded in the Quebec town; despite it reducing the need to import oil from producers in countries like Nigeria and Saudi Arabia, the project had to pass through Quebec—and Quebec was not in favour. Montreal mayor (and former Liberal cabinet minister) Denis Coderre and the organization representing Montreal-area municipalities had come out in opposition to the pipeline. And since a Liberal victory at the next election ran through Quebec, it became increasingly clear that a new oil pipeline might not. The Liberals held forty of the seventy-eight seats in the province and had high hopes of adding another twenty in the next election.

If Quebec was a hard sell, B.C. looked equally foreboding. Christy Clark's B.C. Liberals opposed Kinder Morgan's expansion, saying that support was conditional on five conditions being met—including benefits for First Nations, a "fair share" of the economic spoils for B.C., and a "world-leading" marine-oil-spill response system. But with an election due in the spring of the following year, it became clear to the Trudeau Liberals that, if they could provide enough cover for Clark to say yes, she was of a mind to do so, particularly since she was seeking federal government approval for PETRONAS's $36 billion Pacific North West liquified natural gas project. "I think she would dearly love to say she is the 'premier of yes' when it comes to resource development," said one person involved in the negotiations with the federal government.[37] Ominously, John Horgan, the leader of the B.C. NDP, said he would align with the mayors of Vancouver and Burnaby in opposition to a project he said was not in the public interest.

Opinion polls suggested that there was support in most regions for a plan that advanced both the environment and the economy, and that Trudeau was trusted to make the right decision by a majority of Canadians (unlike his predecessor). He was aided by an NDP premier in Alberta, Rachel Notley, who had already introduced a carbon plan that would cap emissions from the oil sands. In early February, Trudeau travelled to Alberta to reinforce the alliance and reiterate that he was in agreement with Notley's message that taking action on the environment made it possible to build a pipeline to get oil to export markets.

Supplying proof that being in government had forced a drastic realignment of priorities, Trudeau was asked in Edmonton if he would stick to his pledge that a First Nations "no meant no" would be a veto on pipeline projects. He replied that he was committed to a "renewed relationship" and would "respect inherent and treaty rights." The Liberal government looked to "First Nations and Indigenous peoples as partners in all that happens in this land," he said.[38] But that fell far short of the veto on development he had promised during the campaign. The response from a number of influential First Nations figures like lawyer and professor Pam Palmater was that Trudeau had betrayed Indigenous Canadians by failing to live up to his promises.

As Trudeau hit his first one hundred days in office in mid-February, he could point to a hectic blur of international summits, provincial visits, and legislative action back in Ottawa. The middle-class tax cut had been passed; the long-form census, cut by the Harper government, had been restored; and twenty-five thousand Syrian refugees had been admitted. By late February, Canada's six aging CF-18 fighter planes ceased their mission in Iraq, even as the new government increased the size of its military mission against the Islamic State from 650 to 830 personnel, including a force of JTF2 commandos.

The new prime minister was leading a charmed life that culminated in a state visit to Washington, where President Barack Obama all but passed the baton to Trudeau as the defender of the liberal economic order. Obama saw Trudeau as a kindred spirit, which helped the PM reset relations with the White House. After years of Canada being ignored, the U.S. capital—certainly the Democratic part of it—was abuzz with "Justin fever." Amy Klobuchar, a Democratic senator from Minnesota, said at an event organized by the online political news source Politico that the moment was reminiscent of the scene in the movie *The Graduate* where a young Benjamin Braddock is told the future is in plastics. "I said to my daughter: 'One word—Canada. Its time has finally come.'"[39]

Democrats, conscious they might be on borrowed time, lived vicariously through the youthful Canadian leader, who looked set to implement an activist agenda on climate change in a way denied to Obama during the economic crisis and the congressional gridlock that followed. The day of the state dinner was when Trudeau truly went global. Not only did he stand shoulder-to-shoulder with the American president, but there was an affinity between the two that bordered on reverence. An article in London's *The Guardian* newspaper said that Obama had found the Robin to his Batman, while the *New York Post* headline focused on the prime minister's wife: "Meet Sophie Trudeau, the hottest first lady in the world."[40] As the president said during their Rose Garden press conference, "From my perspective, what's not to like?" Trudeau kept referring to "my friend Barack."[41]

The welcome ceremony on the back lawn was typically ostentatious. The two leaders and a cross-section of their cabinets were greeted by the Marine Corps band playing John Philip Sousa's "Liberty Bell March" (more popularly known as the theme to *Monty Python's Flying Circus*), a twenty-one-gun salute, and a colour guard from every branch of the U.S. military. There was a holiday atmosphere to the whole event—as if the Canadians were visiting Disneyland rather than trying to unblock log-jams in the commercial relationship, like the perennial irritant over softwood lumber. This was reflected in Trudeau's decision to bring his mother, his in-laws, his chief fundraiser, and the president of the Liberal Party, while leaving most of the cabinet at home.

The warmth expressed by Obama for Trudeau and Canada was genuine. At the star-studded gala dinner that night, Obama recalled how when he first spoke to Trudeau, it was not just as a political leader but as a fellow father. "We're not here for power. We're not here for fame or fortune, but we are here for our kids," he said. "We're here for everybody's kids, to give our sons and daughters a better world."[42] But the idea propounded by Obama administration officials that we were witnessing a "developing special relationship" was overdone.[43] The president was already a lame duck and it was unclear whether the much-vaunted special relationship would survive the incoming president, particularly if it was Republican candidate Donald Trump, the antithesis of Obama in almost every way.

The reality was that Obama was leaving and Trudeau was just getting started. The state dinner was a source of pride for Canadians, but it was transient—and the prime minister and his entourage were ill-prepared for what was coming next.

EIGHT

ELBOWGATE—AND OTHER EXAMPLES OF DOING POLITICS DIFFERENTLY

WHILE TRUDEAU WAS DELIGHTING the paparazzi in Washington, back in Ottawa staff and officials were busy preparing the all-important first budget, which was being promoted as the first progressive budget in more than a decade. In late March, Bill Morneau, perhaps the most Keynesian finance minister since the elder Trudeau's chancellor Marc Lalonde, showered billions of dollars on cities, First Nations, families, and the elderly. The budget plan, with a cover that looked suspiciously like a mother and daughter walking down a yellow brick road, immediately came in for criticism for plunging the country into deep deficits—$29.4 billion in the first year—with no plan to return to surplus. The election platform had anticipated four years of deficits totalling $26.1 billion; the 2016 budget forecast deficits of more than $113 billion over the subsequent five years. Morneau said the spending would create growth that would "we hope" return the economy to balance "over time."[1]

In his inaugural House of Commons budget speech, Morneau said that after the dark days of the Great Depression and the Second World War, Canadians believed the future could be brighter. They prospered as confidence inspired investment and investment inspired confidence, he said. Since then, people had become less optimistic, but fortunately the Liberals had come to power to restore hope for the middle class. The fact that Canada was not in recession, as had been feared at the time of the election, far less a Great Depression, did not give the new government pause for thought. The budget confirmed that the economy, beyond the energy sector, was largely stable, with non-energy output growing at an annual rate of 2.2 per cent. Exports were showing signs of life, as was investment, and there was not a demand deficit that required a boost in the form of government spending. There was, in fact, no burning requirement to finance spending from the wallets of future taxpayers—except for the fact that the Trudeau government had said it would.

Inside government, the plan was hailed as a triumph of fiscal restraint. "There was a subset of people around the decision-making apparatus, particularly in the PMO, who said, 'Let's get as much of this great shit out of the door as quickly as possible—damn the cost,'" said one person involved in the discussions. "Bill wanted a line in the sand and it was agreed it was negative $30 billion. Growth was more robust, so it came in better. But the deficit could have been $50 billion—and the fact that it wasn't was down to Morneau."[2]

Robert Asselin, who was by then a senior adviser to the finance minister, said that the change of culture in Ottawa encouraged senior bureaucrats in every department to bring forward spending proposals that had been gathering dust for years. "The list of requests was just crazy. I remember getting the letters from ministers and saying, 'This is not serious.' Not only were they not sticking to the platform, they were trying to squeeze us on everything. We had to say no to a lot of things. It was a very long process, the first budget," he said.[3]

In Morneau, Trudeau had found an experienced foil who provided him with the business gravitas he lacked. The finance minister had been executive chair of the country's largest human resource firm, Morneau Shepell, a business founded by his father. With an M.Sc. in economics from the London School of Economics and a resumé that included a stint as chair of the C.D. Howe think-tank, Morneau offered private sector credibility that was in short supply among a markedly corporatist cadre of new recruits. In 2014, while still chair of C.D. Howe, Morneau had spoken at the Liberal convention in Montreal, where he accused the Conservatives of ignoring the economy in favour of playing politics. The following Monday, after his weekend speech, he was forced to step down from the think-tank, as it sought to safeguard its non-partisan reputation.[4] People who work with him talk of a man who commands respect. "He's an easy guy to get along with—he doesn't really lose his cool and he's in it for the right reasons," said one former colleague.[5] But if he provided a degree of adult supervision (on the first budget at least)—like someone walking through the party taking the car keys from beer-swilling teenagers—he had a lot to learn about politics. "By his own admission, he was not a good politician early on—and he found out too late that politics was a big part of his job. But nobody goes into these jobs knowing it all—it's a natural process," said one person who got to know him well.[6]

The Liberals had no choice but to include large-spending measures like the $23 billion Canada Child Benefit and the middle-class tax cut. But in the rush to implement a number of the platform promises, the new government went too far, too fast on some commitments. "We were all so excited to be in power after so long, we wanted to do everything in the first budget, which in retrospect was a mistake," said a senior staffer involved in its crafting. "Indigenous, for example, we were too much in a hurry—we could have held back."[7] Asselin agreed, noting, "The thinking was really about implementing our promises and the platform, but we went too fast on a few things."[8] The budget promised $8.4 billion in new spending for Indigenous education, housing, and clean drinking water. The net result was to raise expectations way higher than the ability of the system to absorb the new money and deliver on it.

Defenders of the government's ambitious agenda say the real commitment was to get relations between the federal government and Indigenous communities back on the right path. They say there has been a qualitative change since the Liberals took office and that, "bit by bit," outcomes are improving when it comes to building schools and cleaning up water supply on reserves. But the promised billions in the budget—$3.7 billion on Indigenous education; $1.2 billion on new housing; $969 million for new schools; $635 million on child and family services; a removal of the 2 per cent spending cap imposed by then Liberal finance minister Paul Martin in 1996; and $40 million to pay for the inquiry into murdered and missing Indigenous women—raised hopes beyond any realistic prospect of satisfying them. "We said we were going to repair the relationship, we said we're going to do everything. But the difference between where things are and where we said they're going to be is striking," said one senior Liberal involved in the file.[9]

With the budget out of the way, Morneau's attention turned to the second part of the Liberal safety-net package (the first being the Canada Child Benefit). In the platform, the Liberals had promised to reverse the Harper government's decision to raise the eligibility age for Old Age Security to sixty-seven from sixty-five (a move the parliamentary budget officer later said would cost Canadians $11.2 billion a year by 2029[10]) and also to negotiate with provinces and territories to enhance the Canada Pension Plan. With fewer companies offering defined benefit pensions, advocates argued that CPP contributions, and therefore benefits, should be increased. Critics pointed out that higher payroll premiums would reduce disposable income for workers and could have an impact on employment levels.

Morneau said he hoped he could reach some kind of agreement with seven of the ten provinces, representing two thirds of the population, by the end of the year. Few gave him much chance of making the first changes in the program's fifty-year history, previous attempts at reform having ended in stalemate. Saskatchewan, British Columbia, and Quebec had all expressed reservations about a mandatory increase to CPP contributions, while Ontario had already introduced its own planned enhancement, the Ontario Retirement Pension Plan. Yet by late June, Morneau had convinced all the provinces except Quebec and Manitoba to sign on to a new CPP deal that increased premiums and raised the amount of benefit available.

He was aided by the federal government's close relationship with Kathleen Wynne's Liberal Ontario government, which said it would abandon its own plans for a pension enhancement if there was a national alternative. That concentrated the minds of the finance ministers around the table, and they were finally persuaded when Morneau proposed to hike the Working Income Tax Benefit for lower earners to cover any increase in premiums. After B.C. proposed to delay the whole project until 2019 and phase it in over six years, Morneau had a deal that would see premiums rise about $7 a month for workers earning $55,000 (rising to $34 a month by 2023). Once fully implemented in 2025, the maximum annual benefit will rise by about a third.

"It was a lucky occurrence—the provincial map in terms of friendliness was at an all-time high," said one person involved in the CPP talks. "We had an Alberta government that, unlike those in the previous forty years, was willing to play ball; a B.C. government in a pre-election phase that was not interested in pushing back on too many things; a Saskatchewan government that was surprisingly easy to deal with on every fed–prov issue, with one exception [carbon pricing]; an NDP government in Manitoba that was on its last legs; an Ontario government with which there was a lot of cross-pollination; a Liberal government in Quebec; and four Atlantic provinces that were Liberal and basically client states of the federal government." [11]

A similar alignment would allow Morneau to strike an equally unlikely deal the following year, when the provinces came calling for renewed funding under the expiring health accords. Much as the Liberals had maligned the Conservative approach to dealing with the provinces, the fiscal reality dictated they adopt the same "take it or leave it" approach. In this case, the proposal was to limit increases in health transfers to a minimum of 3 per cent a year, after a decade of 6 per cent increases. After Morneau and health minister Jane Philpott promised to sweeten the pot with an additional $3 billion over four years for improved home care, it was clear that the general principle was not up for discussion. Over the course of the next year, province after province took the deal on the table—saving the federal government around $65 billion over a decade, compared to the deal the provinces had been seeking. Asselin said the deal went almost unnoticed. "Morneau didn't get enough credit for that. [Philpott] is very popular for the right reasons —she's a stellar minister—but she had nothing to do with it. We phoned all the premiers and squeezed them one by one. It was one of the successes of this government for the fiscal framework—we saved a lot of money," he said.[12]

But if health spending grew in line with the economy, the explosion of social spending was aimed at narrowing the gap in income inequality. One of the architects of the government's Canada Child Benefit and Canada Pension Plan enhancements argues that the measures, along with the increase to the Working Income Tax Benefit (now the Canada Workers Benefit), have been transformative for lower-income Canadians. "In 2025, retired seniors who have contributed to CPP will get up to $27,000 in combined CPP and OAS [Old Age Security], which is in the ballpark of a full-time minimum-wage worker. So we will have a guaranteed annual income for seniors and a guaranteed annual income for parents with kids," he said.[13]

Trudeau noted subsequently that the Child Benefit was the policy decision that has given him most satisfaction. "We took a whole bunch of disparate child benefits, some taxable, some not, and turned them into something clean and solid that has made a huge difference in people's lives, particularly because there were a lot of folks around who said, 'No, it's not going to have much of an impact,'" he stated. "To turn around and see the very tangible impact it's had on the Canadian economy—on the way people feel about the economy, that was an incredibly satisfying piece of policy to be able to put together."[14] The new government's ambitious change agenda meant it was attempting to reinvent the wheel in almost every area of social policy.

Beyond Canada's borders, the government had made some progress in developing a coherent foreign policy. Trudeau had announced that Canada would lead a NATO battle group in Latvia; would conclude the

Canada–European Union trade agreement; was discussing the launch of exploratory discussions about a free trade deal with China; and was bidding for a United Nations Security Council seat in 2021–22. Unfortunately for the Liberals, the articulation of that policy was incoherent. Stéphane Dion, the party's former leader, had landed at the renamed Department of Global Affairs and was attempting to convey the differences between Liberal and Conservative policy. He coined the term "responsible conviction" to make the case that Liberal policy would be principled but less dogmatic than under the Conservatives, and more geared to getting results.

The Tories had little tolerance for the UN, but the Liberals would be in the vanguard of multinational efforts on everything from climate change to peacekeeping. The Conservatives had severed ties with Iran and Russia, but there had been no positive consequences beyond cutting off engagement with murderous regimes with despotic leaders, so the Liberals planned to re-engage with those countries. "Our world is highly imperfect and to improve it we must engage in it with our eyes open, not withdraw from it," Dion said in speech at the University of Ottawa that raised eyebrows, not least in the Prime Minister's Office, which had not been given a heads up about the new direction.[15]

There is not much evidence to suggest that Trudeau had thought deeply about foreign affairs prior to becoming Liberal leader. He had travelled extensively with his father, but his musings on what he saw do not suggest a mind that was greatly engaged in the great geopolitical issues of the day. He recalled being in Bangladesh with Pierre, where the prime ministerial motorcade was stuck in traffic and an old man standing with his bicycle was waiting to cross the street. "I remember watching him for those seconds that our paths intersected and feeling an odd pang to realize that I would never know his story—where he had come from, where he was going, what his life was, with all the events, dreams and anxieties that made him every bit as real and important as I was to myself."[16] But running a G7 country required a more sophisticated analysis than the revelation that individuals are unique, just like everyone else.

In the run-up to the 2015 election, a council of advisers on international affairs was convened, under the joint chairmanship of Liberal MP Marc Garneau and former army general Andrew Leslie, to flesh out the rough themes of idealism and multilateral cooperation that were inherent in Trudeau's instinctive progressivism. Broadly, the plan, collated by foreign policy adviser Roland Paris, was to live up to Canada's Paris commitments on climate; expand trade with China and other fast-growing Asian nations; reaffirm Canada's commitment to counter-terrorism and the coalition against the Islamic State; contribute to NATO "reassurance measures in Eastern Europe"; revitalize Canada's multilateral diplomacy at the United Nations; champion human rights, especially for women, children, minorities, and refugees; contribute peacekeepers to help fragile states; and resume diplomatic relations with "troublesome" countries like Russia and Iran.[17]

Dion's approach was not necessarily at odds with those principles—his speech was judged a "pretty classic Liberal approach to foreign policy" by Gerald Butts. But the muddy messaging and the go-it-alone approach were causing ripples. Advisers in Dion's office recalled friction as the minister ploughed ahead with his own policy. "The feeling was the previous approach wasn't working and you needed to do a ninety-degree turn on it, as opposed to degrees. Dion was prepared to go the whole hog to fundamentally change the game—and that's where there was a disagreement, absolutely," said one person who was there. "He had a lane, he was running ahead into it, and there wasn't much of a discussion or a heads up with others. But when you do that—and you don't bring people along—you're effectively on your own."[18] The sense that the global affairs minister had gone rogue was starting to permeate the Prime Minister's Office, which was not given any notice about the "responsible conviction" speech, with predictable consequences down the road for that most unlikely of diplomats, Dion.

Trudeau had enjoyed five months without a testing foreign policy crisis. But at the end of April 2016, he was forced to make one of those life-and-death decisions that all leaders dread. Two Canadians were kidnapped by Filipino jihadists with allegiances to the Islamic State. One of the men, businessman John Ridsdel, was beheaded almost immediately, but the second, Robert Hall, was a prisoner of the Abu Sayyaf militants in the southern Philippines. It was a test of Canada's no-ransom policy and, to the rookie prime minister, it must have conjured up the spectre of the challenge his father faced at the hands of the Front de libération du Québec in the October Crisis of 1970, when British trade commissioner James Cross and Quebec labour minister Pierre Laporte were kidnapped (Cross was later released, but Laporte was murdered).

The younger Trudeau emerged from a cabinet retreat in Alberta to express outrage at the murder of Ridsdel, and insisted that Canada would not pay terrorists any ransom money. The 2009 case of Canadian diplomats Robert Fowler and Louis Guay suggested that Canada's no-ransom policy was not quite as rigid as the government claimed— the men had been freed after months in captivity in the Islamic Maghreb after a ransom was paid. Leaked U.S. memos at the time suggested that the Canadian government had contributed to the ransom cash.

But Trudeau was adamant. "Paying ransom for Canadians would endanger the lives of every single one of the millions of Canadians who live, work and travel around the globe every single year," he said.[19] The consequence of that decision became clear in mid-June, when Hall's severed head was discovered. The Calgary-born metalworker and part-time actor's friends and family had assembled about $1.4 million in ransom money, but it fell well short of the $16.6 million Abu Sayyaf had demanded to free Hall as well as his Filipina girlfriend Marites Flor and a Norwegian, Kjartan Sekkingstad (both of whom were eventually released).

Trudeau said the 3 a.m. call he received, advising him of Hall's death, was one of his worst moments as leader. He had followed his father's example in staring down terrorists. Pierre said the October Crisis taught him, "It is absolutely essential to have at the helm of state, a very firm hand, one that sets a course, that never alters, that does not attempt to do everything at once out of excitement or confusion."[20] But the person making such fateful decisions pays a price, as Margaret Trudeau noted of her husband on the night Laporte was killed: "I heard him crying . . . he was a shaken man. I watched him grow old before my eyes. It was as if Laporte's death lay on his shoulders alone: he was the one who wouldn't negotiate, he was the man who would now have to take responsibility for the murder of an innocent man. It gave him a new bitterness, a hard sadness I had never seen before."[21]

Gerald Butts said the hostage standoff deeply affected everyone in the Prime Minister's Office. "As a staff, we were very much shaken up by that. We knew the prime minister made the right call, and for the right reasons, but man . . . that's a real thing that someone lost their family member," he lamented. Yet Trudeau had remained as resolute as his father during the October Crisis, to the point where he told his mother, Margaret, that if she or his children were ever kidnapped, he would have to "do his duty" rather than compromise the office to save them.[22] In hindsight, he maintained that the decision was clear. "I'll remember it forever, but it was not necessarily a difficult decision, in the sense that it was obvious you can't negotiate with terrorists and put at risk the lives of millions of Canadians around the world," he said.[23]

Back in Ottawa, with no serious threat to its hegemony, the government decided to make things interesting by reacquainting itself with the old Liberal kryptonite of arrogance and hubris. A harbinger of a political scandal that was to embroil the prime minister in the second half of the year emerged with an advertisement for a $500-per-ticket Liberal Party fundraising event at a Bay Street law firm with then-justice minister Jody Wilson-Raybould—an episode the opposition parties dubbed "cash for access." It was true, as Trudeau pointed out, that the event did not break any fundraising rules. But it hardly matched the Olympian standards of integrity the Liberals had promised on taking office. It didn't even pass the smell test when judged by the government's own accountability code, which said that ministers must avoid the appearance of conflict of interest, as it emerged that the Bay Street firm had actively lobbied the minister. It was a brewing scandal that was not about to go away.

Even more bizarre was the incident when Trudeau employed the weapon in the political armoury that is usually used figuratively, rather than literally—the elbow. Trudeau was in the House of Commons on May 18 and was becoming increasingly frustrated at opposition tactics to delay the Liberal legislative agenda. At one point, the prime minister marched out from behind his desk, "manhandled" the Conservative whip, the late Gord Brown, and elbowed NDP MP Ruth Ellen Brosseau in the chest. An angry confrontation with a number of New Democrats, including then-leader Tom Mulcair, followed, and things nearly turned even more ugly.

The bad blood had been building for some days. The Liberals had nearly lost a vote on a government bill when the opposition parties ambushed them while they were short of members in the chamber—an indication of their inexperience in the dark arts of parliamentary affairs. The Liberals, becoming impatient about the slow passage of their bill on assisted dying, replied with a motion that would have imposed the government's will on procedure in the House, thereby, in the words of the Conservative House leader Andrew Scheer, "unilaterally disarming the opposition." It was that simmering dispute that bubbled over into the physical fracas featuring the prime minister. "It is not appropriate to manhandle other members," Commons Speaker Geoff Regan admonished Trudeau, stating the obvious.

That kicked off a day of mea culpas on Trudeau's part, who apologized to Brosseau for his "unacceptable behaviour." He explained that he had gone over to help Brown through a "gaggle of MPs" who were impeding his progress and slowing the vote. But it was clear that the prime minister had lost his temper. "As he was entering a small circle of us who were standing there, he swore and said, 'Get the bleep out of the way,'" said NDP MP Tracey Ramsey. "He pushed his way into the circle we were standing in, he grabbed [Brown], dragged him out and so doing he elbowed my colleague [Brosseau] quite viciously. She was very physically hurt."[24] Another NDP MP, Niki Ashton, cast doubt on Trudeau's feminism, saying the incident made women feel unsafe in the Commons.

It was with considerable irony that Trudeau was obliged to speak at the National Prayer Breakfast the morning after telling his parliamentary colleagues to go forth and multiply. The preplanned reading was from Romans 12: "Bless those who persecute you: bless and do not curse." The prime minister later returned to the House, where he again lamented his "poor choices." The incident did not have long-term implications beyond reminding Canadians that their political leader retained an impetuosity and immaturity that he had managed to rein in during his first months in office. The Speaker was compelled to find a prima facie breach of privilege, and the House debated the "physical molestation" of Brosseau rather than the assisted-dying legislation. The Liberals were also obliged to back down on their power-grab motion in the face of accusations that they were treating democracy as an inconvenience. If nothing else, Trudeau was living up to his promise to do politics differently—no previous prime minister had ever been accused of molestation in the House.

But as Parliament rose for its summer break, Canadians offered a collective shrug and went on with their vacations. An opinion poll in late June suggested that 56 per cent of Canadians approved of the government and more than half had positive feelings about Trudeau personally. Liberal support had risen from the 40 per cent in the October 2015 election, as many former New Democrats proclaimed themselves happy with the Liberal agenda.[25]

Yet even as Trudeau appeared invulnerable, chinks in the political armour were apparent. A separate Angus Reid Institute poll indicated that more people thought the government relied too heavily on public relations and photo opportunities than believed it was actually getting things done.[26] This was to become a constant refrain from the government's critics and it bears some deconstruction.

The first part of the Angus Reid survey spoke to the concern about the Liberal fixation on brand management. It was clear even before

Trudeau was sworn in that he would take image manipulation and spin to new highs (or lows) in the social media age. The night before he visited the governor general at Rideau Hall, his team sent out a fundraising email in his name, claiming he was about to put his kids to bed, "but before I go . . ." could the recipient pitch in a few bucks? The endless photo opportunities that followed indicated how adept the Liberals quickly became at message control—defined by political scientist Alex Marland as distilling complex ideas into simplified information shared via social media such as Facebook, Instagram, and Twitter, a process that required dumbing down, harmonization, consistency, and centralized decision-making in the prime minister's inner circle.

After the Harper years, when (at least according to the opposition) the prime minister ruled like a feudal landlord abusing tenants who hadn't paid their rent, Trudeau claimed he had no interest in centralizing power. Rule by cabinet was back, he said as he was sworn in. But that is not how it has worked out, according to a number of Liberal MPs. "Too much power is centralized—way, way, way too much power. All the senior advisers are from Queen's Park—including Katie [Telford] and Gerry [Butts]. But Queen's Park is not Ottawa," said one MP.[27]

Perhaps the confirmation of the "Savoie thesis"—the idea promoted by academic Donald Savoie that cabinet has become a sounding board for prime ministers who pay more attention to a select band of courtiers—was inevitable. As Marland noted, *Winnipeg Free Press* editor J.W. Dafoe had observed a similar trend as far back as under Wilfrid Laurier. "A prime minister under the party system as we have it in Canada is, of necessity, an egoist and an autocrat. If he comes to office without these characteristics, his environment equips him with them as surely as a diet of royal jelly transforms a worker into a queen bee. . . . It is in keeping with the genius of our party system that the leader who begins as the chosen chief of his associates, proceeds by stages, if he has the necessary qualities, to a position of dominance," Dafoe wrote.[28]

In the modern era, this model has seen MPs find themselves as the last to know about any given subject, as the "first among equals" principle is abandoned in favour of a more presidential-style leader surrounded by increasingly powerful unelected advisers. Some MPs have balked at the fact that Telford and Butts attended caucus, nominally the preserve of the elected. (Jean Chrétien rarely had staff in caucus, but Ian Brodie, Stephen Harper's first chief of staff, did attend—at Harper's insistence.)

Some who have worked at the sharp end argue there is nothing sinister about the centre coordinating the message the government wants to send out. Eddie Goldenberg, Jean Chrétien's senior adviser, explained in his account of Ottawa life, *The Way It Works*, that the government in which he was a key player tried to involve the whole cabinet in priority-setting, but desisted when it became clear that the cabinet was too large and diverse to be able to take into account the mix of considerations that go into allocating spending priorities.[29] After interviewing ministers during the first term, Goldenberg concluded they were so busy with their own departmental responsibilities, they gave little serious thought to the government's agenda. There is little evidence that things have changed, despite what Justin Trudeau espouses.

The second part of the Angus Reid survey spoke to doubts among voters that the new government was getting things done. In light of its efforts to bring in Syrian refugees and to introduce the middle-class tax cut and the Canada Child Benefit, not to mention its striking of the enhanced Canada Pension Plan deal, this might be judged a little harsh. But the truth was that progress was uneven across the government, with many of the promises kept being relatively low-hanging fruit that, like the reinstatement of the long-form census, required just the stroke of a pen.

In the trenches, some political veterans were noticing an inability to execute by rookie ministers—who were often staffed by rookie chiefs of staff, thanks to the reluctance by the Prime Minister's Office to hire veterans from the Chrétien and Martin eras. "If you charted our new ministers and new chiefs of staff, you'd find out that's where a lot of the problems came from," said one senior Liberal staffer. "My theory is there are three key people—the minister, the chief of staff, and the deputy minister [the senior public servant]. If three out of three are experienced, you're going to kick ass. Two out of three, you're still going to make progress. One out of three you're going to go a little bit backwards, and three out of three rookies and you're heading straight backwards. I think in the first year there just wasn't quite enough experience. The goal was a good one—getting new voices—but execution was flawed."[30] The key to progress seemed to be to have an experienced proponent pushing a file, particularly if it was Butts. "When Gerald had his mind on a file, it would move. But if it wasn't a Gerald file—or didn't have a chief who was experienced in navigating—all of a sudden it would grind to a halt. It has to come from the top. The PM is really interested in a lot of things, but he doesn't own anything. He's political," said the senior staffer.[31]

One measure of the efficiency of government is cabinet decision-making. Some ministers have spoken about the frustration of getting files through the cabinet committees made up of senior ministers that then make recommendations to the whole cabinet. In previous governments, a file would make it to cabinet committee, where it would advance to cabinet or be killed outright. In the early Trudeau years in particular, decision documents like the defence policy review would go in and out of cabinet committees multiple times. Inevitably, that level of indecision creates a backlog, choking up the cabinet decision-making process. "The scarcest commodity in Ottawa is not money, it is ministerial time," said Gene Lang, a former chief of staff to the defence minister in Paul Martin's government.[32] As one parliamentary secretary put it, "When the House is sitting, I have thirty hours of wasted time every week, if you include Question Period, which I do. I have to squeeze in everything else around all this parliamentary stuff."[33]

This fixation on style over substance—the obsession with spin and the problems in delivering on commitments—would come back to haunt the Liberals later in the mandate.

NO AMOUNT OF GLOSS would prove sufficient to cover the series of negative headlines that greeted MPs as they returned to Ottawa in the fall. The first minister in the new government to fall overboard was Hunter Tootoo, the fisheries minister, who had stepped down in early summer, ostensibly to deal with an alcohol problem. But in mid-September, a story in the *Globe and Mail* revealed he had been having a sexual relationship with a young staffer, which he had broken off so he could pursue a relationship with her mother.[34] The story was swiftly followed by the news that Butts and Telford were reimbursed more than $200,000 to move their families to Ottawa from Toronto. The revelation prompted the two senior aides to repay thousands of dollars in costs they conceded were "unreasonable."[35]

Then it emerged that Wilson-Raybould's Bay Street fundraiser was not a one-off, but rather was part of a strategy by the Liberals to fill their coffers by offering access to senior cabinet ministers. An audience with Bill Morneau cost an elite band of Halifax business people $1,500 a head; another $500-a-ticket event in Toronto was organized by businessman Barry Sherman, whose company Apotex lobbied the Department of Finance (the pharma billionaire was found dead with his wife, Honey, under suspicious circumstances in their home in Toronto a year later). Morneau defended the fundraisers, saying "they are in fact open" to all Canadians—an example of his tin political ear.[36]

The cash-for-access events sat uncomfortably with ethical rules Trudeau had unveiled the previous year, which stated "there should be no preferential access or appearance of preferential access"[37] in exchange for political donations. What transitioned the situation from uncomfortable to untenable was a story that Trudeau himself had been the draw at a fundraiser at the mansion of a wealthy Chinese-Canadian businessman, where one of the guests had been seeking Ottawa's approval to open a new bank.[38] The prime minister's explanation that he was merely trying to attract investment dollars to Canada from China was pitiable, and the party was embarrassed into committing to reforms—future events would be held in public spaces and publicized well in advance. The party also promised that event guest lists would be made public after the fact.

Despite the run of bad publicity in the fall of 2016, the Liberals were polling consistently above where they had performed in the election a year earlier—albeit against two parties that were embroiled in internal leadership races.[39] Canadians appeared content with the spirit of political enlightenment promised, if not yet delivered, by the Liberals. However, the final months of the year presented fresh challenges that were to define the rest of Trudeau's mandate—not least of which was the surprise election as president of the United States of one Donald John Trump.

NINE

THE AGE OF TRUMP

ISAAC NEWTON SAID HE lost money in the South Sea Bubble financial collapse because, even though he could track the movement of the stars, he could not calculate the madness of men. That same sense of vexation was apparent at an event at Ottawa's Château Laurier hotel as the U.S. presidential results came in on the night of November 8, 2016. Senior bureaucrats and Liberal politicians in the room looked like deer in the path of an oncoming train. Trump wasn't supposed to win—he was a twenty-five-to-one outsider when he launched his campaign in summer 2015; he was still five-to-one against on election day.[1]

One senior official, shaking his head in disbelief, said the government wasn't prepared for a Trump victory, before leaving early to confer with his colleagues. "Although Ottawa had done some planning for the possibility of a Trump victory, the U.S. election was a shock," said former Trudeau adviser Roland Paris, with some understatement.[2] The government's lack of preparation was borne out by subsequent inquiries by the *Huffington Post*, which discovered through Access to Information requests that the public service provided no contingency plan to Trudeau. There was only one mention of Trump, prior to an email circulated the day before the election that summarized an essay by Brookings Institution scholar Thomas Wright. He argued that Trump viewed the world economy as a zero-sum game, wouldn't have any qualms about leaving trade agreements, and was not afraid of trade wars.[3]

The view that it hardly mattered what Trump thought, because he wasn't going to win, exploded in the early hours of November 9, when the president-elect took to the stage to claim victory. At that moment, Trudeau's game plan became obsolete and his domestic and foreign agenda were subsequently dominated by attempts to react to a man whose views were, in Wright's words, "considerably outside the mainstream." Bureaucrats and politicians all over Ottawa raced to bookshops to acquaint themselves with Trump's business advice tome, *The Art of the Deal*, and the concept of "truthful hyperbole."

Trudeau had accused Stephen Harper of bungling relations with the U.S. and campaigned on repairing them with the expectation that Hillary Clinton would win. The government had gone so far as to invite vice-president Joe Biden to Ottawa in December for a post-election visit, to help ease the transition to the new Democratic administration. The Trudeau and Obama governments had formed a relationship so deep and rich, you could grow oak trees in it. But when the invitation to Biden was extended, no one had contemplated the prospect that it would take place while Donald Trump was measuring the curtains in the White House and the Democrats were yesterday's breakfast.

Trudeau and his team scuttled to react—Butts and Telford made contact with Trump's closest advisers, including Jared Kushner (the president-elect's son-in-law) and Steve Bannon, the former head of Breitbart News, while other intermediaries like former prime minister Brian Mulroney were asked to use their influence with Trump and his associates. Within days, Ottawa attempted to forestall any apprehension of Democrat bias by suggesting that it was willing to renegotiate the North American Free Trade Agreement as a gesture of goodwill. Trump had vowed to tear up the agreement, prompting David MacNaughton, Canada's ambassador in Washington, to volunteer the option of Trudeau and Trump sitting down to "improve" the deal.

Politicians, like gamblers, need to know when to hold 'em and when to fold 'em. But Trudeau's pre-emptive decision to tell one of the planet's most voracious deal-makers that Canada was willing to renego-tiate NAFTA, without even being asked, ranked as one of the great exam-ples of a sovereign government disintegrating like cheap toilet paper. Liberal sources suggested that the mindset was to calm the business community by making it clear that tweaks or adjustments were custom-ary in organic trade agreements like NAFTA. Yet experienced trade nego-tiators suggested that any "improvements" would not be to Canada's benefit. "Naïve would be a polite term," said Derek Burney, prime min-ister Brian Mulroney's chief of staff during the negotiation of the Canada–U.S. Free Trade Agreement.[4]

Trump had called NAFTA "an absolute catastrophe" and "a total disas-ter," but, up to that point, he had not talked specifically about Canada as a source of anxiety. By opening the door to fresh negotiations, Trudeau had given the president-elect the chance to use the U.S.'s massive negotiating leverage. Trump, after all, was a man who coined the bar-gaining maxim "It's give and take—but it's gotta be mostly take." It was an inauspicious start to relations with the man who would be responsi-ble for crumpling up the Liberal government's agenda.

Neither was it a good time for Trudeau to revert to his old habit of self-immolation, but on the death of his father's old friend Fidel Castro, he proved unable to restrain himself. While Trump accurately charac-terized Castro as "a brutal dictator who oppressed his own people for nearly six decades," Trudeau called him "a larger than life leader . . . a legendary revolutionary and orator" and went on to say, "My father was proud to call him a friend."[5] The remarks were noticed in the United States. Republican senator and former presidential candidate Marco Rubio called them "shameful and embarrassing."[6] Trump was in Florida at the time, home to a large Cuban-American population, and had to be talked off the ceiling by his old acquaintance, Mulroney, who explained that the younger Trudeau was not as left-wing as his father.[7]

Trudeau's statement was also the cause of much cringing in the global affairs department, which in the normal course of events would have prepared a staid official obituary. But Trudeau was in Madagascar at the

Francophonie conference, where the statement was crafted. "My under-standing was that it was the PM reacting to someone he knew well and grew up with. Maybe there wasn't the challenge function there should have been. My only thought was that I had no input," said one senior official at global affairs, with noticeable relief.[8]

The only other file that rivalled U.S. relations in importance was the grand bargain to price carbon while also building a pipeline—a trade-off that polling suggested could win support in all regions of the country. In October, Trudeau had demonstrated that he meant busi-ness about setting a minimum carbon tax by announcing his plans in the House of Commons while provincial environment ministers were meeting in Montreal to discuss their options. The timing prompted a walkout by a number of ministers in protest of the abandonment of the cooperative approach the Liberals had been taking up to that point. But the message was clear: adopt a carbon tax (or cap and trade); otherwise Ottawa would impose its own levy—a minimum of fifty dollars a tonne by 2022 (which would add around eleven cents a litre to the price of gas). The umbilical link between the carbon tax and pipelines was clear from the reaction in Alberta, where Premier Rachel Notley said she would only agree to the federal plan if the federal government approved a pipeline.

Ottawa delivered on its part of the bargain in late November, when it announced its decision to approve Kinder Morgan's Trans Mountain pipeline expansion plan. Trudeau had softened up his environmental base by proclaiming a $1.5 billion ocean protection plan in early November, from the deck of the *Sir Wilfrid Laurier* coast guard vessel, with Vancouver harbour as a backdrop. But that did little to sweeten the announcement for many opponents of the pipeline to Burnaby. "I am convinced it is safe for B.C. and right for Canada," he said at a press conference announcing the decision. He also approved a retrofit and expansion of the aging Line 3 pipeline between Alberta and Manitoba but refused to launch new consultations on the Northern Gateway route, effectively killing the project.[9] The Liberals also introduced an oil tanker moratorium on B.C.'s north coast, a decision that blocked pipeline development to Prince Rupert. As the pipeline debate on the West Coast intensified, these two decisions became increasingly controversial.

But at the time, the immediate concern was opposition to Trans Mountain. "If Trudeau wants Clayoquot Sound 2.0 in the middle of Metro Vancouver, he'll get it," declared the Pipe Up network website, referring to the "War in the Woods" protest against logging in the late 1980s and early 1990s. The early rumblings of political opposition that would become increasingly significant were also heard. Vancouver mayor Gregor Robertson and Burnaby mayor Derek Corrigan said they were dismayed by the news, while Andrew Weaver, the provincial Green Party leader, said that Ottawa had betrayed its promise to Canadians about climate change and to First Nations regarding reconciliation.[10] But Trudeau had been elected on a platform of balancing the environment and the economy, and that necessitated upsetting people on both sides of that equation.

TRUDEAU MAY HAVE BEEN caught flat-footed by Trump's victory, but he wasted no time in taking decisive action. In early January, he ousted his testy foreign minister, Stéphane Dion, and replaced him with Chrystia Freeland, the effervescent trade minister who had won good reviews when she walked out of negotiations on the free trade deal with the European Union, in protest against the intransigence of the Belgian region of Wallonia.[11] She, in turn, was replaced by experienced trade lawyer Francois-Philippe Champagne, while immigration minister John McCallum was named the new ambassador in Beijing and replaced by Toronto lawyer Ahmed Hussen. Hussen's appointment set off alarm bells in the security establishment when background checks suggested the former refugee had a niece who was married to an Islamic extremist back in Somalia. Panic subsided after Hussen confirmed he did have a niece by that name—but she was four years old and lived in Toronto.

Dion was offered the dual ambassadorship of Germany and the European Union, which he said he would think about.[12] Another casualty was Maryam Monsef, the fresh-faced Afghan refugee who had been given the Mission Impossible of living up to Trudeau's promise that the 2015 election would be the last held under the first-past-the-post system. Monsef was criticized for her handling of the democratic institutions file and found herself demoted to minister for the status of women.

But it was the sacking of a former party leader that dominated the headlines. A book written in 2018 by one of Dion's advisers, Jocelyn Coulon—*Un selfie avec Justin Trudeau*—claimed that the relationship between Dion and Trudeau was "glacial." Coulon suggested that Dion's chilly response to Trudeau's candidacy in 2007 explained why the relationship was so cool, which may be true. But his contention that the only private meeting the two men had was when Dion was fired is disputed by people who worked with Dion and in the Prime Minister's Office. "That is false," said one of Dion's closest advisers. "Coulon overestimated his access—take a lot of what he said with a massive truckload of salt. Dion would definitely dispute that he and Trudeau had a frosty relationship. But it's Dion—with whom did he have a close relationship? You don't hug the man."[13] Coulon said the only conversation he recalled between the two men, on the government jet, ended in signs of irritation from Trudeau over Dion's insistence on rapprochement with Russia.[14] The prime minister is a man "incurious about the affairs of the world," Coulon remarked. He said the reason Trudeau gave Dion for sidelining him was that he needed "change." That was beyond dispute.

The sense in the Prime Minister's Office was that Dion's academic, sometimes prickly manner would irritate the unconventional new U.S. administration. Freeland's personable style was seen as more complementary, and she had the benefit of knowing some of the incoming members of Trump's cabinet from her time as a business journalist in the United States—a useful thing at a time when Trump was already musing about a 35 per cent border adjustment tax on every export crossing the border, rhetoric that drove down the value of the Canadian dollar.

Gerald Butts admitted that the Prime Minister's Office was blind-sided by Dion's "responsible conviction" speech, with its redefinition of Canadian foreign policy priorities. But he said that was not the reason Dion was shuffled. "Stéphane had his mandate letter, and our style —I think all ministers would back me on this—is that we have a pretty light touch on the reins. The reason we made that switch was because Freeland was better equipped to deal with the Trump administration than Stéphane was. Technically, we were surprised by the 'responsible conviction' speech. Would we have used that message? Maybe not. But if you read the speech it was roughly a pretty classic Liberal approach to foreign policy," he said.[15]

The reorganization went beyond a simple shuffle. Freeland took the U.S. trade file with her from her previous job, while her former chief of staff, Brian Clow, was moved into the Prime Minister's Office to coordinate a whole-of-government approach to Canada–U.S. relations. The response extended beyond the federal government—Trudeau was in touch with premiers, mayors, business leaders, and former politicians across the country to leverage their networks as part of a Team Canada advocacy campaign. The message was that the economic relationship benefitted both countries and that millions of jobs on both sides of the border depended on the continued free flow of goods and services.

Yet, as so often in the past, just as Trudeau was being lauded for his decisive action, he walked all over his own good publicity by doing something ill-advised. In this case, it was the revelation that he had taken his family to Bell Island in the Bahamas as a guest of the Aga Khan. Despite the prime minister's own code of ethics barring sponsored travel, it emerged that he was ferried to the island on a private helicopter owned by the Ismaili Muslim spiritual leader. Once the trip was made public by the *National Post*, the Opposition charged that the hospitality extended by the Aga Khan might be deemed to be a gift that could reasonably be seen to have influenced Trudeau in the exercise of his official duty—in contravention of the Conflict of Interest Act.

There was no evidence that Trudeau made any decisions that benefitted the Aga Khan or any of his interests in Canada, but it later emerged that there was an ongoing official business relationship between the government of Canada and the Ismaili leader at the time. In fact, the Aga Khan Foundation was registered to lobby the Prime Minister's Office and did so to advance a $200 million riverside revitalization project in Ottawa that was close to the Aga Khan's heart.

Trudeau later said his father had formed a firm friendship with the Aga Khan while he was in office, and that in 1983 the two families went on a vacation to the Greek islands. He even revealed that he refers to the Aga Khan as "Uncle K." Yet the younger Trudeau had no interactions with the Aga Khan in the thirty years between that vacation and his election as Liberal leader in 2013, with the exception of his father's funeral in 2000, where he said he felt "instant recognition, instant closeness" to the Aga Khan.

Contact between the two resumed with Trudeau's accession to the Liberal leadership, with dinners and occasional phone calls. Trudeau and his wife met the Aga Khan for dinner at his residence in Paris while the prime minister was attending the UN Climate Change conference in November 2015. Subsequently, Sophie and the Trudeau children went to Bells Cay for a spring break. In mid-July 2016, Sophie contacted the Aga Khan's daughter to inquire whether her family could return to the island over Christmas. Trudeau said it offered the privacy and security the family needed. It was on that trip that the Trudeaus were joined by the Aga Khan and his family, exchanging gifts and enjoying meals where the conversation was "personal and social in nature." Trudeau maintained that he considered the Aga Khan a family friend and that no requests for funding or assistance in any matter were made.

But that was not the view of the ethics commissioner, Mary Dawson, in her review of the affair, given that discussions about business between the Aga Khan and the government of Canada were ongoing at the time of both the March and December trips. "That should have put Mr. Trudeau on notice that such gifts might reasonably be seen to have been given to influence him in the exercise of an official power, duty or function as prime minister, or otherwise give rise to a real or apparent conflict of interest," she said when she reported back later in the year.[16] She found the prime minister guilty of contravening the Conflict of Interest Act on four counts, mainly because of the ongoing business relationship with the Aga Khan.

Dawson's findings prompted a hair-shirt "listening tour" of the country—to help Trudeau "reconnect with Canadians" who did not spend their Christmas vacation on a billionaire's private island. It was not the crime of the century, but it did not resonate well with people hearing the news on their commute to work on a cold Canadian winter morning. And it once more exposed Trudeau's vulnerability—a sense of entitlement that suggested the normal rules don't apply to him. Trudeau quickly attempted to bury the bad news on the tour of town halls—traipsing around the country calling local radio stations to request Tragically Hip songs and telling everyone he was "just there to say 'hi' to people." In large measure, it worked—although he put his foot in it at a town hall in Peterborough, Ontario, where he said that Alberta's oil sands must be phased out. He later claimed he "misspoke."[17]

ONE OF TRUMP'S FIRST acts as president was a win for Canada. He used an executive order to help pave the way for the building of the Keystone XL pipeline, inviting TransCanada Corp. to reapply to build the line and directing the U.S. State Department to make a favourable decision on the application, as part of a strategy to increase domestic oil production.

But the signs were already there that Trump intended to follow through on his election pledge to "tear up NAFTA." At a Senate committee meeting in mid-January, Trump's nominee for commerce secretary, Wilbur Ross, said that every aspect of the free trade agreement would be on the negotiating table. The Americans reserved most of their ire for Mexico's cheap labour and poor environmental standards, but

Ross also took aim at NAFTA's tripartite dispute resolution panels and its rules-of-origin provisions, which govern how much content from outside the NAFTA region is permissible.

The NAFTA action was part of a wider plan that would see the United States cut corporate taxes and business regulation and attempt to reduce its trade deficit, particularly by targeting China. But it was clear from day one that Canada was in Trump's crosshairs—even though he made reassuring noises when Trudeau visited Washington in mid-February. "We have a very outstanding trade relationship with Canada. We'll be tweaking it," the president said at a press conference in the White House. It was to prove the start of an eighteen-month marathon of negotiations that dominated the agenda and the headspace of most of the key political actors in the Canadian government right up until the new NAFTA deal was reached in fall 2018. The result proved to be more than a "tweak."

Trudeau had played his hand well to that point—charming the most conceited president in recent history with a picture of himself. On their first call, Trump had revealed that he had met Trudeau's father—"a dapper dude," in the president's words. Hence, when Trudeau arrived at the White House in February, he handed Trump a picture of himself with Pierre Trudeau at a banquet in New York City in 1981. "He was a man who I knew and respected greatly," Trump said. The visit went as well as could have been expected—the two leaders spoke about the things upon which they agreed—trade, security, energy, middle-class jobs—and were silent on the things about which they might fall out—the environment, softwood lumber, and immigration. There was always the prospect that the president might go off script. In late January, Trump had temporarily banned travellers from seven Muslim countries, prompting Trudeau to tweet that "those fleeing persecution, terror and war" were welcome in Canada "regardless of your faith." It was a shot that Trump chose to ignore as he stuck to his speaking notes and said he would like to see harmonious relations between the two countries. Trudeau left U.S. airspace with the special relationship still intact but likely wondering what might constitute a "tweak."

By then, though, the Canadian delegation had spent enough time with the Trump entourage to ensure that no one got carried away. "Our general sense on the way back from Washington was that this was the first act of a very long play. No one got too excited or thought this was going to be definitive because we knew it could all change by the time we landed," said Butts.[18]

AT HOME, THE LIBERALS were in the middle of a storm of their own making. One of the signature campaign promises in 2015 was ending the first-past-the-post voting system and replacing it with a shiny new, if unspecified, way to choose a federal government. On the campaign trail, Trudeau had promised to make "every vote count." "We are committed to ensuring that the 2015 election will be the last federal election using first-past-the-post," he declared, repeatedly. But in early February 2017, Monsef's replacement as democratic institutions minister, Karina Gould, was dispatched to explain why the government was abandoning the pledge. "*Most* of our electoral pledges have been kept," she said, by way of defence.[19]

Trudeau had aligned himself with reformers, including many younger voters, who argued that the existing system delivered majority governments, without the party in power necessarily winning the majority of the votes. But after winning a majority with 40 per cent of the vote, the prime minister appeared to lose enthusiasm for change. He had advocated a ranked ballot system, which could have delivered Liberal governments until one of the prime minister's progeny was ready to take over the family business, given that it rewards centrist parties that collect a lot of second-place support. While in opposition, he would talk to young voters about political cynicism, suggesting that disaffection with politics was a reflection of a failed system.

But as prime minister, he had now concluded that if he couldn't get the system that would keep his party in power in perpetuity, he'd stick with the one that delivered a whopping majority last time. Trudeau had suggested in a newspaper interview the previous fall that Canadians' motivation to change the system had waned since Stephen Harper was defeated. An all-party committee studying the issue had concluded that there should be a referendum on an unidentified proportional represen-tation voting system, but Monsef had dismissed it as an idea that would exclude women, minorities, and people with "exceptionalities" because they didn't vote in large numbers.

It was, then, no great surprise when Gould's mandate letter as the new minister said it would not be part of her job to change the electoral system. "A clear preference for a new electoral system, let alone a consen-sus, has not emerged," it read.[20] And "There is no clear path forward," said Trudeau in the House of Commons. "It would be irresponsible for us to do something that harms Canada's stability."[21] Behind him, his backbenchers looked glum, as if Trudeau had just announced a campaign to wipe out the Canadian moose.

The reputational damage for the Liberals was significant, even if polling suggested that it did not shift voting intentions among left-of-centre voters permanently. The opposition leapt on the U-turn like lions on a gazelle. "A massive political deception," said Tom Mulcair, who remained NDP leader pending the election of his successor. As he helpfully pointed out, the pledge was made 1,813 times over the course of the election campaign. It helped get the Liberals elected and many voters would never give them the benefit of the doubt again. For those who voted for Trudeau as an antidote to political cynicism, in the hope that he would overturn what they regarded as an unjust electoral sys-tem, it was nothing short of a betrayal.

The Liberals tried to get things back on track with their second bud-get, in late March, but it was a pale imitation of its profligate predeces-sor. "The second budget was just a narrative because we had run out of money," said Robert Asselin, who was an adviser to the finance minis-ter at the time, suggesting that the document contained more verbiage than spending commitments. "The fall statement was much more sig-nificant—we announced infrastructure spending, the [infrastructure] bank, which is big policy because it introduces private financing into infrastructure, which even Harper was timid about. But the second budget was a non-budget."[22]

In November, Bill Morneau had used his fall statement to outline the tens of billions of dollars the government planned to spend on infrastructure projects over the next decade, and to announce the infrastructure bank aimed at attracting private capital into transit and highway projects. But the spring 2017 budget was a snoozer with only one thing in common with its predecessor—there was not even the pretence of balancing the budget. All bets were on the growth plan working and deficits shrinking, as if by magic. The budget was notable only for the heads up it gave that the Liberals intended to tighten tax rules that allowed Canadians to share income with their spouse and adult children. No details on the tax clawback were given, but the government had served notice that it was going to eliminate tax breaks enjoyed by high earners. When the details did emerge later in the year, they would provoke a firestorm that nearly consumed the finance minister.

With disappointments multiplying, the government needed to deliver on one of its big election promises, and in mid-April it took major steps toward the legalization of cannabis by introducing a bill that outlined the end of ninety-four years of failed pot prohibition in Canada. Four years after the then leader of the third party blurted out the commitment at a rally in British Columbia, the framework for a legal system was there in vague form, even if details on taxation, distribution, packaging, and legal driving limits remained works in progress. The proposals were half-baked, but opposition to the idea was muted, particularly given the Liberals' emphasis on trying to squeeze the $7 to $10 billion black market while trying to keep pot out of the hands of kids.

As Bill Blair, the former Toronto police chief who navigated the legalization process for the government, pointed out, one in five Canadian youths were using cannabis and "the profits go to organized crime, with no regard to potency, purity or provenance. This legislation will make Canada safer."[23] Blair, the grizzled former undercover drug cop, was given the difficult task of finding the Goldilocks point where the new pot industry would become successful enough to displace the illicit producers but not so successful that consumption rates would skyrocket. "It's not the government's intent to promote the use of this drug," he said. The fact that he was open about his distaste for cannabis—even though he admitted he had never tried it—gave him a degree of credibility that might not have been offered to a more bohemian career politician with one eye on the tax revenues that would inevitably accrue. The passage of the bill, promised in time for Canada Day 2018, was one of the few things that went according to plan for the Liberal government in the Age of Trump.

By mid-April, the U.S. president had changed his tune from the soothing lullaby he had trilled during Trudeau's visit to the White House two months earlier. In Wisconsin, where he signed an executive order to reinforce protectionist Buy American procurement policies, he vowed to eliminate Canada's "very unfair" supply management system and threatened to tear up NAFTA if Ottawa refused to sign on to substantial changes. The visit was not felicitous for Canada since Wisconsin farmers offered Trump chapter and verse on Canada's protectionist rules on milk, eggs, and poultry, which slap tariffs of up to 300 per cent on imports. Changes by Canadian regulators had also cut U.S. farmers out of the market to supply ingredients used to make cheese and yogurt.

David MacNaughton, the Canadian ambassador in Washington, attempted to deflect the charge, suggesting that U.S. overproduction was to blame for financial losses to American dairy farmers. But there was no putting lipstick on the supply management bovine. The Wisconsin comments marked the first time Trump mentioned a trade violation by Canada—and for once, he was right. That visit gave Trump the excuse he needed to enact his "trade is bad" policy on NAFTA. In late April 2017, one senior member of staff in the Prime Minister's Office was startled to receive a call from his counterpart in the White House, urging Trudeau to call Trump and attempt to talk him out of ripping up NAFTA—which the prime minister proceeded to do.[24]

Bob Woodward's bombshell account of the inner workings of the Trump presidency, *Fear: Trump in the White House*, suggested that the president had called a meeting in the Oval Office and demanded that an executive order be written that would pull the U.S. out of NAFTA. The order was written up by staff secretary Rob Porter, but Woodward alleges that senior economic adviser Gary Cohn (or Porter) simply lifted it off his desk. With no list of tasks to be accomplished, Trump was prone to forgetting his own decisions, and the calculation was that the president might fail to remember how ardent he was about withdrawal.[25]

But that was not before reports in American media had emerged suggesting that Trump was about to act unilaterally, knocking a third of a cent off the loonie. Peter Navarro, the head of Trump's National Trade Council, and Robert Lighthizer, the U.S. trade representative, argued that NAFTA had decimated U.S. manufacturing. Others in the White House, like Cohn, argued that trade deficits could be positive for the United States, since they allowed Americans to buy cheaper goods from elsewhere in North America. It was a member of the pro–free trade faction that called Ottawa seeking Trudeau's assistance. "You never know how much of it is theatre, but it didn't feel that way," said the PMO staff member who had received the call.[26] The unconventional diplomatic manoeuvre proved decisive—Trump later abandoned his threat to pull out of NAFTA unilaterally, citing the arguments made by Trudeau and Mexican president Enrique Peña Nieto as pivotal. But it highlighted the difficulties of dealing with the volatile president.

The sense that the relationship was turning sour prompted Trudeau to take the unprecedented step of inviting former prime minister Brian Mulroney—a Conservative—to appear before a special cabinet committee on Canada–U.S. relations. Mulroney highlighted the importance of "access" in Washington, which ushers in influence. Without it, "you're one of two hundred in the queue," he said.[27] But he said that Canada would have to be prepared to say no in the face of a bad deal, as his government had when it suspended negotiations in 1987, after its primary objective of securing a dispute settlement mechanism was ignored. He referred to his own experience in negotiating agreements like NAFTA and the acid rain treaty, urging ministers to be patient, argue with facts not emotions, and not respond to presidential tweets. Crucially, he advised Trudeau that if a new deal was reached, he would have to "own" it, even if he was forced to make concessions in areas like supply management.

BACK ON THE HOME front, a controversy that had been bubbling for over a year threatened to boil over—the suspension of the second-highest-ranking officer in the Canadian military, Vice-Admiral Mark Norman. The whole affair suggested that it was not just in message control that the Trudeau Liberals were natural heirs to the Harper Conservatives—in the case of the vice-admiral, they proved themselves just as capable of playing the man not the puck.

Trudeau pushed for an RCMP investigation into the leak of classified cabinet discussions over the construction of a naval supply ship project that led to the police accusing Norman of breach of trust. Norman was suspended over claims that he provided allegedly secret information to a company the federal government had hired to build a supply ship for the Royal Canadian Navy. In the eyes of many observers, Norman had been guilty of nothing more than trying to ensure that the ship, the MV *Asterix*, was delivered to the navy on time and on budget—which it was. A federal judge pointed out that there was no suggestion that Norman received any personal advantage for what he was alleged to have done. Yet his life was turned upside down, after he was suspended and his home was raided by the RCMP.

The accusation was that Norman got involved in the political decision to delay approval for the building of the *Asterix* at the Chantier Davie Canada shipyard in Lévis, Quebec. Supply ships provide the life-blood of any navy—fuel, food, ammunition—and Norman had been forced to remove from service Canada's only two supply vessels because they were rusting away. In the words of one former vice-admiral, the navy had been reduced to the status of a "well-armed coast guard."[28] There could be no doubts that Norman was keen for a seaworthy replacement as soon as possible—he told the House of Commons defence committee as much in November 2014.

But shipbuilding is an intensely political activity, and when it was revealed to CBC reporter James Cudmore that the government was putting on hold the $670 million sole-source contract to Chantier Davie (awarded by the Conservatives), it provoked a backlash in Quebec.[29] CBC reported that James Irving, chief executive of the rival Irving Shipbuilding Inc., had "meddled" in the decision, sending letters to several ministers about the deal, saying that his firm could build the ship at lower cost. It was obvious the awarding of the contract had political overtones—the Davie yard was in the riding of Conservative MP Steven Blaney and was signed ahead of a general election. But the only two other yards in the running—Irving in Halifax and Seaspan in Victoria —were already toiling to build the vessels for which they had been contracted under the National Shipbuilding Strategy program.

Project Resolve, as the venture came to be known, was a gamble—it saw Davie buy a commercial container ship and convert it to the navy's specifications. But it was viewed as a viable interim solution until new supply ships could be built at other yards. That was until Irving's letter landed on the desks of four cabinet ministers—Bill Morneau, Harjit Sajjan, and two politicians from Atlantic Canada, procurement minister Judy Foote and Treasury Board president Scott Brison. At an ad-hoc cabinet committee meeting in mid-November 2015, the project was put on hold. In an email to Davie officials "from Mark" that later emerged in court records, an explanation was offered: "Most positive interpretation could be govt just unsure and asking questions; cynical view could be folks manipulating new govt to kill it. Not sure what the truth is."[30]

Cudmore's report appeared the next day and caused panic in the Prime Minister's Office and the bureaucracy. Norman noted in an email to Davie officials that they were "having kittens over references to explicit Cabinet discussions in Cudmore's article. Launching an investigation."[31] Norman's view, expressed in emails to other former colleagues, was that the delay would put defence capabilities at risk. "The blatant politics of this (and too many other similar files) is just beyond what should be reasonable," he said, as he contemplated resigning.

The leaked information served its purpose—Quebec premier Philippe Couillard called Trudeau to tell him the delay at Davie was unacceptable and was putting Quebec jobs at risk. The layoffs at Davie became the focus of questions to Trudeau from journalists, persuading him that it might be a good idea to approve the project—particularly when it emerged that there was an $89 million penalty clause in Davie's contract.

But there was a sense of outrage around the cabinet table—Brison told the RCMP that leaks prevented the new government from doing its job properly. One person with knowledge of the discussion around the government's response remarked that the chief of the defence staff, Jonathan Vance, was left with no alternative but to take a hard line. "Taking information about discussions in a Cabinet room—advising an interested, private party of things that happen in the Cabinet room and advising them on tactics and strategy to manipulate the Cabinet towards a certain result. You can't tolerate that if you're a CDS," he said. "I'm sure [Norman's] motives were to get the navy a ship they needed, but you cannot have an official subverting the process of the democratically elected officials. The cabinet must be able to deliberate in private. He appeared to take it upon himself to help a private company manipulate that process. That's why Vance did what he did. He had to."[32]

But as Brison, a seasoned political veteran who had served in Paul Martin's government, knew well, leaking was a way of life in Ottawa. For one thing, Norman wasn't in the room, or even in Ottawa, when the decision was made. As Norman's defence lawyers pointed out, "Norman appears to be the first person in Canadian history to be criminally prosecuted for a purported violation of Cabinet confidences. This, in circumstances where he was not generally a participant in any Cabinet meetings and did not leak any Cabinet documents." In fact, Norman's lawyers argued that an internal investigation by the Privy Council Office found that at least forty-two people knew about the planned cabinet committee discussion on the ship contract beforehand, and that seventy-three people knew about the outcome of the cabinet meeting about the naval supply ship after it concluded. "The PCO investigation found that there were six separate leaks related to the Ad Hoc Committee alone, including to two separate CBC reporters, Radio-Canada, and the lobbying firm FleishmanHillard," the court document said.[33]

A more experienced, less hypersensitive government would not have launched any kind of inquiry until it knew what its findings would be. Ottawa is notoriously leaky—it always has been—and the worst of the leakers are usually found in the upper echelons of the party in power. (I once wrote a story that sparked a leak investigation under the previous government that was placed under the purview of the person who had leaked the information in the first place.) But, pending the RCMP investigation, the second-highest-ranking military officer in the country was removed from office without any official explanation as to why. The RCMP working theory was that Norman provided information, including cabinet confidences, to Davie to influence decision-makers within government to adopt his preferred outcome. The Mounties staked out his house in the Ottawa suburb of Orléans, before raiding it, to attempt to prove a case that looked as threadbare as a vagabond's vest.

Norman's lawyer, Marie Henein, said in a statement that her client had "at all times served his country honourably and with the sole objective of advancing the national interest and the protection of Canada."[34] She said that Norman was "caught in the bureaucratic cross-fire," which seemed about right. When the case for the defence was filed, Henein made clear that she intended to probe the actions and motivations of Brison in particular. In court documents filed in fall 2018, Norman's lawyers alleged that Sajjan and Foote had advocated proceeding with the project but Brison intervened, at the behest of the Irving family, to persuade his colleagues to put the Davie deal on hold.[35] Brison and the Irvings denied any involvement in the Norman affair, including the idea that the company had engaged in "political meddling."[36]

The case rumbled on in court over the course of the Liberal mandate, but most who followed it, including Ontario Superior Court Justice Kevin Phillips, did not believe that the emails between Norman and the Davie officials were smoking guns. In his ruling to lift a publication ban and unseal parts of the RCMP affidavit, Phillips wrote that it appeared the vice-admiral was merely "trying to keep the contractual relationship together so that the country might get itself a badly needed supply ship."[37]

As the *Ottawa Citizen*'s David Pugliese pointed out in his exhaustive study of the affair, *Man Overboard*, the leak of secret information and cabinet confidences to trusted journalists has been part of the media strategy of every government in memory, including this one. He pointed out that portions of the 2017 budget were provided to CTV days in advance; that "senior Liberal officials" had confirmed the name of Julie Payette as governor general before the appointment was made public; and on and on. Yet because those leaks were sanctioned by government, they were not deemed to breach trust.

In early May 2019, the Public Prosecution Service of Canada (PPSC) acknowledged that it was facing a public embarrassment and dropped the single breach of trust charge against Norman. The Crown said new information had come to light, thanks to Norman's defence team, and that there was no reasonable chance of conviction. The prosecution said that Norman's actions were "inappropriate and secretive" but that no crime had been committed.

Even the defence team wouldn't talk about the nature of the new information but it appears that it came from former Conservative cabinet ministers interviewed by Henein but not the RCMP. Jason Kenney, the newly elected premier of Alberta, told the *National Post* that when he was defence minister he met Norman at a Battle of the Atlantic dinner at the Canadian War Museum in Ottawa in April 2015.

Kenney was mulling the problem of how to supply the navy with food, fuel, and ammunition after a fire aboard its last serviceable supply ship, HMCS *Protecteur*, led to its decommissioning. He said senior officials in the Department of National Defence had recommended a thirty-six-month process to upgrade the navy's supply capacity but Kenney did not want to leave it as a glorified coastguard for three years. Neither, it emerged, did Norman.

He recommended the government go with a proposal from Davie shipyard in Quebec to buy a commercial container ship and convert it. Based on Norman's recommendation, Kenney took the proposal to cabinet and was given approval to fast-track the purchase. "It turned out to be the right call because it came in on budget and on time," he said.[38]

Kenney volunteered all this information to Henein, and it's possible it tipped the balance in Norman's favour. After all, how could Norman be guilty of breach of trust if he was merely following through on a process that had cabinet approval? The fundamental principle of military discipline is that the last order is the good order until it is countermanded—and the Liberals had not issued a countermanding order.

Whatever information was handed on by the defence, the Crown decided it stood no reasonable chance of conviction and stayed the breach of trust charge. Justin Trudeau and the PPSC denied that the charge was dropped to avoid an embarrassing trial during the general election. But, as was clear from the moment the RCMP revealed its evidentiary hand two years earlier, the case was built on sand, particularly without proof that Norman had benefited personally or had any intention of wrongdoing. In the wake of the failed Mike Duffy case, it suggested that a successful prosecution in the murky world of politics, in the absence of demonstrable bribery and corruption, is an exceptionally hard task.

For Norman, the news provided palpable relief. "I'm ready to go back to work," he said, saying the experience would be "surreal" in light of the belief by so many senior government officials that he was guilty.[39]

The federal government attempted to appease Norman by saying it would pick up his legal fees—something it had previously refused to do. But neither the reinstated vice-admiral nor his intrepid lawyer would rule out a civil suit. "No person should ever walk into a courtroom and feel like they are fighting their government," said Henein.

While his reputation was battered, he could console himself with the thought of punitive damages likely coming his way, courtesy of the Canadian taxpayer.

THIS WAS AN UNSAVOURY and unwelcome distraction for a government that needed all hands on deck in the Department of National Defence as it sought to push back Donald Trump's contention that Canada had short arms and long pockets when it came to contributing to its own defence. The department was already in the midst of a furor, thanks to its own minister, Harjit Sajjan, who had dented his credibility and was under intense pressure in Parliament over his claim that he was the "architect" of Operation Medusa in Afghanistan, a land battle between NATO and the Taliban that took place in 2006. Sajjan was an intelligence officer in the Canadian reserves at the time and was praised by senior officers for his role in the battle. But he was forced to concede that he had made a mistake by describing himself as the operation's key planner. The claim did not go down well inside the Forces, where the culture disapproved of "stolen valour" claims.

The opposition parties were merciless, saying that the minister's claims were part of a wider pattern of mendacity on his part. Sajjan had raised the prospect of a "capability gap" in Canada's fighter jet fleet in order to justify the purchase of eighteen Boeing Super Hornets to supplement the aging CF-18s. Canada could not meet its NATO and NORAD commitments simultaneously, Sajjan said, ignoring the fact that it was ever thus. The commander of the air force, Lieutenant-General Mike Hood, had told a parliamentary committee he had enough planes to cope, as long as a decision on a replacement fleet was made within five years.

The real reason behind the purchase, according to the opposition, was to push off the competition to replace the existing jets beyond the next election—ending the prospect that it might be won by Lockheed Martin's F-35, a plane the prime minister had said, in his 2015 election platform, that Canada would not buy. One former chief of the defence

staff, Paul Manson, and twelve other retired senior air force command-
ers wrote to Trudeau asking the government to abandon a plan they
called "ill-advised, costly and unnecessary."[40]

A report in late 2018 by the auditor general, the late Michael Ferguson,
into the crisis facing Canada's fighter jet fleet found that the situation
was even worse than the military was letting on when it said the air
force needed the eighteen new planes. Ferguson found that the RCAF had
only three quarters of the number of technicians it needed, and only
two thirds of the pilots required. The CF-18s were bought in the early
1980s and were expected to be retired twenty years later—yet by pushing off a competition for a replacement fleet, they were now expected
to fly until 2032, by which time they'd be fifty years old. At the press
conference in November 2016, when the chief of the defence staff had
said Canada could not meet its obligations without the new Boeing
planes, he had given the impression that buying the jets would solve the
problem. But as the auditor general made clear, the problems facing
the air force were more systemic than a shortage of aircraft.[41]

The government was less transparent than it should have been, but as
Sajjan's former chief of staff, Brian Bohunicky, explained, the interim
purchase was an attempt to do better than previous ministries—Liberal
and Conservative. "Here's the biggest, completely missed story about
the armed forces and this government," he said. "The Forces risk-manage
in a sophisticated manner, and our air force is very good at getting the
most mission-ready aircraft from an inadequate fleet. . . . But essentially
it comes down to the fact that we risk-manage never being called upon
to fully deliver on both NATO and NORAD missions at the same time. The
story that's been missed is that the Liberal government said, 'That's not
good enough.' For a grown-up, G7 founding member of NATO, that's
not good enough and we're going to be more serious than that."[42] There
were good reasons the story was missed—mainly revolving around the
inability of the defence minister to communicate effectively.

Back in the House of Commons on the Operation Medusa charge,
Sajjan cut an increasingly forlorn figure, on one occasion rising to

apologize eleven times in one Question Period. A decorated war hero and an honourable man he remains, but, as he was forced to admit, the architect of Operation Medusa he was not. The scene in the House of Commons was reminiscent of a particularly graphic wildlife video of hyenas eating a wildebeest.

People who worked with Sajjan recall it as a trying time. "As soon as you start explaining a story like that in the House of Commons, you would be in more trouble. It was awful, but it would have been worse if he had done anything that justified something that simply should not have been said," Bohunicky noted.[43] Yet, despite his lack of natural political craft, Sajjan remains highly regarded by his colleagues. "He's as advertised—the real thing. Very intense, very dedicated, very, very loyal to the PM," said Bohunicky."[44]

That he retained the prime minister's confidence and was not forced to resign suggests that his loyalty and affection were reciprocated. But it may also have had much to do with the broader geopolitical background —the publication of Canada's long-awaited defence review was imminent and Trump was badgering NATO countries at a meeting of leaders in Belgium to raise their defence spending to 2 per cent of national economic output. "Two per cent is the bare minimum for confronting today's very real, very vicious threats," Trump said. "NATO members must finally contribute their fair share and meet their financial obligations."[45] Trump did not restate the U.S. commitment to the Article 5 pledge to defend any member under attack—a commitment that underpinned the NATO alliance.

Trudeau's response—that Canada did more than its fair share by stepping up when asked—sounded hollow, given that Canada barely spent 1 per cent of GDP on defence. The output versus cash contribution argument was the last refuge of free riders everywhere. A more substantive riposte came in a major policy speech from Chrystia Freeland in the House of Commons in early June, followed the next day by the results of the defence review that had been in the works since the Liberals took power. The global affairs minister signalled that her government was set to forsake flower power for hard power. The theme of the speech was that, at a time of American retrenchment, Canada was obliged to step up to preserve the multilateral world order. She was careful not to antagonize Trump, but, like other NATO leaders, she indicated that the U.S. president could no longer be relied upon. "To rely solely on the U.S. security umbrella would make us a client state—such a dependency would not be in Canada's interests," she said.[46] The speech did not even mention Trump, but it offered an eloquent alternative to a world view that eschewed international trade and leaned on nativism and anti-Muslim sentiment.

The Liberals were elected on a promise to merely "maintain current defence spending." But Freeland promised "substantial investment" in the defence review—and so it proved. The next day's defence review revealed a $62.3 billion increase in spending over the subsequent two decades—ostensibly to fully fund the fifteen warships and eighty-eight new fighter jets that were already planned. The "Strong, Secure, Engaged" policy moved the needle on defence spending to around 1.4 per cent of GDP, as the government promised to buy more equipment and increase the size of the regular force by 3,500 troops to 71,500. The plan was to increase annual defence spending from around $19 billion in 2017–18 to $33.4 billion a decade later. It was more money than any government—Liberal or Conservative—had committed in recent years.

As David Perry, senior analyst at the Canadian Global Affairs Institute, noted, the government had committed to spending serious amounts of new money, "if it all gets delivered as promised." But the spending promised in previous defence reviews had failed to materialize when other priorities emerged, and Perry expressed himself "very dubious" about the defence department's ability to spend the money it already had, never mind an extra $47.2 billion in capital spending. His suspicions were vindicated, at least in year one of the brave new world—more than one third of the amount allocated for capital spending in 2017–18 went unspent and was "re-profiled" for spending in future years.[47]

The key to the defence review will be its implementation. But the Liberals deserve credit for a substantive commitment that went far beyond the election promise to maintain defence spending levels at status quo levels—a commitment that effectively meant declining capability. The fact that the Conservatives didn't want to talk about it suggested that the review had found favour with right-of-centre voters. One of its major accomplishments was that it had the uniforms and civilians who inhabit the "two towers" at defence headquarters in Ottawa singing from the same hymn sheet—a rare occurrence in recent years. "Very early on, the instructions to the generals and assistance deputy ministers from [Chief of the Defence Staff Jonathan] Vance and [Deputy Minister John] Forster was that 'If you're not working on something in the Strong, Secure and Engaged book, you're working on the wrong stuff," said Bohunicky, who as Sajjan's chief of staff was involved in providing the political input.[48]

The commitment to spend an extra $62 billion was not made in direct response to Trump. Work on the details was completed before Trump was even elected. "But he made it more important," said Bohunicky. "He made the case easier to make that we needed to be much more serious than our predecessors about funding the armed forces and saying to Canadians, 'We do ask our armed forces to do a lot domestically and internationally, and we have to be upfront about what it really costs. We have an ambitious view of Canada's place in the world. We ask a lot and we envision asking a lot more in the way we see the world unfolding in the years ahead. So all of that was made more important by the way Trump destabilized the dynamics of geopolitics."[49]

As noted earlier, the defence review went in and out of cabinet committees, lending the impression that there was entrenched opposition to committing so much money to defence. Those involved in the process said there was plenty of debate, with more left-leaning ministers arguing that the money could have been diverted to eradicating poverty or solving drinking-water problems in First Nations communities. But the winning view was that it was not a case of either/or.

One of the reasons that the defence proposal won the day was that it was patently clear to all involved that existing commitments to build fifteen new ships and buy a new fleet of fighter jets were drastically underfunded. "In the past, the costing exercises weren't rigorous but there's always political pressure to put a price tag on projects early—for example, the Harper government put a number on the cost of surface combatants for fifteen ships," said Bohunicky. "But it quickly became obvious that their guess at the cost was going to be nowhere near enough. They switched to language that said we're going to build up to fifteen ships, which could mean three. Turns out what they had set aside ultimately was enough for seven or eight ships, so we had to make the case for why Canada needs fifteen ships. There was a very vigorous exercise done to determine what would be needed. They did that modelling in a far more sophisticated way than Defence ever had before and also brought in outside expertise to validate their work."[50]

The argument was persuasive enough for Morneau at Finance to agree to increase the capital budget from $20 billion to $55 to $60 billion. On fighter jets, the Harper government had set aside $9 billion for a fleet of sixty-five new planes. "Nine billion dollars wouldn't even have bought sixty-five planes and sixty-five planes would not meet the needs of the new policy—or the old one for that matter—so we had to do the policy work to explain why eighty-eight planes were needed and what the full cost would be," said Bohunicky.[51]

The "capability gap" that warranted the $6.6 billion interim purchase of eighteen Boeing Super Hornets got barely a mention in the review, as the document said that the government continued "to explore the potential acquisition." But that saga turned from comedy to farce when relations between Canada and Boeing ruptured, after the U.S. giant launched an unfair trade complaint against Bombardier Aerospace of Montreal. The U.S. commerce department subsequently found that Bombardier had used federal government and Quebec subsidies to offer its new passenger jet at below cost. "We won't do business with a company that is trying to sue us and put our aerospace workers out of business," Trudeau said. A panel of adjudicators with the U.S. International Trade Commission reversed the commerce department's decision, but by then the Canadian government had decided to abandon the Boeing purchase and instead buy eighteen vintage F-18s from the Australian government for $500 million.

Freeland's speech and the defence review suggested that Trudeau saw a leadership role that lived up to the (so far empty) boast he had made at the UN General Assembly in 2016: "We're Canada and we're here to help." But the focus on managing the new U.S. administration reduced the capacity to offer an independent role in the world. As Roland Paris noted, Canada had offered a leadership role in the past—be it Louis St. Laurent's role in the creation of NATO; Lester Pearson's help in the development of peacekeeping; Pierre Trudeau's attempts at dialogue between the developed and developing worlds; Brian Mulroney's campaign against South African apartheid; the efforts of Jean Chrétien's foreign minister, Lloyd Axworthy, to achieve a ban on anti-personnel landmines; or even Stephen Harper's global initiative on maternal, newborn, and child health.[52] Yet all of Canada's foreign policy energy was being devoted toward trying to decipher Donald Trump—a task that would have taxed students of Byzantium, not to mention all the psychologists of Vienna. The kind of "strategic and energetic foreign policy beyond North America" called for by Paris and others was simply not an option in mid-2017.

TEN

TEFLON PROPHET IN TROUBLE

LIBERAL POLLING NUMBERS at the mid-point in the mandate remained at, or even above, where they were on election day, but after five hundred days in office, the sense that the honeymoon was over was inescapable. Andrew Scheer was elected Conservative leader in late May 2017; Jagmeet Singh won the NDP leadership in early October of that year. Three in four Canadians would not have been able to pick either one out of a police lineup, while Trudeau had name recognition more traditionally the preserve of rock stars and hockey players. But the polls offered false comfort.

Scheer, in particular, presented a conundrum for the Liberals. For a couple of months, it had looked like Quebec libertarian Maxime Bernier would win the Conservative crown. Bernier himself thought so and made the mistake of holding his victory lap the night before the vote, telling reporters he'd give a more substantive speech the next night (after he won). In the end, he was pipped by the former Speaker of the House of Commons.

Scheer's campaign had been cautious, intent on offering little that was bold or new to avoid offence (and thus pick up second-place support so crucial in a ranked ballot system). The strategy had worked, and it made it hard for the Liberals to present him as scary. Yes, he was openly "pro-life," but like Stephen Harper before him, he promised he would not introduce legislation on abortion. Just minutes after Scheer's victory at a convention hall in suburban Toronto, Liberal MP Adam Vaughan was suggesting that it marked a return of the "old Reform Party." But Scheer neither looked nor sounded like the kind of reactionary dinosaur Vaughan was trying to conjure up.

At thirty-eight, Scheer could afford to bide his time. If he could hold Trudeau to a minority government in 2019, he would be well positioned to move in for the kill four years later—at the grand old age of forty-four. He was at the helm of a party that had proved it could survive defeats, was flush with cash, and, by and large, felt pretty good about itself—which was why a continuity candidate (Scheer) won, and the change candidate (Bernier) did not. With an experienced team around him, Scheer's job was to build a serious, credible alternative to the Liberals and then wait patiently until voters decided to hurl Trudeau by the lapels from the Prime Minister's Office. History was on his side—there have been twenty-two Conservative Party leaders since Confederation (including Scheer) and thirteen of them served as prime minister.

The problems for Trudeau, quite apart from Trump, were mounting. The government was increasingly open to the charge that it was governing by optics and that it had put people in place in ministries because they ticked identity boxes rather than because they had the ability to run complicated government departments. A prime example was the attempt by the government's House leader, Bardish Chagger, a thirty-seven-year-old rookie, to change the procedures in the House of Commons without securing support from the opposition parties first. As far back as the eighteenth century, British prime minister Henry Pelham noted that the legislative branch in the Westminster system is a "great unwieldy body that requires great art and some cordials to keep it loyal."[1] Uniting all your political opponents in a coalition against you is asking for trouble, but that's precisely what Chagger did by proposing changes to the way the House operated, including ending Friday sittings and restricting the ability of the opposition to filibuster bills. The opposition parties maintained that the standing orders could only be amended by consensus. As Murray Rankin, the NDP's House leader, put it, "It's not always the case that the Conservatives and NDP are holding hands on issues of such importance. But we are united on this one."[2]

The Liberals had already been forced to climb down the previous May, when they attempted to ride roughshod over established parliamentary tradition in the motion that gave birth to the War of Trudeau's Elbow on the floor of the House. That highlighted the prime minister's personal frustration and impatience at the failure of his opponents to acknowledge the brilliance of his legislative program. Yet, despite that chastening experience, Chagger ploughed on with her attempted power grab, all the while maintaining that the proposals merely constituted a "discussion paper." Some of the ideas were sound—nothing ever happens in the House on a Friday, so why not do away with those sittings? Introducing U.K.-style time allocation would have been a better use of everyone's time than filibustering, where MPs bring their inflatable travel pillows into the House and attempt to snooze through hundreds of meaningless votes. But there was a principle at stake for the opposition parties. A five-day filibuster in April prompted a rethink, as the government scuttled to find a way to introduce the most modest changes in the discussion paper, as part of its electoral promise to "make Parliament relevant again."

The reason the government was so determined to gain control over parliamentary procedure—and risk the charge of riding roughshod over time-honoured democratic processes—was that its legislative agenda was moving at the pace of coastal erosion. A key contention in *At the Centre of Government*, an account of the limits of power in Canadian democracy by former Harper chief of staff Ian Brodie, is that Parliament matters. "If Parliament is truly dead, a majority government will simply ram its legislation through Parliament," he said.[3] Yet by his calculation, governments have received royal assent on only 60 per cent of the legislation introduced into the House over the last twenty years (excluding appropriation bills, which always pass). The worrying thing for the Liberals was that their conversion rate was significantly lower. A rough calculation suggests that in the first session of the forty-second

Parliament (to the end of June 2018), the Trudeau government had introduced eighty-two bills, of which forty-seven had passed. Excluding the fifteen appropriation bills that simply supply money to keep government ticking over, that success rate was just 39 per cent.[4] Yet, despite their desire to win the battle for time, the Liberals were forced to acknowledge the accuracy of Brodie's conclusion: "Parliament seems to be alive."[5] In the end, a watered-down version of the plan was agreed to. But the government had learned the hard way that the rules governing Canada's most precious of institutions could only be amended by consensus, not parliamentary cosh.

Butts blamed the slow progress of the legislative agenda on opposition parties that were prepared to throw into the works any spanner they could find. "You always want to get more passed than less. In general, we thought we could get things done more cooperatively than we were able to. That was the fundamental misjudgement we had around electoral reform—that neither one of the opposition parties was interested in doing anything other than embarrassing us, especially the Tories," he said.[6] People with more Parliament Hill experience than Butts would point out it was ever thus and that the role of the opposition is to find fault and turn public opinion toward its way of thinking.

But the attempt to change House procedures unilaterally was instructive because it illustrated the growing pains of the party in power—and its leader. As one MP noted, naiveté in yielding control of committees and the creation of an unwieldy, non-partisan Senate had crippled efforts to drive the agenda. The MP offered up a homespun analogy to the decision to cut loose the Liberal caucus in the Senate. "I was playing hockey and on a power play. I was in front of the net and there was a big defenceman cranking me across the back to move me. I thought, 'That puck's going down low, and when he turns, I'm loading one up and smashing him on the side of the head.' The puck comes down low and I did it, right across the side of the head. But then he turned around, grabbed me and mopped the ice with me. I hadn't thought it through. . . . That's sort of what happened with the Senate."[7]

After five hundred days, the record of achievement was decidedly mixed.[8] Among the promises broken already were some whoppers —keeping deficits to $10 billion a year for three years, and electoral reform. And just before Parliament rose, Trudeau failed to deliver on another pledge clearly stated in the campaign literature—that a revamp of the Access to Information Act would apply to the offices of the prime minister and cabinet ministers. The promise to restore trust in Canada's democracy meant being open with information by default, the Liberals committed. But when the revised act was unveiled by Treasury Board president Scott Brison, it fell well short of the standards of transparency that were promised. Instead of being open to access requests, the offices in question would proactively disclose travel and hospitality expenses, Question Period binders, and ministerial briefing notes.

Brison defended the change as being consistent with an open-by-default policy. "Canadians should not have to go through a request-based system to get information that can be proactively disclosed," he argued.[9] More realistically, it was consistent with the realization by all governments, at all times, that if people don't know what you are doing, they don't know what you are doing wrong. As one reporter remarked caustically at the press conference to reveal the changes, under the new legislation, citizens would not be able to request information on what went on behind the scenes to arrive at the decision not to include the PMO or ministerial offices in access requests.

People with knowledge of that decision-making process blame the "third-party promise" for being made in the first place, with no expectation it would have to be enacted. "It would have driven communications underground—it would have inevitably driven people onto unsecure personal networks and we would have spent massive amounts of time going through information and redacting it," said one insider. "We wanted to go further, but there are a great number of impediments in the public service. They want a way to handle these things quickly and with the minimal amount of work on their end. Media requests are only around 15 per cent of the overall load—most are business people looking for competitive information." [10]

There were some positive changes—giving the information commissioner the power to order that government information be released, for example. But it was clear that even the information that would be proactively disclosed would be sanitized before release. A system administered by bureaucrats, zealous in their protection of the public's right to remain ignorant, would continue uninterrupted. [11] Under the new rules, citizens would continue to have reasonable requests for information returned by the bureaucracy with every single word blacked out. The government that had promised to be "open and transparent"—in contrast to its predecessor—was finding it politically profitable to live in the shade of ambiguity. As the information commissioner, Suzanne Legault, had put it in her 2017 annual review, there was a "shadow of disinterest on behalf of the government" in being transparent and the Act was failing in its policy objective to foster accountability and trust. [12]

The waters were rising around the government, and there were too many holes in the dyke for them to be patched properly. And as summer approached, the trickle of troubles was about to turn into a torrent. In at least one case, the Liberals could offer the defence of *force majeure*— the defeat of Christy Clark's Liberals in British Columbia and the formation of an NDP–Green coalition pact sealed on shared opposition to the Kinder Morgan pipeline. NDP leader John Horgan and Green Party leader Andrew Weaver announced they had negotiated a deal that would see an NDP minority survive for a four-year term—an alliance that would give the new government a single-seat margin over the Liberals. "This issue of Kinder Morgan is one that was critical to us," explained Weaver. Horgan had said his party would use every tool available to scuttle the project. [13]

Constitutional experts suggested the provincial and municipal governments opposed to the pipeline could not block an interprovincial project—and that Trudeau and Alberta premier Rachel Notley said Trans Mountain would not be affected by any change of government in

B.C. "This is a foundational principle that binds our country together," said Notley.[14] But the NDP threatened to create uncertainty by forcing Ottawa to defend the theory in court. And Weaver said the two parties were working with First Nations who complained they were not properly consulted.[15] That unpredictability would chew up time and money and have significant repercussions for Ottawa's push for a pipeline to salt water. "It could be a strategy of death by a thousand delays," said Ted Morton, a former Alberta cabinet minister.[16]

During a meeting in Ottawa in late July, both Horgan and Trudeau strained not to mention the pipeline and concentrate on issues they agreed upon, like the fight against opioids, wildfires, and the softwood lumber dispute. But the tension was palpable, especially when Horgan knocked a glass of water off his podium at the joint press conference and deadpanned, "Spills can happen anywhere." Trudeau was quick to chime in, "We'll clear it up," to which the NDP premier quipped, "It's a federal responsibility." It was clear already that there was not much room for compromise.

Just as the Liberals started to hit the barbecue circuit in early July, a story broke that epitomized the perception by many that the government had lurched too far leftward. Robert Fife of the *Globe and Mail* wrote that the government was poised to offer an apology and a $10 million compensation package to former child soldier Omar Khadr for abuses he suffered while detained in a U.S. military prison at Guantanamo Bay, Cuba. It was a decision that made Conservatives incandescent and many Liberals uncomfortable. In an interview with Gerald Butts, it emerged that Fife's story was as much news to the prime minister and his advisers as it was to the rest of the country. "We found out about it during a State dinner in Dublin when the story broke. . . . We were supposed to be brought into the loop two weeks later," Butts said. "But we wouldn't have stopped it. The basic facts are the government of Canada allowed a Canadian citizen to be tortured in Guantanamo."[17] The Supreme Court had ruled in 2010 that federal officials who participated in the U.S. interrogations of Khadr had violated his rights under the Charter and deprived him of fundamental principles of justice.

The apology and compensation was similar to the package received by Syrian-born Canadian Maher Arar after a 2006 judicial inquiry found Canadian officials complicit in his detention in Syria. But Arar was completely innocent. Khadr was guilty, at the very least, of supporting terrorism and, at worst, of killing one American soldier and wounding another. The fifteen-year-old was badly wounded in an exchange of fire with U.S. troops in a firefight in Afghanistan in 2002, where he was accused of throwing a grenade that killed U.S. army medic Christopher Speer.

In the wake of the Supreme Court ruling, it was clear that the Crown was on the hook. But Trudeau made a decision to apologize and compensate, in contrast to his predecessor, who would have litigated until forced to concede. In fact, in the mandate letter given to his justice minister, Jody Wilson-Raybould, Trudeau had expressly asked her to "end appeals or positions not consistent with our commitments, the Charter or our values."[18]

Ralph Goodale, the public safety minister, tried to point the finger of blame in Harper's direction, saying it was his fault for not settling the case. But Harper broke cover for the first time since the election and fired back. "The decision to enter into this deal is theirs, and theirs alone, and it is simply wrong. Canadians deserve better than this," he said on Twitter. Many Canadians agreed with him. There was considerable sympathy toward the efforts of Speer's wife, Tabitha, and Layne Morris, the soldier who was partly blinded by the grenade allegedly hurled by Khadr, when they filed an injunction to prevent Ottawa from paying the former child soldier. Ultimately, it proved unsuccessful.

But the anger caused by the sense that Trudeau had caved in to blackmail from a member of the "first family of terror," as politician Bob Runciman once christened the Khadrs, was hotter than July. Liberals pointed out that Trudeau should not be held responsible for the abuses of previous Canadian governments; Trudeau himself said the Charter protects all Canadians, "there is no picking and choosing." He said he understood why people were angry but insisted a court case would have ended up costing millions of dollars more. "The measure of a society —a just society—is not whether we stand up for people's rights when it is easy or popular to do so but whether we recognize rights when it is difficult, when it is unpopular," he intoned.[19] The deal with Khadr was certainly that—opinion polls suggested that 71 per cent opposed it.

Seven months after the Khadr news broke, the prime minister was holding a town hall in Edmonton when veteran Brock Blaszczyk stood to ask him a question—his prosthetic leg and medals in clear view. Blaszczyk was a corporal in the Princess Patricia's Canadian Light Infantry when he lost a leg to a roadside bomb in Afghanistan in 2010. He wondered how he was not eligible for the lifetime pension option the government had introduced when it had been able to find millions of dollars for Khadr. He was particularly upset by the Liberal election platform that promised, "No veteran will be forced to fight their own government for the support and compensation they have earned," prompting him to ask, "What veterans are you talking about—those fighting for the freedoms and values you so proudly boast about, or those fighting against?"

Trudeau's reply was as tone deaf as any he has ever given. The government was fighting veterans groups in court, he said, "because they're asking for more than we're able to give right now."[20] The crowd started booing and, for once, the Teflon Prophet was in trouble. The Khadr settlement may have been the logical thing to do from a technical and legal point of view. But politically, it didn't sit well with many people, including many Liberal voters. They could have lived with an apology, but not with the financial settlement. In the court of public opinion, Trudeau got it wrong. The prime minister may not have known about the deal when it was proposed, but he signed off on it—it was a clear choice. It was also a gift to the Conservatives and their argument that, under the Liberals, the pendulum of justice rewarded the perpetrators and penalized the victims.

AUGUST TENDS TO BE the Sunday of summer months—nothing much ever happens in Canadian federal politics. But in the heat of summer 2017, Trudeau took the opportunity of a lull in hostilities to shuffle his cabinet and split up the underperforming Indigenous and Northern Affairs ministry.[21] The "agenda and results" unit inside the Privy Council Office had evaluated every major department as part of a deliverology report card, and two departments in particular did not fare well— Democratic Reform and Indigenous Affairs.

As the auditor general, Michael Ferguson, noted in a series of reports, Indigenous Affairs had a long history of inaction and indifference. "There is now more than a decade's worth of audits showing that programs have failed to effectively serve Canada's Indigenous people," he wrote in November 2016. "Until a problem solving mindset is brought to these issues to develop solutions built around people, instead of defaulting to litigation, arguments about money and process roadblocks, this country will continue to squander the potential and lives of much of its Indigenous population."[22] A senior member of Trudeau's team was more succinct: "There's too much poison in the system."[23]

Trudeau acted by splitting Indigenous and Northern Affairs into two: Indigenous Services, under former health minister Jane Philpott, would oversee the delivery of services like water, housing, and welfare, while the incumbent minister, Carolyn Bennett, was told to concentrate on negotiating land claims and treaty rights as minister of Crown–Indigenous Relations and Northern Affairs. Trudeau insisted that his government was moving forward on a "true nation-to-nation relationship," in which the 1876 Indian Act that governs most aspects of Indigenous life would be superseded by new governance arrangements. Philpott assumed responsibility on the day the United Nations Committee on the Elimination of Racial Discrimination took the federal government to task for underfunding children's and family services.

Despite the rhetoric from the government, there had been plenty of false dawns in the past—in fact the recommendation to dissolve Indigenous and Northern Affairs was made by the Royal Commission on Aboriginal Peoples twenty-one years earlier (one of 440 suggested changes, including the creation of an Indigenous parliament). But as the then national chief of the Assembly of First Nations, Phil Fontaine, said in 2000, the promises made by the government of Canada represented the potential for major steps, but the commitments were not fully implemented.

The Liberals pointed out that $11.8 billion in new spending had been pledged in previous budgets. But within months of assuming her new role, Philpott made the astute move of holding a press conference to let the world know precisely how bad things were with Indigenous service delivery. The former family physician detailed the immensity of the problem she was trying to solve—a graduation rate around half the rate of other Canadians, life expectancy fifteen years shorter, vastly higher rates of tuberculosis, soaring rates of incarceration and foster care. Neither did she put a political gloss on areas targeted by the prime minister—while forty boil water advisories had been lifted, another twenty-six had been added. "It doesn't help for anyone to be in denial," she said.[24]

The aim of the press conference was to lower expectations in order to set the new department up for some wins in the future—based on the acknowledgement that the government couldn't fluff the boil water advisory numbers. John Brodhead, a Queen's Park veteran who was chief of staff to the ministers of infrastructure and then Indigenous services, said the commitment to end drinking water advisories on reserves by 2021 would act as an incentive. "It was a bold commitment," he said, "and it's gone just far enough that the public service and communities have rallied around it and [the Department of] Finance has put money into it, and it's getting done. It would have been 2030 at the earliest without that commitment."[25]

Still, three years after Trudeau had responded to the report of the Truth and Reconciliation Commission by promising to implement all of its calls to action, it was clear that not much had been achieved. Seventy-six of those calls fell under federal jurisdiction, but only three had been concluded by the start of 2018 and three others were close to being done. There was little progress in many of the others by the summer of that year—only nineteen were adjudged by the government to be "fully underway." The Liberals were all in on the Indigenous file and had to move the goalposts down the field. Yet after three years, and billions of spending allocated to Indigenous issues, there was not much to show for it.

A House of Commons committee meeting in October 2018 illustrated just how badly governments of all stripes have let down Indigenous and non-Indigenous Canadians. The Public Accounts Committee was meeting to discuss the auditor general's spring report, which had been highly critical of training programs for Indigenous Canadians that had cost the taxpayer $2.7 billion over the previous eight years. Ferguson's office had labelled the shortcomings of Employment and Social Development Canada (ESDC) an "incomprehensible failure." ESDC does not provide services such as occupational skills training, employment counselling, and wages subsidies to employers directly to clients, but instead funds Indigenous "agreement holders" to deliver training. The department is required to monitor the use of funds, which in 2017–18 totalled $342 million. But Ferguson's office found that ESDC did not collect the data or define performance indicators to demonstrate whether objectives of getting Indigenous people into stable employment was working.

The lead public servant on the file, Graham Flack, was asked by MPs why the bureaucracy was relying on data that was clearly out of date to provide services that could not be proven to be effective. Flack said there had been two serious attempts by officials to update the formula used—in 2003 and 2014. But he explained that since funding levels had not grown, attempts at reform had been resisted by the government's Indigenous partners because adjustment would see some of them lose funding. At the same time, he noted that governments were reluctant to risk the political fallout from making changes that would result in a number of recipients deprived of funding. Flack pointed out that in such a scenario there is only one solution—to allocate new funding. In this case, $99.4 million was allocated in budget 2018. "In my experience, that is what it takes to get movement," he said.[26]

So, in summary, the Canadian government had spent billions of dollars on Indigenous employment training but had no real idea on whether it was working. In fact, the only reliable measure of the program's effectiveness—the unemployment rate—suggested that it was not. In 2007, the rate for Indigenous Canadians was just under 11 per cent, nearly double the rate for the rest of the population. A decade later, it was still 11 per cent. Yet, rather than go back to the drawing board, the solution chosen by the men of systems was to throw another $100 million at the problem. It was an instructive example of budget creep and systemic failure.

LATE SUMMER 2017 WAS dominated by two other issues—the flood of asylum seekers streaming across the Canada–U.S. border, and more details on the Liberals' plans to change the taxation rules for small businesses. Neither of them bolstered support for the government.

The first was a flood of mainly Haitians, who had been living in the United States but were concerned about deportation home to Haiti after Trump was elected and promised to revoke their temporary protected status. Instead of risking deportation, many of the tired, the poor, and the huddled masses fled to Canada—a flow the Conservatives blamed on the "false hope" raised by Trudeau's tweet promising migrants would be welcome in Canada.

The idea that people were claiming they were refugees from the United States was ridiculous—and such claims should have been impossible to make. Canada and the U.S. had signed the Safe Third Country Agreement, which meant refugees were obliged to claim asylum at the first official point of entry. If they had landed in the U.S. first and then claimed asylum at an official port of entry in Canada, the law called for them to be sent back, unless they had a blood relative here or were an unaccompanied minor. But there was a loophole in the agreement—it didn't apply if refugees crossed at unguarded border points.

Over the course of the summer, thirteen thousand migrants traversed the border illegally, many at a crossing at Roxham Road, near Saint Bernard-de-Lacolle in Quebec, whereupon they promptly gave themselves up and claimed social assistance, education, health services, emergency housing, and legal aid under the Charter. The Conservatives were aware of the loophole and had tried to close it, but the Americans were not interested, viewing it as an avenue for illegal aliens to deport themselves. The then immigration minister, Jason Kenney, had raised it with his Homeland Security counterpart, Janet Napolitano, who had said it was a "non-starter" because immigration issues could not be raised in Washington without comprehensive reform. "I think that was disingenuous," Kenney said later.[27]

Trudeau tried to reassure Canadians that they could continue to have confidence in the country's immigration system and that the rules were being enforced. But there was no disguising the fact that the system was being gamed—placing huge strains on federal, provincial, and municipal bureaucracies to respond with housing, health care, and screening. The government sent MPs Pablo Rodriguez and Emmanuel Dubourg to speak to Latino and Haitian communities in the U.S., pointing out that claiming asylum in Canada was not a free ticket—and that half of all claims in 2016 were rejected. That was true, but as the migrants were aware, after a health and security screening, they were able to claim a range of social benefits and get a work permit. If their claim was rejected, they could appeal to the Refugee Appeal Division of the Immigration and Refugee Board or ask the Federal Court to review the decision. With a backlog running into the tens of thousands, this was a process that could take years.

It was no surprise that the migrants kept on coming. The majority of new migrants in the spring of 2018 were coming from Nigeria, after obtaining visas to visit the United States. In late May 2018, the U.S. Department of Homeland Security acknowledged it was reviewing a

Canadian proposal to amend the agreement, but it was clear that Trump's hostile attitude toward immigrants—he referred to the countries many of them came from as "shitholes"—was not likely to result in actions that increased their number in the U.S. The opposition called for the entire border to be designated a technical point of entry, something the government deemed unworkable because it would incentivize people to cross at remote locations and evade detection from the RCMP.

The real reason for the government's negative response was that it was not keen to add another log to the fire on which Trump was nursing his wrath to keep it warm. So rather than raise another irritant, migrants continued to cross at Roxham Road, passing a sign that read: "It is illegal to cross the border here—you will be arrested and detained if you cross here." Frustration at the government's inability to stem the flow created discontent in Quebec, as its services were stretched by the new intake of migrants. By June 2018, the numbers had dipped to just 1,263 crossing, but that was still more than enough to outpace the budgeted processing capacity. An independent review of the system by Neil Yeates, a former deputy minister of citizenship and immigration, said the system was at a crossroads, ill-equipped to deal with the large backlog that was building.

Andrew Scheer's Conservatives advocated a harder line and could point to some success on the refugee file during Harper's time in office. Reforms between 2010 and 2012 were aimed at making sure bona fide claimants were approved more quickly and failed claimants removed judiciously. The goal was a system that was "fast, fair and final." Visas were imposed on Mexicans and Czechs because of concerns over bogus claims, and structural changes were introduced to make the system more flexible. Crucially, there was an increase in operating funding aimed at facilitating a system that handled 22,500 claims annually. The changes saw the number of refugee claims fall to 10,227 in 2013, from 25,783 in 2010 (prior to the reforms). By 2017, the intake had soared to 47,425. The backlog was also reduced because failed claimants were actually removed—in 2012–13, 14,490 failed claimants were returned to their country of origin; by 2016–17, that number was just 3,892.[28] The result was a refugee population that "significantly exceeds the funding capacity," according to Yeates. He talked about the "failure of finality" in the appeals process that acted as a "pull" factor in attracting migrants. "Final is a distant goal," he said.[29] While Ahmed Hussen, the immigration minister, was correct in saying that provision of due process to asylum claimants was not a choice, "it's the law," the sense among many Canadians, particularly in Quebec, was that due process should not be an indefinite process.

The flow of migrants did not constitute a "crisis," despite Conservative claims to the contrary. But it was a significant blow to the government's credibility and future prospects. As Stephen Harper pointed out in his book *Right Here, Right Now*, the discontent over immigrants and refugees felt elsewhere in the world had not appeared in Canada because immigration policy was rooted in uniting the aspirations of new arrivals with those of citizens. "Make immigration legal, secure and, in the main, economically driven, and it will have high levels of public confidence," he wrote.[30] But the consensus on mass immigration was showing signs of stress, as the link between the aspirations of new arrivals and citizens became more tenuous—in particular, over the influx of economic migrants gaming the system at the border.[31]

BUT EVEN THE ASYLUM issue didn't shake the government's popularity like the reforms to small business taxation, which emerged as a textbook case of how not to raise taxes. The measures were released in July with more of a whimper than a bang, as a consultation paper aimed at ensuring there were no ongoing tax advantages for those whom Finance Minister Bill Morneau called the "privileged few." The seventy-five-day consultation period was set to end on October 2. But by early September, opposition to the sweeping changes to taxation rules for small businesses was hardening and Liberal MPs across the country were hearing all about it. One person involved in the process noted that the biggest mistake was launching the measures in the dead of summer. "If we'd done it in September, it may have been more of a thing in the House, but we would have had the entire apparatus ready to respond. One of the biggest issues was we launched it on July 17, Morneau went on the road to talk about it for a week—and no one cared—then he went off on vacation for three weeks. Then the slow bubble started to rise," he said.[32]

The draft legislation was aimed at restricting the way business owners, including professionals like doctors, could "sprinkle" their income to family members to reduce the total amount of tax the family paid. Another change was intended to limit a business owner's ability to convert income into capital gains. A third was aimed at restricting the use of private corporations as vehicles to make passive investments. Under the proposal, passive investments would be taxed at the regular income tax rate, not the 10.5 per cent small business deduction rate.

MPs heading to the Liberal caucus retreat in Kelowna, B.C., in early September relayed the message that the outrage against the reforms was real, and that the party could see its donations dry up. The retreat was unusual for the sheer number of lobbyists in attendance, like the Canadian Medical Association, seeking to persuade the government to change tack. "The opposition went after our caucus members, particularly on the fundraising side—most of them didn't give a shit about the public policy, rather it was about their best fundraisers being lawyers and small businessmen and doctors and dentists," said one insider. "We heard a lot of 'I'm going to lose the next election over this.'"[33]

The "squeeze the wealthy" narrative appealed to the PMO, but in the constituencies, Liberal MPs were getting it in the ear. "If they're wondering why we're not doing as well in fundraising, it's the small business tax issue that's responsible," said one MP. "A constituent said to me, 'When you see Justin and he goes to a Laurier Club reception, the ones who pay $1,500, look around and ask him to count how many of the Indigenous community are there, how many women are there in their own right, and how many men under forty are there.' Good question. There wasn't one caucus where this wasn't raised."[34]

Morneau, facing his first real political controversy, and Trudeau said they would make "no apologies" for the plan, which they claimed was intended to forestall the emergence of a two-tier tax system—one for incorporated people and one for everyone else. But to many it looked like an attack on enterprise and aspiration. The government had already upset the small business community by promising higher payroll levies to expand the Canada Pension Plan and by reneging on the promise to lower the corporate tax rate to 9 per cent.

The vacuum of hard information during the consultation period allowed the opponents of the changes to claim the tax dragnet could drive modest-earning small business owners to the wall, including convenience store owners and farmers, even though the finance department said the policy was targeted at the "1 per cent"—the highest of high earners. The government is "threatening to kill family farms," said Conservative MP Mark Strahl, when Parliament resumed.[35] One Conservative MP said it was all she was hearing about in her constituency. "It took us [the Harper government] ten years to get this tone-deaf," she said.[36]

The finance department had been trying for years to stop the explosion of professionals incorporating in order to shield income from tax. The proposal had been raised twice with the late Jim Flaherty, the former Conservative finance minister, and was twice rebuffed. Small businesses were a key Conservative constituency and Flaherty wasn't about to burn votes. It emerged in the Liberal proposals that Trudeau did not consider entrepreneurs to be part of his base. The incoming government had proven more receptive to the finance department's suggestion to impose the tax, especially once it became clear that the changes could raise as much as $3 billion by taxing the "privileged few." Trudeau had raised the top rate of income tax to 33 per cent the previous year, and many entrepreneurs had moved their wealth into private corporations. This was an attempt to follow the money.

Opponents pointed out that the passive investment provisions were important incentives to encourage more people to set up and grow businesses, allowing business owners to save for their retirement and build a cushion for rough business conditions. Jennifer Chan, a forty-four-year-old physician from Winnipeg, was not the type of "fat cat" the government had in mind when it unveiled the policy, but she emerged as the public face of opposition to the tax changes. Chan worked in the most economically disadvantaged postal code in Canada and said she resented the "tax cheat" label. "I just had my 2004 Subaru towed to the garage. We are very fortunate but we're not fat cats and I don't feel like I am cheating the system," she asserted.[37] In particular, she said she felt the changes would hit female doctors, who saved for maternity leave using passive investments.

Despite the pushback, Trudeau and Morneau embraced the "class war" rhetoric with enthusiasm—much to the chagrin of a number of Liberal MPs. "The first press conference Bill did, he softened his position," said one veteran MP. "Then Gerry Butts talked to him. That ended that—he came out harder. I said 'fuck this'—you're going the wrong way. We really missed an opportunity, partly due to Justin's inexperience. Justin shouldn't have gotten involved at all. You have cabinet ministers so if things go south, you can put them on the backbench. Justin shouldn't have been out there—he shouldn't even have been in the discussion."[38]

But he was.

It has been a curious aspect of Trudeau's time in office that he inserts himself into every crisis—as if he can't bear being out of the spotlight. A charitable interpretation is that he feels the need to support embattled colleagues—as he did in fall 2018, when he rushed back from the United Nations General Assembly in New York to field questions in Parliament about the transfer of child murderer Terri-Lynne McClintic to an Indigenous healing lodge. Ralph Goodale, the public safety minister, had been under fire for describing McClintic's horrific murder of eight-year-old Tori Stafford as "bad practices." But by making himself the public face of the decision, Trudeau also made himself the figure of public derision. It was certainly not the way previous prime ministers, like Jean Chrétien or Brian Mulroney, would have handled things. Derek Burney, who was Mulroney's chief of staff, said the most important lesson he learned in the Prime Minister's Office was "time, focus, message." "PMO ran like a fire-house in those days—doing everything. If a minister got into a problem, PMO ran over to try to fix it. My first task was to say to guys in the PMO: 'We are not responsible for all the problems in the government,'" he declared.[39] But Trudeau was not Chrétien or Mulroney.

On the small business tax, Trudeau took on all comers in the House of Commons. In the first Question Period of the fall session, Trudeau said that "the wealthy" were not paying taxes at the same rate as everybody else. "That's not right," he said, sounding like a Sunday school teacher, as he claimed his case was based on social justice and fairness. It was a prime example of the Liberals trying to shore up the progressive vote that backed them in 2015 but which might have been tempted to flirt with the NDP at the next election. Morneau went so far as to criticize the NDP for not supporting the tax measures. The political thinking was that the road to victory in 2019 ran through Quebec and depended on maintaining the support of more than half of self-described left-of-centre voters. They appeared prepared to lose some "blue Liberals," if it meant they kept the "orange" ones.

Yet there were already signs that the Liberals were prepared to tweak the proposals by offering a political counterweight to small businesses in the form of a tax cut—and by making clear that the reforms would not hit farmers and convenience store owners. Government insiders were already whispering that, when the detailed plans became clear, it would emerge that only a relatively small number—36,000—of 1.8 million private corporations would likely be hit by the measures, since they held 80 per cent of the taxable income.

Morneau, in particular, was taking a pounding as the tax revolt turned nasty. He was wounded by the accusation that he engineered the changes so that the pensions consulting firm he'd run before entering politics, Morneau Shepell, could benefit from increased sales of individual pension plans, as business owners shifted their retirement savings from private corporations. The Conservatives latched onto the issue and refused to let go, focusing on the juxtaposition of Trudeau's family trust and

Morneau's wealth with the mom-and-pop business owners they said would be hit by the government's tax reforms.

The Liberals maintained their "fairness" line, but an insight into the true motivation behind the move came in the *New Yorker*, where a profile of former Donald Trump strategist Steve Bannon revealed his friendship with Gerald Butts. The article implied that Bannon had been converted to an idea that polling suggested would be popular with Trump's base, if not the Republican establishment—higher taxes on the rich. The *New Yorker* quoted Butts as telling Bannon, "There's nothing better for a populist than a rich guy raising taxes on rich guys."[40] The downside, though, was that business no longer trusted a government that showed no appreciation for the anxieties experienced by people who put their personal assets on the line as collateral to start a business. Perhaps more importantly, the Liberal reputation for cutting taxes was left in tatters.

Inevitably, the pressure MPs were feeling in their constituencies was brought to bear, and Trudeau and Morneau held a bizarre press conference in a pizza restaurant in Stouffville, Ontario, where the prime minister offered an across-the-board sweetener, in the form of the small business corporate income tax cut that had been promised in the platform but then "deferred" indefinitely. It was recalled to life in an attempt to buy back support from incensed small business owners—thus widening the gap between personal and corporate income taxpayers that the whole reform package had been aimed at closing. The cost was substantial—$2.9 billion over six years, or roughly what the government had hoped to raise from the tax reforms in the first place. The end result was that most small business owners were still angry but would end up better off than they were before Trudeau and Morneau launched their quixotic quest. "When we changed it, it dissipated, as everything does. But it wasn't a fun time," said one person involved in the process.[41]

The first two years in power had been relatively smooth in terms of relations with Canadians, with caucus, and with the media. But the press conference in Stouffville exposed cracks that were set to widen over the course of the mandate. Reporters who tried to direct a question toward Morneau were told by Trudeau that he would take it "because you have a chance to speak with the prime minister." Queries about a potential conflict of interest in Morneau's private business affairs were deflected when Trudeau said that the finance minister had acted on the advice of the ethics commissioner.

Strains in caucus were also breaking into the open, as New Brunswick MP Wayne Long voted against the tax package. Others chose to complain about it behind closed doors or anonymously to journalists eager for signs of dissent. Wayne Easter, a former minister and the respected chair of the finance committee, didn't hold back: "Whoever drafted that doesn't have a clue about the amount of effort that goes into being a small business. . . . The communications made people feel they were being accused of abusing the tax system," he said.[42]

Trudeau was not contrite, but along with the small business tax cut —from 10.5 per cent to 9 per cent—he indicated that the proposal around lifetime exemptions on capital gains would be ditched over fears it might make it more expensive to pass family farms on to the next generation. But the policy on income sprinkling in private corporations remained, and the government said it would introduce a "reasonableness" test for adult family members to demonstrate that they contributed labour or capital before they were eligible for tax deductions.

By mid-October, the government revealed the results of the consultation exercise that had launched the whole saga—only businesses with annual passive income above $50,000 would be hit—the equivalent of around $1 million in savings, which was an asset level the finance department suggested was only reached by 3 per cent of small businesses. In other words, for the vast majority of businesses the government had created a lot of fuss over nothing. The proposals were so complicated that they were revised again in the 2018 budget—but substantively, at least, the tax revolt was over.

What was not over were questions about Morneau's own affairs, which the opposition parties suggested were motivated by a desire to gain personal benefit from the changes. First, it emerged Morneau's personal assets were not in a blind trust, as had been widely assumed, but that he had followed the advice of ethics commissioner Mary Dawson and set up a conflict-of-interest screen that still allowed him effective control over the $40 million in shares in Morneau Shepell he still held. Second, questions were raised about the apparent conflict of interest over his role as regulator and shareholder in his sponsorship of legislation that would increase the use of target benefit pension plans, a potential benefit to Morneau Shepell. (The case for the defence was that the finance minister could not be in a conflict because the decision was of "general application," in that it applied to a "broad class of persons or entities." Since almost every decision of importance applied generally, it meant it was almost impossible to be found in conflict of interest.) Finally, he was accused of profiting from the sale of 680,000 Morneau Shepell shares, just days before he announced tax changes that caused share prices to fall across the board.

The government's agenda was derailed by some questionable decisions on Morneau's part. They allowed the opposition parties to frame a narrative of a very rich man who was taking advantage of tax loopholes to stay rich, while closing loopholes for people less rich than himself. Trudeau's wealth became part of the debate when he was asked about how his own family had used legal structures to lower taxes paid on the assets left by his late father. He avoided a question about whether the Trudeaus paid their fair share of taxes by saying he'd relinquished control of those assets after winning the Liberal leadership. "I no longer have dealings with the way our family fortune is managed," he said.[43]

It was the most intense storm that Morneau and the government had yet faced, and it saw Liberal support drop five percentage points at its peak. But Morneau survived, in part because it emerged that he had donated around $10 million in proceeds from Morneau Shepell shares to charity, but mainly because whatever the shortcomings in his political acuity, nobody really believed he was corrupt. "It all turned around the first week in December, when the Conservatives accused him of insider trading," said one colleague. "He isn't in this for the money. People have no conception of how rich he and his wife are. The idea he was making public policy decisions to boost his shares is laughable."[44] A senior member of Morneau's staff said he was convinced that the finance minister would be exonerated when the facts emerged. "It was a question of surviving politically through the time for the truth to out. I just didn't think anything wrong had been done—and much had been done right. For all the uproar, it had all the hallmarks of something that had been trumped up," he said.[45]

As the government moved toward the end of the fall session, the Category 5 political storm had passed, as had the tempest associated with the finance minister, but it had left damage in its wake. In hindsight, even supporters of the small business tax plan say it was a black mark on the government. "Was it well executed? Probably not," said one person involved in the decision-making process. "It's impossible to come out with a tax measure with no notice—we had to say 'These are our intentions.' The [PMO] liked it because it filled the 'fairness' narrative. I don't think many journalists understood it and thought we were going after small businesses, which was not the case. When it became controversial, the government backed down and we ended up giving more in the form of the small business tax cut. But the real mistake was that in every tax measure, there have to be offsets—there can't just be losers and no clear winners."[46]

It was hard to see any winners in the government's proposals. With tax rates of over 50 per cent in a number of provinces, the sense among many high-net-worth individuals was that the Liberals were out to get them. For voters, the tax increases exposed a prime minister and a finance minister who appeared to be disconnected from the lives of the middle class they claimed to champion, at the helm of a government increasingly desperate for tax revenues to pay for its ambitious agenda and prolific spending.

Former Liberal finance minister John Manley said his philosophy was that government shouldn't take more than half of what people earn. "Once the government is the senior economic partner in the relationship, it distorts behaviour—people shelter income, work less or whatever. I thought the [2016 income tax increase] was too high. But the way they sold it was 'We're asking higher-income Canadians to pay a little more so that we can reduce the burden on people who are struggling, because we're all in this together,'" he said. "People might not like it, but it was a nation-building message. But with the small business tax thing, it was 'The rich aren't paying their fair share—we're going to plug loopholes.' That's not nation-building, that's wedge politics."[47]

For Gerald Butts, the whole affair was an unfortunate distraction. "It was not helpful," he observed. "The worst part was the waste of time —the most precious commodity in this business is time. We spent six months doing that instead of something else."[48] Yet it was the Prime Minister's Office that had embraced the idea enthusiastically because it fit neatly into Trudeau's "fairness" narrative. The tendency among the Anointed is to blame everyone from the Freemasons to the Illuminati for policy failures, but in this instance, culpability rested a little closer to home.

ELEVEN

A ROUGH WOOING IN BEIJING

THE SECOND HALF OF 2017 would teach the Trudeau Liberals some harsh truths about trying to impose their progressive values at home and abroad. The backdrop to the war on the wealthy was the emergence of Jagmeet Singh as the new federal NDP leader in late October. The Liberals had won a comfortable victory in a suburban Toronto by-election in Markham the previous April, in large measure because the NDP won just 3.5 per cent of the vote. The sense was that if the New Democrats could be beaten into submission in the suburbs of Canada's big cities, the Liberals could win comfortably in 2019.

Singh's election as the first ever visible minority federal leader had the potential to upset those assumptions. The dapper Sikh lawyer promised to focus on areas like electoral reform and pipelines, where the Liberals had disappointed progressive voters. But there were hopes among Liberals, and fears among New Democrats, that Singh was all pink turban and no perception. Charlie Angus, the rock-and-roll New Democrat from Northern Ontario whom Singh defeated, had expressed concerns that the NDP was set to "run the 2015 Justin Trudeau campaign in 2019." A string of poor by-election results and management missteps reduced the prospect for the "GQ election" to be a runoff between Trudeau and Singh. By late 2018, Singh was even behind the Green Party's Elizabeth May in the polls, when voters were asked whom they preferred as their next prime minister. Singh was proving a disappoint-ment to many New Democrats, but the Liberals were taking nothing for granted and worked hard in the fall of 2017 to make sure progressive voters stayed loyal.

In early October, TransCanada Corp. killed its controversial Energy East pipeline to the east coast. The company blamed "changed circum-stances" for the decision to pull the plug on the 4,500-kilometre line that would have carried 1.1 million barrels a day of Western crude to Eastern refineries and the export terminal at Saint John, New Brunswick. The approval by Trump of Keystone XL reduced the need for addi-tional capacity—Canada will need an extra 1.5 million barrels of trans-portation capacity a day by 2030; the combination of Trans Mountain, Line 3, and Keystone would add 1.7 million.[1]

Trudeau also blamed market conditions. But there was no doubt the Liberals had played their part. The National Energy Board had announced it would consider Energy East's contribution to upstream and down-stream greenhouse gas emissions—factors that were not considered when permits were granted for Kinder Morgan's Trans Mountain proj-ect and Enbridge's Line 3 pipeline. The political message was clear—the government had taken enough heat from the progressive left for back-ing Trans Mountain and had no intention of risking seats in Quebec, where the project was staunchly opposed on environmental grounds.

The Energy East project was pitched as a "Canadian solution to a Canadian challenge"—displacing imports from Venezuela and Algeria that are not subject to upstream emissions evaluations—and it was pop-ular in Western and Atlantic Canada. But imposing greenhouse gas emis-sion tests from the life cycle of projects made it clear that the Liberals had approved all the pipelines they intended to. The bar was raised to a level TransCanada could not possibly fulfil, given that it did not control the extraction or processing of the product it carried. Dennis McConaghy, a retired former oil executive and author of the book *Dysfunction: Canada After Keystone XL*, called the NEB decision a "terrible blunder." "The decision to re-scope so profoundly is, fundamentally, a mistake by the panel—one implicitly endorsed by the Trudeau government," he said. "If the government couldn't abide any more pipelines . . . , it should have said so explicitly and not deferred the job to the NEB."[2]

The push on progressive values was as relentless abroad as it was at home. On the NAFTA file, huge amounts of energy were being expended trying to figure out how to deal with the enigma wrapped in a riddle that is Donald Trump. Government ministers emphasized the point by circulating a story from Axios, a U.S. politics and business website, that reported on a conversation between the president and his top trade negotiator, Robert Lighthizer:

> "You've got 30 days and if you don't get concessions then I'm pulling out," Trump told Lighthizer [referring to the U.S.–Korea trade deal].

> "Ok, well I'll tell the Koreans they've got 30 days," Lighthizer replied.

> "No, no, no," Trump interjected. "That's not how you negotiate. You don't tell them they've got 30 days. You tell them, 'This guy's so crazy he could pull out any minute.' . . . And by the way, I might."[3]

Trump was approaching the NAFTA negotiations in a similarly provocative fashion, tweeting that both Canada and Mexico were "being very difficult" and that he "may have to terminate." While bread-and-butter issues were being dealt with at the NAFTA negotiating table, the mandate from the president to his negotiators stipulated that the Americans had to win concessions on everything and give up nothing. The overarching goal for Trump was an end to "the theft of American prosperity" in the form of unfair trade surpluses on the part of U.S. trade partners. Chrystia Freeland, the global affairs minister, pointed out that Canada had a manufactured goods deficit with the U.S. and that Canada was not luring blue-collar jobs north. Yet Trump continued to insist on proposals that the Canadian government was not prepared to accept—a sunset clause that would see NAFTA expire every five years; an end to the independent binational panels that arbitrate disputes; an increase in U.S. content in autos in all three countries; and a loosening in Canada's supply managed agricultural sector.

Canada's best hope was the personal relationship between Trudeau and Trump, which survived a demeaning visit to the White House by the prime minister in October. A body language expert hired by the London *Daily Express* interpreted the exchange by the two men. Judi James said Trudeau looked happy to go into body language "suck up" mode with the president. "Trump's thumbs-up gestures imply a fun, easy-going relationship with Trudeau, although it also seems to signal a low level of respect. The comedy point is a subtle way to put down Trudeau's visible status," she said.[4] Trudeau was prepared to suffer some embarrassment in pursuit of continued preferential access to the $752-billion-a-year trading relationship with the United States. But he did not emerge any the wiser about how to strike a free trade deal with a protectionist.

Support for Trudeau's patient strategy remained high, with the Team Canada lobbying effort of premiers, mayors, and former politicians holding firm. Yet in late October, one crack appeared when a memo penned by former prime minister Stephen Harper to the clients of his consulting firm, Harper and Associates, was leaked to the Canadian Press. The "Napping on NAFTA" memo criticized the Trudeau government in several areas—for too quickly rejecting U.S. proposals; for insisting on negotiating alongside Mexico; and for promoting progressive priorities like labour, gender, Indigenous, and environmental issues. "I fear that the NAFTA renegotiation is going very badly. I also believe that President Trump's threat to terminate NAFTA is not a bluff," Harper wrote. He saved most of his vitriol for the Liberals' progressive trade policies, scoffing, "Did anyone really think that the Liberals could somehow force the Trump administration into enacting their agenda—union power, climate change, Aboriginal claims, gender issues?"[5]

The focus on "progressive values" upset other potential trading partners too, who resented being told how to run their own countries. In
November, the prime minister and his trade minister, François-Philippe
Champagne, were in Da Nang, Vietnam, as part of an attempt to res-
urrect the Trans-Pacific Partnership trade agreement, an accord among
eleven countries that had appeared dead after Trump withdrew the
U.S.'s participation. A late-night deal to agree on "core elements" of a
new agreement was made, but Trudeau nearly derailed the whole thing
when he did not attend a meeting of TPP-nation leaders. Cameras showed
a room with ten TPP leaders, including Japanese prime minister Shinzo
Abe, and an empty chair where Trudeau was meant to be. Australian
officials later briefed reporters that Canada had "screwed" the other
countries. Champagne dismissed the reports as a misunderstanding and
said Canada needed time to push for stronger environmental and labour
protections. Changes affecting the auto sector were put off to a later
date, over concerns that they could cut across the NAFTA talks.

But it was worries about cultural industries in Quebec that were the
cause of the greatest angst. The sensitivity over protection of Quebec
content had been exposed the previous month, when Mélanie Joly, the
heritage minister, had attempted to sell a deal with Netflix that gave the
company a pass from tax and regulation in exchange for a $500 million
investment in Canadian content over five years. The deal was excoriated
in Quebec—first, because Joly couldn't say whether this was more than
Netflix was planning to spend in any case; second, because none of the
investment was specifically earmarked for French productions. Joly
seemed taken aback when she was confronted by the host of top-rated
talk show *Tout le monde en parle* with research statistics that suggested if
Netflix were bound by the same rules as Canadian cable companies, it
would have to contribute more than $100 million a year to Canadian
content. It was a roasting the Liberals were intent on avoiding in Vietnam.

The fear was that extended copyright provisions in the TPP might be
used as a lever by the Americans in NAFTA. As a result, Canada sought a
cultural exemption, which it eventually got. But according to people in

the room, there was nothing written down on paper and Canada was not prepared to say that an agreement-in-principle had been reached until it was signed. For their own domestic reasons, the Japanese and Australians wanted a deal and, in the words of one Canadian official, they "pulled the stunt with the empty chair," making it appear as if Trudeau had stormed off to bed in a petulant fit.[6] A renamed Comprehensive and Progressive Agreement for Trans-Pacific Partnership (the "progressive" part being included at Canada's insistence) was eventually signed in January 2018. But if the TPP countries were prepared to indulge Canada's heavy emphasis on issues like labour and the environment, Trudeau soon found out the Chinese were not.

As the relationship with Washington cooled, the affinity with Beijing was warming. Trudeau had made increased trade with China a cornerstone of his foreign policy long before the advent of Trump. But his election gave a renewed urgency to diversify markets. A study by the Canada–China Business Council had suggested that a free trade deal with China made sense—forecasting a multi-billion-dollar rise in exports and thousands of new jobs. The Chinese had long been a willing partner, but the Conservatives had always been wary of their enthusiasm to secure access to Canadian resources. Harper had approved the sale of Calgary oil company Nexen to state-owned CNOOC Ltd. but had emphasized "this is not the beginning of a trend, this is the end of a trend." In the wake of headlines about industrial espionage by Chinese companies in Canada, the moment for renewed trade links was gone. Harper's skepticism about China was apparent in his book *Right Here, Right Now*, in which he lamented China's trajectory to becoming the world's largest economy. He insisted the Asian power's preferential trade access to its competitors, its renewed authoritarianism, its military build-up and foreign aggressiveness "cannot be seen as anything other than a serious threat to the Western democratic model."[7]

But the Liberal election victory reset the relationship—the Trudeau name had carried great weight in China since the prime minister's father opened diplomatic relations with the People's Republic in 1970.

A trade deal between China and Australia, one of Canada's biggest competitors as a source of raw materials and financial services expertise, suggested that an accord between such disparate economies was possible. But Trudeau's visit to Beijing in fall 2016 revealed why any deal with the Chinese was going to be hard work. After an official meeting in Beijing, Chinese premier Li Keqiang said the two countries had agreed to a feasibility study on a trade deal—a suggestion that was refuted by the Canadian side, which was nervous about labour and environmental agreements, government procurement, and the role of state-owned enterprises. The huge imbalance in trade was a clear obstacle—Canada imports around $65 billion of Chinese goods and exports just $20 billion the other way. The key for Canada to any deal was to lower China's government-imposed hurdles that hamper Canadian exporters.

Despite the confusion in Beijing during Trudeau's 2016 visit, both sides had committed to doubling trade by 2025, and exploratory talks were resumed in April 2017. Part of the reason China was so willing was its enthusiasm to buy up Canadian companies. In April, Premier Li asked Trudeau to "relax the restrictions on high-tech exports to China," according to Chinese media. The new ambassador in Ottawa, Lu Shaye, was also lobbying for unfettered access for Chinese state-owned firms. "Investment is investment," he said. "We should not take too much political considerations into the investment."[8] The Liberals sought to oblige, raising the threshold on automatic reviews of foreign takeovers to $1 billion and waving through the Chinese takeover of a Montreal high-tech firm, ITF Technologies, against the advice of Canada's national security agency. But such controversial decisions meant that the Chinese were receptive when the Canadians proposed a return to Beijing for Trudeau in December 2017.

In the eyes of Guy Saint-Jacques, Ottawa's former ambassador to China, the timing was right to launch talks, and he believed they could be concluded within three years—much more quickly than the decade it took the Australians. "In my view, we didn't have much choice," the retired career diplomat recalled.[9] Saint-Jacques said the Chinese were more keen to strike a deal than Canada, but issues around political liberalization were always going to be a problem. Communist Party General Secretary Xi Jinping's comments at the party conference that October had made it clear that there would be more controls and censorship—a new social grading system was planned that would curtail the regime's critics' ability to travel or be promoted. Yet, during his visit in 2016, Trudeau had said he would not agree to free trade negotiations unless they included chapters on the environment, labour rights, state-owned enterprises, and public procurement. Much to Saint-Jacques's surprise, the Chinese agreed to the inclusion of labour protections in any prospective deal.

But after his arrival in Beijing in December 2017, the Chinese gave Trudeau, his ministers, and the travelling media a tough lesson in power politics in the Great Hall of the People in Beijing. It was apparent from the moment the Canadian party arrived that the hosts were going to be assertive. The Canadian media pool camera operator was manhandled and had his shot of Trudeau and Premier Li blocked by Chinese security. Adam Scotti, the prime minister's official photographer, was blocked from entering the official photo shoot. The press conference to round off the visit was on, then it was off.

The belief that the hosts had accepted the fundamentals of the progressive trade agenda was quickly disabused. Whatever was said to suggest that the Chinese would be flexible in accommodating Trudeau's ultra-liberal trade agenda was obviously not shared with the party leadership. Li made clear he was not ready to commit a country with 150 million rural-to-urban migrants to anything that suggested more onerous health and safety obligations, minimum wages, or collective bargaining. Yet, had the Canadian side not insisted on the inclusion of labour rights in the press release, diplomats could have been creative and reached an agreement. China has a trade surplus with Canada and would have liked to have more access to the Canadian market. But Xi was not about to compromise his own extremely illiberal agenda to get it.

In the end, Trudeau left Beijing empty-handed, despite the expectations that he and Li were going to issue a press release announcing the launch of formal talks. Li noted that different national conditions justify different responses. "It is only natural we don't see eye to eye on some issues," he said.[10] Trudeau met with Xi before he left the Chinese capital, and for a time it seemed like an eleventh-hour agreement might be possible. But he had failed to appreciate the three golden rules for doing business in China: never impose your own values, never interpret acknowledgement during a meeting as agreement, and never assume the people in the meeting have the authority to strike a deal.

"Trade that benefits everyone," "putting people first," and "Canadian values on the environment, labour, and gender" meant little to a leadership set on ushering in a new era of glory for China. Trudeau's Twitter feed may have read, "Changing the world a little bit every day," but if he was intent on small steps, he had just come face to face with a regime that planned to change the world by huge leaps. And there was no room for Trudeau's progressive trade agenda in its new world order.

The prospect of rapprochement faded still further when Ottawa blocked the sale of Canadian construction giant Aecon Group, builder of Toronto's iconic CN Tower, to a Chinese state-owned enterprise on security grounds the following May. Canada's intelligence agencies warned that companies owned by the Chinese government were prone to passing on information or technology to Beijing. But China's ambassador in Ottawa, Lu Shaye, in the kind of hyperbolic language the Chinese government has become famous for, said the action amounted to discrimination and urged Canada to rid itself of such "demons" of prejudice against his country. "Canada's rejection of Aecon shows that Chinese enterprises are suffering from unfair treatment," Lu wrote. "I hope Canadians can embrace China as simply a different country and not regard China as a threat just because of our differences. Only by getting rid of such kinds of demons can Canada relieve the burden, co-operate with China and come aboard the express train of China's development."[11]

Tensions deepened further in December 2018 with the arrest in Vancouver of Meng Wanzhou, the chief financial officer of telecom giant Huawei, on allegations that her company had violated U.S. sanctions on Iran. Chrystia Freeland said Canada was just following the terms of its extradition agreement with the United States. But the issue was complicated by President Trump suggesting he might be willing to drop charges in exchange for a trade deal with Beijing, which appeared to confirm the accusations in China's state-run media that the arrest was politically motivated. Canada was caught in the middle, and two of its citizens paid the price. Former diplomat Michael Kovrig and businessman Michael Spavor were detained in what appeared to be reprisals for the Meng arrest.

But despite the deterioration in relations, Trudeau remained sanguine. "For sure the relationship is retrievable. We've been very consistent with China. One of my critiques of the previous government was that they were hot and cold on China. We've been firm and clear that we're always going to stand up for human rights but also find ways to engage in a predictable framework with the world's second largest economy," he said.[12] Yet for all the reassuring rhetoric, as the Trump administration was sounding the bugle-call on a new cold war with China, the Trudeau government was starting to feel the pressure from both protagonists as it tried to steer an independent course.

TWELVE

"TOO INDIAN, EVEN FOR AN INDIAN"

IT HAD BEEN A tumultuous year, but Justin Trudeau's Liberal Party was still sitting comfortably in the polls, almost ten points clear of the Conservatives, and he could reflect on the fact that all but two first-term majority governments in the entire history of Canada had been re-elected.[1] Christmas vacation 2017–18 for the Trudeau pack—Justin; his wife, Sophie; and their children, Xavier, ten years old, Ella-Grace, eight, and Hadrien, three—was a very different affair than the previous year, when they had accepted an invitation from the Aga Khan to holiday with family and friends on the Ismaili spiritual leader's private Caribbean island, Bells Island, using his private helicopter to get there. Trudeau was eventually found guilty of contravening the Conflict of Interest Act on four counts for his little family vacation and so decided to play it safe this time around, skiing on the slopes of Lake Louise in the Rockies.

The Liberals have always had a vulnerable heel when it comes to entitlement issues. The NDP leader Jagmeet Singh summed up the public mood: "It just seems there's these two worlds. There's the world everyone else lives in, where people are struggling to make ends meet. And then there's the world where people who are wealthy and well-connected and powerful think the laws don't apply to them."[2] But while there was widespread disapproval about the Trudeau-family visit with the Aga

Khan, the ethics commissioner's censure did not appear to shift vote intentions—at least not immediately.

The Trudeaus headed to the remote, back-country resort Skoki Lodge, accessible only by ski and sled. In contrast to the luxury of the previous year, conditions at Skoki were spartan, with no Wi-Fi, no power, and no running water. "The outhouse at 25 below was great for the kids," joked Trudeau.[3] The prime minister is an inveterate user of social media, but in its absence he read vociferously and scribbled away at those soft-cover puzzle magazines you can buy at newsstands. His usual exercise regime of boxing and yoga was replaced by skiing and snowboarding.

He returned to work in a buoyant mood. When asked if he was worried that the government's credibility was being impacted by a recurring habit of tossing election pledges into a boneyard of broken promises, he was unapologetic. "We put forward an incredibly ambitious agenda for 2015, where we laid out a plan for a government that was going to be active in changing things and making things better for people in a whole bunch of different ways, and we're delivering on those commitments. We're halfway through the mandate. We've done an awful lot, there's still more to do but I am confident that we're going to achieve the things Canadians expected us to do," he said.[4]

Trudeau was elected on the back of the slogan "Hope and Hard Work." When he stuck to that message track—labouring with diligence and discipline to promote a more compassionate Canada than the one bequeathed by his predecessor, Stephen Harper—he won acclaim at home and abroad. He appeared remarkably unruffled at being one of the most scrutinized people on the planet. "Justin has not changed. Of all the people involved in this process, he's changed the least," said Tom Pitfield, who has known Trudeau most of his life. "He's the exact same person who tried to win that boxing tournament—he's just become more disciplined."[5]

But political troubles are not like flurries on a river—one moment white, then melted forever. They are more like mounds of thick, wet slush that pile up until they block a government's progress. The blizzard that blew away any complacency in Liberal ranks, and forced Trudeau and his advisers to recognize that victory at the next election was not preordained, was the prime minister's ill-fated passage to India in February 2018. What should have been a routine foreign trip, with the prize of securing closer trade ties to one of the world's fastest-growing economies and endearing the prime minister to Indian Canadians across the country, ended up highlighting the more flaky side of Trudeau's personality. The colourful spontaneity Canadians had once found refreshing was suddenly ridiculous for many.

If, as Walt Whitman suggested, human beings are prone to contradict themselves because they are large and "contain multitudes," Trudeau is not that unusual.[6] But if his first fifteen months in office displayed the Jesuit restraint more typical of his father, the visit to India in February, with the whole family in tow, saw his impetuous side come to the fore, with near-disastrous diplomatic consequences. Trudeau said that the impetus behind the visit was his own memories of going on trips with his father. "Going through it now, having my family with me, makes me a better politician and a better dad," he said by way of explanation.[7]

The family was pictured in lavish local costumes in the shadows of the subcontinent's great sites. The eight-day visit was characterized by a threadbare itinerary that looked increasingly like a taxpayer-funded family vacation. Coming so soon after the Aga Khan scandal, it felt to many Canadians like a thumb in the eye. As the attire grew more exuberant, so did the sniping that the Trudeau tour was "too Indian, even for an Indian."[8] The extremely light official diary allowed the Trudeaus time to pose with some of India's top movie stars, like Shah Rukh Khan, who wore a sober Western-style black suit while the Trudeaus wore braided saris and sherwanis. The prime minister capped it off with a performance of bhangra dancing that struck many people as being a Bollywood move too far.

Some senior Liberals back in Ottawa lifted their heads from their hands long enough to point the finger of blame at Sophie for ordering the over-elaborate costumes and persuading the whole family to wear them. "I think there's no question that was more her than him," said one Liberal MP. "But, look, he wasn't forced to wear any of that stuff. There's a theatrical side to him that likes ingratiating himself with people."[9] (Sophie Grégoire Trudeau was asked to contribute to this book but declined.)

It all smacked of the kind of cultural imperialistic tourism that Mark Twain lampooned 150 years ago in *The Innocents Abroad*: "In Paris, they simply opened their eyes and stared at us when we spoke to them in French! We never did succeed in making those idiots understand their own language."[10]

When it was revealed that an Indian Canadian once convicted of the attempted murder of an Indian politician in British Columbia had been invited to an event at the High Commission in New Delhi, the trip was roundly condemned as a disaster. Jaspal Atwal, a former member of the extremist International Sikh Youth Federation, deemed a terrorist group in Canada and India, attended a reception in Mumbai, where he was photographed with the prime minister's wife and Indian-born cabinet minister Amarjeet Sohi. He was also invited to the event in New Delhi, but that invitation was quickly rescinded once the pictures from Mumbai were made public in Canadian media and Atwal was identified as having been convicted of the attempted murder of Malkiat Singh Sidhu, a Punjab cabinet minister, during a visit to Vancouver Island in 1986.

There may have been extenuating circumstances. The Prime Minister's Office encouraged the Canadian national security adviser, Daniel Jean, to talk to reporters—briefings in which Jean suggested that elements within the Indian intelligence service may have been happy to see Atwal embarrass Trudeau for being soft on Sikh separatism. Atwal's name was removed from a blacklist, thus allowing him into India, and Jean suggested he had been cultivated by diplomats at the Indian consulate in Vancouver.

But as any veteran of political campaigns knows, when you're explaining, you're losing. The impression left with many Canadians was that

Trudeau had embarrassed himself, which was his prerogative—and the country, which was not. "If they had Googled the name, this guy [Atwal] would have shown up in two seconds," said Garry Keller, who was a former chief of staff to Conservative foreign affairs minister John Baird.[11] Trudeau's erstwhile allies at the *Toronto Star* wrote it off as "the least successful foray into that country since the repelled Mongol invasions."[12] Similar headlines ran in newspapers around the world. Trudeau said his one regret was he didn't take more suits to India.[13]

When the final bill came in, the trip was revealed to have cost around $1.5 million, including $17,000 to fly Vancouver celebrity chef Vikram Vij to help prepare Indian-inspired meals at the Canadian High Commission. As the opposition pointed out, there were, presumably, plenty of cooks in India who knew the recipe.

"We walked into a buzz-saw—[Narendra] Modi and his government were out to screw us and were throwing tacks under our tires to help Canadian conservatives, who did a good job of embarrassing us," said Gerald Butts, in his evaluation. "But none of that is the core issue. . . . Nobody would remember any of that had it not been for the photographs. We should have known this better than anybody—in many ways we'd used this to get elected. The picture will overwhelm words. We did the count—we did forty-eight meetings and he was dressed in a suit for forty-five of them. But give people that picture and it's the only one they'll remember."[14] Prince Harry, so often depicted in a Savile Row suit, probably felt the same way about the pictures of him on the one occasion he dressed as a Nazi.

The impact was immediate in the polls. What had been a comfortable Liberal lead over the Conservatives was whittled away and the parties spent the following months in a statistical tie. New Conservative leader Andrew Scheer had come in on cat's paws after winning a lengthy leadership race in May 2017 and had spent most of the intervening period consolidating his existing base rather than wooing new voters. Yet suddenly, through no particular enterprise of his own, Scheer was a real contender to be Canada's next prime minister. It was a classic example of a recurring paradox at the heart of Justin Trudeau's Liberal government: brave moves—such as his decision to hold a town hall in Nanaimo, B.C., in early February 2018, in front of an audience that was deeply hostile to his government's decision to back the construction of a crude oil pipeline through the province—that are often undone by silly, unforced errors.

His father, Pierre, had faced an election that was far tighter than it should have been in 1972—just four years after being elected on a wave of "Trudeaumania." Visiting British journalist Jerome Caminda discovered an angry country. Trudeau dominated the front pages of Canadian newspapers through his "flair for physical activity" and his unerring sense of drama, Caminda wrote, but he was losing his audience.[15] Still, Trudeau senior was seeking re-election at a time when unemployment remained high, even as inflation was rising. By contrast, his son has presided over a period of relatively strong growth, with inflation at benign levels and unemployment lower than at any time since the mid-1970s. In the absence of strong economic headwinds, the loss of Liberal audience could be blamed squarely on the prime minister.

Trudeau's handlers continually reminded him that his sense of humour was no laughing matter, advising, "You have many attributes but you're not funny—stick to the script."[16] Yet he struggled to comply, as with his weak attempt at humour with the lady in a town hall who talked about "the future of mankind," only to be corrected by Trudeau, who said he preferred "peoplekind." The seemingly innocuous comment drew ire around the world before Trudeau even had the chance to explain he was joking. "How dare you kill off mankind, Mr. Trudeau, you spineless virtue-signalling excuse for a feminist," wrote professional controversialist Piers Morgan on MailOnline, the most visited English-speaking newspaper website in the world.[17]

Veterans inside the Liberal government kept their heads while the less experienced were losing theirs. "The India trip plays into a narrative that Trudeau's not serious, but voters will not be saying in the polling booth, 'All things being equal, I'd like to vote for him but those

costumes in India were so fucking stupid.' Those people don't exist,"
said one battle-scarred campaign vet.[18] But the backlash was an indication that a politician who has been a pioneer in the use of political image
management on visual-based social media had gone too far.

As traditional media budgets have shrunk, and new outlets for visuals
multiplied, politicians have more ability than ever to communicate
directly with voters. Trudeau has taken full advantage. An analysis by
researchers Mireille Lalancette and Vincent Raynauld of 145 Trudeau
Instagram posts in the year after his election revealed a shrewd strategy
to build a positive, optimistic view of the new prime minister and
Canada. The photos taken by official photographer Adam Scotti were
edited strategically to showcase a "dynamic and outgoing" leader, tend-
ing to his duties with "seriousness and vigour." Elements of Trudeau's
personal brand were highlighted—youth, athleticism, open-mindedness,
empathy, a sunny disposition, and support for feminist causes permeate
the pictures. Trudeau is an ardent runner and jogs wherever he happens
to be in the world. By pure coincidence, a photographer seems to be
available on every occasion. Close to half the pictures contained patriotic symbols.[19] Nothing is left to chance—a picture of Trudeau jogging
with Mexican president Enrique Peña Nieto featured the prime minister
in a pair of Rugby Canada shorts and a T-shirt from the Saskatchewan
Jazz Festival. The Prime Minister's Office tweeted directly to both
organizations along with the picture.[20]

This was hardly the first time that a Canadian prime minister had
tried to manipulate his or her image. William Lyon Mackenzie King set
up the Bureau of Public Information in 1939 to monitor public opinion.
The Harper Conservatives became experts at precisely micro-targeting
the voters they needed—slicing and dicing the electorate because
they knew who their supporters were, where they lived, and whether
they were likely to vote, thanks to a voter information database that
was the envy of their rivals. But Trudeau took political image-making
to another level. One stream of posts saw him expressing reaction to
national and international events like the Fort McMurray fires or the

Bataclan terrorist attack in Paris. "They highlight his compassion, empathy and sensitivity," said the authors of the Instagram study.

By the end of 2017, one columnist calculated that Trudeau had wept openly, or had his eyes well up, at least seven times on camera.[21] In October, he cried as he spoke about the death of his friend Gord Downie, lead singer of the Tragically Hip; a month later, he was in tears as he apologized to residential school survivors in Newfoundland and Labrador; and a few days later he was dabbing his eyes with Kleenex as he delivered an apology to members of the LGBTQ community for decades of sexual persecution by the Canadian government. These were meaningful interventions for the people whose lives had been impacted —but they were frequent. Trudeau's demonstrative nature expanded the palette of emotions accessible to Canadian prime ministers—it was hard to imagine his predecessor exhibiting such vulnerability, or even his own father. But the prevalence of occasions where he brought himself to tears in late 2017 led some to question his sincerity.

Another category of pictures featured Trudeau taking part in pre-planned events like the Pride Parade or visiting baby pandas at the Toronto Zoo. They showed him in casual attire, usually in a shirt with the sleeves rolled up and no tie, "at ease interacting with those around him." Some of the posts offered an insight into his family life—trick-or-treating on Halloween or taking part in Father's Day celebrations. "These posts give an impression of normal family life that appeals to voters who see their own lives reflected in the Trudeau family," said the authors of the Instagram study.[22]

With such a carefully calibrated spin machine at his disposal, it remains a matter of debate how Trudeau, with his bulging Tickle Trunk, got it so wrong in India. Perhaps it was as simple as voters not seeing their own lives reflected in the images of the Trudeaus, dressed up like Bollywood extras, in front of the Golden Temple in Amritsar. One Liberal MP said Trudeau has gone to the empathy well once too often. "What I get at the doorsteps is 'I don't want to hear any more apologies. I don't want to see any more pay-outs. I don't want any more political correctness.

Do them but talk about what you're doing on the economy. Talk about the things that make a difference in my life." The MP said he has a large reservoir of respect for Trudeau. "He's a quick study and he's got more depth than people give him credit for." But he said the opposition tag of him as a lightweight is always there. "That 'lightweight' business is always at the back of people's minds and India confirmed the lightweight image."[23] Whatever the explanation for the trip's shortcomings, it was more bad news to add to an accumulating pile. The potential for spontaneous combustion is always there for Canada's twenty-third prime minister.

ONE SLOW-BURNING ISSUE THAT highlighted how the culture wars had replaced economics at the heart of the political divide was the battle the government chose to fight over the Canada Summer Jobs program, which provides grants to small businesses, non-profits, and public sector organizations to hire full-time students. It was hardly the stuff to have people reaching for their torches and pitchforks. Yet the previous summer, the government discovered that some anti-abortion groups had accessed funding, and new employment minister Patty Hajdu was determined to avoid a repeat by requiring applicants to check a box affirming they respected the values underlying the Charter of Rights and Freedoms, including women's reproductive rights and the rights of gender-diverse and trans-gender Canadians. Failure to do so invalidated the application.

That requirement sparked a court case filed by an anti-abortion group, the Toronto Right to Life Association, explaining why it could not agree with the wording in the application guide, even though it attested that it supported Canadian law, including the Charter and human rights law. The organization had received Summer Jobs money the previous year, something Hajdu's office had deemed an "oversight." The issue became a cause célèbre for many groups, including strong advocates of women's rights who saw it as a freedom-of-expression case. The Liberals were criticized for blocking access to funding provided by all taxpayers, based on the legitimate political beliefs of the applicants.

In the Omar Khadr case, Trudeau had said that the Charter protected all Canadians. "There is no picking and choosing," he stated at the time. Yet in the case of Summer Jobs, it seemed to many people that he had done exactly that, creating a hierarchy of rights, with those the Liberals found most agreeable at the apex. Trudeau denied that anyone's rights were being infringed. "We're not limiting freedom of expression or freedom of belief in any shape or form. We are simply saying organizations with the explicit purpose of limiting and eliminating Charter rights like women's rights do not qualify for government funding," he said.[24]

But it was not just anti-abortion groups who were impacted. Jason Cole, a Baptist pastor in Dartmouth, Nova Scotia, was typical of the moderate faith leaders across the country who felt they had been backed into a corner by the government. He said his church, Regal Heights, was against abortion "but we don't picket against it." In an open letter to the prime minister, he stressed that his church champions Charter rights. But he argued that refusing to tick the attestation box that confirmed the applicant's respect for reproductive rights was a matter of conscience. "In order to apply, as opposed to previous years, I now have to agree with a part of the ideology of the Liberal Party of Canada, which is not proper," he said.[25] Trudeau asserted that he recognized the role that church and faith groups played in promoting strong communities and running day camps for kids. "We're absolutely going to work with them to ensure they can continue to do that," he said.[26]

But the truth was that the Liberals saw what it called "a woman's right to abortion" as a wedge with which to attack the Conservatives, by forcing leader Andrew Scheer to come out and back the anti-abortion groups fighting the attestation requirement in court. Petrified of being branded a proponent of "fear and division," Scheer ignored the issue in the House of Commons. By mid-March, it had been raised just once during Question Period—and even that resulted in baiting from the

Liberal front bench. "Is the member opposite saying she is opposed to reproductive freedom?" asked the combative Hajdu.

What Trudeau may not have banked on was the vocal opposition to the measure from religious and ethnic groups that had largely supported him in 2015. In Mississauga in late January, representatives from the Muslim, Sikh, Jewish, Hindu, and Christian communities met to discuss whether the government was violating their religious freedom. Few statesmen could boast, as Trudeau could, that they had achieved unity among all the Abrahamic and Indian faiths, albeit 100 per cent in opposition. It struck at the vision of the Anointed. Liberal chauvinism on reproductive issues meant there was a refusal to believe in the legitimacy of any dissent to their prevailing orthodoxy. But that attitude produced such a groundswell of moderate opposition that even the timid Scheer was persuaded to break cover.

In an act of reckless abandon, the Conservative leader put forward an opposition day motion saying that non-political, non-activist applicants should be able to access the $200 million program, regardless of whether they ticked the attestation box. Privately, many Liberals shook their heads and wondered why Hajdu had refused to soften the government line on the issue. "I think it was more the minister on Summer Jobs than the prime minister. But he'd see it as a Charter issue and he'll stand by the Charter, even if it's not right," said one Liberal MP. "But the attestation is going to continue to hurt us. The churches are still complaining. I don't think they realized how big a hornet's nest they created."[27] Another MP complained about the "enormous bubble of frustration" created in caucus by the political centre ignoring backbenchers with experience in retail politics as mayors and provincial politicians. "The small business tax reform was the Alamo—a disaster. But the pendulum swung back to the centre and then we gave it another push leftward with the summer youth employment program, which was also warned about," he said.[28]

The India trip was an airburst that cast political fallout across the country. The Summer Jobs program was more contained, but it contaminated some key voting constituencies. Both episodes hurt Liberal polling numbers—in the month after Trudeau returned from his passage to the subcontinent, Liberal support tumbled five points, while that for the Conservatives rose. A Nanos Research poll suggested that one third of male voters who had supported Trudeau in 2015 had since deserted— soft Liberals who had wanted a change but were not impressed with the prime minister's focus on gender and diversity.[29]

YET THE TEMPTATION TO play identity politics was irresistible when it came to Bill Morneau's third budget. Unexpected growth in 2017 had handed the finance minister a multi-billion-dollar windfall, and he proceeded to spend the lot—$6.5 billion on 309 line items. Business groups had urged Morneau to address Trump's tax cuts to help maintain Canada's competitive edge and signal that the government understood that the trade and tax reality had changed. And John Manley, the then president of the Business Council of Canada, urged prudence in the face of uncertainty over NAFTA, rising interest rates, and high household indebtedness.

But the budget ignored all those calls—Morneau insisted he would not be rushed into having a "knee-jerk reaction" and instead said he would focus on long-term issues like "addressing the gender gap." The additional money was sprinkled around voting groups on the left, leaving the deficit projection unchanged at $18.1 billion for 2018–19 and budgetary balance a distant speck on the horizon.

The narrative of helping get women into the workforce in general, and trades in particular, was sold as an investment in economic growth —an offset to an aging workforce. But much of the spending was intensely political and designed to strangle at birth any prospect of NDP leader Jagmeet Singh capturing the imagination of progressive voters. The new Canada Workers Benefit stole the thunder of the NDP's Working Canadians Guarantee; an advisory council was struck to examine the specifics of a national pharmacare program (a central plank in the

New Democrats 2019 platform); $400 million was earmarked to support official languages, aimed at bolstering Liberal support in francophone ridings outside Quebec—and on and on.

The deficit would have been worse if not for $2.6 billion that was planned for infrastructure but didn't make it out the door—hardly a proud boast for a government elected on a ticket to make productive investments that would improve the quality of life for people stuck in traffic jams. As the then parliamentary budget officer, Jean-Denis Fréchette, pointed out in April, the Liberals had only identified projects for half the money in phase one of their infrastructure program—$7.2 billion of $14.4 billion. (Phase two of the program is worth $33 billion over ten years.) Liberal insiders explained that part of the problem was flow of funds—municipalities were only reimbursed after the money was spent, creating an inevitable time lag. Bigger projects like Toronto's SmartTrack and Vancouver's TransLink extensions are part of phase two and will come on stream later. "I think it's a really transformative plan and in ten years, we'll look back and be happy," said John Brodhead, a former chief of staff to the infrastructure minister.[30]

But, in the meantime, it looked like a classic example of Liberal execution not matching Liberal rhetoric. The government judged that Canadians didn't care about deficits, as long they felt they were under control. But there were concerns from Manley, and other more centrist Liberals, that the Trudeau government was not preparing for the tough times ahead. "It is simply not prudent to allow spending to consume all the additional revenue generated by better growth, as the government has done," Manley opined. "What's more, the government's failure to signal in some tangible fashion that it understands the scale of our country's competitiveness challenges is deterring the very investment we need to build the Canada we want."[31]

A common complaint among more fiscally conservative Liberals is that many of the key players in Trudeau's inner circle—including Butts and Telford—learned their politics in Dalton McGuinty's free-spending provincial Liberal government in Ontario—an experiment that did not end well for the Liberals or the taxpayer. "Part of it is because these guys come from Queen's Park and are from that spending mentality," said one person familiar with the budgetary process.[32] There was a sense that the government could have shown a path to balance in its 2016 fall fiscal update and, following the 2017 windfall, balanced the budget within three years. Yet, even after re-profiling billions of dollars in infrastructure money, deficits were projected to remain in double figures well into the next decade. "They like spending—they just like it," said one insider. "A narrative was created and then some artificial priorities were added. Inclusive growth is the right thing to do—putting more women in the workforce—but you need to put real means into it. This is just a narrative and when you go under the surface, there's nothing substantive there. It's government by narrative. Harper was pretty good at that too. But we said we'd be better."[33]

The competitiveness pressures were being felt most acutely in the oilpatch, where there were concerns about lack of market access, high taxes, and constrictive regulation. Market watchers noted a gradual seep of jobs, head office functions, and capital. "It's the slow bleeding of Canada," said Jack Mintz, the president's fellow of the School of Public Policy at the University of Calgary.[34] While in the past, companies would attempt to keep profits out of the U.S., moving functions like sales and marketing to Canada in order to escape a federal corporate tax rate of 35 per cent, there were concerns about the reverse happening after Trump's tax cut to 21 per cent. The combined U.S. federal–state corporate income tax fell from 39.1 per cent to 26 per cent (except in states like Texas, where there is no state rate). But Trump's package offered other advantages, like being able to write off machinery and equipment investment costs from profits, rather than depreciating them. Companies denied they were relocating lock, stock, and oil barrels, but giant energy firms like Encana moved their senior executives from Calgary to Denver, and power and influence followed.

Research by the C.D. Howe Institute think-tank suggested that for every dollar of new investment a U.S. worker enjoyed in 2017, a

Canadian worker attracted just $0.59—the worst performance on record.[35] Morneau was unmoved by the argument, insisting he was confident in the resiliency of the Canadian economy; that growth, employment, and consumer confidence were at satisfactory levels, while measures taken to address personal debt levels had had some success in cooling an overheated housing market. He was dismissive of the primacy of tax rates as a determinant on investment, saying that lower Canadian corporate rates may or may not have had an effect on business investment. "I don't think there's clear evidence to support it," he told Bloomberg.

But tax rates were not the only point of competitive disadvantage. Rich Kruger, chief executive of Imperial Oil, said that a regulatory regime riddled with risk and uncertainty, not to mention limited pipeline capacity to get product to market, was reducing Canada's attractiveness as a place to invest. The regulatory problem was about to get more acute with the passage of Ottawa's major environmental regulation bill, C-69, which broadened the scope of the assessment process and added enhanced consultation with Indigenous groups. Expanded factors taken into consideration included traditional Indigenous knowledge and the extent to which a project helped or hindered the attainment of climate change goals. Direct economic benefits of a project were no longer considered under the new rules.

Critics raised their eyebrows at new regulations that would scrutinize projects according to their "intersection of sex and gender with other identity factors" and the discretionary power of ministers to decide whether they go ahead. "It's our assessment that the bill is likely to increase costs and timelines. We have significant concerns about it," said Kruger.[36] Outgoing Saskatchewan premier Brad Wall warned that the cumulative effect of the carbon tax hikes and new regulations could heat up a Canadian unity issue already bubbling because of the pipeline issue. "The cumulative effect of [the new regulations] and the carbon tax mean we are heading toward an unhealthy debate, just as we did when another Trudeau introduced his energy policy. How is this different from the National Energy Program, in terms of what it will do to jobs and pipelines and so on?" he asked.[37]

Senior political staff handling the file denied that the Trudeau government has been anti-development. "On development we've been small 'c' conservative—pretty pragmatic. How many projects are you aware of that we haven't approved? We did Pacific Northwest—with its massive GHG emissions—but the bottom had fallen out of the market," said one insider. "Energy East didn't die because of our policies; it died because Donald Trump approved Keystone XL pipeline. That project only came to be because Obama was continually blocking Keystone."[38] He pointed out that the government conceded 135 amendments to its environmental protection bill to reflect criticisms from the opposition and industry, including reducing timelines and the minister of environment's ability to kill projects in the preplanning phase. "We want projects to be built and we don't want our approvals to be thrown out of court. It's as simple as that," he said.

Trudeau explained that his government's legislation was aimed at improving on the track record of the Conservatives, which saw projects routinely killed by the courts. "When you actually talk about what's in the bill—less doubling of oversight between the province and federal government, clearer and shorter timelines—these are all things that industry has asked for. And they are likely to get better buy-in from Indigenous people and Canadians in general," he said.[39]

If divisions within the federation were simmering over the competitiveness issue, they were soon set to erupt over the Trans Mountain pipeline. The opposition of John Horgan's NDP government in British Columbia incensed Albertans, particularly after B.C. environment minister George Heyman said his province would seek to regulate bitumen moving through the province. Rachel Notley was an old comrade-in-arms of Horgan's, but in February the NDP premier of Alberta threatened retaliation if B.C. continued to block Trans Mountain. She demanded Trudeau throw the full weight of the federal government behind the pipeline—something he had been loath to do to that point, saying he didn't want "to opine on disagreements between provinces."[40]

But it was becoming clear that, much as it would have preferred to sidestep an interprovincial brawl (not to mention an NDP civil war), Ottawa was not impartial. At a town hall in Nanaimo, B.C., in front of an audience that was vocal and hostile to the government's decision to back the construction of the pipeline, Trudeau ignored the abuse— "You're a snake, you're a liar!" shouted one man—and insisted that pushing forward with the pipeline was a compromise on the environment and the economy that was in the best interests of the country. It was a rare acknowledgment from the prime minister that optimism and the belief in "omni-competence" were not always sufficient to solve intractable problems that sometimes required painful trade-offs.

By making the case he did in Nanaimo, Trudeau was committed to an alliance with Notley, and her contention that the B.C. government had no jurisdiction. For Trudeau, the stakes were high—without a pipeline, Notley would not sign on to a carbon tax plan that critics pointed out would become increasingly untenable if conservative opposition parties won elections in Ontario, Quebec, and Alberta in the coming months. Trudeau gave vent to his frustration in an interview with the *National Observer*. "John Horgan is actually trying to scuttle our national plan on fighting climate change. By blocking the Kinder Morgan pipeline, he's putting at risk the entire national climate change plan because Alberta will not be able to stay on if the Kinder Morgan pipeline doesn't go through," he said.[41]

The prospects of it not going through increased exponentially in early April when the Texas oil giant Kinder Morgan announced it was suspending all activity on the pipeline until May 31 because of the political opposition in B.C. The company said it needed political certainty before it ramped up spending on the expansion of the pipeline, as it moved from clearing trees to laying pipe. The news was delivered to Trudeau as he was heading to the vigil in Saskatchewan for the victims of the Humboldt Broncos bus crash that killed sixteen and injured thirteen members of the junior hockey team. The insensitivity of the timing was a reminder to Trudeau and his team that they were dealing with a foreign multinational motivated solely by maximizing returns to shareholders. The development also made it crystal clear that the health of the federation depended on Ottawa regulating the economy of Canada in the national interest. But it was apparent there would be a political price to pay if the federal government pushed through a pipeline against concerted opposition. The Liberals had attempted to stand on all sides of every issue to that point, but now they were forced to choose.

The City of Burnaby had already said it would not pay RCMP overtime costs related to Trans Mountain because its citizens opposed the project. By mid-April, two hundred people had already been arrested near the Burnaby marine terminal, including Green Party leader Elizabeth May and then-NDP MP and future mayor of Vancouver Kennedy Stewart. The reaction of the federal and Alberta governments was to explore rescue options to satisfy Kinder Morgan's requirements that its shareholders be protected and the B.C. government's threats of obstruction come to an end.

The prospect of Horgan backing down evaporated after an emergency meeting in Ottawa with Trudeau and Notley, at which he reiterated that he intended to ask the courts to declare that B.C. had powers to regulate the pipeline. Kinder's chief executive, Steve Kean, saw the possibility for his company to make a tidy profit on the transaction, aware that when it came to spending public money, governments are generally more emptor than caveat. He and his executive chairman, Richard Kinder, didn't become two of the richest men in Houston by missing the opportunity to sell into a buyer's market—they were acutely aware of how important the pipeline was to Trudeau, given that he had closed down every other alternative route to get crude to the ocean. Kinder Morgan was in the market to sell not only the expansion but the existing pipeline, and the only potential buyers in the time frame set by the sellers were the governments of Canada and Alberta.

At a meeting in Texas in early May, Kean played hardball with Morneau—a tactic that persuaded the finance minister, Gerald Butts, and Morneau's chief of staff, Ben Chin (who had worked on the file in the office of former B.C. premier Christy Clark), that Kinder Morgan was trying to back the government into a corner so it could sell Trans Mountain for a price well above its market value. Morneau had been involved in acquisitions with his own firm, Morneau Shepell, prior to entering politics—but had no experience on the scale of Trans Mountain. To compensate, he pulled together a team of public servants with investment banking backgrounds, including Ava Yaskiel, a head of corporate law at law firm Norton Rose Fulbright, who was on secondment at the Department of Finance; Tim Duncanson, a former investment banker with Onex Corp., who had also moved to become a senior adviser at Finance; and Evan Siddall, vice-president at Goldman Sachs before taking over as president of the Canada Mortgage and Housing Corp.

Instead of bending to Kean's asking price, Morneau sprang his own surprise on the Kinder Morgan CEO—telling him he planned to hold a press conference the next day, where he would offer the Texas oil company insurance against Horgan's political manoeuvres that Kean claimed were the problem. If Kinder didn't want that deal, the indemnity would be transferable to other buyers. At the announcement in Ottawa, Morneau said the government would backstop the project with a full indemnity from losses that were "politically motivated." If Kinder Morgan—or a new operator—lost profits because of Horgan's actions, Ottawa would give them their money back. "We think plenty of investors would be interested in taking on this project, especially knowing the federal government believes it is in the best interests of Canadians and is willing to provide indemnity to make sure it gets built," he said, even as he was aware that it was unlikely anyone other than the federal government would be able to move quickly enough to meet Kinder Morgan's deadline.[42]

Morneau was seeking to call Kinder Morgan's bluff and to establish a floor price for the project lower than the company's asking price. There had been similar interventions before in Canadian history—Brian Mulroney's Conservatives had taken a stake in the Hibernia oil platform, off Newfoundland, in 1993, when the project was close to collapse.

Ottawa's 8.5 per cent stake has paid back billions of dollars in dividends since the oil started to flow in 1997. But Trudeau and Morneau were playing a high-risk game with public money, in which the political fortunes of the Liberal government and the viability of the federation were at stake.

Morneau's tactic certainly focused minds on both sides, and at a meeting with Kean in Toronto, he explained why he could not pay a hefty premium with public money. With Siddall and Duncanson leading talks, the two sides hammered out an agreement-in-principle.[43] With just days to go before Kinder Morgan's May 31 deadline, a deal was done and Ottawa found itself in the pipeline business. Trudeau's government agreed to pay $4.5 billion to buy the Trans Mountain project, including the existing pipeline that dated back to the 1950s, the terminal assets, the management team, the workforce, and the right to build an expansion that would triple daily capacity to 890,000 barrels a day. It did not include construction costs estimated by one investor at $6 billion.

Conservative leader Andrew Scheer said Trudeau was using taxpayers' money to buy his way out of his own failure. But Morneau insisted that the transaction represented a "sound investment opportunity"— and some institutional investors agreed. One New York hedge fund owner remarked that, if the already profitable pipeline was built, he expected the federal government to make a $2 billion profit on the asset when it was sold. "I would be shocked if the Canadian government didn't make money," he said.[44] Still, the "if" was a big caveat. It remained to be seen whether the Trudeau Liberals had the stomach to force through construction in the face of entrenched opposition, or crack down on civil disobedience, particularly if it came from First Nations. Environmentalists and Indigenous activists promised to make Trans Mountain another Standing Rock, the pipeline protest in North Dakota that saw armed soldiers and police in riot gear clear an encampment. "The cutest, progressivist, boy-bandiest leader in the world is going fully in the tank for the oil industry," said American environmentalist Bill McKibben in *The Guardian*.[45]

In the House of Commons, Jim Carr, then the natural resources minister, blamed the Harper government for setting the environment and
the economy in opposition. "They pitted us against each other. It polarized us. That's not who we are," he said. But it was very much who
we were in the spring and early summer of 2018. There were divisions
between provinces that supported and that opposed the pipeline, and
between provinces that supported and that opposed carbon pricing.
Any consensus that had existed over Trudeau's grand bargain on the
environment and the economy was unravelling. A government elected
on promises of positive politics and inclusiveness had taken decisions
that had increased polarization in the country.

THIRTEEN

TAKING ON THE TARIFF MAN

IT WAS AS IF a spell had been broken and the idea that Justin Trudeau could be a one-term wonder was no longer an implausible prospect. Through the first half of 2018, his government seemed to be at the mercy of every wind, not least because the prime minister kept making headlines for all the wrong reasons. Whether he had become complacent, or even just bored with the limits on his emotional vocabulary, he repeatedly made mistakes that upset small, but significant, subsets of the electorate.

The Liberals had not quite reached that stage where the social movements they had been espousing turned against them—the leftist tilt of policy was too relentless to alienate the progressive voters Trudeau needed to keep onside. But the Aga Khan vacation, the India trip, the gender-focused budget, the summer jobs program, the Trans Mountain acquisition, and rising opposition to a carbon tax all chipped away at the sense of near infallibility Trudeau had enjoyed during his first two years in power. After so many mistakes, Trudeau would find that each blunder became more pronounced as the public's patience grew thinner.

Yet the one file where Trudeau's performance was ranked consistently higher than his overall approval rating was Canada–U.S. relations —particularly his dealings with Trump and the president's increasingly shrill demands on the trade front. After Trump's visit to Wisconsin in

April 2017, where he threatened to rip up NAFTA because of Canada's restrictive policies on dairy exports, there was growing pessimism among Canadian officials about the future of the trade relationship. Those fears had only grown as negotiating teams from all three NAFTA countries had met to hammer out a modernized deal and the United States had started putting so-called poison pill proposals on the table.

At a cabinet retreat in London, Ontario, in January 2018, Trudeau struck what many people judged the appropriate tone—civil and positive, flexible but emphatic. "People know that we remain positive and hopeful, but we know this particular administration can be somewhat unpredictable and we are prepared for anything. We have contingency plans," he said.[1] One of those appeared to be faith in the ability of Republican senators and business groups like the U.S. Chamber of Commerce to rein in Trump's worst protectionist excesses. But the more people like Chamber president Tom Donohue warned that pulling out of NAFTA would be a major mistake, the more emboldened Trump appeared to be to do just that. He complained to the *Wall Street Journal* that Canada was running a US$17 billion trade surplus with the United States, despite his own country's calculations suggesting it was the U.S. that had a surplus of US$12.5 billion in 2016.[2]

Trudeau continued to emphasize that the prospect of a reconstituted NAFTA could be a "win-win-win" for the three partners. But that was a fundamental misread of the author of *The Art of the Deal*. For Trump to win, it meant others had to lose, and Ottawa's negotiators found themselves increasingly forced to make concessions at the bargaining table. Trump was said to be annoyed that Canada had not joined him to gang up on Mexico and force auto jobs north. Instead, Canada formed a united front with Mexico against Trump's demands.[3] This avoided the very real prospect of Trump dividing, then conquering, even if the president were later able to prise away the Mexicans and strike a separate agreement.

The phony war threatened to get very real in March when Trump warned he would apply tariffs on steel and aluminum imports on national security grounds, having been convinced by his trade adviser, Peter

Navarro, that the U.S. industry could only be protected by building a fortress around America to block trans-shipped Chinese metals. The Trudeau government was able to leverage the network of contacts it had built in the previous eighteen months to seek an exemption for Canada. The prime minister called close Trump ally Blackstone Group CEO Steve Schwarzman, who reputedly said that he carried influence with the president because he is richer (and thus, in Trump's world view, smarter) than him. Harjit Sajjan, the defence minister, called his American counterpart James Mattis and pointed out that, far from being a national security threat, Canada supplies the U.S. with much of the aluminum it uses in its fighter jets.

Former prime minister Brian Mulroney made the case to his friend Commerce Secretary Wilbur Ross, while the Chamber of Commerce's Donohue called Mitch McConnell, the U.S. Senate majority leader, and Paul Ryan, the then Speaker of the U.S. House of Representatives. But the pivotal intervention was Trudeau's call to Trump. The prime minister's civility and willingness to be portrayed as the junior partner paid off, as Trump agreed to exempt Canada and Mexico for thirty days. Trump had made it clear he saw a direct link between the tariffs and NAFTA negotiations. "We have large trade deficits with Mexico and Canada. NAFTA, which is under renegotiation right now is a bad deal for U.S.A. . . . Tariffs on steel and aluminum will only come off if new and fair NAFTA is signed," he tweeted.

The exemption was proof that Trudeau had Trump's ear, but if the prime minister thought he had talked the president around, he had misjudged his man. Trump is a protectionist from the tips of his polished Oxfords to the top of his unique comb-over, and it was clear that, while steel and aluminum tariffs were off the table, they could quickly reappear if he didn't receive satisfaction at the negotiating table. The comments by Wilbur Ross on CNBC that the U.S. was asking for Canada and Mexico to give up some privileges they had enjoyed under NAFTA "and we are not in a position to offer anything in return" had been dismissed as a bluff.[4] But it increasingly looked as if Trump wanted complete

capitulation from Canada, as he complained about how his closest trading partner was "very difficult, very spoiled" during negotiations.

After the exemption, there were hopes that the president might accept
a "skinny" NAFTA, a slimmed-down version of the agreement focused on
increasing the North American content in autos that would have had
the benefit for the president of not requiring congressional approval.
But as those hopes rose, Trump stood on the south lawn of the White
House in late May and said that Canada and Mexico had been taking
advantage of the U.S. for a long time. "I'm not happy at their requests.
But I will tell you, in the end, we will win and we will win big," he said.[5]

The "gaping differences" between the two sides, in the words of U.S.
Trade Representative Robert Lighthizer, centred on the American insistence on a "sunset clause" that would have blown up the modernized
NAFTA after five years and potentially forced everyone back to the negotiating table. In the eyes of the Canadians (and Mexicans), this would
hurt investment because it would create uncertainty. Trump's team also
disliked the Chapter 19 binational dispute resolution panels that had
almost been a deal breaker when Brian Mulroney was negotiating the
initial agreement with Ronald Reagan in 1987. Chapter 19 gave the U.S.,
Mexico, and Canada the right to challenge each other's anti-dumping and
countervailing duty decisions in front of an expert panel that included
members from the countries involved in the dispute. For the Canadian
side, this was seen as crucial, since it would provide the agreement with
enforceable rules not subject to mercurial executive decisions.

Other irritants included Canada's supply-managed agricultural
sectors. Relations were increasingly rocky between Lighthizer and
Canadian global affairs minister Chrystia Freeland, even while Finance
Minister Bill Morneau and his American counterpart, Steve Mnuchin,
were working well together. Morneau and his wife, Nancy McCain,
were even invited to Mnuchin's wedding to his fiancée, Louise Linton,
in Washington.

The desire to grab the "skinny NAFTA" deal that appeared within
grasp persuaded Trudeau to be flexible in what he might be prepared to

give up, particularly regarding the managed dairy sector, just as Canadian negotiators had been when they landed trade deals with the European Union and the Trans-Pacific Partnership countries. Canada was also prepared to give up on Chapter 11, the arbitration mechanism that allowed investors in a NAFTA country to bring proceedings directly against another NAFTA government. Since Canada had been the subject of the highest number of investor-state arbitration claims, the Trudeau government was not sad to see it go.

But Chapter 19 and the sunset clause were different. The former bound the U.S. to decisions made by a tribunal comprising of representatives from both countries. As Fen Osler Hampson detailed in his book *Master of Persuasion: Brian Mulroney's Global Legacy*, in the original negotiations, Mulroney was prepared to walk away from a free trade agreement with the United States unless there was an arbitration process independent of the U.S. court system. Just three hours before the deadline, Mulroney talked to Ronald Reagan and asked him how it was possible for the U.S. to conclude a nuclear arms deal with the Russians but not a trade deal with its closest neighbour and ally. Mulroney got his dispute settlement mechanism.[6]

But, whereas Reagan believed the prosperity and security of the U.S. was enhanced by a more cooperative global system, Trump subscribed to the "every country for itself" school of thought. He was increasingly persuaded by Lighthizer and his trade adviser, Navarro, that the recent history of trade liberalization should be rolled back and U.S. multinationals investing overseas forced to repatriate their capital. In that scenario, a combination of lower corporate taxes and punitive tariffs would persuade American manufacturers to relocate their production to the United States.

As a consequence, in early June, "skinny NAFTA" died and Wilbur Ross announced that Canada, Mexico, and the European Union would be subject to a 25 per cent tariff on steel and a 10 per cent levy on aluminum. Canada and the U.S. were in a trade war. Ross cited lack of progress on NAFTA as the reason for the imposition of the tariffs, but they were applied under an obscure provision in the U.S. trade law that allowed the administration to apply duties on imports it deemed a threat to national security. As Lighthizer told a Senate committee in late July, the real target was China, but it was deemed necessary to prevent a "hole in the net" that would allow steel from China and other places to flow into the U.S. through Canada. "That's the context. Nobody is declaring war on Canada or saying they are an unfriendly neighbour. They're obviously not, they're a great ally and certainly one of America's closest friends and closest trading partners. But if you decide that you need to protect an industry, you can't be in a position where the protection is of no value because everything comes in through the capital of Canada," he said.[7]

Notwithstanding the absence of steel being trans-shipped through Ottawa, the mood in Canada's capital was outrage, with added exasperation. Trudeau had resisted the urge to score domestic political points by insulting a man so vain it seemed conceivable he drank his own bathwater. Some Canadian prime ministers used to wind up Washington. Jean Chrétien was once overheard telling the Belgian prime minister, "I like to stand up to the Americans. It's popular—people like it, but you have to be careful because they're our friends." But Trudeau had sacrificed his own self-respect in pursuit of a renewed NAFTA deal in the national interest. And it hadn't worked. Trump was like the school bully with the class dweeb—acquiescence was interpreted as submissiveness.

Trudeau was forced to take the only course left open to him, as he held an impromptu press conference in Ottawa, along with Chrystia Freeland, to announce retaliatory measures worth $16.6 billion. The trading system agreed to with the General Agreement on Trade and Tariffs in 1947 had proven resilient to challenges in the ensuing seventy years, mainly because outlaw nations had found themselves on the receiving end of massive retaliation. Trudeau said that using a national security provision as an excuse for the U.S. tariffs was an "affront" to the long-standing security partnership between two countries that had fought side by side in Flanders, Normandy, Korea, and Afghanistan.

The response was carefully calibrated, Freeland explained—"precisely reciprocal" in value and comprising consumer goods from swing states ranging from yogurt and pizza to coffee and maple syrup; from chocolate and strawberry jam to bourbon and playing cards. The products were carefully chosen, she said, so that Canadian producers and consumers were less badly affected because there was a ready Canadian-produced substitute.[8]

Even then, when every fibre of his body must have been screaming to retaliate, Trudeau maintained a sense of serenity. "The government of Canada is confident that shared values, geography and common interest will overcome protectionism," he said.[9] Trudeau revealed that he'd attempted to repeat his eleventh-hour intervention from March, when he'd convinced Trump to grant Canada a temporary exemption from steel and aluminum tariffs. Members of Trump's team called contacts in Trudeau's office and urged the prime minister to try to broker a deal with the president. During the resulting phone call between the two leaders, on May 25, Trump is said to have justified the U.S. action as a response to previous Canadian aggression. "Didn't you guys burn down the White House?" he reportedly asked Trudeau, a reference to the War of 1812, when British troops burned down the presidential residence in retaliation for an American attack on York, present-day Toronto.[10] Trump may have been joking. But he also may not.

Trudeau said he'd made an offer to visit Washington to finalize a modernized NAFTA. "There were the broad lines of a decent win/win/win that I felt required the final deal-making moment. But I got a call from vice-president [Mike] Pence, who impressed upon me a pre-condition to us getting together—that Canada accept a sunset clause. I had to highlight there was no possibility of any Canadian prime minister signing a NAFTA deal that included a five-year sunset clause,"[11] he said.

But Trump decided against seeking a compromise—and heading into a meeting of G7 heads of government that week in Charlevoix, Quebec, the prospects for "win/win/win" looked very far away indeed. In the run-up to the meeting, both Trudeau and Freeland took to the

U.S. airwaves to protest the American action. On Trump's nemesis, cable network CNN, the global affairs minister said Canadians were "hurt and insulted" at being classed as a national security threat. Larry Kudlow, Trump's economic adviser, was dispatched to respond on the rival, Trump-friendly network, Fox News, to suggest that the Canadians were overreacting and compare the dispute to a "family quarrel."

Trump's actions were proving controversial at home, as well as abroad, as Republican congressmen complained about the impact of retaliatory measures in their home states. It was pointed out that, in 2002, President George W. Bush had imposed steel tariffs that were withdrawn eighteen months later because they adversely affected GDP growth and employment in the U.S. But the lessons of history were lost on the president and he charged into Charlevoix like a bull travelling with his own china shop. He caused controversy even before he left U.S. airspace, by suggesting that Russia be reinstated into the G7, four years after it had been expelled for annexing Ukraine's Crimea. Canada, among others, swiftly made it clear the idea was a non-starter.

In the buildup to the summit, the media predicted it would end up being the "G6 plus 1," with the countries on the receiving end of Trump's tariffs using the opportunity of having the president there in person to air their collective grievances. Which is exactly how it turned out. But in the early going, relations were cordial enough. Trump ambled toward his host on the front lawn of the Manoir Richelieu in Charlevoix, overlooking the St. Lawrence, as glum as if he were heading to lunch with the Clintons. But the grip-and-grin went well and the two leaders looked as if they could do business.

It was over the weekend that relations between the president and everyone else turned polar and an all-out trade war appeared imminent. The agenda in Charlevoix had shifted from trade to issues not close to Trump's heart—climate change and empowering women. He created a stir by arriving late to the gender-focused breakfast session and ducked out of the summit early to begin his twenty-hour journey to Singapore, where he was meeting North Korean leader Kim Jong-un. But before he left, he held a press conference that repeated the position that Canada and other trading partners must eliminate their trade barriers, including supply management for Canada's dairy sector, if they wanted new trade deals with the United States. Trump said that a deal was "close" on a sunset clause that would reopen NAFTA after five years.

After the president left, Trudeau held his own press conference, in which he reiterated Canada's position that it would not be "pushed around" by the U.S. president over the tariff dispute. He stressed that Canada could never agree to the sunset clause provision. Trump, who was watching the press conference from Air Force One, en route to Singapore, took grave exception to the prime minister's comments and immediately started retaliating on Twitter, calling Trudeau "very dishonest and weak" and threatening to impose tariffs on automobiles. Noting that he had ordered American officials to withdraw from the joint communiqué being penned in Charlevoix, he later dispatched his top advisers to bad-mouth Trudeau on the U.S. network shows the next day. "PM Justin Trudeau of Canada acted so meek and mild during our @G7 meetings, only to give a news conference after I left saying 'U.S. tariffs were kind of insulting' and he 'will not be pushed around,'" Trump tweeted. The following morning on the U.S. cable networks, Navarro called the Canadian prime minister a "backstabber" who deserved a "special place in hell."

Trudeau kept his head down, while Freeland said that "Canada does not conduct its diplomacy through ad hominen attacks."[12] Trump's adviser Kudlow gave some semblance of an explanation for Trump's hair-trigger reaction (beyond the suggestion from former CIA director Michael Hayden that the president is "unstable, erratic, and thin-skinned")—namely, that the U.S. president could not permit any show of weakness on the eve of a summit with North Korea. But the assault on one of America's closest allies was unprecedented, and it amplified the hurt and anger already being felt in Canada.

Behind the scenes, senior Canadian officials, including ambassador David MacNaughton, were bandying about the idea of a national effort similar to the Second World War "Victory Gardens"—a symbolic but material patriotic mobilization that saw individual Canadians build vegetable plots to help the war effort. The government was wary to be seen advocating such an effort, but it was keen to broaden the involvement of individual Canadians by encouraging them to express their displeasure by boycotting U.S. goods. The great patriotic trade war against American gherkins and strawberry jam was launched on July 1, Canada Day, when the government's retaliatory action against U.S. steel tariffs came into effect. The Trudeau government didn't need to artificially stoke the anger felt by Canadians—one poll suggested that nearly 80 per cent of people opposed Trump's tariffs.

The government's job was made that much easier by another inflammatory Trump tweet on his way to Singapore that suggested he intended to punish "the people of Canada" for comments Trudeau made in his Charlevoix press conference. "That's going to cost a lot of money for the people of Canada," he wrote. The leader of one of the U.S.'s great trading partners was, in Trump's words, "weak" and "dishonest," while Kim Jong-un, the leader of the world's most repressive regime, was "a great personality" and a "very talented man." Brian Mulroney, the former prime minister, was still being used by Trudeau as a bridge to the Trump administration and he urged patience. "This too will pass," he said, as he dismissed the grounds for Trump's complaints. "How the hell can you have an unemployment rate of 3.8 per cent [the U.S. rate] if your trade arrangements are so bad? The answer is, they're not."[13]

How did things get so off track that the government of Canada was tacitly appealing to the economic nationalism of its citizens? It was a long way from Trump's first press conference with Trudeau, where he talked about the "very outstanding" trade relationship between the two countries that would require nothing more than a "tweak." Was such a downward spiral inevitable? Canadians seemed prepared to give Trudeau that most essential of commodities for all politicians—the benefit of the doubt—based on Trump's mercurial personality and style. But critics like Brian Lee Crowley and former Stephen Harper adviser Sean Speer, at the free-market Macdonald Laurier Institute think-tank, pointed out that Trudeau himself had said that a key measure of any Canadian government is how it manages the Canada–U.S. relationship, regardless of whether it agrees with the incumbent in the White House.

Lee Crowley and Speer argued that Ottawa had made a series of miscalculations and errors that provoked the Trump administration and exacerbated bilateral tensions, putting the NAFTA negotiations at risk.[14] They cited Canada's initial negotiating position of proposing a deal that was "more progressive" through the insertion of "ideological causes completely at odds with Trump's priorities. This was both a distraction and needlessly provocative," they wrote. Much the same could be said about the agenda at the G7 summit in Charlevoix, which focused on issues like gender and the environment, knowing this would "annoy and isolate" the president, they contended, with some justification.

Trudeau's China policy of pursuing a free trade deal while downplaying national security concerns were also cited as potential irritants. The Liberals had waved through a number of dubious takeovers and only blocked the acquisition of construction giant Aecon by a Chinese state-owned enterprise after being pressured into undertaking a full-scale national security review. Lee Crowley and Speer pointed out that a Canadian warship, HMCS *Vancouver*, engaged in military exercises with the Chinese navy in May—a move that the Americans doubtless interpreted as being at odds with efforts to resist Chinese claims and militarization in the South China Sea. The Trudeau government failed to recognize the evolving political landscape in Washington and adjust accordingly —"a costly and regrettable mistake," the authors concluded.

That mistakes were made is undeniable. The "progressive" agenda irritated Wilbur Ross, in particular, according to people who spoke with him. But the stark fact was that Trudeau was trying to strike a trade deal with a protectionist. No amount of tweaking could easily reconcile those differences.

What had klaxons ringing all over Ottawa was Trump's threat to impose a 25 per cent duty on all autos imported into the United States —including those from Canada. The Peterson Institute for International Economics looked at the impact of the duty, and the inevitable retaliation, and concluded that the measure would kill 624,000 jobs in the U.S. and reduce auto production by 4 per cent.[15] The feeling in Ottawa was that the damage to the Canadian manufacturing sector would be existential, given that it employed 130,000 to 140,000 people. The prospect of U.S. job losses was causing growing discomfort among U.S. Senate Republicans. "I think there's a jailbreak brewing," said Bob Corker, a Republican senator from Tennessee who was trying to rein in the administration.[16]

Powerful Republicans like Senate majority leader Mitch McConnell of Kentucky started to express concerns about the impact on their home states. "We make Toyota Camrys and the price of steel seems to be headed up. We're the home of bourbon—proudly—and the price of bourbon seems to be headed up. So there is a concern," he said.[17] Trump appeared to confirm the imposition of tariffs was a grand game of poker at an event in Fargo, North Dakota. "We can't lose," he said. "Just play the game for a little while."[18]

By mid-summer, MPs were already hearing about the human collateral from tariffs on steel. Robert Dimitrieff, president of a specialty steel company, Patriot Forge, in Brantford, Ontario, told the international trade committee he employed 250 people but said the company would close "within a few months" unless it received some relief from tariffs. As a snapshot of Canadian industry, Patriot was typical for its reliance on the U.S. economy. It shipped 90 per cent of its products to the United States and was doubly wounded by Canadian retaliation because it imported most of its alloy from specialty steel producers in the U.S.

The auto business was four times the size of the steel industry, and as Jerry Dias, the head of the country's biggest union, Unifor, said, "There's not an assembly plant in the country that could survive a 25 per cent tariff."[19] The sense of fear about the prospect of "carmaggedon" was palpable among Canadian business owners. Bob Verwey, president of Owasco, a Whitby, Ontario–based car and RV business, told MPs his house, his family, and the jobs of 220 employees were on the line. "I believe Trump is a bear and we shouldn't be poking him too much," he said. But as United Steelworkers national director Ken Neumann pointed out, "If you don't poke the bear, he's going to eat your lunch."[20] Charlie Chesbrough, a senior economist at Cox Automotive, said he thought the threat was a negotiating ploy to get a NAFTA agreement on the president's terms. He said that even if Trump did impose auto tariffs, manufacturers would be reluctant to close Canadian plants and shift production south unless they were convinced the president's protectionist policies were going to outlive his administration.[21]

But the Canadian government was forced to try to fathom the unfathomable—the Trump Doctrine of foreign policy. This was summed up by editor-in-chief of *The Atlantic* Jeffrey Goldberg, in three pithy quotes: "No friends, no enemies" (Trump didn't believe the United States should be part of any alliances); "Permanent destabilization creates American advantage" (keeping allies and adversaries perpetually off-balance benefitted the U.S.); and "We're America, bitch" (Trump didn't feel the need to apologize for anything the U.S. did). The president pursued policies that undermined the Western alliance, empowering Russia and China, but they allowed him to direct a middle finger at a world that no longer respected American power and privilege, Goldberg wrote.[22]

That reckless lack of concern about international relationships that had seemed immutable for seventy years shaped Canadian foreign policy far beyond the NAFTA negotiations. As Chrystia Freeland had outlined in her long exegesis of foreign policy in the Age of Trump the previous year, the core notions of territorial integrity, human rights, democracy, respect for the rule of law, and aspiration to free trade were all under threat—and Canada as an "essential country at this time in the life of our planet" was obliged to step up.

But Canada's conspicuous dependence on the U.S. market made independent action tricky. Canadian foreign policy in the post-war era has often been a tug-of-war between the polar opposite pulls of romanticism and realism. As extolled by Canada's former ambassador in Washington, Allan Gotlieb, in a memorable 2004 lecture, this is the pressure created by Canada's "idealistic vocation" to promote democracy and reduce inequities in the world, and the realpolitik that puts the national interest ahead of all other considerations. Gotlieb explained that the two have not always pulled in opposite directions, but successive governments have usually been dominated by one approach or the other.

Gotlieb was critical of foreign policy under the current prime minister's father that "swung erratically between the poles of aggressive nationalism and unrealistic internationalism," noting, "For Trudeau, one day it was brass-knuckles realism, the next feel-good idealism."[23] As a senior diplomat, Gotlieb urged Trudeau the elder to avoid those areas where Canada's direct interests were minimal, to bypass multilateral forums where rhetoric ruled, and to concentrate on tasks where Canadians derived the most benefit and could have the most impact.[24] The advice was increasingly ignored. Trudeau's policy dissipated under Brian Mulroney, where the "bedrock reality principle was that the U.S. was a friend and ally, not a power against which one sought counterweights." But it re-emerged under Jean Chrétien, whose activist foreign minister, Lloyd Axworthy, saw Canada as an "agent of change." The result was policy "characterized by a profound lack of coherence, then by an increased anti-American inflection," according to Gotlieb.[25] Trudeau and Freeland share a sense of missionary zeal, but Trump's election had dictated that policy was often less virtuous and free-wheeling than either might like. Finger-wagging at world powers like China and India had proven counterproductive, and the "values-based" foreign policy had to be downplayed so as not to rile the president.

When Trump withdrew the U.S. from the Obama-brokered nuclear deal with Iran in May 2018, Trudeau's response was muted. Before Trump's announcement, the prime minister said he hoped the agreement would stay in place, but afterwards he had nothing to add. Canada had its own problems with Iran—relations were basically on ice, with little prospect of them thawing until Tehran allowed Iranian-Canadian Maryam Mombeini, the widow of a university professor who died in an Iranian prison, to return home. (The Liberals even supported a Conservative motion in June, calling for the government to cease diplomatic talks with Iran and list the Islamic Revolutionary Guard as a terror group, such was the frustration with the Mombeini case.) But the "essential country" rhetoric might have suggested a more vocal response in support of allies like Britain, France, and Germany, who were keen to maintain the deal that saw Iran agree to limit its nuclear capacity in exchange for an easing of economic sanctions. Canada's influence in the world came from working with the United States and its big European allies—yet in the case of Iran, it sat on the fence.

A similar ploy was used at the UN the previous December, when Canada abstained on a General Assembly resolution that repudiated Trump's decision to move the U.S. embassy in Israel to Jerusalem—a resolution that France and Britain had both supported. By and large, Canada did not live up to the rhetoric of setting its own "clear and sovereign course" in foreign affairs—unless it suited the Liberal Party's domestic political agenda. Many Jewish voters in Canada had moved to the Conservatives because of Stephen Harper's staunch support, which his critics derided as "Israel, right or wrong." But this lack of support from the Jewish-Canadian community allowed Trudeau to criticize the Jewish state with relative impunity. The Trudeau government had followed its Conservative predecessor in voting against UN resolutions condemning Israel—thus breaking with Liberal tradition (under Jean Chrétien in 2000, Canada had backed a resolution condemning Israel's "excessive force" against Palestinians). But after Israeli snipers used live ammunition against Palestinian protestors at the border of the Gaza strip, Trudeau said the Israel Defense Forces' (IDF) response was "inexcusable."

Tens of thousands of Palestinians had protested the transfer of the U.S. embassy to Jerusalem, leaving sixty dead in clashes with the IDF. A Canadian-Palestinian doctor, Tarek Loubani, was wounded, prompting

Trudeau to make the strongest criticism he had yet levelled at Israel. "Canada calls for an immediate independent investigation to thoroughly examine the facts on the ground—including any incitement, violence and the excessive use of force," he said in a statement.[26] While the U.S. blamed the deaths on Hamas, Trudeau made no mention of the Islamist group that controls Gaza and encouraged the protests. Jewish groups like the Canadian Friends of Simon Wiesenthal Center called Trudeau's statement unbalanced because it failed to condemn Hamas or point out that some protestors were "attempting to enter a sovereign nation to carry out terrorism."[27]

In this instance, for domestic political reasons, Trudeau risked upsetting Trump. A statement blaming Israeli forces while ignoring the role of Hamas played well with progressive voters, for whom Israel was the antagonist and Palestinians merely peaceful civilians. Canada resumed its position astride the fence when it opposed a United Nations Human Rights Council vote to establish an investigation into the deaths at the Israel–Gaza border, on the grounds that it was pushed by Muslim countries and was biased against Israel. But Freeland continued to say that Canada supported a "neutral" inquiry into the use of live ammunition by the IDF.

There was another instance in late summer when the Trudeau government allowed its romantic instincts to prevail. A tweet by Freeland calling for the release of two women's rights activists, including Samar Badawi, sister of imprisoned writer Raif Badawi, provoked an angry response from the peevish Saudi Arabian crown prince, Mohammed bin Salman. Canada had been working for months to try to gain the release of civil and women's rights activists arrested and imprisoned in a Saudi crackdown the previous May—an effort that included one-on-one calls between Freeland and her Saudi counterpart. Officials at the Canadian embassy in Riyadh recommended that the government make a public statement, and Freeland's tweet was issued. Another tweet in Arabic from the embassy in Saudi Arabia followed and prompted the Saudi foreign minister, Adel al-Jubeir, to register his "concern."[28]

The Saudi prince called the intervention "blatant interference in the Kingdom's domestic affairs," expelled the Canadian ambassador, froze bilateral trade, and dumped Canadian assets. The anger was artificial on both sides, and the damage slight. But the Saudis had sent the message to other Western countries to keep their own counsel on the kingdom's right to imprison, behead, and crucify its citizens, or risk losing access to its markets. For their part, the Trudeau Liberals were able to engage in their particular brand of pulpit diplomacy, preaching to the rest of the world without having to back up the rhetoric with resources. Canada's former Saudi envoy, Dennis Horak, was quoted as saying Freeland's tweet was a "serious overreaction" and "went too far." "It was a situation that didn't need to occur . . . to sort of yell from the sidelines, I don't think is effective," he told Reuters.[29] Freeland could claim to being on the side of the angels when the Saudis murdered journalist Jamal Khashoggi in their consulate in Turkey in October 2018. But the fact remained that Samar Badawi was less likely to be released after Canada's involvement than she was before. What the incident had revealed was that Canada was impotent when it came to transforming the behaviour of other states. As Gotlieb pointed out, Canada's role as a middle power will never be regained, but this unrealistic sense of utopianism, millenarianism, and visionary crusading offered the mirage of power and influence.

A more realistic picture of Canada's hard power capabilities was revealed at a meeting of leaders of the North Atlantic Treaty Organization countries in Brussels in mid-July, where this country sat uncomfortably in the bottom half of contributing nations. Trump barrelled into Belgium with the subtlety of a tornado in a glasshouse, immediately living up to his "no friends, no enemies" credo. He claimed that Germany had become "captive to Russia" because of a gas pipeline deal and criticized "delinquent" allies for underspending in their own defence. At a time when the majority of NATO partners had not reached their agreed target of spending 2 per cent of GDP on their militaries, Trump demanded they commit to 4 per cent.

The Canadian government's "Strong, Secure, Engaged" defence policy, released in spring 2017, planned to inject $62.3 billion into the Canadian military—a dramatic increase in spending on new equipment like warships and fighter jets. But even that did not put Canada anywhere close to 2 per cent of GDP—an aspirational figure to which Stephen Harper had signed on in 2014 but which the defence review tacitly admitted Canada had no intention of ever achieving. At the time of the NATO meeting, Canada sat eighteenth out of twenty-nine countries when it came to defence spending as a percentage of GDP.[30] Trudeau repeatedly pointed out that it was the quality of output, rather than the quantity of inputs, that mattered. Canada was spending 30 per cent of its expenditure on new equipment, while other countries lumped in costs for pensions and other soft spending. Prior to the NATO leaders meeting, Trudeau had visited Canadian troops in Latvia, where they were leading a NATO mission.

But there were very real fears that Trump had no interest in preserving NATO, and that he might repeat his performance from Charlevoix, where he had withdrawn the U.S. from the final communiqué. If Trump had openly questioned America's commitment to Article 5, NATO's mutual defence clause, it could have torpedoed the alliance and seen U.S. troops withdrawn from Europe. Deterrence was dependent on political unity. To stave off such an eventuality, Jens Stoltenberg, NATO's secretary general, pointed out that 2017 had seen the biggest increase in defence spending across Europe and Canada in twenty-five years.

After a chaotic twenty-eight hours at NATO, Trump decided not to blow up the organization, instead declaring it a "fine-tuned machine" that had caved into his demands to speed up increases in military spending.[31] After days of complaining that the U.S. was being taken advantage of by its allies, Trump said that America's commitment to NATO "remains very strong."[32] It was a perfect example of Jeffrey Goldberg's summation of the Trump Doctrine in action—"permanent destabilization creates American advantage."

The Trudeau government had responded to the threat of American isolationism by saying that Canada would chart a sovereign course to help ensure the survival of the post-war, multilateral, rules-based order. In reality, American pre-eminence meant that Canada was obliged to tack in whatever direction the capricious U.S. captain chose to sail.

FOURTEEN
—————

"A GREAT DAY FOR CANADA"

THE FORTY-THIRD ELECTION CAMPAIGN began in earnest in the steamy summer of 2018, when most of the country was dozing at the cottage. A prime minister under pressure on a number of fronts decided it would be a good time to shuffle his cabinet while no one was looking, giving new ministers time to learn their files. The shuffle allowed Trudeau to calibrate his front bench to address the fresh challenges facing the government—in particular, Trump's agenda and the election of a new and feisty Progressive Conservative premier, Doug Ford, in Ontario, who had already made known his intention to derail the Liberal carbon tax. The other big test was the asylum seekers issue. The appointment with the greatest potential to improve the electoral prospects for the Liberals was the introduction of former police chief Bill Blair in the newly minted role of minister for border security and organized crime reduction, taking over the "irregular migration" file from immigration minister Ahmed Hussen.

Elsewhere, Dominic LeBlanc moved from Fisheries to become the new minister for intergovernmental affairs and internal trade. LeBlanc is hard to dislike, and the calculation was that he could blunt opposition to the carbon tax and shepherd the provinces to give some meaning to the Canada Free Trade Agreement, signed the year before but as useless as a pulled tooth up to that point. Jim Carr, who had offered a steady hand at Natural Resources, was moved to the newly named International Trade Diversification department, over concerns about overreliance on the U.S. relationship. The livewire former trade minister, François-Philippe Champagne, was given the responsibility for infrastructure—a file that helped the Liberals win the 2015 election but which had since become a liability because the government was unable to get the money out of the door fast enough. Champagne was deemed to be a good communicator in both official languages, with the added bonus that he'd do what he was told. Most of the other changes were cosmetic and politically motivated—designed to maintain the fifty–fifty gender split, pander to particular demographic groups, or help raise the profiles of MPs who might face tight electoral battles the following year.

The shuffle gave the prime minister the opportunity to add five new members to his already bulging ministry—including Jonathan Wilkinson, the new fisheries minister who was in tough in Vancouver thanks to the Trans Mountain pipeline; Mary Ng, a former staffer in the Prime Minister's Office and the only Chinese-Canadian member of cabinet; and Filomena Tassi, an Italian-Canadian from Hamilton, Ontario. The tokenism of the latter two appointments—both were political rookies—provoked quiet outrage among a number of experienced male members in Trudeau's caucus, particularly given Ng's close friendship with chief of staff Katie Telford.

As the prime minister surveyed the electoral landscape that summer, there were reasons to be cheerful. The Liberals were statistically tied in most credible polls and had a leader who consistently polled above his two major rivals.[1] The party was in much better shape organizationally than it had been when Trudeau became leader. In his 2011 election post-mortem, former party president Alf Apps had concluded, "The Conservative Party is able to calibrate its voter contact to each voter's profile with laser-like focus. The Liberal Party is flying half-blind and well behind when it comes to election technology and digital know-how."[2]

Things had improved on the technology front by the 2015 election, but the party structure remained federated and cumbersome. At the convention in 2016, Trudeau used his political capital to transform the party from an exclusive club into a more open political movement. The leader's proposal streamlined the party constitution, doing away with the concept of membership and allowing anyone who registered for free as a Liberal to vote in leadership and nomination contests. It also centralized the party structure and boiled down the eighteen provincial and territorial constitutions. There were fears among some grassroots Liberals that this shift would give the leader and party executives too much power. But Trudeau argued successfully that it was necessary to end the problem of "factional battles and hyphenated Liberals, the regional chieftains and behind-the-scenes power-brokers, the closed insular thinking that almost killed this party."[3]

Anna Gainey, who was party president during the modernization process, said that the 2015 victory was achieved in spite of the structural barriers. "It was a bit like insider baseball—the language that was spoken, the constitution, the rules—there were people who had been around long enough and understood it. But I felt it was not conducive to bringing in those three hundred thousand supporters, who were interested in the party but didn't want to spend ten dollars to become a member. They wanted to be connected. So we tried to bring the party to a place where it was more modern and accessible," she explained.[4] The decision to abolish fees came at a cost—memberships brought in $2.2 million for the party in 2015. But the Liberal fundraising base had broadened—in 2017, the party raised $13.9 million from 64,444 contributors. (The Conservatives outstripped that number, raising $18.8 million from 94,786 donors—but spent nearly $5 million more than the Liberals in fundraising activities.[5])

But if the Liberals had gotten their own house in order, wildfires were blazing across the country—literally and figuratively—that were about to make life uncomfortably hot for the prime minister.

IN LATE JUNE, the *National Post* reported a story about eighteen-year-old allegations against Trudeau, claiming that, at a music festival in B.C. intended to raise money to build a backcountry lodge in honour of his late brother, he had "groped" a female reporter. The unsigned editorial in the August 14, 2000, edition of the *Creston Valley Advance*, a small community paper, took Trudeau to task for allegedly "inappropriately handling" the reporter. "Shouldn't the son of a former prime minister be aware of the rights and wrongs that go along with public socializing? Didn't he learn, through his vast experiences in public life, that groping a strange young woman isn't in the handbook of proper etiquette, regardless of who she is, what her business is or where they are?" it asked.[6] The *Post* revealed that the editorial's author was the reporter who made the allegations. But she refused to speak publicly and, starved of a first-hand account, the story withered.

Trudeau claimed to have no memory of any "negative interactions," but for the self-described feminist who insisted that every survivor must be believed, the story was a problem, casting a shadow over his role as an advocate for women's issues and the #MeToo movement. Not long before the allegations surfaced, he had dropped quadriplegic MP Kent Hehr from cabinet over allegations of inappropriate touching and comments. Yet there were no repercussions for the prime minister's own alleged indiscretions.

The claims, and the indignation on the right that the "mainstream media" had ignored the story, added fuel to the sense that the culture wars and polarization that had characterized the U.S. election in 2016 were spilling north of the border. It became clear that the assertive push toward "inclusive" policies by the Trudeau government had sparked a counterreaction on the right. Ford's election in Ontario was more a consequence of voter fatigue with a tired and corrupt provincial Liberal government, but once installed, the premier was quick to set down markers for his populist conservative regime—cancelling green energy contracts, threatening to invoke the "notwithstanding" clause to halve the size of Toronto city council, and joining

Saskatchewan's court case against the federal government over the carbon tax.

As the parties of the left and right hurtled in opposite directions, away from the quiet majority of befuddled voters in the centre of the spectrum, both the Liberals and Conservatives began to use the coded language of dog-whistle politics to reach their base. At an open-air rally in Quebec, Trudeau was heckled by a woman later identified as belonging to a group that liked neither Islam nor immigration. After delivering a stump speech so dull that birds were in danger of falling from the sky, he could be seen on video walking toward the woman, and when she accused him of betraying the Québécois, he replied that "racism has no place" in Canada. When he was challenged on the issue at a news conference, he said hate speech and the politics of division were a "dangerous path" to go down, adding that he intended to call out the rise in extreme populism. It was political gold for the prime minister, allowing him to equate the far-right views of the heckler with Scheer's Conservatives. At his own nomination meeting the previous week, he had denounced a Conservative Party that was ready to exploit ruptures created by global populism—conveniently overlooking his own appeals to tribal divisions.

His attempt to animate the Liberal base was aided by members of the Conservative caucus, who seemed intent on validating the charge that they were stoking the politics of "fear and division." A Conservative senator questioned the politics of Liberal MP Omar Alghabra, who was born in Saudi Arabia; the same MP was called "an overt Islamist" by another Tory; and then former Conservative foreign affairs minister Maxime Bernier criticized Trudeau's "cult of diversity" and his promotion of "extreme multiculturalism." Bernier had chafed under Scheer's leadership, after being narrowly pipped for the crown in 2017. When his thoughts on multiculturalism were disowned by the party establishment, he decided to leave what he called "an intellectually and morally corrupt" Conservative Party to form his own libertarian "People's Party," scorching the electoral earth behind him as he departed.

Bernier, like others including Stephen Harper in his book *Right Here, Right Now*, saw Canada as ripe for a rejection of the status quo and establishment political figures. He attempted to jump on Trump's populist bandwagon by calling for a reduction in low-skilled immigration. But unlike Trump, Bernier wanted less, not more, protection for trade and workers—a call at odds with the forces that have propelled populism around the world. If there was an appetite for a populist figure in federal politics who could "make Canada great again," by protecting its citizens from the forces of globalism, it was far from clear that it was the libertarian Bernier, who seemed to exist in a bubble of his own self-narrative.

For the Liberals, a split in the Conservative ranks was a welcome respite, since it forced Scheer to concentrate on consolidating his party at the Conservative Party conference in Halifax at the end of August, rather than focusing on the government's shortcomings. History suggests that the Conservatives only win when the right is united and the NDP is polling strongly. In the past forty years, the party has had an average of 38 per cent support in elections where it was united, but that number was cleaved in half during the three elections when it was split. By carving off even a small percentage of Conservative support, Bernier made a Liberal victory in 2019 much more likely. Compared to the relatively bloodless Scheer, the Liberals now had a populist hobgoblin to rally against. The Liberal Party revealed that Bernier's musing on multiculturalism enabled them to raise 77 per cent more funds than in previous issues-based campaigns, and to increase the number of registered Liberal supporters. The battle lines were being drawn. For many progressives, the barbarians were at the gates.

As he chastised those benighted individuals who disagreed with him, Trudeau sought to reinforce that he and the rest of the Anointed were on a morally higher plane by making another public apology. The news that the prime minister was set to seek atonement for events that had happened long before he was born provoked groans of derision from people who found Bernier's message appealing. But on this occasion, there were additional concerns. Trudeau's contrition up to that point had been relatively benign. For gay men and women drummed out of the public service; the descendants of Sikhs turned away on the *Komagata Maru*; survivors of Newfoundland's residential schools; and members of the Tsilhqot'in First Nation, which saw six of its chiefs hanged in 1864, the prime minister's formal apologies may have offered some comfort. But on this occasion—a formal apology for Canada's 1939 decision to turn away the MS *St. Louis*, a ship carrying 907 German Jews fleeing the Nazi regime—the Liberals used the apology to justify government policy on migrants crossing into Canada from the United States.

Omar Alghabra, the parliamentary secretary to the trade minister, tweeted that Canada should reconcile its promotion of human rights globally with mistakes made at home. "We turned away asylum seekers without giving them due process and dignity. We must learn from our history," he said.[7] The tweet provoked a storm of protest from people accusing him of making a direct historical comparison between the Holocaust and the fate facing today's "irregular" migrants. Alghabra denied he was equating the two, but his insistence that "those who don't learn from history are doomed to repeat it" suggested that he saw parallels.

To the government's critics, a senior Liberal was attempting to manipulate sympathy for Holocaust victims to justify the government's managerial shortcomings. Refugees who land in Canada are obliged to receive due process under the Charter, but that process was becoming too prolonged for many. In early September, the *Toronto Star* reported that, since April 2017, only 398 of 32,173 people who crossed the U.S.–Canada border illegally had been deported. Most were still waiting for their asylum claims to be heard—the average wait time had grown to twenty months, from fourteen months two years earlier. Of the 398 failed refugee claimants, 146 were sent back to the United States, where 116 of them had citizenship.[8]

The public consensus on immigration relied on the system being fair and well managed. But that consensus was being sorely tested. In November 2018, federal immigration minister Ahmed Hussen said

Canada would increase its immigration target to 350,000 by 2021, an announcement that seemed designed to flush out the Conservatives. With Bernier's fledgling party promising to cut the number of permanent residents arriving in Canada from the current target of 330,000 in 2019 to around 250,000, there was growing pressure on the Conservatives to follow suit. The party's immigration critic, Michelle Rempel, admitted that it might be the politically expedient thing to do. "If I was taking the easy route, I'd just say 'Cut immigration.' . . . But the reality is we have to reform the system. It isn't working by any metric," she said. "What Bernier doesn't understand is that for the people looking at his party, there is only one number that is sufficient—and that's zero," she said.[9]

An August 2018 survey by the Angus Reid Institute set off alarm bells that the consensus that has characterized Canadian attitudes toward immigration for the previous four decades was in danger of shattering. The poll found that the number of respondents who felt that immigration levels should stay the same or be increased, which had registered at over 50 per cent for forty years, had fallen to 37 per cent. Half of those surveyed said they would prefer to see the federal government's 2018 immigration target of 310,000 new permanent residents be reduced. Rempel said the consensus was under pressure because the Liberals had bungled aspects of immigration policy like the "irregular" border-crossing file. "The consensus is not breaking down, but the public is looking at what is happening with the asylum seekers and they don't think the social contract criteria are being met," she said. "The debate shouldn't be about numbers but about the process by which we set those numbers."[10]

Unlike many other centre-right parties, the federal Conservatives had long been pro-immigration. In 2015, levels remained at a historically high rate, with 271,833 new permanent residents landing in Canada. During the Harper government's term of office, 2.8 million people arrived as permanent residents in Canada, mainly from countries like the Philippines, India, China, and Pakistan. The mix was heavily weighted toward those chosen for their skills and education levels—in

2015, 63 per cent were economic class migrants, 24 per cent arrived under the family reunification program, and 13 per cent were refugees.

But the complexion of the immigration system was changing under the Liberals—by 2021, economic class migrants were projected to fall as low as 56 per cent of the total of 350,000, with family reunification numbers increasing by more than one third to account for 27 per cent of the total and refugee numbers rising to 15.5 per cent of the total. While the increased number of family members admitted into the country played well in ridings with large immigrant populations, the changes were helping to erode support for mass immigration.

Trudeau defended the integrity of the system. "Every single person who arrives in this country, whether they arrive at the airport, or through a border crossing between official border crossings, they get a full security screening, they get processed into our refugee stream and their case will be evaluated in accordance with Canadian law and principles. There are no loopholes and shortcuts, in that our refugee system continues to apply to everyone who arrives in this country," he said.[11] But regardless of the reassurance offered by the prime minister, support was on the decline thanks to illegal migration, porous borders, and an increase in the proportion of non-economic migrants.

IF BERNIER'S DEFECTION WAS a happy distraction for Trudeau, he was less enamoured with two late-summer Category 4 political storms that threatened to devastate his political prospects: a Federal Court of Appeal decision to quash the government's approval of the Trans Mountain pipeline it now owned, and the inking of a U.S.–Mexico trade deal.

The court decision came out of clear blue skies, invalidating the federal cabinet's construction permits because it said the Liberal government had failed to adequately consult First Nations whose rights were affected by the pipeline. In addition, the court said the National Energy Board had not reviewed the impact of increased tanker traffic on marine life, particularly the southern resident killer whales of the Salish Sea. Trudeau's efforts to modernize the energy board, overhaul the environmental assessment process, and introduce a "world-leading" marine safety system were discounted by the three justices of the court of appeal, who ruled that the Liberals had not followed their own rules on the duty to consult.

Pipeline construction had only just started, but the decision forced workers off the job until the government was able to complete a new phase of consultations with First Nations, and the NEB had reviewed the impact on the marine environment of increased tanker traffic. The decision talked of a "short delay," but it was clear that the scheduled December 2020 service date for the pipeline was no longer feasible. The court's ruling left the Trudeau Liberals' "clean environment, strong economy" strategy in tatters.

The prime minister had staked his personal credibility and the better part of $15 billion of taxpayers' money on getting the pipeline built. As columnist Andrew Coyne pointed out, the Liberals had tried to be all things to everyone, "both for saving the planet and for building pipelines, both for Aboriginal reconciliation and for resource development, both for progressive social values and for free trade."[12] Yet on pipelines, the Liberals had allowed the options to dwindle to one, only to find they had no lawful authority to build it. Even MPs on the government side lamented there was no clause making the purchase price conditional on a positive court decision.[13] The grand chess strategy of building a pipeline and imposing a carbon tax was already under pressure as successive provincial governments expressed their ardent opposition to a new tax. The major court delay imperilled the project even more.

The response of Alberta premier Rachel Notley was immediate—she announced her decision to pull out of the pan-Canadian agreement on climate change and freeze the province's carbon tax at thirty dollars per tonne (still twenty dollars per tonne higher than the inaugural federal rate). When Manitoba's premier, Brian Pallister, said in early October that his province was also out, it created the prospect that Trudeau might be forced to impose the carbon price backstop on provinces making up more than half of the country's population. Moreover, in one of his first acts, Ontario's new premier, Doug Ford, had cancelled the province's cap-and-trade regime and joined Saskatchewan in its court battle contesting Ottawa's jurisdictional right to impose the tax.

Andrew Scheer made it clear that he saw the cost to the average family of the carbon tax as the ballot question in the 2019 election, urging Trudeau to "bring it on."[14] The Liberals were equally enthusiastic to resolve a dispute over pricing carbon that had been rumbling on since Stéphane Dion's Green Shift in 2008. "The Conservatives are going to a playbook that is very cynical and accentuates the negative part of their world view, while it accentuates a lot of the positive ones of ours," said Gerald Butts. "If we allow them to reduce it to the carbon tax, then it will be a much more difficult issue for us. But if it becomes a litmus test on whether we have a real policy on the environment, then we're going to do pretty well."[15]

A study released in late September suggested a path through the carbon tax minefield for the Liberals. Canadians for Clean Prosperity, a non-partisan group led by Mark Cameron, Stephen Harper's ex–policy director, suggested that most households, regardless of income level, would receive more money in a carbon "dividend" than they would pay in tax, if the federal government returned the proceeds directly to taxpayers.[16] In late October, the Liberals unveiled a plan that looked remarkably similar to Cameron's—a carbon tax rebate that the government claimed would see 80 per cent of households financially better off in provinces that declined to adopt their own pricing plans—namely Ontario, Saskatchewan, New Brunswick, and Manitoba. Trudeau announced details of the program at a speech in Doug Ford's riding in Toronto, arguing that a price on carbon emissions was a critical part of Canada's commitment to fighting climate change.

The idea that taxpayers might end up better off from a carbon tax was counterintuitive and rabidly derided by Conservatives. Ford called it a "temporary vote-buying scheme."[17] But the announcement provided some ballast to an environment-energy plan that was listing badly, as province after province came out in opposition to the federal plan. It was curious why the debate over carbon pricing evoked such passion. Gas prices rose eleven cents over the course of 2018—a similar amount to that envisaged under the Liberal plan over five years (before any tax rebate). But rational debate over the most cost-effective way to lower carbon emissions had already descended into a tribal brawl over values. The Conservatives believed that the Liberals were putting the special interests of the privileged few ahead of the wider interests of the average voter. The Liberals discounted any opinion that dissented from their own—namely, that putting a price on carbon would protect the environment and grow the economy.

The consequences of getting it wrong became apparent in late 2018, when yellow-vest-wearing protesters in Paris—"*gilets jaunes*"—brought the French capital to a standstill in protests over the country's carbon tax and its impact on gas prices. Cars were torched, stores looted, and the iconic Arc de Triomphe was vandalized with graffiti, before Emmanuel Macron's government relented and cancelled the next tax rise. In response, Trudeau said there were crucial differences between Canada and France. "The only way to move forward and protect future generations from the impact of climate change is to make sure you are supporting families now who are worried about the changes that are happening in the economy. That's why at the heart of our plan to put a price on pollution, we're saying: 'If in Ontario it's going to cost you an extra $250 a year as an average family, we'll make sure you get an extra $300 a year, so that you can be supported through this change.' That's the approach that I think was not quite evident in the French approach and that's where I think they are trying to get to now."[18]

On trade, the surprise U.S.–Mexico deal in late summer put pressure on Canada to accept similar terms or risk being shut out of the trilateral trade pact. The bilateral deal had some clauses that were good for Canada —new auto-industry rules would raise wages in Mexico and help stem the flow of jobs south. But the Mexicans had also agreed to a number of concessions on intellectual property that would increase drug prices and had caved on the Chapter 19 dispute resolution clause that the Trudeau team considered a red line because it offered some guarantees that trade relations would not be entirely at the mercy of an unpredictable president.

Trump turned up the heat as he made the U.S.–Mexico announcement in the Oval Office, saying the choice for Canada was a negotiated deal or a 25 per cent tariff on Canadian-made autos. He was clear that any deal would be dependent on ending tariffs of nearly 300 per cent on dairy products, and he set an October 1 deadline in order to allow him to deliver a text of the deal to Congress and set up a final signing by the end of November. As the deadline approached, Trump signalled his unhappiness with the Canadian side during his closing press conference at the United Nations General Assembly. He said he had purposely refused to meet Trudeau and made public his dislike for Chrystia Freeland. "We're very unhappy with the negotiations and the negotiating style of Canada. We don't like their representative very much," he said. "We're thinking about just taxing cars coming in from Canada."[19]

The rhetoric soared into the realm of fantasy. Trump said that every time he had a problem when negotiating with Canada, he would pull out and display a picture of a Chevrolet Impala, a car assembled at the General Motors plant in Oshawa, Ontario. For their part, Canadian officials said Trump had never shown them any such photograph.[20] There was a grim irony in the news that came in November—a month after Trump had resolved his differences with Canada on the trade front—that GM planned to close the Oshawa plant at the end of 2019, as part of a global restructuring plan. But the Canadian negotiators had no inkling of GM's plans, as they hammered out a new agreement.

Over the next month, the two sides crashed antlers over Chapter 19 and dairy. Emboldened by the belief that Congress would not agree to a bilateral deal, the Canadian side refused to back down. Finally, on the eve of the deadline, after a tense weekend of negotiations, U.S. trade representative Robert Lighthizer emailed the Canadian negotiating team huddled in the Prime Minister's Office in Ottawa's Langevin Block to say that the Americans were prepared to leave the dispute resolution system untouched. In return, the Canadian side granted more access to its dairy sector.

According to Gerald Butts, the Americans were never really serious about dismantling Canada's supply management system for dairy, eggs, and poultry. "They didn't care so much about market access, they cared about us undercutting prices in third markets. It was way more about skimmed milk and baby formula being sold to Asia than it was about accessing the Canadian market," he said.[21] Canada was not exporting any significant quantity of either product, but the Americans were worried about the future. Ironically, the best way to ensure that Canadian producers kept their international ambitions in check was to leave supply management in place.

The concessions enabled the announcement of a tentative new trilateral deal—the United States Mexico Canada Agreement (USMCA)—to replace NAFTA, just thirty minutes before the deadline expired. Lighthizer had been the public face of the U.S. negotiating team, but even he offered credit to Trump's son-in-law, Jared Kushner, who had been asked to help out on trade early in the presidency and had opened a back-channel communication link to Telford and Butts. The thirty-seven-year-old real estate tycoon married to Trump's daughter, Ivanka, had managed to keep the talks on track when it seemed they might derail. As relations between Freeland and Lighthizer became strained, particularly after the "Taking on the Tyrant" panel, Kushner kept the talks going—finally getting down to the wire by asking what was non-negotiable. When the answer came back that it was Chapter 19, Kushner got Lighthizer on a conference call with Telford and Butts. "Together the four of them worked through some of the outstanding issues that led to a breakthrough in the negotiations, ultimately leading to the success of the deal," one Washington source told Reuters.[22]

It was a tame ending to an eighteen-month drama that saw Canada–U.S. relations sink to their post-war nadir. Many Canadians wouldn't soon forget the disrespect shown to one of America's most staunch allies. But at the same time, the sense of relief was palpable—there was a collective realization that being outside a trade deal with the United States could have been an existential threat to Canada's future prosperity. Freeland may not have been popular in Washington, but her performance won rave reviews at home. "She's a star and everyone knows it," wrote columnist Margaret Wente.[23]

Like any opportunistic leader, Trudeau claimed victory—arguing that the deal was a "great day for Canada." It was a reaction as instinctive as the mammalian diving reflex or blushing, but the claim was short on facts to support it. It was true that the team led by chief negotiator Steve Verheul had negotiated away some of Lighthizer's more draconian demands—a Buy American provision that would have capped Canadian companies bidding for U.S. government contracts; a requirement that 50 per cent of the components in cars made in Canada be American made; the abolition of supply management; and the sunset clause that would have automatically ended the deal after five years.

But the claims of a great coup were hollow. Trump had used what he called "the power of tariffs" to bully his trading partners into making concessions, the full extent of which were not clear when the deal was agreed. One provision in the agreement allowed the U.S. to vet any prospective deal between Canada and a "non-market player"—China— and to terminate the USMCA with six months' notice if it didn't like the terms. As one former State Department official put it, Canada had been "deputized" in the trade war against China.[24] Another clause instituted quotas on how many cars could be built in Canada (although the limit was much higher than current production). Both provisions set unwelcome precedents and amounted to what should have been unacceptable constraints on Canadian sovereignty.

Meanwhile, tariffs on steel and aluminum remained in place. Canada retained Chapter 19, but there was speculation that Trudeau had made it his "red line" because he knew Trump didn't care that much and would concede it, thus giving him a win. But the "win," such as it was,

was the avoidance of catastrophic defeat. Gerald Butts, who spent long hours as part of the team shuttling between Ottawa and Washington, said the final deal played out more or less as he thought it would. He disputed the idea that Chapter 19 was a ruse. "Early on, our strategy was [that] the most important thing to come out of it with was a real trade agreement—and real trade agreements have real rules that can be enforced by mechanisms that are indigenous to the agreement itself. That's why Chapter 19 was so important," he said. "You could make the argument that the World Trade Organization didn't exist when the original deal was signed, so why not just fall back on WTO rules? But the real answer to that is volume—the amount of trade that is transacted between Canada and the U.S. It's the same way that people make the case for special gun courts or white-collar crime courts. It's the volume of the transactions that require a dedicated thing. Lighthizer finally drew the conclusion that he wasn't going to get a deal without it, so they gave up on it."

Butts said he believes the sovereignty concerns have been overblown. "The 'China clause,' as people have called it, where it started and where it ended, gives a good indication of how important it is. It started off that if any one of the three NAFTA partners signed a trade deal with China, the other two could kick them out of the agreement. We came a long way from that. We knew the Americans needed a rhetorical win on that, because they're trying to make the argument they're organizing the right-thinking world against the Chinese on trade. But once they made it a six-month withdrawal notice, then it's automatically what they could do today anyway. I don't think it changes anything and let's not forget that every trade agreement is an abrogation of sovereignty," he advised.[25]

But there was no hiding from the reality that Canada had entered a new era of managed trade, in which the U.S. had accrued undue influence over the country's economic growth. Steel and aluminum tariffs remained in place, and it was implicitly understood that a quantitative cap would be placed on Canadian production if and when they were removed. "This is a silent job killer and it's not good for Canada," said James McIlroy, a veteran trade consultant. A more realistic summation of the deal came from Larry Kudlow, Trump's economic adviser: "Canada gave very graciously."[26]

FIFTEEN

THE CULTURE OF SPENDING

IT WAS AS IF Justin and Sophie were sitting on the couch watching a charity concert on television and the Liberal leader turned to his wife and said, "You know, we should make a donation." That is not how it happened, but a tweet sent out on the prime minister's account in early December 2018 summed up for many people much of what they found disagreeable about the Trudeau Liberals. The tweet in question was to comedian Trevor Noah, the driving force behind the Global Citizen Festival concert in South Africa, featuring Beyoncé and Jay-Z among others, in celebration of Nelson Mandela's centenary. "Hey @Trevornoah —thanks for everything you're doing to celebrate Nelson Mandela's legacy at the @GlblCtzn festival," read the Trudeau account tweet. "Sorry I can't be with you—but how about Canada pledges $50M to @EduCannotWait to support education for women & girls around the world? Work for you? Let's do it."

Few argued with the cause. But the glib fashion in which it was announced gave the impression that Trudeau had made a private dona-tion on the spur of the moment. The reality was that the money was part of a package of measures on global gender equality announced at the G7 meeting in Quebec in summer 2018. The tweet had been planned for three weeks, but it upset people who felt that it encapsulated the worst traits of their prime minister in 280 flippant characters—an impulsive, arrogant, profligate friend of the stars, using public money as if it were his own to burnish his reputation.

Another relatively innocuous story pointed to the culture of spending that had taken root in Ottawa. It emerged that the RCMP had spent $23 million buying more than six hundred new cars for use at the G7 summit in Quebec and had subsequently placed them on a government surplus website to sell them second-hand—some with as few as 77 kilometres on the clock.[1] The case reflected a wider malaise that relied on the indifference of the majority to the government's natural inclination to spend, spend, spend.

When the Liberals said in their first budget that deficits would be quadruple what they had promised in their election platform, they signalled to the broader public service that they had permission to spend. It was a sign that the culture in Ottawa had changed and that the bureaucracy could dust off proposals that had been sitting on shelves during the Harper years. The Conservatives had their moments of frivolous spending—who could forget Bev Oda's $16 orange juice or the $2 million "fake lake" at the G8/G20 media centre in 2010? But these were exceptions, and the Harper government's deficit reduction action plan chopped billions of dollars from public service spending. In their last budget, the Conservatives projected they would spend 12.9 per cent of GDP on programs in 2017–18 if they were re-elected. In reality, the Trudeau government spent 14.5 per cent of GDP—or $28 billion more —that year. Waste had become embedded in the way the government did business. The fall update forecast that the national debt would reach $787 billion in 2023–24, 20 per cent higher than the $617 billion owed in Stephen Harper's last year in office.

The principal reason for the increase was a huge hike in government transfers to individuals—elderly and child benefits increased dramatically. There was a good argument to make that this may not have been the best use for the money, even if the budget had been in balance, which it wasn't.[2] Poverty for seniors and children was much lower than for the general population—roughly half the rate when it came to the elderly—and was already declining.[3] At the same time, income levels were on the rise across the country in the decade prior to 2015. (The national median income rose 10.8 per cent. Lone-parent families were better off; couples with children were better off; even little old ladies were better off.)[4] Yet the Liberals had identified a political problem and were determined that massive government support would be required to solve it.

Bill Morneau defended the decision. "We had a clear objective in 2015 to deal with the fact that the benefits of growth in the decade before were going disproportionately to some sectors of the population. We know that led to a sense of discontent and anxiety among middle-class Canadians. Our goal was to make sure that everybody gained." But wasn't everyone gaining already? "Everybody was gaining, but the gains were going disproportionately to smaller subsets of the population. Our goal—and it's a goal that has been satisfied—was making sure that we put in place policies that enabled everyone to be successful. Three years later, we've had significantly increased workforce participation among women, among new immigrants, among youth, among Indigenous Canadians. Our goal is to have all Canadians be successful to address the demographic challenge. That's been achieved over the last three years," he said.[5]

The example offered by the Department of Finance was that a median-income couple on $110,000 (after tax), with two children, ended up around $2,000 a year better off. The Liberals said that these investments would eventually help lift 652,000 people out of poverty. But the cost would add to deficits projected by the finance department to persist into the middle of the century. It was, the Opposition charged, "a raid on future generations." It would be churlish to argue that the lives of many Canadians were not improved as a result of increased federal transfers —they were. But, as the finance minister's fall 2018 economic update in late November made clear, the land was not as strong as the Liberals wanted Canadians to believe, and the fiscal problems the government had created were structural and enduring.

On the plus side, surging demand in the United States had created strong tax revenues, growth was forecast at a respectable 2 per cent, unemployment was below 6 per cent—a forty-year low—and the debt-to-GDP ratio was ticking gently downward. The Bank of Canada said in late 2018 that investment intentions were strong, corporate profits were high, and Canada was proving successful at attracting foreign investment in knowledge industries, software design, and tech services.

The government received another boost in early October 2018, with the news of a $40 billion energy megaproject on the West Coast that was expected to provide a major economic boost to northern British Columbia. LNG Canada said it would create thousands of jobs as the Royal Dutch Shell–led liquefied natural gas project in Kitimat, B.C., proceeded to construction. Trudeau hailed the announcement as a sign of confidence in the Canadian economy and the government was able to claim that the country had a solid economic base with some justification. "Global investment is flowing into Canada because we're doing interesting and positive things that they want to be part of. It's not as strong as it should be in the oil and gas sector—that's where we are losing investment—but in all other sectors, we're doing very well," he said.[6]

Yet the prime minister and his finance minister had made scant provision for a recession that was already overdue. The country was set to face a reckoning—the debt-to-GDP ratio would not keep falling if the economy started to shrink. As two experienced political operators, the aforementioned Sean Speer and Morneau's former adviser, Robert Asselin, wrote in *Policy Options*, the government's fiscal policy should be sustainable over the long term. "The hard truth is that policy-makers will have almost no policy leverage when the next recession hits—which, according to historical trends, tends to occur every eight years or so."[7]

In the meantime, while there was growth, it was patchy and the benefits were not being felt by everyone. Economists argued that the focus on the low unemployment rate offered a misleading sense of well-being. The government boasted about rising wages, but in truth they barely outpaced inflation—in the Liberal government's first three years in power, real wages averaged gains of just 0.3 per cent, versus 1 per cent for the previous decade

There were other signs of distress. By late 2018, the housing market had recorded three quarters of contraction, and Alberta's oilpatch was enduring something of an existential crisis, as jobs and investment continued to bleed south of the border. When Trudeau appeared to speak at a Chamber of Commerce event in downtown Calgary in late November, the hotel was besieged by angry Albertans, and he was booed when he spoke at another event by pro-pipeline protestors, who chanted, "Build that pipe." Former Encana chief executive Gwyn Morgan noted with alarm how his former company had "exported" itself to the United States. He blamed Trudeau and the Liberal government for a litany of bad policy decisions—from the oil tanker ban off the West Coast to killing the Northern Gateway pipeline; from the introduction of "upstream emissions" in pipeline regulatory hearings to Bill C-69, the impact assessment act—that he said had all but killed Canada's most economically important industry.[8]

Some in Alberta believed that the Liberal government was deliberately trying to sink the oil industry and that the purchase of the Trans Mountain pipeline was a smokescreen. Morneau dismissed that idea as "an absurd proposition," pointing to the $4.5 billion investment in Trans Mountain as "indicative of our absolute desire to make sure we resolve a very important challenge."[9] Ottawa tried to cool the anger bubbling in Alberta with a pre-election giveaway, in the shape of a $1.6 billion federal financial support package for the oilpatch. But it was a band-aid solution. Westerners saw themselves on the receiving end of a sustained assault on their interests by Ottawa, at the same time as more politically favoured parts of the country were benefitting.

The news that Quebec was set to receive increased equalization payments came at the same time that Trudeau effectively vetoed the prospect of the Energy East pipeline project being revived. "There is no support for a pipeline through Quebec," he told CTV. As veteran *Calgary Herald* columnist Don Braid noted, Alberta separatism was out in the

open again, after being dormant for forty years. Trudeau had provoked an almost identical response in the West to the rage that greeted
his father's National Energy Program in the 1980s. Celebrity investor
W. Brett Wilson told Braid that he felt Alberta was being pushed out
of Confederation. "I'm not a separatist, I'm a frustrated nationalist,"
he said. But the number of people on the prairies who wanted to exit
Confederation was growing, and the "grand bargain" was in trouble.[10]

The apparently forked-tongue promise to bring Alberta crude to
market by pipeline while simultaneously introducing a climate change
strategy that included a carbon price was bogged down on both fronts.
The hope was that a majority of Canadians in all provinces would find
the proposal to be an acceptable compromise. But as McGill University's
Andrew Potter and Christopher Ragan noted, it had become clear that
the result had been an even more polarized debate, with partisans on
each side "stacking up like sea containers in a busy port."[11] Potter and
Ragan argued that treating two distinct economic policies as "politically conjoined twins" had reduced the room for compromise and that
a more sensible strategy would have been to "delink" the pipeline and
carbon pricing, pursuing each policy on its own merits. It was a classic
example of the men (and women) of systems in the Prime Minister's
Office overestimating the "omni-competence" of government and failing to take account of the principles of individual human motion outlined by the eighteenth-century economist Adam Smith.

Trudeau ranked the decision to proceed with the linked pipeline
and carbon pricing package as the toughest he had made while in office.
"Any decision you make around the big things that have a significant
impact on people's lives, and the decisions you make that are balancing
various entrenched competing interests . . . are decisions you know
there are a lot of people who are going to take issue with and disagree
with," he said. But, in the teeth of the controversy, he remained totally
unburdened by doubt about the righteousness of the decision, insisting,
"Any issue where you have to say, 'I'm not doing this because it's going
to make me popular, I'm doing this because it's the right thing to do,'

are always those decisions where you have to really be comfortable that you're doing it because you deeply believe and feel it's a step in the right direction for the country." [12]

The fall update's principal admission was that more needed to be done to address Canada's competitiveness challenge that had been exacerbated by policy decisions on the environment, energy, and U.S. corporate tax cuts. "Canada is a small economy and its domestic savings are never going to be enough to support the level of government and business investment required, so we need to attract foreign capital," said Craig Alexander, chief economist at Deloitte Canada. [13] The lack of productivity advances left the Canadian economy stuck in a cycle of low growth and stagnating incomes. Morneau touted his $14 billion plan to allow businesses to write off investments in machinery and other assets more quickly, unveiled as part of the fall update, as an appropriate response to changes to the tax structure in the United States.

But concerns over Canada's competitive position persisted, and were heightened by news in early December 2018 from General Motors that it was planning to close its Oshawa, Ontario, assembly plant at the end of 2019. Just days after Morneau had boasted that the Canadian economy was strong and the middle class was making progress, Canadians were confronted with the prospect of the auto industry moving, plant by plant, back behind Donald Trump's tariff walls. With an aging population and slowing labour force growth, the government was faced with the challenge of maintaining revenues in the long term. "At this stage of the business cycle, I don't think the government should be running deficits," said Deloitte's Alexander." [14]

Compared to its international peers, Canada was in reasonable fiscal shape. But many critics worried the government was running structural deficits that were not going to disappear with economic growth. Trudeau maintained that the "productive investments" his government was making would grow the economy and balance the budget, but in late December 2018, the finance department said that, by its estimates, Canada would remain in deficit until 2040. Those worries were starting to resonate with voters, according to some pollsters. An opinion poll by the Angus Reid Institute asked people who said they would consider voting Liberal at the next election whether they agreed or disagreed with maintaining deficits rather than the balanced budget Justin Trudeau promised in his election platform. Four in ten of those who considered themselves "likely" or "maybe" Liberal voters disagreed.[15]

But the man who made those promises was unapologetic about breaking them. "That's where you have to make a decision. Is the fact that kids will have more nutritious lunches because their parents have an extra three hundred bucks or five hundred bucks a month to buy better groceries, is that going to make enough of a difference in their lives to make our economy grow to make that a worthwhile investment? If taking money to invest right now in better public transit, does that mean more people will be able to afford their homes and get better jobs and go to school without having to buy a car, and does that create growth? Absolutely. The question is, how do we best invest in the future? That was a question at the core of the 2015 election campaign."[16]

As is typical of all Young Turks, Trudeau's mind was barely darkened by misgivings that he might be wrong—that the investments his government was making might not really be paying off and that Canada had committed itself to a disastrous spiral of debt, just as a global economic downturn looms.

His supporters argued caveat emptor—that he had done nothing that he didn't say he would do as far back as 2014. "Having been there at the very beginning of the prime minister's leadership bid—the whole thing is very much what he presented and what he stands for, which is 'strengthen the middle class to grow the economy,'" opined Ben Chin, former chief of staff to the finance minister and now senior advisor in the Prime Minister's Office. Chin said the rejection of trickle-down economics was at the core of it, noting, "That comes with a more enlightened view of ourselves—the 'better angels' view of being Canadian. It's been pretty constant."[17] Rodger Cuzner, the veteran MP from Cape Breton, said the public face Trudeau presents is who he is, and what he believes in. "These are anything but policies to win votes. He's taken on underrepresented Canadians. He wants to find more opportunities to get women engaged in the workforce. We're sitting on an untapped resource, so women, Indigenous Canadians, youth, persons with disabilities. I think middle-aged white guys in this country think, 'Fine, you're doing this for these people, what are you doing for me?' It will be our challenge going into the next election to persuade them, they'll benefit from us," he said.[18]

Liberals took comfort from the fact that opinion surveys throughout 2018 showed Trudeau out-polling his rivals. "When you're comparing the guy to perfection, he can really bug you. But given the alternatives of him or him or him, it's different," said Chin.[19] Yet the potential for a close shave in 2019 was there. Pollster Bruce Anderson at Abacus Data said that about eight million voters—or around one quarter of the electorate—were "persuadable." That is, they could be persuaded to give Trudeau a second term, or to vote for a new government because they were unhappy about things the government had done.[20] The challenge for the opposition parties was to present common-sense, moderate options to potential non-partisan swing voters.

Canadians tend not to think in terms of the political spectrum. One Liberal MP observed that on the doorsteps he rarely heard complaints about the party being too far left. "Rather they say things like, 'Why are you making so many apologies?' or 'The 50 per cent female cabinet is just window dressing; what about the real issues?' But to me that's code for 'Let's come back to the centre,'" he said.[21] Gerald Butts dismissed talk about the Liberals drifting leftward. "The biggest divide at the last election was generational, not ideological . . . ," he said. "The only people who think in right and left terms these days write for newspapers."[22] But it's not just journalists who still locate political opinions on one or more geometric axes—and who feel that the extreme middle is ill-served. A number of Liberal MPs interviewed for this book said they feel there is a gap in the political market. "A lot of people who think the Liberals have gone too far left think the Conservatives are too far right," commented one backbencher. "Where would Joe Clark or John Manley go today? The truth is you've got be polarized to attract attention."[23]

As much as Trudeau has been quick to point his finger at his political opponents for being willing to exploit the ruptures caused by political polarization, he has been equally swift to capitalize on them himself. One Liberal MP scoffed at the idea that the Harper government was more guilty of playing the politics of division. "That's nonsense. We're more polarizing than they were and I don't think that's sunk in yet. I don't think Justin intuits that—or if he does, he thinks it's worth the gamble and he thinks we can win on that kind of polarization," he said.[24]

Trudeau came to power promising "evidence-based policy," but empirical evidence was largely ignored in the backbone commitment of his election campaign—the promise to reverse "the historic decline of the middle class."[25] The case can be made that there was no decline. As economist Thomas Sowell noted, facts are there to be marshalled for a position already taken. "Momentous questions are dealt with essentially as conflicts of visions," he said.[26] The Anointed make much of their compassion for the less fortunate and their concerns about pollution and war, Sowell observed, "as if these were characteristics that distinguish them from people with opposite views on public policy." It has to be thus, he argued, because if compassion and caring were common features on both sides, the debate would be about methods, probabilities, and empirical evidence. "That clearly is not the vision of the Anointed," he concluded.[27]

The problem for Trudeau, as the country moved toward the forty-third general election, was that his methods had not changed the world as dramatically as he might have wished. Ushering in a gender-balanced cabinet and legalizing cannabis won him international acclaim. But an Abacus Data poll in late 2018 suggested that 37 per cent of Canadians felt the country was on the wrong track, with many expressing concerns over wages and the cost of living.[28] An Angus Reid Institute survey late in the year revealed that Trudeau's approval rating had fallen to a net negative 23 per cent (just 35 per cent approved of his performance;

58 per cent disapproved). When he was elected in 2015, Trudeau had a net positive 34 per cent rating—nearly twice as many people approved of him then as they did three years later. Even Donald Trump's approval rating was higher.[29] The golden boy who had appeared on the cover of *Rolling Stone* magazine under the headline "Why Can't He Be Our President?" had become a prophet without honour at home.

SIXTEEN

DUMPSTER FIRE

EVENTS EARLY IN 2019 exploded the fantasy that Trudeau had rewritten the political rule-book, shaking the faith of even the most rock-ribbed Liberals. The announcement by Treasury Board president Scott Brison that he planned to resign from politics prompted a mini-cabinet shuffle in early January. Jane Philpott was moved from Indigenous Services to replace Brison at Treasury Board, which was passing curious given the progress she appeared to be making. But it was the shuffling of Jody Wilson-Raybould from the justice department to the more junior post of veterans' affairs minister that raised most eyebrows (Seamus O'Regan was shifted from the veterans' affairs department to replace Philpott at Indigenous Services, while David Lametti, a former professor law who represented a Montreal riding became the new justice minister).

Very little about the game of ministerial thrones made much sense, particularly Wilson-Raybould's demotion. Her bruised pride was evident from her demenour at the swearing-in ceremony at Rideau Hall —a stark contrast to the joy she displayed three years earlier when she was named as justice minister, the highest office in the government of Canada ever attained by an Indigenous Canadian. Given Trudeau's mantra that no relationship was more important to him than the one with First Nations, it defied logical analysis. Wilson-Raybould was the architect of the framework guiding the Liberal Party's Indigenous reconciliation policy. She had, as she pointed out in a highly unusual post-shuffle statement, achieved everything in her mandate letter as justice minister "and much beyond it," including the assisted dying bill and the legalization of pot.[1]

But her statement also hinted at why she'd been moved—her willingness to "speak truth to power" in her role as attorney general of Canada, the government's top legal adviser.[2]

The reasons for Wilson-Raybould's demotion became clearer in early February, following a *Globe and Mail* story that alleged she was pressured as justice minister to intervene in the corruption prosecution of Quebec construction giant, SNC-Lavalin, and was punished for refusing to do so. The story claimed Wilson-Raybould was pressed to get involved in the case, after the director of the Public Prosecution Service refused to negotiate a remediation agreement with SNC over allegations of corruption committed by former executives of the company (SNC was prepared to admit its guilt and pay a fine to avoid the prospect of a conviction that could bar it from federal contracts for up to ten years).[3]

SNC lobbied the Prime Minister's Office extensively to argue in favour of a remediation agreement—and there was undoubtedly sympathy in the PMO for the claim that prosecution could cost thousands of jobs in Quebec (and put at risk a number of Liberal seats in the province). The attorney general had the legal power to take over the case from the director of Public Prosecutions, provided that information was made public. Subsequent testimony made it clear Wilson-Raybould was asked to get involved but she refused to do so—effectively sealing her fate as justice minister, once Brison had made his intentions known.[4] By mid-February, she had resigned from cabinet and sought guidance from a retired Supreme Court justice on whether she could tell her side of the story. Yet, while she remained muzzled by solicitor-client privilege, Liberal insiders whispered to journalists that Wilson-Raybould was difficult to work with, while Trudeau blamed her publicly for the fiasco. The prime minister expressed himself "surprised and disappointed," saying Wilson-Raybould had an obligation to raise the matter with him, if she felt the government had broken the rules, and that she had not done so.[5]

There was the sense of a ministry in disarray, as Trudeau answered questions from the media about the affair in a Winnipeg Transit depot, a backdrop dripping with symbolism as he effectively threw his former justice minister under the bus. The Prime Minister's Office had lost control of the narrative and Trudeau was behaving in a way that validated those old "Just Not Ready" attack ads.

By the time the saga entered its second week, the prime minister was showing signs of desperation, spitting out bloopers like a broken slot machine. He claimed that Wilson-Raybould would still be justice minister if Scott Brison hadn't resigned. It quickly became a social media meme. "If Scott Brison hadn't stepped down, [defenceman] Erik Karlsson would still be an Ottawa Senator," wrote one hockey fan.[6] Brison's spouse, Max St. Pierre, joined in the fun. "It's ok, I usually blame my husband for everything too," he tweeted.[7] What should have been a passing storm had blown up into a potential election issue—mainly because the prime minister had excited opinion rather than calmed it. For a government that had proven itself so adept at branding, it looked horribly inept at reacting. Even low information voters, disinterested in the minutia, could register that Trudeau looked as uneasy as a man caught clubbing baby seals. Keith Beardsley, who was deputy chief of staff for issues management in Stephen Harper's government, said Trudeau and his advisers didn't seem to have a firm grasp of what their message should be, "as if they expect Trudeau's charisma to see them through."[8] But the Liberals' prime asset had become their biggest liability.

A catalogue of self-inflicted wounds made a bad situation worse. For a government with a reputation for slick communications, there was a failure to act nimbly and snuff out emerging bad news—instead of admitting to mistakes and apologizing, Trudeau typically plunged into an ocean of platitudes and set off with confidence for the opposite shore.

The scale of the government's troubles became apparent when Gerald Butts, Trudeau's self-described "best friend" and "closest adviser," resigned, saying allegations that he was guilty of pressuring Wilson-Raybould were becoming a distraction for the government. His resignation did not make those allegations go away and it was a curious decision, given the absence of any evidence against him. His position was not untenable and his resignation added fuel to accusations of a cover-up.

(It later emerged that Wilson-Raybould had made Butts's departure one of the conditions for any compromise agreement to heal internal divisions.)[9]

Butts denied any wrongdoing, saying he "honoured the unique role of the attorney general"[10] in the SNC case, though his role in it remained opaque in his resignation statement.

It was an inglorious end to his time in government for a man who was the architect of the 2015 election victory and who had been integral to everything the Liberals did in office—from the economy and environment "grand bargain" to the negotiations with the Trump White House. His departure was cheered by some backbench Liberal MPs who blamed him for being an obstacle to their progress into cabinet. But the simple truth was that Butts, almost as much as Trudeau, had resuscitated a Liberal Party that was displaying the vital signs of a "resting" Norwegian blue parrot that had been nailed to its perch.

For the prime minister himself, the silence in his office the day after Butts's departure must have been deafening. In his resignation statement, Butts said the Prime Minister's Office is "larger and more important than any of its staff."[11] But as Trudeau's principal political confidante, chief electoral strategist, and senior policy adviser, his exodus left a void. The Anointed's intellectual bellwether had left the building.

By the time all the evidence was in, it was pretty clear lines had been crossed. The guidelines on the role of the attorney general suggest he or she may be informed about partisan considerations before making a decision but, crucially, should not be directed toward a particular outcome.

Gripping testimony at the parliamentary justice committee, first by clerk of the Privy Council, Michael Wernick, then by Wilson-Raybould, offered inconsistent versions of events. The clerk said that in a meeting he attended between Trudeau and his justice minister, the prime minister made it clear she was the "decider" in the SNC case. He said Trudeau and his staff had always acted with the highest level of integrity and predicted that Wilson-Raybould's grievance was with him, over a phone call he'd made to her in mid-December 2018, in which he told her the prime minister and her parliamentary colleagues were "quite anxious" about the SNC case and the potential impact on jobs. Wernick said the conversation fell within the boundaries of what was lawful and appropriate. "I was informing the minister of context," he said.[12] When it was pointed out to him that Wilson-Raybould was removed from her position for not bowing to pressure, Wernick said she was not fired but accepted another position in cabinet and at no time raised any concerns of impropriety with the prime minister or ethics commissioner.

What he and Trudeau may not have bargained on was the bravura performance by Wilson-Raybould before the committee, after which Canadian public opinion united behind her belief that she was treated harshly. She portrayed herself as a "truth-teller"—an Indigenous person who had seen the consequences of the rule of law being abused.[13] The public was in her pocket early on in a calm, but incendiary, half-hour opening statement that detailed allegations of "inappropriate" pressure exerted by the prime minister, by advisers in his office, and from Wernick that culminated in "veiled threats." She detailed a "consistent and sustained" effort to secure a remediation agreement for SNC by a "barrage of people hounding me and my staff."[14] Even after she had made it clear that she intended to side with the director of Public Prosecutions and refuse to negotiate a deal with the engineering company, advisers in the Prime Minister's Office tried to get her to change her mind. "We can have the best policy in the world but we need to get re-elected," she said she was told by Mathieu Bouchard, an adviser in the PMO.[15] She had a very different recollection to Wernick of the tenor of the phone call they had in mid-December, in which he said he merely informed her of "context." She said Wernick told her Trudeau was "quite determined" to get a deal for SNC and was going to "find a way to get it done one way or another." She said she was warned she was on a "collision course" with the prime minister.[16]

In a recording of the phone conversation that Wilson-Raybould later released to the justice committee, she said she was under no illusions that "the prime minister gets things that he wants" and that she was "waiting for the other shoe to drop."[17]

She didn't have to wait long. She was demoted within weeks of that conversation and, as she testified, the top bureaucrat in her department was told by Wernick that her replacement could expect to have an early conversation with the prime minister about a remediation agreement with SNC.[18]

Trudeau's first public appearance after her testimony was at the Canada Space Agency where he announced that the country was going, not to the dogs as many feared, but to the moon. That announcement was overshadowed by questions to the prime minister about SNC. He took issue with Wilson-Raybould's "characterization" of events but his already tarnished halo was now bent out of shape.

Trudeau had promised to do politics differently but it was his Treasury Board president, Jane Philpott, who gave her leader a lesson in political principle when she abruptly resigned from cabinet. Philpott remains a close friend of Wilson-Raybould and left cabinet ostensibly because she had lost confidence in Trudeau's leadership in the SNC-Lavalin affair. "There can be a cost to acting on one's principles but there is a bigger cost to abandoning them," she said in her resignation letter.[19]

As one of the most popular and hard-working ministers in cabinet, her resignation further upset members of caucus already angry about their lack of access to the prime minister.

"The disappointment is palpable. This is a crisis and he [Trudeau] has been found wanting," said one senior caucus member. "The caucus is united in a desire to get re-elected. It is not necessarily united in a desire to be elected behind him."[20]

Yet no leadership contenders were immediately apparent. Trudeau would survive the storm, "but not without damage," said another MP.[21]

The first signs of an effective response to Wilson-Raybould's allegations came with Butts' appearance at the justice committee. He did not present any evidence that would have exonerated the allegations of a pattern of interference in the independence of the attorney general. But he offered a calm counter-argument to the points she raised. "I am firmly convinced that nothing happened here beyond the normal operations of government," he said.[22]

It was not a wholly convincing argument. Butts said that he and his office respected the role of the attorney general and acted with integrity at all times—any pressure, such as it was, was merely to seek a second opinion on the remediation deal. This was pushed because the PMO was concerned the attorney general had not done her due diligence.

Yet, as a matter of law, nobody's opinion mattered except those of the director of Public Prosecutions and the attorney general. To even question the decision meant the office of the attorney general was not being respected.

Even on the subsequent cabinet shuffle, the explanation did not ring true.

Butts said that Wilson-Raybould had to be moved out of the justice department, after she turned down the opportunity to become Indigenous services minister, because to leave her there would set a bad precedent and make cabinet unmanageable. More likely, Trudeau saw an opportunity to take advantage of Brison's resignation and remove a thorn from his side.

Butts's testimony did at least provide an alternative version of events to Wilson-Raybould's account of an uncontrollable government machine running roughshod over prosecutorial independence.

Trudeau tried to normalize a crisis that had paralyzed the government for a month at a press conference in Ottawa on March 7. His advisers had suggested his appearance to answer questions on SNC would involve a display of contrition—perhaps he might conjure up the image of life in Stornoway, the residence of the leader of the Official Opposition, to coax a tear, it was suggested.

But when he was asked directly whether he was apologizing for anything, he doubled down on his talking point that the government was merely protecting jobs, while respecting the integrity of the rule of law. "I continue to say there was no inappropriate pressure," he said.[23] He had just made a statement in which he had hinted at humility—that he asked his staff to follow up with Jody Wilson-Raybould on the prospect of her intervening in the SNC case, even though she had told him she had made her mind up not to during their meeting on September 17 last year. He said he had asked her to revisit her decision and thought she was open to doing so, but since the SNC story broke, he had come to understand she was not. He said that fact was not clear to him because of an "erosion of trust" between the former attorney general and Butts. "I was not aware of that erosion of trust but I should have been," he said. "I acknowledge we need to make adjustments."[24]

But this was the pretense of humility, not the true embodiment of it. Trudeau added no new information and there was no admission that lines were crossed. It was yet another example of Trudeau acting as a prime minister so convinced of the righteousness of his agenda, he discounted behaviour he would not have tolerated from his political opponents. Trudeau sees himself in a special position as one of the Anointed, cast in the role of rescuing people treated unfairly by society. While capable of contrition for aberrations committed long before he was born, he has never shown true remorse for anything he has done in office. The certainty that his path is wise and noble provides special dispensation for moral lapses—the prerogative born from a lifetime of privilege means that rules, and even laws, can be broken with a clear conscience.

The subtitle of Thomas Sowell's *The Vision of the Anointed* is: *Self-Congratulation as a Basis for Social Policy*. Few Canadian governments have been as vainglorious as this one. The idea that some of his own ministers might not share his conceited vision clearly did not occur to Trudeau. Wilson-Raybould was open to a compromise to avert open civil war in the Liberal Party. However, it reportedly required Trudeau, not only to clean house in his own office by firing Butts and Wernick, but also to admit that his office acted inappropriately in its attempts to convince her to consider granting SNC a deferred prosecution agreement.[25]

In the wake of Butts's resignation, Canada's highest-ranking public servant also decided to exit the stage. Wernick told Trudeau that he would retire since he was no longer trusted by the opposition.

Yet when it came to an admission of guilt, Wilson-Raybould might as well have tried to persuade the prime minister to ban Tim Horton's doughnuts as concede he harassed her.

The Liberals tried to cauterize the wound by ejecting Wilson-Raybould and Philpott from caucus for their public dissent over the government's handling of the SNC-Lavalin affair.

There was disquiet among MPs about Trudeau's leadership but it was outweighed by resentment about the lack of *esprit de corps* displayed by the two former ministers—both parliamentary rookies without deep roots in the Liberal Party—that threatened their re-election.

In private meetings in early April, Trudeau told the two they would be removed and then announced the move publicly at a caucus meeting in front of cheering Liberal MPs.

"The trust that previously existed between these two individuals and our team has been broken," Trudeau told the room. "Whether it's taping conversations without consent, or repeatedly expressing a lack of confidence in our government and in me personally as leader, it's become clear that Ms. Wilson-Raybould and Dr. Philpott can no longer remain part of our Liberal team."[26]

Trudeau called Wilson-Raybould's act of covertly recording a phone call with Wernick "unconscionable."

The ejections may have rallied a shaken caucus but beyond the Ottawa bubble many Canadians sympathized with the former justice minister's response that she did what she was required to do, "based on principles and values that must always transcend party."

However, while she was able to boast about her conduct from a vantage point on the moral high ground, the net result was a setback to the agendas closest to her heart—gender equality and Indigenous reconciliation.

The only winner from the Liberal civil war was Andrew Scheer, who said the message sent was clear: "If you tell the truth, there is no room for you in the Liberal Party of Canada."[27] While voters have not embraced Scheer, they had cooled sufficiently on Trudeau that opinion polls suggested the Conservatives had edged ahead of the Liberals in the spring of 2019.

The media coverage of the SNC saga conjured up Nixonian images of an arbitrary, vengeful prime minister, prepared to go to great lengths, perhaps as far as obstructing justice, for partisan ends.

It also highlighted a worrying lack of shrewdness in the Liberal ranks. The sense that Trudeau and his team had completely lost the plot was bolstered by the leader's threat to sue Scheer for his claim the prime minister had engaged in corrupt conduct, accusations Trudeau's lawyer, Julian Porter, said were "false and defamatory statements."[28] Rather than withdraw his comments, Scheer repeated them outside the House of Commons, beyond the protection of parliamentary immunity, in the hope that Trudeau might follow through with the lawsuit and have the whole murky affair play out in court, where all the actors would be under oath. If the prime minister was seeking sympathy for comments that were "beyond the pale of fair debate," he was to be disappointed —the view that the lawsuit ploy was the most ill-advised "since Oscar Wilde sued the Marquess of Queensbury" was held widely by political commentators, who noted that attempts to involve the courts to pronounce on what might constitute fair debate by previous prime ministers had come to naught.[29] [30]

For a story in which the prime minister insisted there was nothing to see, it had proven ruinous to Liberal fortunes—costing Trudeau two ministers, his most trusted adviser, the country's senior public servant, his reputation for probity, and the party's lead in the polls.

The reality was probably more prosaic than any "-gate" suffixed scandal. A charitable reading of events suggests Trudeau was guilty of behaving in precisely the vindictive manner he so often laid at the door of his predecessor, by removing an uncooperative voice from a front-line cabinet position.

But it hardly lived up to the level of accountability Trudeau had promised when sworn in. "Openness and transparency will be our constant companion and we will work to restore Canadians' trust in their government and in our democracy," he said then.[31]

The SNC-Lavalin affair suggested voters were hoodwinked in 2015—Trudeau promised he would govern without cynicism. In reality, he compounded contemptuous behaviour with the other besetting sin of modern politics—creating unrealistic expectations.

Scheer may have overreached in calling for his resignation. But the mere suggestion that Trudeau should step down over a Canadian-style Watergate was a very long way from the kinder, sunnier style of government he promised. As the SNC affair played out, all the frustrations about Trudeau's hubris and hypocrisy bubbled to the surface and put his job at serious risk. It had taken seven years to build the Trudeau narrative—and just two months to burn it to ashes.

IF TRUDEAU HAS BEEN losing his audience, it is entirely possible he will be able to win it back. As the most experienced leader on the federal stage, he also has the advantage of a campaign team of winners intent on building a positive narrative to remind people why they voted for him in the first place.

In the wake of the SNC scandal, Trudeau flirted with mud-slinging by accusing Andrew Scheer of being soft on racism.

But the Liberal team is confident that they can depict a selfless and empathetic leader who is taking action on the environment, First Nations, and gender not because they are vote-winners but because he believes it is the right thing to do. "Justin speaks his mind, which some feel is a liability," said Tom Pitfield, who will again run Trudeau's digital campaign. "But that also reinforces his authenticity. He speaks to people like he's having a beer with a friend. He is another kind of populist —one that uses his ability to relate to people as a way to bring them together." Pitfield explained that the likelihood the Conservatives will go low with negative attacks on Trudeau and the Liberals offers the opportunity to own the positive, hopeful narrative. "You appeal to people's higher order preferences—you show them you are going to provide them with the help and relief they need; that their fears are the same things that are keeping Justin up at night—which they are—and focus on those types of things again from a policy perspective. From a positive place, you own that hopeful narrative again." [32]

Yet, as with his father in 1972, just four years after Trudeaumania, Trudeau's time in office has drained the enthusiasm from some people who voted for him the last time but who feel they have been deserted by the man who promised to change the world—or at the very least the voting system. The government has not lived up to as many of its promises as the majority governments that preceded it. It has failed to deliver on its agenda for First Nations and others, and has blatantly broken promises on electoral reform and balanced budgets. Many voters who projected their own visions onto the Liberals have been left disenchanted by Trudeau's policies on small business taxes, Omar Khadr, the summer jobs program, and illegal migration. Still others, particularly in the West, rave and seethe unhealthily about the Liberal project when it comes to the carbon tax and non-existent pipelines. And then there has been the prime minister's own behaviour.

Trudeau is no political neophyte. He has been an MP for more than a decade. Nobody made him wear a sherwani when he was in India or dance the bhangra.

Nobody forced him to manhandle the Conservative whip and elbow an NDP MP on the floor of the House of Commons because he was frustrated at the slow passage of government legislation.

No one compelled him to describe Fidel Castro as a "larger than life leader, a legendary revolutionary and orator."

Neither was the prime minister coerced into the helicopter that whisked him off to a vacation on the Aga Khan's Caribbean island, in contravention of the Conflict of Interest Act.

He was not bound to pay Omar Khadr $10 million in compensation or to defend the government's court case against veterans "because they're asking for more than we're able to give right now."

There was no necessity to launch a sustained campaign of "inappropriate" pressure to get his attorney general to change her mind on a criminal prosecution, risking allegations about obstruction of justice. Nobody forced him to demote her when she refused to do so.

The principles of open and accountable government mean the prime minister sets the general direction of government policy and establishes standards of conduct. He is not a cog in something turning—he operates the machine.

Statesmen as far back as Cicero, the Roman consul, have compared politics to navigation, where sometimes you run before the wind, sometimes you tack, and sometimes you catch a tide. But as Cicero noted, all this takes years of skill and study. Successful statesmen adapt inflexible principles to changing political circumstances, he said. But Trudeau lacks the guile and experience of a Jean Chrétien, or even a Stephen Harper, and that might explain why his popularity has tumbled by 50 per cent. He has been quick to blame those who disagree with him for indulging in the "politics of fear and division." But there are few more divisive figures on the political scene than Justin Pierre James Trudeau, the "man of systems" who has found that moving different pieces around the chessboard is more difficult than he might have imagined.

Many Canadians may not be able to verbalize their disquiet, but veteran Canadian-American columnist David Brooks gave a pretty good summation of leadership in his book *The Road to Character*. "The best leader goes along with the grain of human nature, rather than going against it. He prefers arrangements that are low and steady to those that are lofty and heroic," he wrote. "As long as the foundations of an institution are sound, he prefers change that is constant, gradual and incremental to change that is radical and sudden."[33] Trudeau's time as prime minister has been the antithesis of what Brooks judged to be sound leadership—arrangements that are lofty and heroic, change that is radical and sudden.

He has agitated a tendency prevalent across the Western world—the rise of authoritarian populism—that was noticeably absent in Canada prior to his election. The Canadian economy has proven remarkably resilient during Trudeau's term in office, so the white-hot anger directed toward the prime minister is not induced by economic distress. Rather, its rise can be explained by a cultural backlash. As Steven Pinker noted in his 2018 book, *Enlightenment Now,* voters who are male, religious, less educated, and in the ethnic majority feel like they have become strangers in their own country, abandoned by the progressive policies that predominate—values they don't share or understand.[34]

Trudeau has needled those voters by relentlessly using polarizing rhetoric and hammering in the wedge of identity politics. He is perhaps fortunate that none of his immediate adversaries are overtly channelling the brewing resentment against climate change, women's empowerment, or Indigenous issues.

Trudeau has remained the compelling political figure of his time. His personality dominates the dramatis personae of the Canadian stage; his charisma ensures that he continues to win people's attention. The global media once again turned to Trudeau as the anti-Trump after the president cancelled a trip to a cemetery for American war dead near Paris on Remembrance Day 2018, due to rainy weather. Trudeau and other leaders marched down the Champs-Elysées, sheltering under umbrellas. Meanwhile, footage of the Canadian prime minister getting soaked the previous summer at a memorial event for the abortive Dieppe landing, where he noted the rain wasn't rain "it was bullets," went viral. Boredom, as much as cynicism, was the reason so many Canadians turned away from politics. Trudeau has proven an effective antidote to the belief that Canadian politics always tends toward the least exciting outcome. Whether he was dancing bhangra or taking the opportunity to have himself photographed galloping through a field on horseback, Trudeau could rarely be accused of lethargy or insipidness.

The public wants to feel a personal connection with their prime minister, and it remains a constant source of amazement that someone raised in the most exceptional way imaginable can connect with everyday Canadians. The danger of being seen as out of touch always lurks —such as when the news broke of his vacation on the Aga Khan's island. Yet there is something to Gerald Butts's contention that "people want Justin to do well"—there remains a generation that saw him grow up in public and feels an affinity not awarded to other politicians. But even men of good intentions should be judged on results. The less charitable way to interpret Justin Trudeau's unswerving conviction to "do what is right" is as an ideologically blinkered crusade that will not be swayed by fact or circumstance. The "hopeful narrative" Canadians have been sold is as much a fairy tale as the fable involving magic beans, a beanstalk, a thwarted giant, and a golden-egg-laying goose.

In the vision of the Anointed, there is an unlimited supply of golden eggs. Yet, in the messy real world, there are only rising debt levels and unintended consequences. For many Canadians, this preening prime minister has proven himself too vaulting, too capricious, and too extravagant. Politicians sometimes forget they are appointed, not anointed. But like anyone elevated, there will come a day when he is demoted and it will be because voters have tired of the idiosyncrasies that once amused them. In the words of seventeenth-century playwright John Webster, "Whether we fall by ambition, blood, or lust, like diamonds we are cut with our own dust."[34]

ACKNOWLEDGEMENTS

This book is the product of the brasserie rather than the library (many thanks to Michael Hannas and Sarah Chown at Metropolitain in that regard). That is, it is the output of a working journalist, ferreting for information from sources in the salons of Ottawa rather than from the dusty shelves of the Library of Parliament. This was an act of necessity—the primary sources needed to write the definitive account of Justin Trudeau's rise to power and his first mandate do not yet exist—or if they do, they are not public.

During my research, I noted with awe and envy the wealth of memoirs and internal documents, including cabinet conclusions, that time had made available to author John English for his epic two-part biography of Pierre Elliott Trudeau. This is not that book. Instead, it is an attempt at a first draft of history (if you don't include Twitter), developed in the course of filing three or four political columns a week for the *National Post*.

Many thanks to my editors at the *Post*, former editor-in-chief Anne-Marie Owens and executive producer, news, Jordan Timm, for their patience and encouragement while I attempted to juggle both duties. I confess to them now that I was jittery about being able to pull it off. But in hindsight, I think the columns benefitted from the book research, and the book was enhanced by me talking to contacts every day. Thanks, too, to my colleagues in the Postmedia parliamentary bureau for their serenity and professionalism in the face of their frequently absent bureau chief.

This project would not have happened without Doug Pepper, vice-president and publisher of Signal/McClelland & Stewart at Penguin Random House Canada. Doug has been my guiding star on an unfamiliar path, combining infectious enthusiasm with wise counsel. Journalistic colleagues who have become authors lament the transition during the writing period from "the book" to "the damn book" to, finally, "the effing book." Doug made the process relatively painless. I'd also like to thank the excellent team at Penguin Random House Canada—managing editor Kimberlee Hesas, cover designer David Gee, copy editor extraordinaire Tara Tovell, and my publicist, Shona Cook.

The manuscript was read by my Liberal-leaning friend Andrew Balfour, whose frequent contribution was that I was being too hard on the government. Meanwhile, Christian Paas-Lang provided outstanding help with fact-checking and endnotes. Christian is an aspiring but already accomplished journalist, and I hired him in the hope that he will return the favour ten years from now, when he is running one of Canada's major media organizations. Thanks to both. Any errors are mine.

A line at the bottom of a list of acknowledgements is a poor return for the love and support provided by my extraordinary wife, Dana Cryderman, during the writing and editing process. She is a career diplomat, a job that requires the right quantities of oil and vinegar. She read the manuscript and made several suggestions to make the narrative a little less caustic.

For most of that time, Dana was pregnant with our son, William Alfred, who was born just as I was finalizing the manuscript in January 2019. He was welcomed home by his captivated elder brother, James, and sister, Fiona. He is snoozing on my chest, aged three weeks and five days, as I type this.

As the singer, bon vivant, and sometimes philosopher Rod Stewart once observed, "You go through life wondering what it's all about but at the end of the day, it's all about family." My only regret is that my father, Jim, is not around to read this book. But to Dana, James, Fiona and William, and my mother, Anne, I love you. Thank you for teaching me how to be content.

John Ivison

Chelsea, Quebec
February 2019

NOTES

INTRODUCTION: THE VISION OF THE ANOINTED

1   David Olive, *Canadian Political Babble: A Cynic's Dictionary of Political Jargon* (Toronto: John Wiley & Sons Canada, 1993), 39.

2   Louise Sassoon, "Bizarre Footage Shows 'World's Sexiest Politician' Justin Trudeau Taking a Tumble Down Stairs," *Daily Mirror*, October 21, 2015, https://www.mirror.co.uk/news/world-news/bizarre-footage-shows-worlds-sexiest-6677939.

3   Andrew Coyne, "Trudeau, Morneau: Middle-Class Phonies," *National Post*, October 17, 2017, A1.

4   Angus Reid Institute, "Majority of Canadians Disapprove of Justin Trudeau for the First Time Since He Became Prime Minister," March 19, 2018, http://angusreid.org/federal-issues-march2018.

5   Interview, Gerald Butts, 18/7/18.

6   Foreign Staff, "Richard Nixon Predicted Justin Trudeau Would Be Canadian PM," *The Telegraph*, October 21, 2015.https://www.telegraph.co.uk/news/worldnews/northamerica/canada/11944646/Richard-Nixon-predicted-Justin-Trudeau-would-become-Canadian-PM.html.

7   John English, *Citizen of the World: The Life of Pierre Elliott Trudeau Volume One 1919–1968* (Toronto: Vintage Canada, 2007), 3.

8   Interview, confidential source.

9   English, *Citizen of the World*, 219.

10 Ian Brown, "The Challenge," *Globe and Mail*, October 3, 2015, F1.

11 Quoted in ibid.

12 Interview, Ben Chin, 11/9/18.

13 Justin Trudeau, *Common Ground* (Toronto: HarperCollins Canada, 2014), 289.

14 Interview with another former senior Liberal staffer, who asked to remain anonymous because he is not authorized to speak publicly by his current employer. A number of people interviewed for this book had similar commercial restrictions and so are referred to as "confidential sources."

15 The 39 per cent passage rate is my calculation. The 60 per cent average was worked out by Ian Brodie, Stephen Harper's former chief of staff, in his book *At the Centre of Government: The Prime Minister and the Limits on Political Power* (Montreal: McGill-Queen's University Press, 2018), 88.

16 Interview, confidential source.

17 Interview, confidential source.

18 Interview, confidential source.

19 John Ivison, "First Nations a Litmus Test for Liberals," *National Post*, December 16, 2015, A4. The last Conservative budget projected program expenses, as a percentage of GDP, to be 12.9 per cent in 2017/18, or $282.7 billion. The 2018 Liberal budget estimated Trudeau's government would spend 14.2 per cent of GDP on program expenses in that year, or $304.6 billion.

20 John Ivison, "John Ivison: The 'Slow Bleeding' of Canada Is about to Get Underway—and Only Morneau Can Stop It," *National Post*, April 29, 2018, https://nationalpost.com/opinion/john-ivison-the-slow-bleeding-of-corporate-canada-is-about-to-get-underway-and-only-morneau-can-stop-it.

21 Thomas Sowell, *The Vision of the Anointed: Self-Congratulation as a Basis for Social Policy* (New York: Basic Books, 1995), 3.

22 Interview, William A. Macdonald, 17/5/18. Bill was a senior partner at McMillan Binch and was instrumental in recruiting John Turner to the firm after he stepped down as finance minister in 1976. He has been a director of companies such as Imperial Oil and Rio Algom and has advised governments around the world for the past fifty-five years. In his eighties, he remains an astute observer of the Canadian scene, kept young by "an active engagement in the future."

23 Interview, William A. Macdonald, 18/9/18.

24 Sowell, *The Vision of the Anointed*, 111.

25 Adam Smith, *The Theory of Moral Sentiments* (London: R. Chapman, 1809), Part VI, Section II, Chapter II, 318.

26 Interview, David Coletto, 18/5/18.

27 Abacus Data research suggests that of those who identified themselves as "left" or "centre-left" in a post-election survey, 44 per cent supported the Liberals, 30 per cent NDP, and 11 per cent Conservative. Those numbers were identical in an April 2017 study. By April 2018, a survey suggested they were 45 per cent Liberal, 30 per cent NDP, and 13 per cent Conservative—that is, Liberal support among left-of-centre voters did not shift.

28 Interview, David Coletto, 18/5/18.

29 Interview, confidential source.

30 Andrew Potter, "Partisans Need to Make a Choice—Do We Define Ourselves by What We Believe in or by What We Despise?" *Ottawa Citizen*, July 20, 2018, https://ottawacitizen.com/news/national/potter-partisans-need-to-make-a-choice-do-we-define-ourselves-by-what-we-believe-in-or-by-what-we-despise.

31 Interview, Gerald Butts, 18/7/18.

32 Stephen J. Harper, *Right Here, Right Now: Politics and Leadership in the Age of Disruption* (Toronto: McClelland & Stewart, 2018), 170.

ONE: PASSION OVER REASON

1 Trudeau, *Common Ground*, 30.

2 Susan Delacourt, *Justin Trudeau: Can He Bring the Liberal Party Back to Life?* (Toronto: Toronto Star Newspapers Limited, 2013), iBooks, 80.

3 New Edinburgh News (@newednews), "Thx to Joyce D. for sharing a 1981 NEN photo, featuring @JustinTrudeau, brothers & friends playing in New Ed's lanes," Tweet, October 21, 2015, https://twitter.com/newednews/status/656822554628259840.

4 Interview, confidential source.

5 Trudeau, *Common Ground*, 34.

6   Deborah Brooker, "Margaret Trudeau Today: A TV Career, a New Man —and Her Kids," *Ottawa Citizen*, February 9, 1983, https://news.google.com/newspapers?id=ouhfAAAAIBAJ&sjid=_-4FAAAAIBAJ&pg=1352%2 C4315355.

7   John English, *Just Watch Me: The Life of Pierre Elliott Trudeau: 1968–2000* (Toronto: Knopf Canada, 2009), 311.

8   Trudeau, *Common Ground*, 37.

9   English, *Just Watch Me*, 312.

10 Trudeau, *Common Ground*, 35.

11 Ibid., 39.

12 Ira Urquhart, "Mrs. Trudeau's Front-Page Fling," *Washington Post*, March 14, 1977, https://www.washingtonpost.com/archive/lifestyle/1977/03/14/mrs-trudeaus-front-page-fling/0ebd5557-4a56-4320-828d-f5be8d6972b7.

13 Trudeau, *Common Ground*, 54.

14 Mark Kennedy, "Trudeau Goes Public with His Personal Life," *Ottawa Citizen*, October 18, 2014, A8.

15 Trudeau, *Common Ground*, 48.

16 Ibid., 55.

17 Interview, Seamus O'Regan, 15/12/18.

18 English, *Just Watch Me*, 610.

19 Trudeau, *Common Ground*, 62.

20 Justin Trudeau, "I Was Deeply Insecure: Justin Trudeau on Growing Up, Raising Sons and What It Means to Be a Man," March 26, 2018, https://www.chatelaine.com/living/justin-trudeau-what-is-a-man.

21 Trudeau, *Common Ground*, 72.

22 Interview, Marc Miller, 23/5/18.

23 "An 18-Year-Old Justin Trudeau on Quebec Sovereignty," *The National* video (CBC Player), 1:53, 1990, https://www.cbc.ca/player/play/2379931230.

24 Trudeau, *Common Ground*, 81.

25 Interview, Marc Miller, 23/5/18.

26 Trudeau, *Common Ground*, 91.

27   Interview, Gerald Butts, 18/7/18.

28   A biographical thread common to Trudeau, Butts, Katie Telford, and
     Telford's husband, lobbyist Rob Silver, is their shared history in university
     debating. Butts was president of the Canadian University Society for
     Intercollegiate Debate in 1992–93, a position Silver held seven years later.
     Telford was a member of the English Debating Society at the University of
     Ottawa and met Silver at a debate competition at Western University.
     From: Delacourt, *Justin Trudeau*, 30.

29   Interview, Gerald Butts, 18/7/18.

30   Trudeau, *Common Ground*, 82.

31   Ibid., 92.

32   Ibid., 96.

33   Ibid., 98.

34   Interview, Marc Miller, 23/5/18.

35   Mark Twain, *The Innocents Abroad* (Ware: Wordsworth Editions Ltd., 2010), 427.

36   Trudeau, *Common Ground*, 107.

37   Ibid., 134.

38   Ibid., 137.

39   Ibid., 137.

40   Ibid., 139.

41   Robert Frost, "Stopping by Woods on a Snowy Evening," Poetry Foundation,
     https://www.poetryfoundation.org/poems/42891/stopping-by-woods-on-a-
     snowy-evening.

42   John Gray and Tu Thanh Ha, "'Je t'aime, papa,'" *Globe and Mail*, October 4,
     2000, A1.

43   Peter Scowen, "Hardly the Keeper of the Trudeau legacy," *National Post*,
     October 7, 2000, A15.

44   Justin Trudeau, "Something I'm Passionate About," *Globe and Mail*,
     February 3, 2001, A11.

45   John Ivison, "Political Career a 'Far-Off Possibility,' Trudeau Says," *National
     Post*, April 11, 2006, A9.

46 Interview, Elizabeth Gray-Smith, 6/6/18.

47 Interview, Seamus O'Regan, 15/12/18.

48 Ibid.

49 Trudeau, *Common Ground*, 150.

50 Jane Taber, "Justin Trudeau Is off Eligible-Bachelor List," *Globe and Mail*, October 22, 2004, A3.

51 Trudeau, *Common Ground*, 155.

52 Shinan Govani, "A Beach Built for Two: Sophie and Justin Honeymooning in Mauritius," *National Post*, May 30, 2005, A1.

53 Trudeau, *Common Ground*, 157.

54 Ian Brown, "The Challenge," *Globe and Mail*, October 3, 2015, F1.

55 Laura Stone, "'A Family Affair': Canada's Next First Lady? Lunch with Sophie Grégoire-Trudeau," Global News, March 23, 2015, https://globalnews.ca/news/1897750/a-family-affair-canadas-next-first-lady-lunch-with-sophie-gregoire-trudeau.

56 Interview, Seamus O'Regan, 15/12/18.

57 Interview, Justin Trudeau, 18/12/18.

58 Ibid.

59 Interview, Seamus O'Regan, 15/12/18.

60 Interview, confidential source.

61 Glen McGregor, "Fortunate Son," *Ottawa Citizen*, February 14, 2013, A1.

62 Ingrid Peritz, "One Dashing Quebecker Signs on to Play Another," *Globe and Mail*, July 13, 2006, A1.

63 Simona Rabinovitch, "An Officer and a Gentleman," *Globe and Mail*, August 1, 2006, R1.

64 Ibid.

65 English, *Citizen of the World*, 111.

66 Trudeau, *Common Ground*, 160.

67 Ivison, "Political Career a 'Far-Off Possibility, Trudeau Says.'"

68 Ibid.

69 Roy MacGregor, "The Man Who Would Be King," *Globe and Mail*, November 25, 2006, A4.

70 Trudeau, *Common Ground*, 164.

71 Delacourt, *Justin Trudeau*, 17.

72 Trudeau, *Common Ground*, 165.

73 MacGregor, "The Man Who Would Be King."

74 Ibid.

75 Ibid.

76 Trudeau, *Common Ground*, 168.

TWO: TESTING THE WATER WITH BOTH FEET

1 Jane Taber, "Liberals Welcome Trudeau, Bid Adieu to Graham," *Globe and Mail*, February 23, 2007, A1.

2 Trudeau, *Common Ground*, 169.

3 Taber, "Liberals Welcome Trudeau, Bid Adieu to Graham."

4 Trudeau, *Common Ground*, 170.

5 Konrad Yakabuski, "The Son Also Rises," *Globe and Mail*, September 20, 2008, F3.

6 Trudeau, *Common Ground*, 176.

7 Interview, confidential source.

8 Trudeau, *Common Ground*, 197.

9 Interview, Alex Lanthier.

10 Ibid.

11 Ingrid Peritz, "Justin Trudeau Captures Liberal Nomination in Montreal," *Globe and Mail*, April 30, 2007, A4.

12 Don Macpherson, "He's Still Daddy's Boy," *Montreal Gazette*, May 1, 2007, A23.

13 Elizabeth Thompson, "Dion Chastizes Justin Trudeau," *Montreal Gazette*, May 8, 2007, A14.

14 Interview, confidential source.

15 Interview, Alex Lanthier, 8/5/18.

16 Trudeau, *Common Ground*, 193.

17 Sonia Verma, "'I Don't Have Anything to Prove,'" *Globe and Mail*, October 2, 2010, F3.

18 Irwin Block, "Trudeau Launches Campaign in Papineau," *Montreal Gazette*, September 25, 2008, A10.

19 John Ivison and Don Martin, "How a Rout Became a Bout," *National Post*, October 11, 2008, A1.

20 Trudeau, *Common Ground*, 220.

21 Yakabuski, "The Son Also Rises."

22 Interview, confidential source.

23 Interview, confidential source.

24 Interview, Rodger Cuzner, 4/10/18.

25 Canwest News Service, "Bloc Quick to Trash Trudeau's Youth Plan," *Montreal Gazette*, February 26, 2009, A10.

26 Verma, "'I Don't Have Anything to Prove.'"

27 Josh Visser, "Liberals Apologize for Late Delivery of Dion Video," CTV News, December 3, 2008.

28 Trudeau, *Common Ground*, 228.

29 Ibid.

30 Michael Ignatieff, *Fire and Ashes: Success and Failure in Politics* (Toronto: Random House of Canada, 2013), 58.

31 Ignatieff, *Fire and Ashes*, 80–81.

32 Trudeau, *Common Ground*, 212.

33 Ignatieff, *Fire and Ashes*, 158.

34 Trudeau, *Common Ground*, 229.

35 Peggy Curran, "Trudeau Keeping His Eye on the Prize," *Montreal Gazette*, May 5, 2011, A2.

36 "Trudeau Won't Run for Liberal Leadership," *Montreal Gazette*, October 14, 2011, A6.

37 John Ivison, "If Rae Leaves, He'll Be Hard to Replace," *National Post*, February 8, 2013, A4.

38 Interview, Alex Lanthier, 8/5/18.

39 John Ivison, "From Piece of S--- to Peace on Earth," *National Post*, December 15, 2011, A1.

THREE: LIVING IN THE LIMELIGHT

1 Stanford Graduate School of Business, "Stephen Harper, 22nd Prime Minister of Canada," YouTube video, 55:18, February 28, 2018, https://youtu.be/FXXY1eowaEw?t=1934.

2 Interview, Gerald Butts, 18/7/18.

3 John Ivison, "The Right Name for the Job," *National Post*, January 17, 2012, A4.

4 Ibid.

5 Trudeau, *Common Ground*, 242.

6 Interview, Tom Pitfield, 31/10/18.

7 Delacourt, *Justin Trudeau*, 108.

8 Rick Bell, "Tick Talk," *Calgary Sun*, May 16, 2018, A4.

9 Trudeau, *Common Ground*, 246.

10 English, *Citizen of the World*, 272.

11 Stephen Rodrick, "Justin Trudeau: The North Star," *Rolling Stone*, July 26, 2017, https://www.rollingstone.com/politics/politics-features/justin-trudeau-the-north-star-194313.

12 Gloria Galloway, "PM Says He Regrets Brazeau Comments," *Globe and Mail*, August 2, 2017, A4.

13 Interview, Justin Trudeau, 18/12/18.

14 Interview, Rodger Cuzner. 5/10/18.

15 Interview, Patrick Brazeau.

16 Trudeau, *Common Ground*, 248.

17 FactPointVideo, "Justin Trudeau—Patrick Brazeau Charity Boxing Match —English Coverage of Complete Fight," YouTube video, 16:13, April 1, 2012, https://www.youtube.com/watch?v=XuSpZ3_5pTc.

18   Trudeau, *Common Ground*, 248.

19   Interview, Patrick Brazeau.

20   Bruce Arthur, "Justin Trudeau Relives Boxing Breakthrough after Sun TV Low Blow," *Toronto Star*, September 26, 2014.

21   Interview, confidential source.

22   Interview, confidential source.

23   "Rodger Cuzner's The Thrilla on the Hilla," Global News video, 1:12, March 20, 2016, https://globalnews.ca/video/2572374/rodger-cuzners-the-thrilla-on-the-hilla.

24   Interview, Patrick Brazeau.

25   Interview, confidential source.

26   StraightGoodsNews, "Justin Trudeau, Quebec Separation -021412," YouTube video, 2:27, February 14, 2012, https://www.youtube.com/watch?v=ayd3z5bT1Gs.

27   Interview, Gerald Butts, 18/7/18.

28   Ian Brown, "The Challenge." *Globe and Mail*, Saturday, October 3, 2015, F1.

29   Trudeau, *Common Ground*, 255.

30   Interview, confidential source.

31   Interview, confidential source.

32   Interview, confidential source.

33   Delacourt, *Justin Trudeau*, 100.

34   Trudeau, *Common Ground*, 262.

35   Interview, confidential source.

36   Interview, Gerald Butts, 18/7/18.

37   Brown, "The Challenge."

38   Delacourt, *Justin Trudeau*, 34.

39   Interview, Gerald Butts, 18/7/18.

40   Ibid.

41   Trudeau, *Common Ground*, 263.

42   Ibid., 265.

43 Delacourt, *Justin Trudeau*, 39.

44 Interview, Tom Pitfield, 31/10/18.

45 Ibid.

46 Interview, confidential source.

47 Interview, confidential source.

48 Trudeau, *Common Ground*, 268.

49 Ibid., 298.

50 Justin Trudeau, *Common Ground*, "Select Speeches," 300.

51 John Ivison, "Trudeau Supports Oil Sands Sale," *National Post*, November 20, 2012, A4.

52 Interview, confidential source.

53 Delacourt, *Justin Trudeau*, 10.

54 Ibid., 124.

55 Interview, confidential source.

56 John Ivison, "Passion over Reason," *National Post*, March 2, 2013, A6.

57 Interview, confidential source.

58 Interview, confidential source.

59 Ivison, "Passion over Reason."

60 McGregor, "Fortunate Son."

61 Ibid.

62 Ibid

63 Joan Bryden, "Garneau Leaving Liberal Leadership Race, Feels Trudeau Can't Be Stopped," Canadian Press, March 13, 2013, https://globalnews.ca/news/408450/garneau-leaving-liberal-leadership-race-feels-trudeau-cant-be-stopped.

64 Daniel Leblanc, "Team Justin Opens up Its Playbook," *Globe and Mail*, March 2, 2013, A12.

65 Ibid.

66 Ibid.

67 Trudeau, *Common Ground*, 306.

68 Daniel Leblanc, "Newly Crowned Trudeau Sets Out to Rebuild the Liberal Party," *Globe and Mail*, April 14, 2013, https://www.theglobeandmail.com/news/politics/newly-crowned-trudeau-sets-out-to-rebuild-the-liberal-party/article11205979.

69 William Shakespeare, *Antony and Cleopatra*, 1.5.74–75.

70 John English, "Politics Made Pierre. Lightning Strikes Twice?" *Globe and Mail*, April 18, 2013, A17.

FOUR: NO SMALL DREAMS

1   Daniel Leblanc and Steven Chase, "Tories Target Trudeau's Stand on Terror," *Globe and Mail*, April 20, 2013, A17.

2   "String of Terror Incidents 'No Reason to Commit Sociology,' Stephen Harper," Canadian Press, April 25, 2013, https://nationalpost.com/news/politics/string-of-terror-incidents-no-reason-to-commit-sociology-stephen-harper.

3   Steven Chase, "PM Steps Up Attack on Trudeau over 'Root Causes' of Terrorism," *Globe and Mail*, April 26, 2013, A5.

4   John MacLachlan Gray, "Why Can't Politicians Act Like Normal People?" *Globe and Mail*, January 24, 2001, R1.

5   John Ivison, "Trudeau's Next Step on Senate," *National Post*, May 28, 2013, A4.

6   Gary Mason, "The West Knows Where Trudeau Stands," *Globe and Mail*, June 7, 2013, A15.

7   Sean Silcoff, "Trudeau Offers to Repay Groups for Speeches," *Globe and Mail*, June 17, 2013, A4.

8   Linda Diebel, "How Chrystia Freeland Became Justin Trudeau's First Star," *Toronto Star*, November 29, 2015, https://www.thestar.com/news/insight/2015/11/29/how-chrystia-freeland-became-justin-trudeaus-first-star.html.

9   Interview, Gerald Butts, 29/10/18.

10 Ibid.

11 Bill Curry and Steven Chase, "Trudeau's Pot Use Fans Legalization Debate," *Globe and Mail*, August 23, 2013, A1.

12 Aaron Wherry, "How Does Justin Trudeau Really Feel about Electoral Reform? Let's Go to the Tape," CBC News, October 21, 2016, https://www.cbc.ca/news/politics/wherry-trudeau-electoral-reform-opinion-1.3814319.

13 Michael Adams, "The Youth Vote Is Key for Today's Trudeaus," *Globe and Mail*, August 26, 2013, A9.

14 Tim Harper, "Trudeau Could Get Burned by Risk-Taking," *Toronto Star*, August 26, 2013, A3.

15 David Dodge and Richard Dion, "Economic Performance and Policy during the Harper Years," *Policy Options*, October 19, 2016, http://policyoptions.irpp.org/magazines/october-2016/economic-performance-and-policy-during-the-harper-years.

16 John Ivison, "Harper's Future Tied to Economy," *National Post*, September 6, 2013, A4.

17 Dodge and Dion, "Economic Performance and Policy during the Harper Years."

18 Ivison, "Harper's Future Tied to Economy."

19 Interview, Robert Asselin. 7/5/18.

20 Terence Corcoran, "Carbon Pricing Just Hot Air," *National Post*, October 31, 2013, A1.

21 John Ivison, "The Right Honourable Offence," *National Post*, November 2, 2013, A1.

22 English, *Just Watch Me*, 618.

23 Susan Delacourt, *Shopping for Votes: How Politicians Choose Us and We Choose Them* (Madeira Park: Douglas & McIntyre, 2013), 225.

24 Andrew Coyne, "Trudeau's Gaffes Harder to Ignore," *National Post*, November 12, 2013, A7.

25 Lee Berthiaume, "Trudeau Unapologetic over Absences," *National Post*, December 11, 2013, A4.

FIVE: JUST NOT READY

1 Morley was sentenced to sixteen months in prison after admitting to two false accounting offences. He claimed to have mistakenly continued to claim housing expenses after the mortgage was repaid.

2   "MP Becomes First Ever Person to Forget He Had Paid off His Mortgage,"
    Daily Mash, 14 May, 2009, https://www.thedailymash.co.uk/politics/
    politics-headlines/mp-becomes-first-ever-person-to-forget-he-had-paid-off-
    his-mortgage-200905141760.

3   Reader's letter to the author at the time of the sponsorship scandal.

4   Interview, confidential source.

5   Gloria Galloway and Josh Wingrove, "Trudeau Shakes up Senate," *Globe
    and Mail*, January 30, 2014, A1.

6   Interview, Alex Lanthier. 8/5/18.

7   John Paul Tasker, "Senate Passes Budget Bill with No Amendments as
    Parliament Breaks for Summer," CBC News, June 22, 2017.

8   For example, the consistently reliable Nanos Research had the Liberals at
    34 per cent support on February 15, compared to 28.7 per cent for the
    Conservatives and 23.2 per cent for the NDP.

9   Q Media Solutions, "Sunny Ways—Liberal Party of Canada," YouTube
    video, 7:23, October 20, 2014, https://www.youtube.com/watch?
    v=XjKlhjU508c.

10 Daniel Leblanc and Jane Taber, "Liberals Accelerate Strategy to Attract
    Centre-Right Voters," *Globe and Mail*, February 24, 2014, A6.

11 John Ivison, "Trudeau's Pile-on Plan," *National Post*, February 22, 2014, A1.

12 "PrimeTime Politics," CPAC video, 1:58:29, February 11, 2014, http://www.
    cpac.ca/en/programs/primetime-politics/episodes/30396042.

13 Campbell Clark, "Trudeau Borrows Strategy from Obama's Re-election
    Campaign," *Globe and Mail*, February 24, 2014, A6.

14 John Ivison, "Twin Gaffes Dumb and Dumber," *National Post*, February 25,
    2014, A4.

15 Ibid.

16 Andrea Hill and Jordan Press, "Trudeau Apologizes for Ukraine Gaffe,"
    National Post, February 26, 2014, A4.

17 Interview, confidential source.

18 John Ivison, "Trudeau Bumbles to Top of Polls," *National Post*, June 20,
    2014, A1.

19 Lee Berthiaume, "Justin Trudeau Says Current Liberal MPs Must Vote Pro-Choice on Abortion," *Ottawa Citizen*, June 18, 2014.

20 "Abortion Opponents Not Welcome to Run for Liberals in 2015, Trudeau Says," CTV News video, 1:52, May 7, 2014, https://www.ctvnews.ca/politics/ abortion-opponents-not-welcome-to-run-for-liberals-in-2015-trudeau- says-1.1810805.

21 Ivison, "Trudeau Bumbles to Top of Polls."

22 "Trudeau on Liberal MP's 'Bozo Eruption' Remark: 'I Understand His Frustration,'" CTV News, May 27, 2014, https://www.ctvnews.ca/politics/ trudeau-on-liberal-mp-s-bozo-eruption-remark-i-understand-his- frustrations-1.1840106.

23 Josh Wingrove, "Trudeau Says Anti-Abortion Candidates Not Welcome in Party," *Globe and Mail*, May 8, 2014, A6.

24 Daniel Leblanc, "Liberals Open to Anti-Abortion Viewpoints, Trudeau Says," *Globe and Mail*, May 20, 2014, A4.

25 Josh Wingrove, "'Very Intoxicated' 19-Year-Old Won't Be Charged in Trudeau Break-in," *Globe and Mail*, August 26, 2014.

26 John Ivison, "Fall Session and the War against Ennui," *National Post*, September 5, 2014, A4.

27 Ignatieff, *Fire and Ashes*, 145.

28 John Ivison, "Trudeau has benefit of the doubt; Tories just can't seem to capitalize on recent success," *National Post*, Wednesday, September 4, 2014, A4.

29 Brad Lavigne, *Building the Orange Wave: The Inside Story Behind the Historic Rise of Jack Layton and the NDP* (Madeira Park: Douglas & McIntyre, 2013), 268.

30 Kim Mackrael and Steven Chase, "Going It Alone," *Globe and Mail*, October 4, 2014, A10.

31 Mackrael and Chase, "Going It Alone."

32 Canuck Politics, "'Whip Out Our CF-18s and Show Them How Big They Are': Trudeau," YouTube video, 1:29, October 13, 2014, https://www. youtube.com/watch?v=qjPIzODJJjE.

33 John Ivison, "Firsthand Accounts of Fatal Ottawa Shooting: 'There Was a Very Real Sense That Nothing Will Ever Be the Same Again,'" *National Post*,

October 22, 2014, https://nationalpost.com/news/canada/there-was-a-very-real-sense-that-nothing-will-ever-be-the-same-again-john-ivison-witnesses-attack-on-hill.

34 John Ivison, "Canada's Loneliest Hero," *National Post*, October 20, 2016, A1.

35 John Ivison, "Anti-Terror Bill Needs Closer Look," *National Post*, February 3, 2015, A4.

36 John Ivison, "Mulcair Does His Job on Spy Bill," *National Post*, February 19, 2015, A4.

37 Dale Smith, "Mulcair Says NDP Opposes Anti-Terror Bill, Liberals 'Intimidated,'" *Toronto Sun*, February 18, 2015.https://torontosun.com/2015/02/18/mulcair-says-ndp-opposes-anti-terror-bill-liberals-intimidated/wcm/d3a3f06d-0fc7-402a-890b-c519f3499887

38 Ivison, "Mulcair Does His Job on Spy Bill."

39 John Ivison, "PM Damaged by String of Bad Hires," *National Post*, April 1, 2014, A4.

40 Interview, confidential source.

41 Margaret Wente, "Bad Judgment, Naked Opportunism," *Globe and Mail*, February 14, 2015, F2.

42 John Ivison, "How to Make a Liberal Restless," *National Post*, March 31, 2015, A1.

43 Jane Taber, "Liberals' Latest Angst: It's All about Eve," *Globe and Mail*, April 11, 2015, A14.

44 Sohi credits Brian Mulroney's Conservative government for his release and was able to thank the former prime minister in person when Mulroney addressed Trudeau's cabinet in 2017 on Canada–U.S. relations. Sohi had arrived in Canada in the 1980s but returned to India as an activist on land reform. He was arrested and accused of being involved in terrorist activities, but his local MP, David Kilgour, took the case to the Mulroney cabinet, which pressed the Indian government to release him on the basis he was being held on false charges. From Min Dhariwal, "Amarjeet Sohi Thanks Former PM Brian Mulroney for Role in Freeing Him from Indian Prison," CBC News, April 7, 2017.

45 Interview, confidential source.

46 John Ivison, "Trudeau Falls to New Low in Poll," *National Post*, July 23, 2015, A1.

47 John Ivison, "Tory Ads Target Trudeau, Not Tom," *National Post*, May 25, 2015, A1.

SIX: THE ROAD TO RIDEAU HALL

1 John Ivison, "Race to the Ballot Box on Tax Cuts," *National Post*, July 15, 2015, A4.

2 Interview, confidential source.

3 John Ivison, "Trudeau Tax Plan a Big Gamble," *National Post*, May 5, 2015, A1.

4 Ivison, "Trudeau Tax Plan a Big Gamble."

5 Statistics Canada data suggests median after tax income rose to nearly $57,000 in 2015, from $48,000 in 2000—all numbers in constant 2016 dollars. From Statistics Canada, "Chart 1—Median After-Tax Income, Median Market Income and Median Government Transfers for Families and Unattached Individuals, Canada, 2000 to 2016," *The Daily*, March 13, 2018, https://www150.statcan.gc.ca/n1/daily-quotidien/180313/cg-a001-eng.htm.

6 April also showed a contraction, so as Canada moved toward an election, there was the very real prospect that the country was technically in recession, defined as two quarters of negative growth.

7 Jane Taber, "Candidate Quits Due to Grits' Support for Bill C-51," *Globe and Mail*, June 16, 2015, A4.

8 Interview, confidential source.

9 John Ivison, "Trudeau as Boy Scout," *National Post*, July 19, 2015, A1.

10 John Ivison, "The Class War Isn't Working," *National Post*, May 20, 2015, A4.

11 Mark Kennedy, "Trudeau Attacks Not Working," February 26, 2014, A1.

12 Interview, Gerald Butts, 18/7/18.

13 Ibid.

14 Ibid.

15 Steven Chase, "Leaders Set Tone in Bruising First Debate," *Globe and Mail*, August 7, 2015, A1.

16   Interview, Dwight Duncan, 26/10/18.

17   Interview, Gerald Butts, 18/7/18.

18   Interview, Tom Pitfield, 31/10/18.

19   Interview, confidential source.

20   Interview, Tom Pitfield, 31/10/18.

21   Ibid.

22   Ibid.

23   Campbell Clark, "Canadians OK with a Deficit, Poll Finds," *Globe and Mail*, August 27, 2015, A4.

24   Interview, Robert Asselin.

25   John Ivison, "Trudeau Opens Door to Deficits," *National Post*, August 25, 2015, A7.

26   Interview, confidential source.

27   In the event, growth did dip 0.1 per cent in the second quarter, sending the country into a brief technical recession. Growth ended the year up 0.9 per cent, but that masked a drop of 4 per cent in Alberta and contractions in the other energy producing provinces, Saskatchewan and Newfoundland and Labrador. From Statistics Canada, "Gross Domestic Product, Income and Expenditure, Second Quarter 2015," *The Daily*, September 1, 2015, www150. statcan.gc.ca/n1/daily-quotidien/150901/dq150901a-eng.htm.

28   John Ivison, "Deficit Remains a Dirty Word," *National Post*, August 28, 2015, A1.

29   Interview, confidential source.

30   Liberal Party of Canada, "Which Is It, Tom? Karl Marx or Margaret Thatcher?" September 2, 2015, https://www.liberal.ca/which-is-it-tom-karl-marx-or-margaret-thatcher.

31   John Ivison, "The Conservatives Hold 13 Seats in Atlantic Canada. They're in Danger of Losing 10," *National Post*, September 25, 2015, https://national-post.com/opinion/john-ivison-the-conservatives-hold-13-seats-in-atlantic-canada-theyre-in-danger-of-losing-10.

32   Daniel Leblanc, "In Quebec, Trudeau Aims to Connect," *Globe and Mail*, September 23, 2015, A4.

33 John Ivison, "From Coast to Coast, the Anger at Harper's Distinctive Brand of Governance Is Palpable," *National Post*, October 16, 2015, https://nationalpost.com/news/politics/from-coast-to-coast-the-anger-at-harpers-distinctive-brand-of-governance-is-palpable.

34 Ivison, "From Coast to Coast, the Anger at Harper's Distinctive Brand of Governance Is Palpable."

35 David Olive, *Canadian Political Babble* (Toronto: John Wiley & Sons Canada, 1993), 77.

36 He didn't make it. Saxton lost Vancouver North to Liberal Jonathan Wilkinson. John Ivison, "B.C. Races Reflect Canada," *National Post*, October 19, 2015, A6.

37 John Ivison, "Voters Want Change, But Afraid to Give Liberals Too Much Power," *National Post*, October 17, 2015, A7.

38 English, *Just Watch Me*, 111.

SEVEN: BECAUSE IT'S 2015

1 Nicholas Soames, "Sweat and Tears Made Winston Churchill's Name," *The Telegraph*, May 4, 2011, https://www.telegraph.co.uk/news/politics/av-referendum/8493345/Sweat-and-tears-made-Winston-Churchills-name.html.

2 Interview, Gerald Butts, 18/7/18.

3 Alex Marland, *Brand Command: Canadian Politics and Democracy in the Age of Message Control* (Vancouver: UBC Press, 2016), xviii.

4 Robyn Urback, "Robyn Urback: Brace Yourselves—Four More Years of PM PDAS," *National Post*, November 11, 2015, https://nationalpost.com/opinion/robyn-urback-justin-trudeaus-pdas-are-making-things-uncomfortable-for-some-of-us.

5 Interview, confidential source.

6 Interview, confidential source.

7 He accepted and was subsequently appointed Canada's permanent representative at the United Nations. Other members of the transition team included communications director Kate Purchase, former chief of staff Cyrus Reporter, and future deputy secretary to the cabinet for results and delivery Matthew Mendelsohn.

8 Interview, Seamus O'Regan, 15/12/18.

9 Interview, Derek Burney, 11/10/18.

10 Mike Blanchfield, *Swingback: Getting Along in the World with Harper and Trudeau* (Montreal: McGill-Queen's University Press, 2017), 196.

11 Mark MacKinnon, "Friends Abroad,'" *Globe and Mail*, October 24, 2015, F5.

12 John Baird, "Statement by the Honourable John Baird, Minister of Foreign Affairs Canada, to the Sixty-Sixth Session of the United Nations General Assembly" (New York, September, 26, 2011), https://gadebate.un.org/sites/default/files/gastatements/66/CA_en_fr.pdf.

13 Blanchfield, *Swingback*, 196.

14 Roland Paris, "The Promise and Perils of Justin Trudeau's Foreign Policy," in *Justin Trudeau and Canadian Foreign Policy*, eds. Norman Hillmer and Philippe Legassé (London: Palgrave Macmillan, 2018), 23.

15 Paris, "The Promise and Perils of Justin Trudeau's Foreign Policy," 22.

16 Campbell Clark, "Trudeau Pledges Climate Leadership," *Globe and Mail*, December 1, 2015, A4.

17 Andrew Coyne, "How Many World Leaders Does It Take to Fix Climate Change?" *National Post*, December 1, 2015, A1.

18 David Akin, "3 Bureaucrats Spent $12Gs Dining in Paris, and We Picked Up the Bill," *Toronto Sun*, August 23, 2016, https://torontosun.com/2016/08/23/politicians-racked-up-whopping-1-million-bill-in-paris/wcm/0ecdde9a-cce4-47e5-89af-fd485770a097.

19 Clark, "Trudeau Pledges Climate Leadership."

20 Interview, confidential source.

21 Jorge Barrera, "Trudeau: A Liberal Government Would Repeal, Amend All Federal Laws That Fail to Respect Indigenous Rights," APTN National News, October 15, 2015, https://aptnnews.ca/2015/10/15/trudeau-a-liberal--government-would-repeal-amend-all-federal-laws-that-fail-to-respect--indigenous-rights.

22 John Ivison, "John Ivison: Ron Giesbrecht, Chief of 80 Member Kwikwetlem First Nation, Earned $914,219 Tax Free Last Year," *National Post*, July 31, 2014, https://nationalpost.com/opinion/john-ivison-ron-giesbrecht-chief-of-80-member-kwikwetlem-first-nation-earned-914219-tax-free-last-year.

23 Canada. Office of the Auditor General of Canada, *2018 Spring Reports of the Auditor General*. [Ottawa], 2018, http://www.oag-bvg.gc.ca/internet/ English/parl_oag_201805_e_43018.html.

24 English, *Just Watch Me*, 48.

25 Ibid., 57.

26 Lawrence Martin, "The Lessons of Pierre Trudeau's First Four Years," *Globe and Mail*, November 10, 2015, A13.

27 Allison Jones, "Syrian Refugees Arrive on Government Aircraft in Toronto," Canadian Press, December 11, 2015, https://www.therecord.com/news--story/6169601-syrian-refugees-arrive-on-government-aircraft-in-toronto.

28 Lauren Pelley, "These Syrian Refugees Named Their Son after Justin Trudeau but Now, Their Optimism Is Fading," CBC News, February 27, 2018. https://www.cbc.ca/news/canada/toronto/syrian-refugee--update-1.4545226.

29 John Ivison, "Liberals Lament Uncivil Service," *National Post*, December 21, 2015, A1.

30 Ibid.

31 Campbell Clark, "Trudeau Brings in Tony Blair's Guru to Help Grits Deliver the Goods," *Globe and Mail*, February 22, 2016, A4.

32 Interview, confidential source.

33 Interview, confidential source.

34 By contrast, the Conservative platform in 2011 made one hundred commitments and achieved 95 per cent of them. Rachel Curran, "How Governments Get Stuff Done," *Policy Options*, December 26, 2017, http:// policyoptions.irpp.org/magazines/december-2017/how-governments-get-stuff-done.

35 Scotiabank, "Pipeline Approval Delays: The Costs of Inaction," February 20, 2018, https://www.gbm.scotiabank.com/content/dam/gbm/ scotiaeconomics63/pipeline_approval_delays_2018-02-20.pdf.

36 John Ivison, "B.C. Moving to 'Yes' on Pipeline," *National Post*, April 13, 2016, A1.

37 Ivison, "B.C. Moving to 'Yes' on Pipeline."

38 "Trudeau Backs Away from Election Pledge on First Nation Veto," APTN
National News, February 4, 2016, https://aptnnews.ca/2016/02/04/trudeau-
election-pledge-on-first-nation/.

39 John Ivison, "It's Justin Time in Washington," *National Post*, March 10, 2016, A1.

40 Michelle McQuigge, "World Takes Note of Trudeau, Obama Rapport,"
Canadian Press, March 11, 2016, https://www.ctvnews.ca/politics/world-
takes-note-of-trudeau-obama-rapport-1.2813534.

41 John Ivison, "Budding Bromance," *National Post*, March 11, 2016, A4.

42 Blanchfield, *Swingback*, 219.

43 John Ivison, "U.S. Tunes in to Canada," *National Post*, March 9, 2016, A1.

EIGHT: ELBOWGATE—AND OTHER EXAMPLES OF DOING POLITICS DIFFERENTLY

1 Bill Curry and Robert Fife, "Spending in Search of Growth," *Globe and Mail*, March 23, 2016, A1.

2 Interview, confidential source. The deficit eventually came in at $17.8 billion,
as a result of lower than expected spending—partly because infrastructure
money did not flow as quickly as was intended.

3 Interview, Robert Asselin, 7/5/18.

4 Glen McGregor, "Bill Morneau Resigns from C.D. Howe Institute after
Liberal Convention Speech," *Ottawa Citizen*, May 20, 2014, https://
ottawacitizen.com/news/local-news/bill-morneau-resigns-from-c-d-howe-
institute-after-liberal-convention-speech.

5 Interview, confidential source.

6 Interview, confidential source.

7 Ibid.

8 Interview, Robert Asselin, 7/5/18.

9 Interview, confidential source. As one indication of how slow progress is,
the government's list of long-term drinking water advisories on reserves
fell by a net of just fourteen to ninety-one systems in the nearly two years
between the start of 2016 and a review in early 2018, despite the influx of
cash. That number is intended to reach zero by 2021.

10 Bill Curry, "Bigger CPP Could Cut into Federal Tax Take," *Globe and Mail*, June 24, 2016, A8.

11 Interview, confidential source.

12 Interview, Robert Asselin, 7/5/18.

13 Interview, confidential source.

14 Interview, Justin Trudeau, 18/12/18.

15 Campbell Clark, "Liberals' New Foreign Policy Ends up in Familiar Territory," *Globe and Mail*, March 30, 2016, A3.

16 Trudeau, *Common Ground*, 44.

17 Paris, "The Promise and Perils of Justin Trudeau's Foreign Policy," 20.

18 Interview, confidential source.

19 Steve Chase and Robert Fife, "PM Rules out Ransom for Hostages as Rescue Mission Explored," *Globe and Mail*, April 27, 2016, A1.

20 English, *Just Watch Me*, 102.

21 English, *Just Watch Me*, 97.

22 Interview, Gerald Butts, 29/10/18.

23 Interview, Justin Trudeau, 18/12/18.

24 Laura Stone, "'It Is Not Appropriate to Manhandle Other Members,'" *Globe and Mail*, May 19, 2016, A1.

25 John Ivison, "Trudeau 2.0 Takes the Stage," *National Post*, June 23, 2016, A1.

26 Ibid.

27 Interview, confidential source.

28 Marland, *Brand Command*, xv.

29 Eddie Goldenberg, *The Way It Works: Inside Ottawa* (Toronto: McClelland & Stewart, 2006).

30 Interview, confidential source.

31 Ibid.

32 Interview, Gene Lang, 17/5/18.

33 Interview, confidential source.

34 Robert Fife, "Messy Tootoo Love Triangle Helped Spur Resignation from Cabinet," *Globe and Mail*, September 12, 2016, A1.

35 Laura Stone, "Real Estate, Legal Fees Hike Moving Costs," *Globe and Mail*, September 22, 2016, A14.

36 Robert Fife and Steven Chase, "Liberals Avoid Scrutiny for Contentious Fundraisers," *Globe and Mail*, October 26, 2016, A3.

37 Justin Trudeau, "Message to Ministers: Open and Accountable Government," November 27, 2015. https://pm.gc.ca/eng/news/2015/11/27/open-and-accountable-government#Standards_of_Conduct.

38 Robert Fife and Steven Chase, "Trudeau Attended Fundraiser with Chinese Billionaires," *Globe and Mail*, November 22, 2016, A1.

39 NDP leader Tom Mulcair lost a vote on a leadership review at the party's convention in Edmonton in April, prompting a race that featured Ontario MPP Jagmeet Singh and caucus members Charlie Angus, Guy Caron, and Niki Ashton. Singh was chosen by the members in October 2017. Rona Ambrose was chosen interim Conservative leader after the 2015 election, and a race to succeed Stephen Harper, featuring fourteen candidates, concluded with a victory for Andrew Scheer on May 27, 2017.

NINE: THE AGE OF TRUMP

1 Lucinda Shen, "Here's How Much You Could Have Won Betting on Trump's Presidency," *Fortune*, November 9, 2016, http://fortune.com/2016/11/09/donald-trump-president-gamble.

2 Paris, "The Promise and Perils of Justin Trudeau's Foreign Policy," 24.

3 Althia Raj, "Trump's 'Stunning' Win Caught Canada's Public Servants Unprepared, Documents Suggest," *HuffPost Canada*, January 19, 2018, https://www.huffingtonpost.ca/2018/01/19/trumps-stunning-win-caught-canadas-public-servants-unprepared-documents-suggest_a_23338240.

4 John Ivison, "The Rush to Seem Relevant," *National Post*, November 15, 2016, A6.

5 John Ibbitson, "Trudeau's Words on Castro a Reminder Canada Willing to Go Its Own Way on Cuba," *Globe and Mail*, November 26, 2016, A1.

6   Cleve R. Wootson Jnr., "Trudeau Called Castro a 'Remarkable Leader.' Twitter Wondered What He Would Say about Stalin," *Washington Post*, November 26, 2016.

7   Interview, Brian Mulroney.

8   Interview, confidential source.

9   The $7.9 billion pipeline had been approved in June 2014 by the Harper government, subject to 209 conditions, but the Federal Court of Appeal quashed those permits two years later, saying the proponent, Enbridge, had failed in its duty to consult First Nations. The Trudeau government's refusal to launch fresh consultations killed the project.

10   Greens of British Columbia, "Andrew Weaver Responds to Kinder Morgan Trans Mountain Approval," November 29, 2016.

11   The Canada–EU deal was eventually signed in November, 2016, after nearly a decade of negotiation. Freeland's calculated withdrawal was credited with putting pressure on intransigent regions like Wallonia to sign. Within days of her walking out, EU officials urged Freeland to return to the table and the deal was signed. "Walking out was important because it created a crisis and made it their problem," she said. From Adrian Morrow and Robert Fife, "Freeland Talks Tough on Trade with Trump," *Globe and Mail*, February 8, 2017, https://www.theglobeandmail.com/news/world/foreign-affairs-warns-trump-of-retaliation-if-border-tariffs-imposed/article33955105.

12   Dion was eventually appointed ambassador to Germany, but the European Union role was downgraded to "special adviser."

13   Interview, confidential source.

14   Jocelyn Coulon, *Un selfie avec Justin Trudeau* (Montreal: Québec Amérique, 2018).

15   Interview, Gerald Butts, 29/10/18.

16   John Ivison, "Trudeau Broke Ethics Rules, Watchdog Finds," *National Post*, December 21, 2017, A1.

17   Bill Curry, "Trudeau Says He 'Misspoke' about Phasing out Oilsands," *Globe and Mail*, January 24, 2017.

18   Interview, Gerald Butts, 29/10/18.

19 John Ivison, "Electoral Reform Will Cost Trudeau," *National Post*, February 2, 2017, A2.

20 Laura Stone, "Trudeau Abandons Electoral Reform Pledge," *Globe and Mail*, February 2, 2017, A1.

21 Aaron Wherry, "Opposition Accuses Trudeau of 'Betrayal,' as Liberals Abandon Promise of Electoral Reform," CBC News, February 1, 2017.

22 Interview, Robert Asselin, 7/5/18.

23 John Ivison, "Weeding out Crime," *National Post*, April 15, 2017, A8.

24 John Ivison, "Call Trump to Save NAFTA, White House Staff Told PM," *National Post*, May 9, 2017, A1.

25 Bob Woodward, *Fear: Trump in the White House* (New York: Simon & Schuster, 2018).

26 Ivison, "Call Trump to Save NAFTA, White House Staff Told PM."

27 Fen Osler Hampson, "Justin Trudeau Is Using Brian Mulroney's NAFTA Playbook," *Globe and Mail*, May 12, 2018, O9.

28 David Pugliese, "Man Overboard," *National Post*, January 12, 2018, https://nationalpost.com/feature/man-overboard.

29 James Cudmore wrote the story saying that the cabinet committee had elected to delay the project at Davie Shipyard on November 20, 2015, and on January 12, 2016, he announced he was joining Harjit Sajjan's office as a policy adviser. Cudmore has since moved to the office of democratic institutions minister Karina Gould. In October 2018, NDP MP Charlie Angus asked the CBC's ombudsman to review the corporation's policy around the protection of confidential sources, given Cudmore's involvement in the Norman case.

30 Pugliese, "Man Overboard."

31 Ibid.

32 Interview, confidential source.

33 David Pugliese and Brian Platt, "Vice-Admiral Mark Norman's Defence Lawyers Intend to Probe Actions of Liberal Minister: Court Filings," *National Post*, October 13, 2018, https://nationalpost.com/news/canada/vice-admiral-mark-normans-lawyers-offer-detailed-look-at-defence--strategy-in-new-court-filings.

34 Henein Hutchison LLP, press release, 28/4/17.

35 Pugliese and Platt, "Vice-Admiral Mark Norman's Defence Lawyers Intend to Probe Actions of Liberal Minister: Court Filings."

36 Email to Postmedia, Pugliese, "Man Overboard."

37 Robert Fife and Steven Chase, "Judge Lifts Publication Ban on RCMP Case against Vice-Admiral Norman," *Globe and Mail*, April 21, 2017. https://www.theglobeandmail.com/news/politics/judge-lifts-publication-ban-on-rcmp-case-against-vice-admiral-norman/article34791139.

38 John Ivison, "New Evidence That Exonerated Mark Norman May Date from Stephen Harper's Time as PM," *National Post*, May 9, 2019. https://nationalpost.com/opinion/john-ivison-new-evidence-that-exonerated-mark-norman-may-date-from-stephen-harpers-time-as-pm.

39 CBC News, "Federal Prosecutors Drop Breach of Trust Charges against Vice-Admiral Mark Norman," May 8, 2019. https://www.cbc.ca/news/politics/mark-norman-breach-trust-charge-dropped-1.5127463.

40 John Ivison, "Fighter Jet Deal 'Makes No Sense,' Liberals Told," *National Post*, February 23, 2017, A7.

41 John Ivison, "Fighter Jet Saga an Epic Fiasco," *National Post*, November 21, 2018, A1.

42 Interview, Brian Bohunicky, 22/8/18.

43 Ibid.

44 Ibid.

45 Robert Fife, "Citing Manchester, Trump Rebukes NATO over Defence Spending," *Globe and Mail*, May 25, 2017, A1, https://www.theglobeandmail.com/news/politics/trudeau-touts-canadas-anti-terror-fight-as-trump-pushes-nato-to-do-more/article35111815/.

46 John Ivison, "Canada Signals a Break with U.S.," *National Post*, June 7, 2017, A1.

47 Murray Brewster, "DND Unable to Spend Billions in Equipment Funds, Pushing Projects beyond Next Election," CBC News, May 30, 2018, https://www.cbc.ca/news/politics/sajjan-dnd-equipment-funds-1.4683606.

48 Interview, Brian Bohunicky.

49 Ibid.

50 Ibid.

51 Ibid.

52 Paris, "The Promise and Perils of Justin Trudeau's Foreign Policy," 28.

TEN: TEFLON PROPHET IN TROUBLE

1   Roger Ellis and Geoffrey Treasure, *Britain's Prime Ministers* (London: Shepheard-Walwyn, 2005).

2   John Ivison, "Liberal Power Grab Backfires," *National Post*, March 24, 2017, A4.

3   Brodie, *At the Centre of Government*, 87.

4   Author's calculation based on LEGISinfo data, Parliament of Canada, www.parl.gc.ca/Legisinfo.

5   Brodie, *At the Centre of Government*, 89.

6   Interview, Gerald Butts, 29/10/18.

7   Interview, confidential source.

8   The TrudeauMeter website suggested that 44 of 224 promises had been enacted, 30 had been broken, 63 were in progress, and 87 had not been started. From "TrudeauMeter," 2018, https://trudeaumetre.polimeter.org.

9   John Ivison, "'Used as a Shield against Transparency,'" *National Post*, June 21, 2017, A4.

10 Interview, confidential source.

11 Releases could be blocked if the information sought was obtained in confidence; if its release might impair federal–provincial relations; if it might impact international affairs or defence; if it interferes with law enforcement; if it might lead to the commission of an offence; if it relates to an investigation or audit; if it threatens the safety of an individual; if it provides personal information; etc.

12 Canada. Office of the Information Commissioner of Canada, *Annual Report, 2016–17*. [Ottawa], June 2018, http://www.oic-ci.gc.ca/eng/rapport-annuel-annual-report_2017-2018.aspx.

13 Justine Hunter, "BC Greens Strike Deal to Force End of Liberal Era, Support NDP Government," *Globe and Mail*, May 30, 2017, A1.

14 Shawn McCarthy and Robert Fife, "PM Defends Trans Mountain as BC Greens, NDP Gear up for Fight," *Globe and Mail*, May 31, 2017, A1.

15 *HuffPost Canada*, *The Discourse*, and APTN pulled together a Trans Mountain database in July 2018, that suggested that of the 140 First Nations and other Indigenous groups along the pipeline's route, 41 had signed mutual benefit agreements in support, 14 were involved in legal challenges in opposition, and 85 did not have agreements. From Brenna Owen, "We've Got New Trans Mountain Data and We're Sharing It," *HuffPost Canada*, July 3, 2018, https://www.huffingtonpost.ca/2018/06/28/new-trans-mountain-data_a_23470638.

16 McCarthy and Fife, "PM Defends Trans Mountain as BC Greens, NDP Gear up for Fight."

17 Interview, Gerald Butts, 29/10/18.

18 Justin Trudeau, Prime Minister of Canada, "Minister of Justice and Attorney General of Canada Mandate Letter," November 12, 2015, https://pm.gc.ca/eng/minister-justice-and-attorney-general-canada-mandate-letter-november-12-2015.

19 Robert Fife and Jeff Gray, "PM Says Settling Khadr Case Saved Tens of Millions of Dollars," *Globe and Mail*, July 14, 2017, A1.

20 John Ivison, "PM Is in Fight He Can't Win," *National Post*, February 6, 2018, A1.

21 The shuffle also saw B.C. MP Carla Qualtrough move to Public Works and Procurement from Sports and Disabilities, where she was replaced by Calgary MP Kent Hehr, who was demoted from Veterans Affairs. Hehr's replacement was Trudeau's old friend Seamus O'Regan. Moncton MP Ginette Petitpas Taylor replaced Philpott at Health. Newfoundland MP Judy Foote stepped down from Public Works for family reasons.

22 David Akin, "Report Card Gives Liberals an Incomplete," *National Post*, January 24, 2017, A1.

23 John Ivison, "Is This a New False Dawn on Indigenous File?" *National Post*, August 29, 2017, A1.

24   Campbell Clark, "In Outlining the Gap in Indigenous Care, Philpott Sets Stage for Change," *Globe and Mail*, January 23, 2018. https://www.theglobeandmail.com/opinion/in-outlining-the-gap-in-indigenous-care-philpott-sets-stage-for-change/article37715083.

25   Interview, John Brodhead, 23/4/18.

26   John Ivison, "Add $100M to Jobs Tire Fire," *National Post*, November 2, 2018, A1.

27   John Ivison, "Border Jumpers Given a Free Pass," *National Post*, May 5, 2018, A6.

28   Neil Yeates, *Report of the Independent Review of the Immigration and Refugee Board: A Systems Management Approach to Asylum.* [Ottawa]: Immigration and Refugee Board, April 10, 2018, https://www.canada.ca/en/immigration--refugees-citizenship/corporate/publications-manuals/report-independent--review-immigration-and-refugee-board.html.

29   Ibid.

30   Harper, *Right Here, Right Now*, 137.

31   A survey by Angus Reid suggested that half of Canadians felt the 2018 target of 310,000 new arrivals was too high, a departure from the consensus of previous years. From Angus Reid Institute, "Immigration in Canada: Does Recent Change in Forty Year Opinion Trend Signal a Blip or a Breaking Point?" August 21, 2018, http://angusreid.org/canadian-immigration--trend-data.

32   Interview, confidential source.

33   Ibid.

34   Interview, confidential source.

35   John Ivison, "Liberals Double Down on Bad Idea," *National Post*, September 27, A1.

36   John Ivison, "Focus Should Be Creating More Wealth," *National Post*, August 24, 2017, A4.

37   John Ivison, "Ire Over Being Branded a Tax Cheat," *National Post*, August 30, 2017, A4.

38   Interview, confidential source.

39 Interview, Derek Burney, 11/10/18.

40 Ryan Lizza, "Firing Steve Bannon Won't Change Donald Trump," *New Yorker*, August 15, 2017, https://www.newyorker.com/news/ryan-lizza/firing-steve-bannon-wont-change-donald-trump.

41 Interview, confidential source.

42 Bill Curry and Gloria Galloway, "Liberal Government's Own MPs Take Issue with Tax Reforms," *Globe and Mail*, September 13, 2017, A1.

43 Robert Fife and Steven Chase, "PM Dodges Questions about His Taxes," *Globe and Mail*, September 20, 2017, A4.

44 Interview, confidential source.

45 Interview, confidential source.

46 Interview, confidential source.

47 Interview, John Manley, 4/5/18.

48 Interview, Gerald Butts, 29/10/18.

ELEVEN: A ROUGH WOOING IN BEIJING

1 John Ivison, "One Pipeline Is Not Treated Like the Other," *National Post*, September 9, 2017, A5.

2 Ibid.

3 Jonathan Swan, "Scoop: Trump Urges Staff to Portray Him as 'Crazy Guy,'" *Axios*, October 1, 2017, https://www.axios.com/scoop-trump-urges-staff-to-portray-him-as-crazy-guy-1513305888-c1cbdb89-6370-4e13-98ed-28c414e62a35.html.

4 Katrina Turrill, "Donald Trump and Melania Greet the Trudeaus—but What Does THIS Hand Gesture Mean?" *Daily Express*, October 13, 2017, https://www.express.co.uk/life-style/life/865980/donald-trump-melania-news-justin-trudeau-body-language.

5 Alexander Panetta, "'Napping on NAFTA': Harper Blasts Trudeau Government Handling of Negotiations," Canadian Press, October 27, 2017, https://www.cbc.ca/news/politics/harper-nafta-napping-trudeau-1.4376523.

6 Interview, confidential source.

7   Harper, *Right Here, Right Now*, 46.

8   Robert Fife and Steven Chase, "Beijing Pressing for Full Access to Canada's Economy in Trade Talks," *Globe and Mail*, March 24, 2017, A1.

9   John Ivison, "China 'Won't Wait Forever' on Trade Deal," *National Post*, December 4, 2017, A1.

10 John Ivison, "Beijing Ambush Nixes Trade Deal," *National Post*, December 5, 2017, A1.

11 Lu Shaye, "China Is Not a Threat to Canada—and Doesn't Deserve Unfair Treatment," *Globe and Mail*, May 29, 2018, A13.

12 Interview, Justin Trudeau, 18/12/18.

TWELVE: "TOO INDIAN, EVEN FOR AN INDIAN"

1   The exceptions were Alexander Mackenzie's government in 1878 and R.B. Bennett's in 1935—on both occasions, the country was in the depths of recession.

2   John Ivison, "Trudeau suffers stings, bites in Aga Khan vacation report," *National Post*, December 20, 2017. It should be noted that Singh—who is the son of a psychiatrist, attended an expensive private high school in the U.S., wears bespoke suits and a Rolex watch, and is rich enough to forgo a salary from the NDP—is not an average Canadian either.

3   John Ivison, "Trudeau's Not for Turning," *National Post*, January 17, 2018, A1.

4   Ivison, "Trudeau's Not for Turning."

5   Interview, Tom Pitfield, 31/10/18.

6   Walt Whitman, *Song of Myself* (Boston: Charles River Editions, 2018), 51.

7   Interview, Justin Trudeau, 18/12/18.

8   Outlook Web Bureau, "Trudeau Family's Attire Too Flashy Even for an Indian," *Outlook India*, February 21, 2018, https://www.outlookindia.com/website/story/trudeau-familys-attire-too-indian-even-for-an-indian/308603.

9   Interview, confidential source.

10 Twain, *The Innocents Abroad*, 423.

11 John Ivison, "Trudeau's Sloppy Stance on Diplomacy," *National Post*, February 24, 2018, A4.

12 Star Editorial Board, "Justin Trudeau's Very Bad Trip to India May Carry a Steep Cost," *Toronto Star*, February 22, 2018, https://www.thestar.com/opinion/editorials/2018/02/22/justin-trudeaus-very-bad-trip-to-india-may-carry-a-steep-cost.html.

13 Interview, Justin Trudeau, 18/12/18.

14 Interview, Gerald Butts, 29/10/18.

15 English, *Just Watch Me*, 173.

16 Interview, confidential source.

17 Piers Morgan, "How Dare You Kill off Mankind, Mr. Trudeau, You Spineless Virtue-Signalling Excuse for a Feminist," *Daily Mail*, February 6, 2018, https://www.dailymail.co.uk/news/article-5358761/PIERS-MORGAN-dare-kill-mankind-Mr-Trudeau.html.

18 Interview, confidential source.

19 Mireille Lalancette and Vincent Raynauld, "Instagram, Justin Trudeau, and Political Image-Making," *Policy Options*, April 9, 2018, http://policyoptions.irpp.org/magazines/april-2018/instagram-justin-trudeau-and-political-image-making.

20 Eric Andrew-Gee, "Picture Perfect," *Globe and Mail*, August 13, 2016, F1.

21 Gary Mason, "For Trudeau, the Water Works," *Globe and Mail*, December 1, 2017, A17.

22 Lalancette and Raynauld, "Instagram, Justin Trudeau, and Political Image-Making."

23 Interview, confidential source.

24 Ivison, "Trudeau's Not for Turning."

25 John Ivison, "PM's Abortion Stance Defies Common Sense," *National Post*, January 20, 2018, AA6.

26 Ivison, "Trudeau's Not for Turning."

27 Interview, confidential source.

28 Interview, confidential source.

29 Campbell Clark, "Justin Trudeau Is Losing the Male Voter. Can the PM Win Him Back?" *Globe and Mail*, March 25, 2018, https://www.theglobeandmail.com/opinion/article-justin-trudeau-is-losing-the-male-voter-can-the-pm-win-him-back/.

30 Interview, John Brodhead, 23/4/18.

31 John Manley, "Morneau Misses Mark on Canada's Challenges," *Globe and Mail*, March 2, 2018, B4.

32 Interview, confidential source.

33 Ibid.

34 Ivison, "The 'Slow Bleeding' of Canada Is about to Get Underway—and Only Morneau Can Stop It."

35 William Robson, "Sorry, Mr. Morneau, but There's No Denying That Canada's Competitiveness Is Dismal," *Financial Post*, May 10, 2018, https://business.financialpost.com/opinion/sorry-mr-morneau-but-theres-no-denying-that-canadas-competitiveness-is-dismal.

36 John Ivison, "Oil Industry Strains to Move Forward," *National Post*, July 18, 2018, A4.

37 John Ivison, "In Canada, Energy Projects on the Line," *National Post*, August 8, 2017, A1.

38 Interview, confidential source.

39 Interview, Justin Trudeau, 18/12/18.

40 John Ivison, "Time for Bold Leadership on Pipeline," *National Post*, February 3, 2018, A5.

41 Kelly Cryderman, "Trudeau Ratchets up Pipeline Pressure on B.C," *Globe and Mail*, February 16, 2018, A1.

42 John Ivison, "Pipeline, Politics and Powerplays," *National Post*, May 17, 2018, A1.

43 Campbell Clark, "How the Deal Was Done," *Globe and Mail*, June 2, 2018, B1.

44 John Ivison, "Divided We Stand," *National Post*, May 30, 2018, A1.

45 John Ivison, "Pipeline Decision Splits Country," *National Post*, May 31, 2018, A1.

THIRTEEN: TAKING ON THE TARIFF MAN

1   Adrian Morrow and Bill Curry, "Trump Strikes Softer Tone in Latest NAFTA Comments," *Globe and Mail*, January 13, 2018, A3.

2   Ibid.

3   Adrian Morrow, "The President Aimed His Fire at Canada with War of 1812 Remark," *Globe and Mail*, June 7, 2018, A4.

4   Jonathan Swan, "Trump Has No Interest in NAFTA Concessions, Says Top Official," *Axios*, October 26, 2017, https://www.axios.com/trump-has-no-interest-in-nafta-concessions-says-top-official-1513306466-9b329fc4-adbc-40db-9720-199514e0c1d2.html.

5   John Ivison, "Trump Tirade a Prelude to 'Skinny' NAFTA?" *National Post*, May 24, 2018, A4.

6   Fen Osler Hampson, *Master of Persuasion: Brian Mulroney's Global Legacy* (Toronto: Signal, 2018), 30.

7   Peter Zimonjic, "Early NAFTA Deal with Mexico Could Secure Concessions from Canada, U.S. Trade Representative Says," CBC News, July 26, 2018, https://www.cbc.ca/news/politics/us-steel-lighthizer-national-security-1.4763290.

8   John Ivison, "John Ivison: For All Trudeau's Efforts to Be the Trump Whisperer, Canada Is Now Fighting a Trade War," *National Post*, May 31, 2018, https://nationalpost.com/news/politics/john-ivison-steel-tariffs-deal-a-blow-to-trudeaus-reputation-as-the-trump-whisperer/

9   John Ivison, "Cue Canada's $16.6B 'Retaliation' after Trump Ignites Global Trade War," *National Post*, June 1, 2018, A1.

10 Jim Acosta and Paula Newton, "Exclusive: Trump Invokes War of 1812 in Testy Call with Trudeau over Tariffs," CNN, June 6, 2018, https://www-m.cnn.com/2018/06/06/politics/war-of-1812-donald-trump-justin-trudeau-tariff/index.html?r=https%3A%2F%2Fwww.google.com%2F.

11 Ivison, "Cue Canada's $16.6B 'Retaliation' after Trump Ignites Global Trade War."

12 Robert Fife, "Show Down," *Globe and Mail*, June 11, 2018, A1.

13 John Ivison, "Ready for the Gherkin War," *National Post*, June 13, 2018, A1.

14   Brian Lee Crowley and Sean Speer, "A US–Canada Trade War Rages on
      —and We Are Not Blameless," Macdonald-Laurier Institute, July 6, 2018,
      https://www.macdonaldlaurier.ca/us-canada-trade-war-rages-not-blameless.

15   Sherman Robinson et al., "Trump's Proposed Auto Tariffs Would Throw
      US Automakers and Workers Under the Bus," Peterson Institute for
      International Economics, May 31, 2018, https://piie.com/blogs/trade-
      investment-policy-watch/trumps-proposed-auto-tariffs-would-throw-us-
      automakers-and.

16   Brett Samuels, "Corker: I Think There's a Jailbreak Brewing in Opposition
      to Trump's Tariffs," *The Hill*, June 24, 2018.

17   John Ivison, "Trade Hopes Hinge on Congress," *National Post*, June 29, 2018, A1.

18   Ibid.

19   John Ivison, "The Human Face of Trade," *National Post*, June 27, 2018, A1.

20   Ibid.

21   John Ivison, "Time to Get Tough against Trump Tactics," *National Post*, June
      12, 2018, A1.

22   Jeffrey Goldberg, "A Senior White House Official Defines the Trump
      Doctrine: 'We're America, Bitch,'" *The Atlantic*, June 11, 2018, https://www.
      theatlantic.com/politics/archive/2018/06/a-senior-white-house-official-
      defines-the-trump-doctrine-were-america-bitch/562511.

23   Allan Gotlieb, "Romanticism and Realism in Canada's Foreign Policy,"
      Policy Options, February 1, 2005, http://policyoptions.irpp.org/magazines/
      canada-in-the-world/romanticism-and-realism-in-canadas-foreign-policy.

24   English, *Just Watch Me*, 66.

25   Gotlieb, "Romanticism and Realism in Canada's Foreign Policy."

26   Robert Fife, "PM Calls for Probe into Israel's 'Excessive Force' against
      Civilians," *Globe and Mail*, May 17, 2018, A1.

27   Ibid.

28   Amanda Connolly, "'I'm in Shock': The First 24 Hours of the Saudi–Canada
      Tweet Feud Left Canadians Reeling," Global News, December 7, 2018, https://
      globalnews.ca/news/4737329/canada-saudi-arabia-tweet-fight-dennis-horak.

29   Connolly, "'I'm in Shock.'"

30   NATO Public Diplomacy Division, "Press Release: Defence Expenditure of
     NATO countries (2011–2018)," July 10, 2018, 3, https://www.nato.int/nato_
     static_fl2014/assets/pdf/pdf_2018_07/20180709_180710-pr2018-91-en.pdf.

31   Jonathan Lemire and Jill Colvin, "Trump Dishes up Fresh Dose of Chaos
     Aimed at May, Londoners," *Associated Press*, July 12, 2018, https://www.
     apnews.com/191883cbd468439499c495b0410ac3a2.

32   Ibid.

FOURTEEN: "A GREAT DAY FOR CANADA"

1   In Nanos Research's tracking poll of "preferred prime minister" in early
     October 2018, Trudeau's twelve-month high was 48.3 per cent and his year
     low was 34.3 per cent. Andrew Scheer's high was 27.7 per cent, while
     Jagmeet Singh's was 10 per cent. From Nanos Research Group, "Liberals 38,
     Conservatives 32, NDP 17, Green 6 in Latest Nanos Federal Tracking,"
     October 2, 2018, http://www.nanos.co/wp-content/uploads/2018/10/
     Political-Package-2018-09-28-FR.pdf.

2   Delacourt, *Shopping for Votes*, 312.

3   Joan Bryden, "Liberals Embrace Trudeau's Plan to Transform Party into Open
     Movement," Canadian Press, May 28, 2016, https://www.theglobeandmail.
     com/news/politics/liberals-embrace-trudeaus-plan-to-transform-party-into-
     open-movement/article30197832.

4   Interview, Anna Gainey, 20/9/18.

5   Elections Canada, "Registered Party Financial Returns," Conservative:
     http://www.elections.ca/WPAPPS/WPF/EN/PP/SummaryReport?
     act=C23&returnStatus=1&reportOption=1&selectedReportType=11&query
     Id=f7de82129530458a9358d9151f4ec2b7 and Liberal: http://www.elections.
     ca/WPAPPS/WPF/EN/PP/SummaryReport?act=C23&selectedEvent=0&
     reportOption=1&returnStatus=1&selectedReportType=11&selected
     ClientId=36035&queryId=f7de82129530458a9358d9151f4ec2b7&display
     Introduction=False&displayDescription=False.

6   Douglas Quan, Adrian Humphreys, and Marie-Danielle Smith, "Why an
     18-year-old Groping Allegation against Trudeau Is Not a #MeToo
     Moment," *National Post*, June 23, 2018, A6.

7   John Ivison, "History Morphs in Lecture," *National Post*, September 11, 2018, A6.

8   Nicholas Keung, "Canadian Border Agency Has Deported 398 'Illegal Migrants' out of 32,000," *Toronto Star*, September 8, 2018, https://www. thestar.com/news/immigration/2018/09/07/canadian-border-agency-has-deported-398-illegal-migrants-out-of-32000.html.

9   John Ivison, "Can Canada's Immigration Consensus Hold?" *National Post*, November 9 2018, A4.

10 Ibid.

11 Interview, Justin Trudeau, 18/12/18.

12 Andrew Coyne, "Trudeau Liberals Fall to Earth," *National Post*, August 31, 2018, A4.

13 Interview, confidential source.

14 John Ivison, "Study Boosts Liberal Carbon Tax Plan," *National Post*, September 20, 2018, A4.

15 Interview, Gerald Butts, 29/10/18.

16 The model suggested that households earning $60,000 to $80,000 in Ontario would pay an additional $239 in 2019 in direct and indirect costs, rising to $509 in 2022, as the tax increased. But rebates per household would be $350 in 2019 and $836 in 2022. The difference was explained by the tax proceeds from industrial emitters being returned to households. From Canadians for Clean Prosperity, "Report: Carbon Dividends Would Benefit Canadian Families," September 21, 2018, https://www.cleanprosperity. ca/2018/09/21/1073.

17 Shawn McCarthy and Laura Stone, "Liberals Unveil Rebate Plan, Bringing Carbon-Tax Battle to Ford," *Globe and Mail*, October 24, 2018, A1.

18 Interview, Justin Trudeau, 18/12/18.

19 David Akin, "Trump Trashes Canada's Top Trade Negotiator but His Ottawa Emissary Thinks Freeland Is OK," Global News, September 27, 2018. https://globalnews.ca/news/4491165/trump-trashes-freeland-ambassador-says-she-is-ok.

20 Interview, confidential source.

21 Interview, Gerald Butts, 29/10/18.

22 David Ljunggren and Steve Holland, "How Trump's Son-in-Law Helped Salvage the North American Trade Zone," *Reuters*, October 1, 2018, https://www.reuters.com/article/us-trade-nafta-kushner-insight/how-trumps-son-in-law-helped-salvage-the-north-american-trade-zone-idUSKCN1MC04M.

23 Margaret Wente, "Chrystia Freeland, Warrior Princess," *Globe and Mail*, Tuesday, October 2, 2018, https://www.theglobeandmail.com/opinion/article-chrystia-freeland-warrior-princess.

24 Alexander Panetta, "Trump's Silent Victory in USMCA," *Politico*, October 11, 2018, https://www.politico.com/newsletters/pro-canada-preview/2018/10/11/trumps-silent-victory-in-usmca-324371.

25 Interview, Gerald Butts, 29/10/18.

26 John Ivison, "PM's Claim of Victory Is Hollow," *National Post*, October 2, 2018, A4.

FIFTEEN: THE CULTURE OF SPENDING

1 Marie-Danielle Smith, "Federal Government Spent Millions on 631 New Cars for G7 Summit. Now, It's Trying to Sell Most of Them," *National Post*, November 5, 2018, https://nationalpost.com/news/politics/the-federal-government-spent-23-million-buying-631-new-cars-for-the-g7-summit-now-its-trying-to-sell-most-of-them-off.

2 The report said that revenues rose $20 billion, or 6.9 per cent, from the previous year, to $313.6 billion. Expenses rose in lockstep by $20 billion, or 6.4 per cent, to $332.6 billion—on top of a 6 per cent increase the previous year, creating a budgetary deficit of $19 billion. From: Canada. Department of Finance, *Annual Financial Report of the Government of Canada, 2017/18*. [Ottawa], October 19, 2018, https://www.fin.gc.ca/afr-rfa/2018/index-eng.asp.

3 Using the low income cut-off after-tax threshold (below which people would have to devote a larger share of their income than average to necessities like food, shelter, and clothing), the census showed the number of poor seniors across Canada had declined from 6.7 per cent in 2005 to 5.1 per cent ten years later. The proportion of eighteen- to sixty-four-year-olds beneath the LICO threshold also fell—from 11.7 per cent to 9.9 per cent—but in

percentage terms that was still double the number of poor seniors. From: Brian Murphy, Xuelin Zhang, and Claude Dionne, "Low Income across Groups," *Low Income in Canada—A Multi-line and Multi-index Perspective*, Statistics Canada, catalogue no. 75F0002M, https://www150.statcan.gc.ca/n1/pub/75f0002m/2012001/chap3-eng.htm.

4   The median income increase of 10.8 per cent in the decade prior to 2015, masked huge increases in provinces like Newfoundland and Labrador (up 29 per cent), Saskatchewan (36.5 per cent), and Manitoba (20.3 per cent). From: Statistics Canada, "Household Income in Canada: Key Results from the 2016 Census," *The Daily*, September 13, 2017, https://www150.statcan.gc.ca/n1/daily-quotidien/170913/dq170913a-eng.htm.

5   Interview, Bill Morneau, 22/11/18.

6   Interview, Justin Trudeau, 18/12/18.

7   Sean Speer and Robert Asselin, "Fiscal Policy Must Be Sustainable over the Long Term," *Policy Options*, July 16, 2018, http://policyoptions.irpp.org/magazines/july-2018/fiscal-policy-must-be-sustainable-over-the-long-term.

8   Gwyn Morgan, "Gwyn Morgan: A Great National Energy Champion Is Leaving Canada, Thanks to Trudeau," *Financial Post*, November 21, 2018, https://business.financialpost.com/opinion/gwyn-morgan-a-great-national-energy-champion-is-leaving-canada-thanks-to-trudeau.

9   John Ivison, "PM Says 'This Is a Crisis,' Calgary Says: We Know," *National Post*, November 23, 2018, A1.

10 John Ivison, "Western Alienation as the Buffalo in the Room," *National Post*, December 19, 2018, A4.

11 Andrew Potter and Christopher Ragan, "Was Trudeau's 'Grand Bargain' Just a Little Too Clever?" *Globe and Mail*, November 9, 2018, https://www.theglobeandmail.com/opinion/article-was-trudeaus-grand-bargain-just-a-little-too-clever.

12 Interview, Justin Trudeau, 18/12/18.

13 John Ivison, "Are Canadians Seeing Real Economic Progress?" *National Post*, September 17, 2018, A1.

14 Ibid.

15 Angus Reid Institute, "Liberal Love-in? Trudeau's Approval among His Base Tops What CPC, NDP Bases Feel for Scheer, Singh," October 16, 2018, http://angusreid.org/trudeau-scheer-singh-base.

16 Interview, Justin Trudeau, 18/12/18.

17 Interview, Ben Chin, 11/9/18

18 Interview, Rodger Cuzner, 4/10/2018.

19 Interview, Ben Chin, 11/9/18

20 Bruce Anderson, "It's Not All about Their Base: Canada's 2019 Election Will Hinge on These Voters," *Maclean's*, August 20, 2018, https://www.macleans.ca/opinion/its-not-all-about-their-base-canadas-2019-election-will-hinge-on-these-voters.

21 Interview, confidential source.

22 Interview, Gerald Butts, 29/10/18.

23 Interview, confidential source.

24 Interview, confidential source.

25 Justin Trudeau, "Speech by Liberal Party of Canada Leader, Justin Trudeau, at the 2014 Biennial Convention in Montreal," Liberal Party of Canada, February 22, 2014, https://www.liberal.ca/speech-liberal-party-canada-leader-justin-trudeau-montral-qc-2. In reality, median household income rose 10.8 per cent to $70,336 between 2005 and 2015.

26 Sowell, *The Vision of the Anointed*, 2.

27 Ibid., 5.

28 The Abacus Data poll of November 1, 2018, suggested that 40 per cent felt the country was heading in the right direction and 23 per cent were unsure. From: Bruce Anderson and David Coletto, "For Most Canadians, the World is in Trouble," Abacus Data, November 1, 2018, https://abacusdata.ca/problemsfacingcanada_poll.

29 Angus Reid Institute, "Winter of Discontent: As Justin Trudeau's Approval Deteriorates, Can Andrew Scheer Sustain Gains?" December 19, 2018, http://angusreid.org/wp-content/uploads/2018/12/2018.12.18-federal-politics.pdf. A RealClearPolitics aggregate of polls suggested that Trump's

approval rating was minus 10 per cent, with 42 per cent approving of the job he was doing and 52 per cent disapproving.

SIXTEEN: DUMPSTER FIRE

1 John Ivison, "Wilson-Raybould couldn't hide her disappointment at move from justice minister," *National Post*, January 14, 2019. https://nationalpost. com/opinion/john-ivison-wilson-raybould-couldnt-hide-her-disappointment-at-move-from-justice-minister

2 Ivison, "Wilson-Raybould couldn't hide her disappointment at move from justice minister."

3 Robert Fife, Steven Chase, Sean Fine, "PMO pressed Wilson-Raybould to abandon prosecution of SNC Lavalin," *Globe and Mail*, February 7, 2018.

4 John Ivison, "The government needs to let Jody Wilson-Raybould speak," *National Post*, February 9, 2018. https://nationalpost.com/opinion/john-ivison-the-government-needs-to-let-jody-wilson-raybould-speak?utm_term=Autofeed&utm_medium=Social&utm_source=Twitter#Echo-box=1549662757

5 Maura Forrest, "Trudeau goes on the attack after former justice minister Jody Wilson-Raybould's shock resignation," *National Post*, February 12, 2019. https://nationalpost.com/news/politics/jody-wilson-raybould-resigns?video_autoplay=true

6 John Ivison, "Trudeau has nobody but himself to blame for mishandling Wilson-Raybould and SNC Lavalin," *National Post*, February 15, 2019. https://nationalpost.com/opinion/john-ivison-for-mishandling-wilson-raybould-and-snc-lavalin-trudeau-has-nobody-to-blame-but-himself?utm_term=Autofeed&utm_medium=Social&utm_source=Twitter#Echobox=1550275774

7 Ivison, "Trudeau has nobody but himself to blame for mishandling Wilson-Raybould and SNC Lavalin."

8 Ivison, "Trudeau has nobody to but himself to blame for mishandling Wilson-Raybould and SNC Lavalin."

9 David Cochrane, "Wilson-Raybould set multiple conditions for ending rift with Trudeau, say sources," CBC News, April 3, 2019. https://www.cbc.ca/news/politics/wilson-raybould-trudeau-philpott-snc-lavalin-1.5083792

10 Gerald Butts, resignation statement, February 18, 2019.

11 Butts, resignation statement.

12 John Ivison, "With nothing to lose, Wernick displays admirable candour," *National Post*, February, 22, 2019.

13 John Ivison, "Wilson-Raybould's testimony may cost Trudeau his job," *National Post*, February 28, 2019.

14 Ivison, "Wilson-Raybould's testimony may cost Trudeau his job."

15 Ivison, "Wilson-Raybould's testimony may cost Trudeau his job."

16 Ivison, "Wilson-Raybould's testimony may cost Trudeau his job."

17 Jody Wilson-Raybould, written submission to the House of Commons Standing Committee on Justice and Human Rights, March 26, 2019.

18 John Ivison, "Look for PM to ride out this storm: only a caucus revolt will bring him down," *National Post*, March 1, 2019.

19 John Ivison, "A real loss for the Liberals; Trudeau gets lesson in politics and principles," *National Post*, March 5, 2019.

20 John Ivison, "This is a crisis and he has been found wanting," *National Post*, March 6, 2019.

21 John Ivison, "This is a crisis and he has been found wanting."

22 John Ivison, "We are left with suspicious minds," *National Post*, March 7, 2019.

23 John Ivison, "Trudeau isn't feeling it and concedes only to an erosion of trust," *National Post*, March 7, 2019.

24 John Ivison, "Trudeau isn't feeling it and concedes only to an erosion of trust."

25 Cochrane, "Wilson-Raybould set multiple conditions for ending rift with Trudeau, sources say."

26 Brian Platt, "Tuesday Night Massacre: Trudeau ejects Jody Wilson-Raybould, Jane Philpott from Liberal caucus," *National Post*, April 2, 2019. https://nationalpost.com/news/politics/jody-wilson-raybould-says-shes-been-kicked-out-of-the-liberal-caucus?video_autoplay=true

27 Platt, "Tuesday Night Massacre," *National Post*, April 2, 2019.

28 Letter to Andrew Scheer from Julian Porter, QC, March 31, 2019.

29 Letter, Julian Porter, March 31, 2019.

30 Andrew Coyne, "Trudeau's lawsuit threat all part of a cunning play for sympathy," *National Post*, April 8, 2019, https://nationalpost.com/opinion/andrew-coyne-trudeaus-lawsuit-threat-all-part-of-a-cunning-play-for-sympathy

31 Justin Trudeau, "Statement by the Prime Minister of Canada on the swearing in of the 29th ministry," November 4, 2015. https://pm.gc.ca/eng/news/2015/11/04/statement-prime-minister-canada-following-swearing-29th-ministry

32 Interview, Tom Pitfield, 31/10/18.

33 David Brooks, *The Road to Character* (New York: Random House, 2015), 266.

34 Steven Pinker, *Enlightenment Now: The case for Reason, Science, Humanism, and Progress* (New York: Viking, 2018), 340.

35 John Webster, *The Duchess of Malfi* (J.M Dent and Company, 1896), 5.5.93–95.

INDEX